# POLICE DEVIANCE

**Second Edition**

**Thomas Barker**
*Jacksonville State University*

**David L. Carter**
*Michigan State University*

**anderson publishing co.**
2035 reading road
cincinnati, ohio 45202
(513) 421-4142

**POLICE DEVIANCE**
**Second Edition**

Copyright © 1991 by Anderson Publishing Co./Cincinnati, OH

ISBN 0-87084-100-9
Library of Congress Catalog Number 90-82315

Kelly Humble *Managing Editor*

Cover Design by John H. Walker

# ACKNOWLEDGMENTS

Preparation of a book is a process that is laborious, exciting, tedious, informative, educational, and a relief to have completed. We are indebted to many people who contributed to this bittersweet experience, not the least of which are those who used the first edition regularly enough to warrant publication of the second edition.

We are particularly grateful for the contributions of authors who wrote original articles for this book and whose biographies appear in the text. In addition, we would like to acknowledge the input of those persons who have given their advice and feedback on various elements of the book and the subject of police deviance. They include Bob Trojanowicz, Larry Gaines, Darrel Stephens, Bill Tafoya, Dan Dearth, Donna Hale, and Rick Holden.

We also express our special appreciation to Bill Simon of Anderson Publishing Company. We thank Bill not only as our publisher but also as our friend of several years for the many contributions he has made to the field of criminal justice. Bill's humor, advice, openness, and genuine sense of caring are attributes we cherish.

Finally, we owe our heartfelt thanks and support to our families. They have tolerated our erratic hours, our meandering across the country "in search of new knowledge," and the occasional deviation from our usually pleasing temperaments—to them we dedicate this book.

# PREFACE TO THE SECOND EDITION

Despite our years of study on the subject, our knowledge of police deviance continues to evolve. It seems that just as one dimension of the phenomenon becomes clear, other dimensions become clouded. This reflects the inherent nature of the social sciences. Try as we might to explain and categorize human behavioral changes with the relative certainty that our colleagues in the physical sciences explain the laws of nature, that comparative end appears to be beyond our reach. With this limitation in perspective (and reluctantly accepted), we have endeavored to define and explain the broad problem of police deviance and the associated administrative issues. Our intent is to present issues, offer current knowledge and speculation on the issues, and describe the parameters of behavioral and administrative responses within the framework of a police deviance typology.

Since publication of the first edition of *Police Deviance,* some relevant factors have occurred. For example, the Supreme Court issued its ruling in *Garner v. Tennessee,* police officer drug use became more visible as a problem, new research has been conducted on police misconduct review procedures, and new court decisions have been made on issues of police liability. In addition, reviews of the first edition pointed out some issues which should have been addressed but, we must admit, did not occur to us (but should have). All of these changes are reflected in the second edition, in addition to more original articles and a slight change in the book's organization.

Our goal has been to offer ideas and perspectives in the hope of generating debate and policy-oriented action in dealing with police misconduct. We ask the readers of this book—particularly students contemplating a career in law enforcement—that you keep an important point in mind: The problems of police deviance described herein reflect the exception rather than the rule. The descriptions of police misconduct represent the minority of officers whose behavior taints their peers. Despite this fact, it remains important to recognize that those officers who are deviant tread on the most sacred foundations of this society—our constitutional rights and the trust we empower to law enforcement agencies. The gravity of this malpractice is sufficient reason to carefully study the problem.

Thomas Barker
Jacksonville State University

David L. Carter
Michigan State University

# PREFACE TO THE FIRST EDITION

This book deals with multiple facets of a special problem facing the police—the problem of deviant police behavior. The topics discussed herein address both ethical and pragmatic concerns for those interested in policing as a profession and the practice of policing in a democratic society.

In the past, the behaviors examined in this book have not been openly discussed by members of the police establishment. The "Blue Curtain of Secrecy" has always surrounded the improper actions of police officers. Police organizations, as formal agents of government and representatives of the criminal justice system, have had to maintain a profile that was too frequently a facade of efficiency, integrity, and fairness. It was believed to be in the best interest of the police to resist the "deviant" label for its members or the department. This belief still exists for many police departments and administrators. However, the reform efforts by progressive police executives and professional associations has created a climate more open to discussion—a climate which recognizes the need to assess these problems and propose remedial strategies.

Compounding the enigma of secrecy has been the sparse research and scholarly discussion concerning the multiple types of police deviance. Research is difficult under ideal conditions, but when the group under study is suspicious of interlopers, is inherently powerful by virtue of its office and has a vested interest in maintaining the "proper" organizational appearance, research problems are increased. Fortunately, this situation has changed somewhat in recent years as reflected by research projects and the publication of scholarly works on various forms of improper police behavior. However, there has been no attempt to assemble the information on these subjects together in one usable text. Consequently, professors of courses dealing with these subjects (such as the authors), as well as other professionals interested in the phenomenon, have had to accumulate the materials from a variety of sources. To alleviate this problem, the authors have reviewed the literature to identify the best available and most representative works on deviant police behavior. Because of voids in the literature, the authors have also incorporated previously unpublished works and articles written especially for inclusion in this book. To further enhance understanding of the phenomenon, a conceptual framework of police misbehavior is proposed in the introduction. It is our hope that this book eliminates the "hit and miss" approach by providing the best available collection of material on the subject.

The authors have contributed equally to this book in terms of concept, format, article selection, and theoretical underpinnings. The text is truly a mutually collaborative effort which concisely integrates the somewhat diverse philosophies of the writers. The result is a strong analytic approach to the understanding of improper police behavior.

Thomas Barker
Jacksonville State University

David L. Carter
Michigan State University

# CONTENTS

ACKNOWLEDGMENTS .................................... *iii*

PREFACE TO THE SECOND EDITION ..................... *v*

PREFACE TO THE FIRST EDITION ....................... *vii*

PART I—FUNDAMENTAL CONCEPTS ..................... 1

1. A Typology of Police Deviance ............................ 3
   *Thomas Barker and David L. Carter*

2. Administrative Guidance and Control of Police
   Officer Behavior: Policies, Procedures, and Rules ........... 13
   *David L. Carter and Thomas Barker*

3. Police Ethics, Integrity, and Off-Duty Behavior: Policy
   Issues of Officer Conduct ............................... 29
   *David L. Carter and Darrel W. Stephens*

4. Peer Group Support for Police Occupational Deviance .......... 45
   *Thomas Barker*

PART II—OCCUPATIONAL DEVIANCE ................... **59**

5. The Touchables: Vice and Police Corruption
   in the 1980s ......................................... 61
   *John Dombrink*

6. An Overview of Issues Concerning Police Officer Drug Use ..... 101
   *David L. Carter and Darrel W. Stephens*

7. An Empirical Study of Police Deviance Other Than Corruption .. 123
   *Thomas Barker*

8. Sexual Misconduct by Police Officers ..................... 139
   *Allen D. Sapp*

9. Police Lies and Perjury: A Motivation-Based Taxonomy ........ 153
   *Thomas Barker and David L. Carter*

10. Deception By Police ................................... 169
    *Jerome H. Skolnick*

# PART III—ABUSE OF AUTHORITY ...... 195

11. Theoretical Dimensions in the Abuse of Authority
by Police Officers ..................................... 197
    David L. Carter

12. Police Use of Deadly Force: Exploring Some Key Issues ........ 219
    Mark Blumberg

13. Execution Without Trial: Police Homicide and the Constitution ... 241
    Lawrence W. Sherman

14. Theoretical Considerations of Officer Profanity and
Obscenity in Formal Contacts With Citizens ............... 275
    Mervin F. White, Terry C. Cox, and Jack Basehart

15. A Taxonomy of Prejudice and Discrimination by Police Officers .. 299
    David L. Carter

# PART IV—MANAGING POLICE DEVIANCE ............. 317

16. Controlling and Reviewing Police-Citizen Contacts ............. 319
    Herman Goldstein

17. Police Disciplinary Procedures: A Review of
Selected Police Departments ........................... 351
    David L. Carter

18. Investigation and Review of Complaints Against
Police Officers: An Overview of Issues and Philosophies ...... 373
    Paul West

19. Civil and Criminal Liabilities of Police Officers ............... 405
    Rolando V. del Carmen

# EPILOGUE ..................................... 427

# AUTHOR INDEX ................................ 429

# SUBJECT INDEX ............................... 433

# ABOUT THE AUTHORS ......................... 437

# PART I: FUNDAMENTAL CONCEPTS

# 1

# A TYPOLOGY OF POLICE DEVIANCE*

## Thomas Barker and David L. Carter

Police officers are a unique occupational group. They fulfill important functional and symbolic roles in our society, representing one of the most important protectors of individual and group liberties. Paradoxically—whether or not we wish to admit it—police officers can also pose a significant threat to these same liberties.

Functionally, the police are charged with the ethical, just, and humane enforcement of laws, provision of service, and maintenance of order. In this charge, law enforcement officers are vested with a significant amount of authority to restrict the freedom of movement of persons and to lawfully subject such persons to embarrassment or indignity in the course of the investigation, search, and/or arrest processes.

Symbolically, police officers are not only the most overt symbol of the criminal justice system but they also clearly represent a potential legitimate source of restraint in a free society. Policing in a democratic and free society is the most difficult form of police work. Police officers have the responsibility of maintaining order, but doing so within strictly limited legal constraints. Furthermore, police practices are viewed, to some extent, as the gauge by which we measure sanctity from government, oppression, and adherence to constitutional guarantees. In many ways, police integrity is the window through which we assess the rectitude of all governmental actions. What they do and how they do it affects the perceptions of how we view the fairness and honesty of the entire criminal justice system.

Given these responsibilities, the officer who violates the covenants of proper behavior has both trespassed on the fundamental precepts of a free society and violated the symbolic contract of propriety in government. Such behaviors are obviously dysfunctional in that their ramifications reach from the pragmatic con-

---

* This chapter was written expressly for inclusion in this book.

siderations of liability and organizational control to the more conceptual concerns of respecting constitutional guarantees. As a result of these concerns, the authors have addressed the diversity of problems associated with deviant police behavior in the hope of articulating specific issues concerning the problems and potential remedies.

Police deviance is a generic description of police officer activities which are inconsistent with the officers' official authority, organizational authority, values, and standards of ethical conduct (which are usually implied, rather than stated). Deviance can encompass a plethora of behaviors for which an officer can be disciplined. Plitt (1983) reviewed a large number of cases (supported by court decisions) where officers have been disciplined. Included in these behaviors, as illustrations of deviance, are:

> Abuse of sick leave, failure to adequately enforce traffic laws, lying/ perjury, lying about drug use of an acquaintance, failure to investigate possible crimes while off duty, commission of a crime, threatening another with physical violence, unexcused absences from work, use of excessive force against a citizen, unacceptable job performance, use of offensive language, cohabitation, off-duty drunkenness, excessive parking tickets, leaving duty to conduct personal business, off-duty firearms incidents, failing to complete reports, failing to obey a direct order, conduct unbecoming an officer, recommendation of an attorney, misuse of firearms, accepting gratuities, unauthorized release of police records, falsifying overtime records, failure to report misconduct of a fellow officer, failure to inventory confiscated property or evidence, sleeping on duty, cheating on a promotional exam, sexual improprieties, patronizing a bar while on sick leave, and refusing to take a polygraph exam [abstract from Plitt, 1983:95-98].

This synopsis illustrates the variability of improper behaviors or rule violations in which police officers have engaged. The enigma facing the student of police deviance is threefold: (1) To conceptualize these behaviors in a concise, comprehensible typology; (2) to understand both the functional and causal dynamics of the behaviors; and (3) to evaluate the ramifications of the behaviors on the police organization. This book approaches these problems through a "descriptive/prescriptive" approach. First, the authors present a series of readings which address different forms of deviance. These are followed by prescriptive presentations that consider how the problems impact both the management and practice of policing.

## Problems in Defining Deviant Police Behavior

In light of the different approaches which have been taken to describe police deviance, the authors feel a brief review of the literature is apropos.

*Use of Force.* Sherman (1980) defined police violence as the justified and unjustified use of any physical force (including deadly force) against citizens. Friedrich (1980) was somewhat more specific, inferring that the police use of force included any forceful activity—either legitimate or illegitimate—which produces physical or emotional injury. Kania and Mackey's (1977) definition integrates these two perspectives by defining "excessive force" as violence to a degree that is more than justified to effect a legitimate police function. They further observed that:

> ..."police brutality" is also excessive violence, to a more extreme degree, and includes violence used by the police which does not support a legitimate police function. Force and violence are not synonymous. Force implies the exertion of power to compel or restrain the behavior of others...[while violence] refers to the usage of manual restraints, blows, and weapons [Kania and Mackey, 1977:29].

*Misconduct.* Another aspect of police deviance—misconduct—was defined by Lynch and Diamond (1983) as police officers' violations of (1) formally written normative rules; (2) traditional operating procedures; (3) regulations and procedures of both the police and other public service agencies; and (4) the criminal and civil laws. In a broader context, Geller (1984) classified police misconduct in five categories: brutality, harassment, corruption, violation of constitutional rights, and the failure to take required or appropriate action.

*Corruption.* While corruption is but one example of this general category of police deviance, the literature views it as a particularly unique and serious form (Barker and Wells, 1982). The definitions of corruption abound and are influenced by the values and orientation of the researcher, the reactive measures of officers in research projects, police department policy definitions, and criminal statutes dealing with corruption as an offense. Common controversies center on what the "dividing line" is between corrupt and non-corrupt behavior. Is simple acceptance of a gratuity, such as a free meal, corruption? If not, would the expectation of reciprocity by the business person who provided the free meal to the officer constitute corruption? Can an officer be deemed corrupt by following informal customs of the department (relating to gratuities) or is specific intent required? Certainly these issues are not easily resolved.

The broadest definition of police corruption is any forbidden act which involves the misuse of the officer's official position for actual or expected material reward or gain (Barker and Roebuck, 1973). Corrupt acts contain three elements: (1) They are forbidden by some law, rule, regulation, or ethical standard; (2) they involve the misuse of the officer's position; and (3) they involve some actual or expected material reward or gain. The material reward or gain can be in the form of money, goods, services, and/or discounts. While this definition may not meet the required elements for criminal prosecution in many jurisdictions, it provides insight to understand the problem as well as criteria to be assessed for disciplinary action in cases of a less serious or noncriminal justice.

## THE DEVIANCE TYPOLOGY

The definitions cited above address many critical behavioral problems in policing; however, some issues of impropriety are not clearly encompassed. Discrimination, violations of civil rights, verbal mistreatment, and sexual harassment are among several dysfunctional behaviors which must be included in an examination of improper police actions. Since these behaviors are only peripherally included in the previous definitions, the authors propose an alternate explanatory model by defining police deviance in a two-point typology: (1) Occupational deviance and (2) abuse of authority.

### Occupational Deviance

Police occupational deviance is the deviant behavior—criminal and non-criminal—committed during the course of normal work activities or committed under the guise of the police officer's authority (Barker, 1977). The authors perceive police occupational deviance manifesting itself in two forms—*police corruption* and *police misconduct*—both of which specifically apply to the officer's role as an employee rather than to the practice of policing, per se.

The functions and relationships that workers have with each other, their clients, service recipients, and society take on special meanings when viewed within the occupational environment. In many respects, the way we view the world and the world views us is a result of our occupation. For example, rather firm stereotypes are associated with physicians, college professors, construction workers, and police officers, each with a stereotype precipitated by the general occupational image. Additionally, every occupation—regardless of its position on a continuum of status and esteem—has its particular form of norm/rule-violating behaviors (deviant behavior) or forms of deviance that take on special meaning because of the worker's identity.

Some forms of occupational deviance are common to individuals with similar work environments. For example, sleeping on the job by members of occupations engaged in shift work (e.g., nurses, police officers, military); betrayals of trust by members of "trust occupations" (e.g., ministers, attorneys, persons in national security industries); and employee thefts/deceptive practices (e.g., retail sales, utility workers, repair services). However, many forms of deviance may be committed only by those who are in a given occupation. For example, only physicians can write fraudulent drug prescriptions and college professors may publish "research results" from false data in order to gain promotion, merit, and tenure. Similarly, only police officers can threaten to arrest in exchange for sexual favors or accept money in lieu of issuing a traffic ticket. The common elements in all of these acts are that they are committed by "normal" persons during the course of their occupational activity and the behavior is a product of the "powers" inherent in their occupation.

Even though every occupation may provide the opportunity for deviant acts, there are few occupations like policing, where members are placed into work settings with so many opportunities for deviance. This phenomenon is particularly aggravated by the authoritarian nature of policing and the subcultural solidarity associated with law enforcement. Moreover, the ramifications of police deviance can be disastrous. A cop engaging in corrupt acts is not only subverting his/her authority but is also denigrating public trust in the police. The officer who commits a theft during the course of a criminal investigation not only violates the criminal law but also damages the relationship between the community and the entire criminal justice system. The effectiveness of law enforcement activities may be seriously impaired by police occupational deviance.

## Abuse of Authority

The second element in the typology—abuse of authority—may be defined as any action by a police officer without regard to motive, intent, or malice that tends to injure, insult, trespass upon human dignity, manifest feelings of inferiority, and/or violate an inherent legal right of a member of the police constituency in the course of performing "police work" (Carter, 1984; Carter, 1985). Within this context, abuse of authority addresses three areas of police deviance. First is *physical abuse* which incorporates "brutality" and "police violence." Physical abuse occurs when a police officer uses more force than is necessary to effect a lawful arrest or search, and/or the wanton use of any degrees of physical force against another by a police officer under the color of the officer's authority.

Second is *psychological abuse*. This includes circumstances wherein a police officer verbally assails, ridicules, discriminates, or harasses individuals and/or places a person who is under the actual or constructive dominion of the officer in a situation where the individual's esteem or self-image are threatened or diminished. Threats by an officer of physical harm to an individual or the unjustified threat of an arrest are examples of psychological abuse.

The third classification is *legal abuse,* a type which will typically occur independently without physical or psychological abuse. It is defined as the violation of a person's constitutional, federally protected, or state-protected rights by a police officer. An improper search, stopping a person without legal grounds, or the improper release of confidential criminal history information are all examples of legal abuse.

## Synthesizing the Typology

Figure 1-1 illustrates the relationship between occupational deviance and abuse of authority. While certain behaviors will transcend the typology contributing to reciprocal deviant effects, the reader should recognize that there is a fundamental distinction between the categories based on the locus of behavior. Abuse of authority has an external locus as an action against the police clientele. That is, the officer's behavior toward citizens is inconsistent with legal and policy constraints imposed on the policing function. Viewed in another context, the officer is engaged in the practice of policing but his/her behavior may be deemed deviant if the officer exceeds the lawful authority of the office. Because the behavior is inconsistent with law and/or policy, it is, by definition, deviant regardless of the officer's intent.

Figure 1-1
POLICE DEVIANCE TYPOLOGY

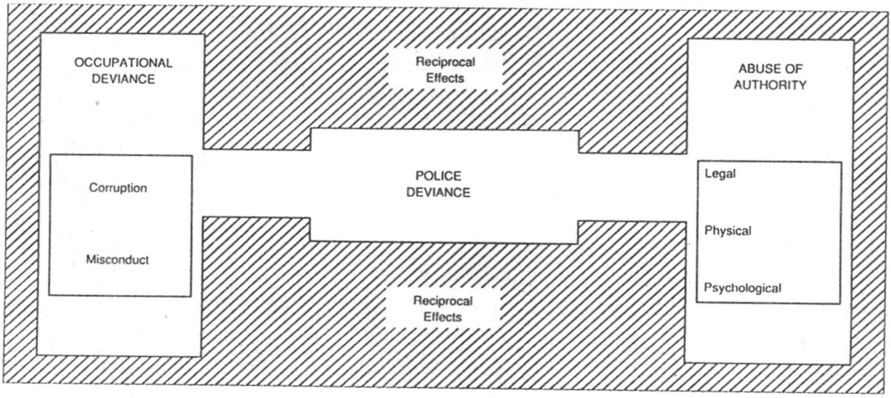

For example, an officer may believe that a person has narcotics in his/her car. Even though no probable cause, consent, exigency, or other legal justification exists, the officer may go ahead and conduct the search with the intent of confiscating the contraband. The intent of getting the narcotics "off the street" may be the rationale behind the officer's actions; however, the search is still unlawful, thereby making the officer's behavior deviant *vis-à-vis* legal abuse of authority. Similarly, an officer may physically abuse a person in retaliation for being spat upon or verbally assail a criminal suspect in the hope of obtaining a confession. In each of these instances the behavior is focused on the officer's authoritative relationship with the public, hence, it is externally directed. Furthermore, the behavior is inconsistent with constitutional guarantees and established police practices, thereby being deviant.

Occupational deviance, on the other hand, has an *internal locus*. It is concerned with how an officer performs as an organizational member rather than the method by which the officer discharges his/her police duties. Notably, the deviant behavior will have violated an organizational rule or breached a trust in the office. Accepting a bribe, sleeping on duty, drug use, and accessing confidential information for personal use are all illustrations of police occupational deviance. While such behaviors may have an indirect effect on the police constituency—particularly regarding integrity and the public trust—the inherent quality of such activities is directly associated with personnel practices and administrative control. Certainly, one must conclude that improprieties such as these are dysfunctional regarding the police mission.

Three other notable distinctions exist between "abuse of authority" and "occupational deviance." The first distinction deals with motivation. Whereas abuse of authority is largely motivated by the officer's intent to accomplish a direct or peripheral police goal, occupational deviance is largely prompted by the personal benefit, gratification, or convenience of the individual officer. The second distinction concerns the police department's liability. Since abuse of authority has an external locus, such behavior is likely to establish liability under 42 U.S.C., Section 1983 of the Civil Rights Act for the deprivation of the constituent's civil rights. Such liability will be less pervasive with occupational deviance. The third distinction is that there is greater peer tolerance for abuse of authority than for occupational deviance. The former, as noted previously, typically seeks to achieve a legitimate end while addressing the frustration and stressors most officers have experienced thereby establishing a common bond of understanding for the behaviors. Conversely, occupational deviance is more likely to be viewed as "wrong" by other organizational members and will typically not engender the same amount of peer support.

## Building on the Typology

The definitions and concepts of the typology establish a foundation to functionally examine improper police behavior. Primarily, it permits the reader to understand how a wide range of deviant behaviors can relate to the organizational setting. Moreover, it serves as a common starting point to examine improper police practices.

Understanding police deviance has important ramifications for the police administrator. Through a conceptual understanding of the various forms of deviance, police managers can focus training and supervision to minimize the potential for deviance (and liability). As a result, the organization will have more robust administrative control as well as providing better service to the community.

In contributing to the accomplishment of these ends, the first part of this book presents fundamental concepts relating to all forms of police deviance. This begins with the typology presented in this chapter followed by a discussion of policies, procedures, and rules as they serve to enhance the formal control mechanisms of the organization. Next, a more conceptual approach to organizational control is discussed with respect to police ethics, integrity, and values with particular emphasis on the policy dynamics of these issues. Part I concludes with a discussion of police misconduct and peer group support.

Part II of the book focuses on specific issues of occupational deviance including corruption, sexual assault, lying, and the emerging problem of police drug use. Part III addresses issues of the abuse of authority including deadly force, less than deadly force, and discrimination.

The final section concentrates on the management of police deviance. Exploring police disciplinary systems, complaint review mechanisms, and departmental liability provides insight into how police deviance can affect the organization. Moreover, the material in this section offers direction on the problems in the hope that they can be remedied.

# REFERENCES

Barker, T. and J. Roebuck (1973). *An Empirical Typology of Police Corruption.* Springfield, IL: Charles C Thomas Co.

Barker, T. and R.O. Wells (1982). "Police Administrators: Attitudes Toward the Definition and Control of Police Deviance." *FBI Law Enforcement Bulletin.* (March): 8-16.

Carter, D.L. (1985). "Police Brutality: A Model for Definition, Perspective, and Control." In A. Niederhoffer and A.S. Blumberg (eds.) *The Ambivalent Force: Perspectives on the Police.* 3d ed. New York: Holt, Rinehart and Winston.

Carter, D.L. (1984). "Theoretical Dimensions in the Abuse of Authority by Police Officers." *Police Studies.* (7:4): 224-236.

Friedrich, R.J. (1980). "Police Use of Force: Individuals, Situations, and Organizations." *The Annals.* (November): 82-67.

Geller, W.A. (1984). "Police Misconduct: Scope of the Problems and Remedies." *ACJS Today.* (February): 6-8.

Goldstein, H. (1977). *Policing in a Free Society.* Cambridge, MA: Ballinger Publishing Company.

Kania, R. and W.C. Mackey (1977). "Police Violence as a Function of Community Characteristics." *Criminology.* (May): 27-48.

Lynch, G.W. and E. Diamond (1983). "Police Misconduct." In S.H. Kadish (ed.) *Encyclopedia of Crime and Justice.* New York: The Free Press.

Plitt, E. (1983). "Police Discipline Decisions." *Police Chief.* (March): 95-98.

Sherman, L.W. (1980). "Causes of Police Behavior: The Current State of Qualitative Research." *Journal of Research in Crime and Delinquency.* (January: 69-96).

# STUDY QUESTIONS

1.  Explain in your own words the differences between the functional and symbolic roles of the police in our society. What are the ramifications of these roles in the study of police deviance?

2.  The authors maintain that traditionally there have been problems in defining deviant police behavior. This observation was followed by a discussion of the literature on the issue. Based on your reading of the cited literature, what is the principal concern on the definitional problems?

3.  In discussing the meaning of police corruption the authors ask these questions: "Is simple acceptance of a gratuity—such as a free meal—corruption? If not, would the expectation of reciprocity by the business person who provided the free meal to the officer constitute corruption? Can an officer be deemed corrupt by following informal customs of the department (relating to gratuities) or is specific intent required?" Based on your perceptions of corruption, how would you answer these questions?

4.  In your opinion is there value in the authors' approach of explaining police deviance through the typology presented? Why or why not?

5.  How might a police administrator use the "occupational deviance/abuse of authority" typology in dealing with employee problems in "the real world"?

# 2

# ADMINISTRATIVE GUIDANCE AND CONTROL OF POLICE OFFICER BEHAVIOR: POLICIES, PROCEDURES, AND RULES*

## David L. Carter and Thomas Barker

An inherent responsibility in minimizing acts of police deviance is instituting an efficient and effective system of administrative guidance and control. This can be accomplished in many ways—adherence to sound management principles, defining authority and responsibility, specifying accountability, stringent supervision, leadership and specification of organizational direction. In order to insure that administrative guidance and control occurs, the police chief executive should set up a formal directive system composed of both verbal and written directives (Wilson and McLaren, 1977:136). The verbal system consists of staff conferences and briefings that take place at all levels of the organization. The written directive system sets goals, defines policy, establishes procedures, and outlines the rules and regulations of the organization. Together, they provide guidance to the members of the police department as well as establishing a means of accountability.

While the need for written directives is generally acknowledged, there remains a clouded visage of the concepts policy, procedures, and rules as they apply to the actual organizational setting. Confusion ranges from the specific meaning of the terms to the actual role for such organizational guidelines. Without clearly understanding these concepts the ability to direct and control is diminished.

## DEFINING CRITICAL CONCEPTS

The clarification of terms and concepts is the initial step which must be taken in describing the dynamics of a written directive system. While an organizational member may possess an intuitive understanding of a "policy," "procedure," and "rule," difficulty arises when one attempts to articulate the distinction between the concepts. Misunderstanding at this basic level will systemically lead to more complicated problems as written directives are promulgated by the organization. In this regard, the following definitions are proposed.

---

* This chapter was written expressly for inclusion in this book.

*Policy.* The principles and values which guide the performance of a departmental activity. Policies are "attitude forming" in the sense that they tell departmental personnel how to think about performing their duties (Hoy, 1982:301).

A policy is *not* a statement of what must be done in a particular situation. Rather, it is a statement of guiding principles that should be followed in activities which are directed toward the attainment of departmental objectives. Policy is formulated by analyzing objectives and is based upon police ethics and experience, desires of the community, and mandate of the law. Policy is articulated to inform the public and department employees of the principles which will be adhered to in the performance of the law enforcement function (Los Angeles Police Department, 1982).

*Objective.* A desired end for which effort is expended that contributes to the mission of the department and, if attained, contributes to the fulfillment of the department's defined purpose.

*Procedure.* A method of performing an operation or a manner of proceeding on a course of action. It differs from policy in that it directs action in a particular situation to perform a specific task within the guidelines of policy. Both policies and procedures are objective oriented. However, policy establishes limits of action while procedure directs responses within those limits (Carter and Dearth, 1984).

*Rule.* A specific requirement or prohibition which is stated to prevent deviations from policy or procedure. Rules allow little deviation other than for stated exceptions. A violation of a rule typically involves an internal investigation and may result in disciplinary action. A *regulation* is synonymous with a rule. As stated earlier, policies are "attitude-forming" and guide judgments; rules are "behavior-forming" and govern behavior.

*General Order.* A written directive that pertains to the permanent policies and procedures for general departmental operations for the indefinite future. The general order is the medium by which policy, procedures, and/or rules on a specific issue or entity are presented to organizational members.

*Special Order.* A written directive of policy and procedure that affects a specific unit (as opposed to the total department), a specific event, or circumstance of a temporary or self-canceling nature.

*Memoranda.* Written information not warranting a formal order which is used to direct any organizational unit(s) or all personnel in specific situations or to inform them of specific departmentally recognized events (e.g., training schools, court decisions, Law Enforcement Week observance, etc.).

*Written Directive.* A generic term used to collectively describe policies, procedures, rules, regulations, orders, and memoranda (*Standards for Law Enforcement,* 1984).

*Departmental Manual.* The collection of amalgamation of all the department's policies, procedures, and rules into a single sourcebook. The phrase "Standard Operating Procedures" (SOP) is frequently used synonymously with Departmental Manual.

As can be seen, there are important distinctions between these concepts which must be recognized in order for them to optimally influence organizational operations. As observed by Couper, "[the] ability of a police agency to perform its functions adequately is based on its ability to define and understand its proper objectives [and] to translate those objectives into precise policies and operational procedures" [1983:13]. To achieve this end, there must be clarity concerning what directives are and their specific role in the organization.

## THE ROLE AND PURPOSE OF WRITTEN DIRECTIVES

The policy of a police department indicates the police position on major issues while concomitantly providing the police agency with a set of standards for which it can be held accountable (Garmire, 1982). Policies are leadership tools which facilitate organizations to direct the actions and decisions of people within the agency. As a result of these needs to direct and provide accountability, "policies are anticipative [in that] they seek to guide future actions and decisions" [Hudzik and Cordner, 1983:289].

Many police departments have no written policies governing basic operations. However, even these agencies will have a written history—sometimes a legacy—of letters from the chief, memoranda, etc. Documents such as these can serve as policies even though they are not written as such or contained in one place. Even when written policies do exist, they are too often poorly developed, ineffective, and even harmful to the organization [c.f., Wilson, 1985:128].

As noted by Walker (1983), policy, in practice, is frequently made by officers on the street—such as the use of discretion when making an arrest or the manner in which an officer deals with the homeless. Three problems result from this situation. "First, it is a *hidden* policy-making process, with no open review. Second, it results in *inconsistent* policy, since there is nothing to insure uniformity among different police officers" [Walker, 1983:70]. Third, they are reactive, not a product of planned organizational direction. Nevertheless, one can be assured that if the chief is silent on issues which require policy statements, policy or custom will be made by the street officers.

A formal process of establishing procedures as well as a uniform method for their application is an inherent necessity in maintaining organizational control. As noted by Goldstein

> ...[there] is an obvious need for some procedure by which an individual police officer can be provided with more detailed guidance to help...decide upon the action [he/she ought to take in dealing with the wide range of situations which [the officer] confronts and in exercising

the broad authority with which [he/she] is invested. Viewed in somewhat different terms, the challenge is to devise procedures which will result in police officers employing norms acceptable to society, rather than their personal norms, in their exercise discretion [1972:167].

Thus, directives "provide employees with a clear understanding of the constraints and expectations relating to the performance of their duties" [Standards for Law Enforcement, 1984:12-1].

The existence of formally stated policy, as articulated by the chief, will identify the role of the law enforcement agency and set the tone for both formal procedures and expected officer behavior. For example, the department's "policing style" (e.g., watchman, service, or law enforcement as proposed by Wilson, 1968); its approach to community relations; the rigor to which it enforces traffic laws; the agency's treatment of social assistance (as opposed to crime-related) calls; and the demeanor of the officers will all be reflected in the chief's policy perspective.

Written directives are essential for a police organization in order to maintain organizational control, accountability, and ensure compliance with a myriad of legal stipulations. The police department can operate more efficiently (i.e., best utilize its resources) and more effectively (i.e., performing its assigned tasks and achieving objectives with intended results) with written directives. At a more conceptual level, formalized orders will give the department direction, they will establish expectations, and provide outcomes which can be measured as a means to determine if the department is fulfilling its responsibilities to the citizens it serves (Carter and Dearth, 1984). Where written directives exist, internal investigations and inspection units can insure compliance.

In assessing the purpose of formally promulgated policies, procedures, and rules, there are three factors which have been touched on above and warrant specific attention: (1) Organization and administrative considerations; (2) the limitation of discretion; and (3) issues of departmental and individual liability.

## Organization/Administrative Considerations

Although policies are not a substitute for the managerial responsibilities inherent in recruiting, training, planning and leadership, properly formulated and drafted policies can accomplish the following:

1. Assure a greater degree of consistency of action among a large number of individual officers who are confronted by wide varieties of tasks.
2. Clarify findings, directives and mandates laid on law enforcement by legislation or judicial pronouncement.

3. Establish and clarify priorities among law enforcement functions.
4. Enhance police training and give consistent guidance to new recruits.
5. Enhance community relations. (Traffic Institute, 1981:1)

The likelihood of assuring a greater degree of consistency of action among police officers is increased when the organization has a departmental manual.

The departmental manual stipulates—through its policies, procedures, and rules—the management philosophy of the department. This gives organizational members important information on their role and behavior in the agency. More specifically, the manual stipulates responsibilities of each division, position, and rank. Therefore, the persons filling those organizational positions know *what* they are responsible for and *to whom* they must report (i.e., the chain of command).

Another important administrative purpose of the manual is that it clearly specifies *how* each organizational task is to be performed (i.e., procedures). This will ensure consistency—hence reliability—of task performance, serve as a mechanism to minimize both internal and external discrimination (c.f., Carter, 1986), provide for comprehensive task accomplishment, ensure compliance with legal mandates, and act as an important mechanism for organizational control.

The rules or regulations which accompany the policies and procedures in the manual specify what actions must or must not be taken in a particular situation. For example, when an employee does not follow a rule, disciplinary action generally will be taken. Thus, the department manual informs all organizational members what is expected of them. It tells them what behavior is mandated or permissible and the consequences for misconduct. Through written policies, procedures, and rules the organization can provide guidance to the officers, control their behavior, and provide more effective service to the community.

## The Limitation of Discretion

Discretion can be defined as "the authority conferred by law to act in certain situations in accordance with an official's or an agency's own considered judgment and conscience" [Walker, 1983:54]. The range of police discretion has been well documented in the literature as well as the issues associated with the limitation of discretionary authority (c.f., Walker, 1983; National Advisory Commission, 1973; Davis, 1971; President's Commission, 1967).

Police discretion can never be eliminated; nor should it be. There is no way that laws, policies, procedures, or rules can be written to cover the myriad situations that police officers encounter. Discretion is an integral part of the police role. However, written directives in the form of policies and procedures set discretionary limits for the decisionmaker—regardless of his/her level in the organization—instead of specifying the decisions to be made (Robbins, 1976). Written rules or regulations are obviously an exception. Generally speaking, the only room for discretion where a rule is concerned is whether or not the rule applies to the specific situation (Traffic Institute, 1986:2). As noted in the *Resource Manual on Police Discretion and Rulemaking,* "written directives... should not eliminate the use of discretion by the police officer. However, they [should] structure and guide discretionary actions" [1980:2]. From this perspective, written directives should be viewed as *structured discretion* (Davis, 1971). Structured discretion can be classified as being either *programmed decisions* or *unprogrammed decisions* (Robbins, 1976).

Programmed decisions are standing decisions (e.g., general orders) which are used to guide personnel in the performance of generally routine tasks. For example, arrest and booking procedures, police report writing, emergency vehicle operations, traffic law enforcement policies, and news media relations are all areas that have a generally defined response mode, yet there is latitude for discretion.

Unprogrammed decisions are more akin to special orders. These are special purpose decisions that frequently require creativity and greater amounts of judgment. While there are still limitations on personnel behaviors, the limits are much broader thereby permitting more discretion. Hostage situations, handling special events, dealing with a natural disaster, and new program research are all illustrations of unprogrammed decisions.

Thus, when developing written directives, administrators must be cognizant of the discretionary issues associated with the activity being regulated and structure that discretion in a manner consistent with law, ethics, the need for goal attainment, and organizational philosophy.

## Issues of Department and Individual Liability

A great deal of literature is available describing the liabilities of local governments, their officials, and individual police officers (c.f., del Carmen, 1986). The current discussion will be strictly limited to a brief review of the provision of the Federal Civil Rights Act, *Civil Action for Deprivation of Civil Rights* (42 U.S.C. 1983), in order to illustrate the important role a department manual can play in a police department's liability.

In 1978, the United States Supreme Court ruled in *Monell v. Department of Social Services* (436 U.S. 658, 98 S. Ct. 2018) that not only individuals but also municipalities could be civilly liable for the deprivation of civil rights. Specifically, the court stated:

Local governing bodies...can be sued directly under Section 1983 for monetary, declaratory, or injunctive relief where...the action that is alleged to be unconstitutional implements or executes a *policy statement* (emphasis added), ordinance, regulation or decision officially adopted and promulgated by the body's officers (436 U.S. at 690).

As a result of this decision, municipalities can be sued when the execution of a government's policy or custom inflicts the injury. When a body of official policies—such as a departmental manual—is conceptually weak and contains provisions that are contradictory, vague, and/or outright unlawful, the municipality's liability may geometrically increase. Similarly, if the organization fails to adopt formal policies and, instead, relies on "unwritten rules," the liability question becomes more complex.

First, the "unwritten rules," if continually relied on, become custom and may virtually have the same effect as written directives. Furthermore, this problem is compounded by the fact that it is more difficult to defend allegations against unwritten customs. Moreover, a local government could be held liable for gross negligence if it showed a "deliberate indifference" to training and supervision of its personnel [*Owens v. Haas* 601 F.2 1942 (2d Cir, 1979), *Turpin v. Maillet* 619 F.2d 196 (2d Cir. 1980)].

The term "supervision" includes the provision of organizational guidance and delineation of policies, procedures, and rules. One should consider that if city officials permit the promulgation of an inadequate departmental manual, this may be paramount to "deliberate indifference."

Individual officers may also be defendants in Section 1983 actions if the officers' official behavior deprives an individual of their civil rights. An important defense for officers in such cases may focus on whether the officers' actions were performed in "good faith." Suffice it to note that if an officer can show that his/her actions were consistent with established (i.e., formally promulgated) procedures, this is an important element of the good faith defense. [NOTE: The municipality may not assert a "good faith" defense in civil rights cases (*Owen v. City of Independence* 45 U.S. 622, 100 S. Ct. 1398, 1980)].

There are many complexities involved with the liability of governments, officials, and employees under the rubric of 42 U.S.C. 1983. It therefore behooves responsible police administrators to become aware of these issues and ensure that adequate protections are in place. This is particularly true given the dramatic increase in Section 1983 Civil Rights cases filed against all departments of government nationwide in recent years.

## LIMITATIONS ON ORGANIZATIONAL DIRECTIVES

When police organizations begin to develop directives, there is a tendency to overregulate the behavior of employees. It is not uncommon to see a limited number of policies and procedures, while the development of rules addressing officer conduct appear to proliferate exhaustively. The fundamental reason for this is most likely the desire to have personnel who are above reproach and who have high standards of integrity. Furthermore, departments attempt to anticipate undesired behaviors and establish regulations to avoid the circumstances which may contribute to misconduct. If officers are involved in undesired behavior, then wide-ranging rules will provide grounds for disciplining the officers.

While it is argued that directives should be comprehensive and as exhaustive as possible, there are bounds within which they must remain. These include:

*Job Relatedness*—to regulate the conduct of officers, particularly regulations associated with off-duty behavior, the department must be able to demonstrate that the regulation is job-related and required as an integral element of the police officer's responsibilities.

*Legal Consistency*—Many types of law interact with the management of a law enforcement agency. Administrators must ensure that any directives issued are consistent with the mandates of criminal law and procedures, administrative law, labor law, civil rights, and applicable city ordinances.

*Consistency With Departmental Missions*—Promulgated policies, procedures, and rules are designed to be in support of the agency's mission, goals, and objectives. Administrators must ensure that this systemic integrity is retained.

*Issues of Authority*—When directives mandate certain actions, the department must ensure that those mandates are consistent with the employee's official police authority as well as his/her organizational authority.

*Reasonableness*—While a paranoia about officers behavior appears to surface when discussing rules of conduct, administrators must strive to ensure that those regulations are reasonable and fundamentally fair. In part, this includes leaving some latitude for unprogrammed discretion and trust in the officer's judgment. Reasonableness particularly becomes an issue when controlling duty conduct.

*Consistency With Union Contract*—If the department has negotiated a collective bargaining agreement, new directives need to be consistent with the provisions of the contract. Should regulations contrary to the agreement be deemed necessary, administrators need to seek a waiver of the provisions from the collective bargaining unit and/or attempt to build the desired changes in with the next contract negotiation. An autocratic approach, mandating directives that conflict with the contract will typically produce problems in direct proportion to the original issue of regulation.

While these are the general limits on organizational directives, other factors are worthy of consideration. At the least, directives and the disciplinary system must not violate the constitutional rights of employees. Guarantees of freedom from regulation on non-job-related actions are minimal due process rights in the disciplinary system are essential. When the system is fair and protects the rights of the officers, it will be a cooperative system. Thus, not only will compliance be higher but there will also be fewer challenges as well as having a negative effect on morale.

Promulgating directives within the above limits alone will not establish effective administrative control. The department also has a responsibility to train employees about the nature and application of directives. Similarly, there must also be effective supervision to reinforce the rules and procedures. If supervision is lax, a subliminal message is sent to the employees that they have a wider range of behavioral flexibility than is intimated through the directives.

# EVALUATING DEPARTMENTAL DIRECTIVES

If a comprehensive directive system is developed, as discussed thus far, it is incumbent that each order within that system be carefully evaluated. The *Guidebook for Law Enforcement Manual Development* observed that "any policy and procedure manual, no matter how well written, will need periodic review, updating, and revision...[therefore requiring] review on a regular basis" [1980:4-4]. The evaluation process, simply stated, determines whether the directives work or not. There is rarely a simple test which can assess many factors and then, somewhat intuitively, decide the future direction (or existence) of the directive.

Some policies and procedures may be evaluated on a quantitative basis. However, there are many inherent validity and reliability problems with quantitative measures in law enforcement activities. Moreover, quantitative measures typically cannot clearly assess the conceptual essence of a policy. As a result, it is suggested that the evaluative process be predominantly a structured qualitative activity that answers questions in six dimensions: (1) concept, (2) structure, (3) operation, (4) comprehension, (5) fundamental fairness, and (6) jurisprudence.

> *Concept*—Was the subject matter addressed by the directive an important issue in police management? Was the subject matter addressed in the proper format (e.g., policy, procedure, rule, general order, special order, memorandum)? Was the subject matter conceptually sound and consistent with accepted principles of organization and administration.
> *Structure*—Was the directive prepared in such a manner that personnel know what is prescribed or prohibited? Was the directive explicit and clear with respect to organizational expectations? Was the directive

written in a manner that was easy to understand without conflict and
duplication?

*Operations*—Could the procedures and rules be easily and reasonably
followed? Does the directive seek and accomplish intended results?
Does the directive's application ease or complicate the department's
activities?

*Comprehension*—Did the directive address all issues and alternatives
reasonably related to the subject matter addressed? Did the directive
provide guidance through its policy statement and procedures? Was
the directive clearly articulated in a straightforward manner?

*Fundamental Fairness*—Did the directive treat all persons at issue—
whether they were criminal suspects, general citizens, police department employees, or other persons with whom the organization has
official contact—in an equitable, impartial, non-discriminatory, ethical, and fundamentally fair manner?

*Jurisprudence*—Were the mandates of the directive consistent with
current criminal statutory and case law? Did the directive adequately
protect police personnel, the police department, and the jurisdiction
from liability? Was the directive consistent with the principles of
administrative law?

Administrators and others evaluating directives should use these assessment
questions as guideposts to determine the utility of departmental orders. While
there is no formula for determining acceptability, the administrator's experience
and intuition will guide him/her in the evaluation process once the cumulative
answers to these questions are digested. Weaknesses, once identified, should be
corrected and then be reinforced by training as appropriate.

# ADMINISTRATIVE CONTROL AND NONCOMPLIANCE OF DIRECTIVES

In consideration of the previous discussions, one may conclude that written
directives are important to the police organization because they:

*Inform officers of expected standards of behavior.

*Inform the community of the departmental mission, goals, values,
policies, procedures, and expected standards of officer behavior.

*Establish a common foundation for execution of the police process to
enhance operational consistency, equal protection, and due process.

*Provide grounds for discipline and counseling of errant officers.

*Provide standards for officer supervision.
*Give direction for officer training.

In light of these responsibilities, it is apparent that directives play a central role in administrative control of the organization. If officer behavior goes beyond the bound permitted by the directives, then the organization must take some form of remedial action regarding the errant employee. That action may be punitive, corrective, or a combination.

An important aspect in reviewing officer misconduct, before assessing the remedial sanction, is to understand the nature of the procedural violation. It is suggested that this can best be viewed by determining if the officer's behavior was malfeasant, misfeasant, or nonfeasant.

*Malfeasance* is the intentional commission of an act which is prohibited by law or directive, or the intentional unjust performance of some act of which the party had no right. If an officer is malfeasant in his/her behavior this is indicative that the officer deliberately violated a rule or procedure; e.g., an officer takes a gratuity despite a departmental rule prohibiting it; an officer accesses the department's computerized information system for his/her own personal use, or the officer commits perjury on the witness stand in order "to get" a criminal.

Generally speaking, such wanton behavior warrants disciplinary action and the internal ajudication process should be initiated as soon as possible. In *rare* circumstances, one may find that there was a sound reason for the officer's behavior. Should this appear to be the case, the department should nonetheless conduct an internal investigation to document the mitigating circumstances with the adjudication phase taking these circumstances under consideration. In cases of malfeasance it is essential for the integrity of the system to remain intact in order to maximize administrative control. This does not mean that discretion and leniency cannot be used when mitigation exists. Rather, it means that process will be followed and all organizational members know that the department considers such behavior serious and will scrutinize each case closely.

*Misfeasance* is the performance of a duty or act that one is obligated or permitted to do, in a manner that is improper or negligent. That is, an officer may perform his/her required duties in a "sloppy" or incorrect manner. Improper completion of reports, improper searching of arrestees, unsafe operation of a police vehicle, or aggressively "reprimanding" a citizen for a traffic violation are illustrations of misfeasance. In these cases the officer's intent is usually in keeping with the spirit of the department's responsibilities, however, the officer simply fails to perform the tasks properly.

Importantly, some of the officer's improper behavior may be attributed to the department. Misfeasance many times can be related to an officer's training, or lack thereof. That is, the officer's actions may simply be a result of the officer not knowing or understanding the proper method of performing tasks. In such cases, when action is taken against the officer for violations of procedures or rules (and typically misfeasance is a procedural violation), the department must also look at its responsibilities to ensure it has properly prepared the officer to perform his/her duties. Sanctions for misfeasant behavior should involve "positive discipline"— that is, it should have a remedial orientation rather than a punitive one.

*Nonfeasance* is the failure to perform an act which one is obligated to do either by law or organizational directive. If the failure to perform an obliged act is the result of a deliberate decision to violate the law or directive, it is malfeasance. If, however, the omission is a result of the officer's failure to recognize the obligation, then the behavior is nonfeasance. An officer who performs a "stop and frisk" but does not meet the standards of *Terry v. Ohio* would fall into this category. Similarly, the officer who responds to all minor theft and does not complete a report because there is virtually no chance of catching the perpetrator or recovering property may also be nonfeasant.

In dealing with nonfeasant employee behavior the department must once again consider its contribution to the rule and procedural violations. Poor supervision can be a significant contributor to nonfeasance as can limited training. In such instances, disciplinary sanctions should, as in the case of misfeasance, have a remedial component to correct the problem.

In practice, noncompliance with departmental directives will not neatly fit exclusively into one of these categories. Rather, the behavior will transgress the typology. The value in viewing misconduct from this perspective is to better analyze the problems in order to be fair to the officer(s) involved and to develop preventive mechanisms to minimize the potential of future problems. The administrator must recognize that police misconduct is not exclusively a problem generated by the problem employee. The problems may also be manifestations of systemic weaknesses, both in supervision and training, which also need to be addressed.

## SUMMARY

A formal directive system in both verbal and written forms is essential for the administrative guidance and control of police officer behavior. However, many police organizations have no written policies, rules, or procedures. Barker and Wells, in a survey of police agencies in one state, found that 24 percent had no written rules and regulations covering 16 patterns of police deviance (1982). As one would suspect, this was related to the size of the department. Forty percent of the smaller departments, under 9 members, had no written rules and regulations, but only 2 of the departments with over 20 members had no written rules and regulations. Even those agencies with written policies, procedures, rules, and regulations may not have a properly formulated system that is communicated to and understood by the members of the department. The IACP, in a 1975 survey of police agencies at all levels, found the following deficiencies in many departments with a written directive system:

*Not current—most had never been updated since originally issued.

*Not usable—did not accurately reflect the current position of chief administrator.

*Were not clearly written.

*In conflict, in many instances with other existing policies, procedures, rules and regulations, thereby creating confusion at upper and lower levels.

*Not distributed to operations-level personnel, and, in many cases, not even to supervisory or management personnel.

*Frequently, only one copy was in existence.

*Not compiled.

*Not enforced.

*Attempted to include too much—policies, procedures, rules and regulations were grouped together under one general heading (IACP, 1975).

Nevertheless, the perceptive police administrator knows that a written directive system is the cornerstone for administrative guidance and control. Written directives serve as the basis for remedial action, discipline, and termination. They not only provide control, they give guidance and help protect the agency from liability. Inculcating an effective system of directives in the police department's operating system provides an important foundation for responsible police management.

# REFERENCES

Barker, T. and R.O. Wells. "Police Administrators Attitudes Toward the Definition and Control of Police Deviance." *FBI Law Enforcement Bulletin.* (March, 1982): 8-16. Vol. 51(9).

Carter, D.L. (1986). "Hispanic Police Officers' Perceptions of Internal and External Discrimination." *Police Studies.* (Winter, 1986).

Carter, D.L. and D.K. Dearth (1984). *"An Assessment of the Mission,"* Texas Police Department. Unpublished Consultation's Report.

Couper, D.C. (1983). *How to Rate Your Local Police.* Washington: Police Executive Research Forum.

Davis, K.C. (1971). *Discretionary Justice.* Urbana, IL: University of Illinois Press.

del Carmen, R.V. (1986). "Civil and Criminal Liabilities of Police Officers." In T. Barker and D. Carter (eds.) *Police Deviance.* Cincinnati: Anderson Publishing Co.

Garmire, B. (ed.) (1982). *Local Government Police Management.* 2d ed. Washington: International City Management Association.

Goldstein, H. (1972). "Police Policy Formulation: A Proposal for Improving Police Performance." In H.W. More (ed.) *Critical Issues in Law Enforcement.* Cincinnati: Anderson Publishing Co.

*Guidebook for Law Enforcement Manual Development* (1980). Olympia, WA: Washington Association of Sheriffs and Police Chiefs.

Hoy, V.L. (1982). "Research and Planning." In B. Garmire (ed.) *Local Government Police Management. 2d Ed.* Washington: International City Management Association.

Hudzik, J. and G. Cordner (1983). *Planning in Criminal Justice Organizations and Systems.* New York: MacMillan Publishing Company.

International Association of Chiefs of Police (1975). *A Manual of Model Police Traffic Services: Policies.* Gaithersburg, MD: International Association of Chiefs of Police.

Los Angeles Police Department (1982). *Departmental Policy and Procedure Manuals.*

Manning, P.K. (1977). *Police Work.* Cambridge, MA: MIT Press.

Matulia, K.J. (1983). "The Use of Deadly Force: A Need for Written Directives and Training." *The Police Chief.* (May: 30-34).

*Monell v. Department of Social Services,* 436 U.S. 658, 98 S. Ct. 2018 (1978).

National Advisory Commission on Criminal Justice Standards and Goals (NAC) (1974). *Police.* Washington: U.S. Government Printing Office.

*Owen v. City of Independence,* 445 U.S. 62, 100 S. Ct. 1398 (1980).

*Owens v. Haas,* 601 F.2d 1242 (2d Cir. 1979).

President's Commission on Law Enforcement and Administration of Justice (1967). *The Challenge of Crime in a Free Society.* Washington: U.S. Government Printing Office.

*Resource Manual of Police Discretion and Rulemaking* (1980). Austin, TX: Texas Advisory Commission on Intergovernmental Relations.

Robbins, S. (1976). *The Administrative Process.* Englewood Cliffs, NJ: Prentice-Hall.

*Standards for Law Enforcement Agencies* (1984). Fairfax, VA: Commission on Accreditation for Law Enforcement Agencies.

Traffic Institute (1986). *Policy and Administrative Control, 2d Ed.* Evanston, IL: Northwestern University.

*Turpin v. Mailet,* 619 F.2d 196 (2d Cir. 1980).

Walker, S. (1983). *The Police in America.* New York: McGraw-Hill.

Wilson, J.Q. (1985). "Police Administration." In W.C. Terry (ed.) *Policing Society.* New York: John Wiley and Sons.

_____ (1968). *Varieties of Police Behavior.* Cambridge, MA: Harvard University Press.

Wilson, O.W. and R.C. McLaren (1977). *Police Administration.* New York: McGraw-Hill.

# STUDY QUESTIONS

1.   In your own words, distinguish between a policy, a procedure, and a rule. Why do you think there is so much confusion about these management tools?

2.   Discuss the relationship between organizational directives and police deviance (i.e., How are they related?).

3.   Historically, police departments did not want to promulgate policies and procedures in writing. Rather, they preferred to follow "custom." Why do you think this practice was prevalent? What was(were) the disadvantage(s) of simply relying on custom?

4.   You are an assistant to the Chief of Police. As a result of various complaints and an internal investigation, it has come to your attention that a few officers are active members of a White Supremacy Group. As far as you can tell, none of their on-duty actions reflect racism nor does it appear that the officers have used any type of police privilege to further the racist movement. After examining departmental directives, you find nothing related to police membership in racist or radical groups. You do find a policy supporting the fact that officers can exercise their constitutional rights. The Chief wants directives prohibiting, or at least controlling, such memberships. You are assigned the task. How would you approach this assignment?

5.   If organizational directives are developed based on need using a sophisticated process, why is there a need for regular evaluation and review of policies, procedures, and rules?

# 3

# POLICE ETHICS, INTEGRITY, AND OFF-DUTY BEHAVIOR: POLICY ISSUES OF OFFICER CONDUCT*

## David L. Carter and Darrel W. Stephens

An unresolved debate frequently addressed in law enforcement discipline cases is the ability of a police administrator to discipline officers for behavior that was performed while the officer was off duty. Cases have ranged from officers being drunk in public; consensual sex and cohabitation without benefit of marriage; consorting with known felons; participation in racist organizations; engaging in homosexual activity; and use of controlled substances, to name only a few. On one extreme, civil libertarians argue that the police organization has no authority to dictate off-duty behavioral standards because such dictates violate the officer's rights. At the other end of the spectrum, advocates of strict behavioral accountability maintain that given the nature of the police mandate, the organization can and must articulate very rigid standards of behavior that extend into the officer's off-duty hours. As in most debates, it appears that "the truth" lies in the middle of this spectrum.

Inherent questions associated with the issue of off-duty conduct which must be faced include: What are the ethical standards incumbent for police officers? Is there a higher standard of integrity required for police officers compared to nonsworn citizens? What legal precedent exists with respect to expectations of officer integrity? What are organizational values and their role in officer behavior? Does public opinion play a role in officer behavioral standards? What policy actions can administrators take to effectively deal with this debate? These questions focus not only on pragmatic matters of police administration but also on the philosophy of police responsibility. This makes definitive answers to the questions difficult to ascertain. The issues, therefore, are discussed in light of their history and present thought culminating in policy recommendations.

## ETHICS IN POLICING

All ethical principles are founded in philosophies which are moral, legal, and social in character. Ethics synthesize philosophical principles which have ele-

*This chapter was written expressly for inclusion in this book.

ments of *application* in the performance of one's duty and establish standards of behavioral propriety in the context of what is acceptable to society.

As noted sociologist Emile Durkheim observed, "there is no form of social activity which can do without the appropriate moral discipline" [Durkheim, 1958:14]. Attorneys, physicians, business persons, psychologists, and the clergy all have fundamental ethical principles they rely on in the decisions they make which are either directly or collaterally associated with their vocation. Similarly, the police have important ethical mandates bent on their behavior.

The International Association of Chiefs of Police (IACP) promulgated both the Law Enforcement Code of Ethics and the Canons of Police Ethics in 1957 as philosophical guides for police behavior and decision-making. The Code of Ethics...

> ...is a pledge [to be made by each law enforcement officer] to discharge fundamental law enforcement duties to the best of ability, to conduct personal affairs so as to reflect credit on one's Department, to enforce the law impartially, and to recognize the public trust implied in the job [Felkenes, 1984:212].

Both the Code and the Canons clearly articulate the recognition of higher standards of conduct for police officers on and off duty. Specifically, the Law Enforcement Code of Ethics states, in part...

> ...I will keep my private life unsullied as an example to all;...Honest in thought and deed in both my personal and official life, I will be exemplary in obeying the laws of the land and the regulations of my department... I recognize the badge of my office as a symbol of *public faith,* and I accept it as a public trust to be held so long as I am true to the ethics of the police service...[Emphasis added]

Similarly, the Canons of Police Ethics places significant responsibilities on officers with specific attention to the officers' off-duty behavior. Notably, "Article 6—Private Conduct" of the Canons states, in part,...

> The law enforcement officer shall be mindful of [his/her] special identification by the public as an upholder of the law. *Laxity of conduct or manner in private life*...cannot but reflect upon the police officer and the police service. The community and the service require the law enforcement officer lead the life of a decent and honorable [person]....
> [The officer] will so conduct [his/her] *private life that the public will regard [him/her] as an example of stability, fidelity, and morality.* [Emphasis added]

These standards have been a part of the underlying philosophy of police behavior for two decades. Their impact, however, is difficult to measure. How do we assess ethical behavior? Has the department officially incorporated these standards as policy? Are officers trained in ethics? If no formal adoption or training has occurred, can the department effectively argue that officers must adhere to these ethical principles as a matter of "professional responsibility?" If police administrators expect officers to subscribe to these principles, they must affirmatively act to incorporate those expectations in the administrative control structure.

## ETHICS AND INTEGRITY: A PRAGMATIC INTEGRATION

Since certain types of conduct—such as cohabitation, public drunkenness, or marijuana use—have become increasingly tolerated by wide and varied segments of society; the question has been posed, "Why should there be a special standard for police officers on these matters?" It is argued that the answer to this question focuses on two factors related to ethics and integrity. First, since the police have the responsibility for enforcing the law, the violation of the criminal law (even misdemeanors and ordinance violations) by a sworn officer is, at the least, an abrogation of the officer's oath of office. How can one be relied upon to perform law enforcement responsibilities if adherence to even the most basic of obligations incurred with the position cannot be maintained?

To argue the oath of office and one's vested authority as a police officer is nullified simply because the officer is off duty or out of the immediate jurisdiction raises these questions: Is there not an ethical obligation and public expectation for a physician to render aid when out of the office; for a minister to give counsel while out of the church; or for an attorney to give *pro bono publico* advice to an indigent? Certainly, these are realistic obligations to humankind which these vocations possess. The police officers' lot is similar.

It would be the rare officer, indeed, who would not respond to a person's call for distress or who would fail to render assistance in an emergency regardless of the officer's geographic location or duty status. The argument that the responsibility of an officer's position does not follow into private life fails to take in account the value system necessary to be a police officer. It further fails to consider the community expectation of the police to "practice what they preach."

A factor which complicates the off-duty argument is that many departments have limited the 24-hour responsibility to "life-threatening" situations. Departments taking this approach discourage officers from doing anything other than calling the police unless action is necessary to protect a life or stop a crime in progress. This restriction has developed over the years to address liability issues, to minimize the potential for officer injuries, to reduce the department's financial obligations to officers who take official action while off duty, and to limit the pressures of the 24-hour responsibility. Restrictions such as these preclude officers from getting involved in minor off-duty incidents, yet they clearly communicate not only the expectation but the obligation an officer has to intervene in situations where an emergency exists. With this communication, it is argued, officers must recognize the department's responsibility to establish rules related to off-duty conduct.

The second issue to be addressed is that police wrongdoing cuts to the heart of integrity. Is there a higher standard of integrity or behavior required of police officers than other members of society? The evidence suggests there ought to be. For example, the police selection process itself is evidence of the required higher standards for police personnel. The rigors of criminal history checks, extensive background investigations, and in some jurisdictions polygraph examinations for police applicants, are indicative of the desire to select persons for police service who have demonstrated the highest of behavioral standards in their personal history. While successful court challenges have been made against certain physical standards in the police selection process, the standards for persons with a reliable character and absence of criminal history have remained solidly intact. Thus, it is clear from the outset of one's entry into the police service there is an expectation by police management for officers to have a higher standard of integrity. Moreover, supervision, rules, and the disciplinary process are designed to, among other things, ensure officers are held accountable to that standard.

This accountability must be ensured by police management through its discipline, administrative controls, and the development of proper values among officers. As such, standards of behavior are commonly established to which officers must adhere. These are standards—somewhat conceptually similar to "status offenses"—which are not and cannot be required of the general public. For example, some police departments have rules that officers cannot frequent certain bars or establishments in their jurisdiction; socially consort with convicted felons; cohabit without benefit of marriage; participate in "conduct unbecoming an officer"; or may require officers to be neatly groomed and live within the incorporated limits of the jurisdiction they police. These are standards which, if violated, can result in officer discipline but do not apply to the general public.

While police managers impose rules and processes to deal with this type of conduct there is also evidence that in some cases peer group control gives support to a higher standard of integrity. That is, the research suggests that the occupational culture of the police, while having its own forms of accepted deviance (e.g., "cooping" or accepting minor gratuities such as free coffee), also has its own standards of behavior. Generally speaking, police officers expect higher standards of behavior from their peers than from members of the general society. While turning in fellow officers who deviate from that standard may not always occur, there is the strong likelihood that the informal sanction of peer group rejection may occur (c.f., Blumberg and Niederhoffer, 1985).

Whether they like it or not, the police are indeed subjected to a double-standard on the issue of integrity. As noted by Elliston...

> One standard applies to ordinary citizens, and a second—a higher standard—applies to the police. Conduct in their personal life, which might otherwise be disregarded, is subject to reproach, discipline, and even dismissal. If an officer's lawn is a garbage heap or his children dirty, he may hear from his sergeant...if a police officer engaged in sex outside of marriage, he could be disciplined. If he committed adultery, he could be dismissed from his job...an officer risks compromising his career for flagrant violations of society's mores—even if legal and private. [1985:280].

## Police Integrity and the Courts

On a few occasions the courts have been directly faced with this issue. In *Calvert v. Pontiac,* 288 Mich 401 (1939), a Michigan court stated that a police officer is a person...

> ...whose character must be above reproach and whose truthfulness must be above suspicion. [The officer's] veracity and integrity must be relied upon in the performance of [his/her] duties and the trial of criminal cases (288 Mich at 404).

Similarly, in *Royal v. Ecorse Police and Fire Commission,* 75 NW2d 841 (1956), the court stated that a police officer's intent on retaining a position on the force can expect, as in the military, to be held to a higher standard of conduct.

This is conceptually supported by a U.S. Supreme Court case wherein a different and higher standard of conduct for military personnel was upheld. In *Parker v. Levy,* 417 U.S. 733 (1974), the Court upheld the court martial's finding of "conduct unbecoming an officer" because of the need to foster an orderly and dutiful fighting force. The underlying theme of the Court's logic focused on the need for administrative controls that maintain organizational integrity in furtherance of the protection of the country. The conceptual relationship between the Court's logic in this case and the authors' argument is based on two factors.

First, there is a recognition that most law enforcement agencies are organized as a paramilitary structure. Generally speaking, this includes a fairly rigid chain of command, ranks with defined organizational responsibility, stringent standards for personnel control, utilization of government resources to maintain order and provide services, highly structured administrative control mechanisms, characteristics of the traditional bureaucracy, and articulated expectations of personnel performance and behavior. The similarities have been noted in varying degrees by the courts and the literature. With the recognition that their mission and authority is different, similar standards of organizational integrity are necessary in order to properly perform their respective missions.

Second, because of the significant powers possessed by the police to arrest, conduct searches and seizures, and use force, there is a recognition that strong controls must be in place to reduce the potential for abuse of these powers. Just as the court found the military needed to maintain a dutiful and orderly fighting force in *Parker v. Levy, supra,* the police need a dutiful and orderly force to fulfill their mission to protect citizens and the democratic process.

More recently, a Minnesota court of appeals upheld the firing of an officer on the grounds of his competency and fitness for duty based on the officer's *off-duty* behavior. In its decision that an officer's off-duty conduct can be regulated by a police department, the court of appeals stated that a police department can demand its officers maintain a higher level of conduct than that expected from society, *Thompson v. City of Appleton,* 366 NW2d 326 (1985).

While legal precedent on the issue is not exhaustive, there is sufficient evidence to suggest the genesis of a trend. This trend, as illustrated above, with jurisprudential roots going back to 1939 and extending to current cases, articulates the need for law enforcement officers to maintain a level of integrity higher than the average citizen because of the authority and responsibilities the public entrusts to the police.

## Values

An important trend in the maintenance of police integrity is the inculcation of values in police personnel—both formally and informally. The police department must infuse a belief system among its officers to accept certain responsibilities and standards of conduct as being proper. The propriety affects both their on-duty and off-duty behavior so that they will not only be good employees but also good citizens. This may be accomplished through leading by example, ongoing training on values and value systems, and articulation of expectations and value statements.

Importantly, the process of inculcating values cannot be coercive, rather it must be consensual. To be effective it is a long-term process which integrates ethics, the departmental mission, professional responsibility, fairness, due process, and empathy. A department which attempts to coerce values will meet with little success.

Chief David Couper of the Madison, Wisconsin Police Department promulgated the mission and values statement illustrated in Table 3.1. The statement clearly indicates managerial philosophy as well as expectations of employees. It establishes important values (e.g., belief in dignity, protecting rights, openness, etc.) that Chief Couper expects of his employees. It is a consensual statement extolling that "we" subscribe to these values in performing the job of law enforcement.

---

### TABLE 3.1

#### MADISON, WISCONSIN POLICE DEPARTMENT VALUES STATEMENT

We have developed a mission statement that attempts to capture the values that "drive" and direct our organization:
WE BELIEVE IN THE DIGNITY AND WORTH OF ALL PEOPLE. WE ARE COMMITTED TO:
   Providing high-quality, community-oriented police services.
   Protecting Constitutional rights.
   Problem solving.
   Teamwork.
   Openness.
   Planning for the future.
   Providing leadership to the profession.
We are proud of the diversity of our workforce which permits us to grow and which respects each of us as individuals and we strive for a healthful workplace [Madison Police Department *Newsletter,* December 26, 1986].

---

In 1987, the Michigan State Police (MSP) established a values statement as shown in Table 3.2. The reader will note that the MSP value statement (a) is more formal than the Madison statement and (b) specifically addressed off-duty conduct. Despite these differences, the MSP statement addresses the same fundamental concepts and expectations of employees. Importantly, it must be recognized that the articulation of the value statement is only the beginning. For it to have meaning, it must be taught and practiced by all personnel throughout the chain of command regardless of their rank or assignment.

---

### TABLE 3.2

#### MICHIGAN STATE POLICE STATEMENT OF VALUES

The Michigan Department of State Police has been entrusted with duties and responsibilities to preserve, protect, and defend people and property and maintain social order. The public trust mandates that all members exemplify the highest standard of conduct both on and off duty.
   Departmental members shall uphold all laws and function in an ethical, courteous, impartial and professional manner while respecting the rights and dignity of all persons.

Tables 3.3 and 3.4 illustrate the value statements of the Newport News, Virginia and Houston, Texas Police Departments, respectively. These values are significantly more detailed than the Madison and MSP examples, notably through the strong sense of moral obligation dedicated to the police organization and police services. On the specific matter of police integrity, the Houston value statement contains supporting commentary...

> The integrity of the Department must not be compromised. There can be no question or suspicion among the citizenry regarding Department ethics. It is imperative that the Department maintain the highest levels of integrity and credibility, ensuring that its standards are sufficiently high so there is not even a perception among citizens that questionable practices exist. Professionalism, in this sense, means adherence to impeccable integrity and careful protection of all citizens' rights. It also includes the maintenance of equally high levels of accountability from those authorized to enforce the law [Houston Police Department, undated:7]

This statement should leave no question in the mind of officers about the department's position and expectation concerning improper behavior.

Subscribed values enhance the quality of organizational life not only because of their "moral" implications but also because they induce people to behave in a certain manner because it is "right." Clearly, compliant behavior is far more desirable than complete reliance on negative control mechanisms.

The inculcation of values and the adherence to a higher standard of integrity will not necessarily make officers role models for the public. However, the adoption of values will provide a basis for making officers more conscientious employees. It will also serve as a basis for letting the community know the organization's fundamental beliefs in carrying out its responsibilities.

## The Environment for Integrity

Administrative mandates for high moral fiber are set forth in departmental codes of conduct and the managerial philosophies of administrators. For example, one police executive of an American city, commenting on substance abuse by officers, stated ...

> The police officer profession must be above suspicion by all members of society. Police officers are entrusted with many powers and

## TABLE 3.3

### NEWPORT NEWS, VIRGINIA POLICE DEPARTMENT VALUES

VALUE #1

The Newport News Police Department is committed to protecting and preserving the rights of individuals as guaranteed by the Constitution.

VALUE #2

While the Newport News Police Department believes the prevention of crime is its primary responsibility, it aggressively pursues those who commit serious offenses.

VALUE #3

The Newport News Police Department believes integrity and professionalism are the foundation for trust in the community.

VALUE #4

The Newport News Police Department is committed to an open and honest relationship with the community.

VALUE #5

The Newport News Police Department is committed to effectively managing its resources for optimal service delivery.

VALUE #6

The Newport News Police Department is committed to participating in programs which incorporate the concept of a shared responsibility with the community in the delivery of police services.

VALUE #7

The Newport News Police Department actively solicits citizen participation in the development of police and programs which impact their neighborhood.

VALUE #8

The Newport News Police Department believes that it achieves its greatest potential through the active participation of its employees in the development and implementation of policies and programs.

VALUE #9

The Newport News Police Department recognizes and supports academic achievement and employees and promotes their pursuit of higher education.

---

### TABLE 3.4

#### HOUSTON, TEXAS POLICE DEPARTMENT PHILOSOPHY AND VALUES

---

The mission of the Houston Police Department is to enhance the quality of life in the City of Houston by working cooperatively with the public and within the framework of the United States Constitution to enforce the laws, preserve the peace, reduce fear, and provide for a safe environment.

The articulated values of the Houston Police Department in support of this mission are:

* Policing the community involves major responsibility and authority. The police cannot carry out their responsibilities alone; thus they must be willing to involve the community in all aspects of policing which directly impacts the quality of community life.
* The Police Department believes it has a responsibility to react to criminal behavior in a way that emphasizes prevention and that is marked by vigorous law enforcement.
* The Police Department adheres to the fundamental principle that it must deliver its services in a manner that preserves and advances democratic values.
* The Department is committed to delivering police services in a manner which will best reinforce the strengths of the city's neighborhoods.
* The Department is committed to allowing public input in the development of its policies which directly impact neighborhood life.
* The Department will collaboratively work with neighborhoods to understand the true nature of the neighborhood's crime problems and develop meaningful cooperative strategies which will best deal with those problems.
* The Department is committed to managing its resources in the most effective manner possible.
* The Department will actively seek the input and involvement of all employees in matters which impact job performance and manage the organization in a manner which will enhance employee job satisfaction and effectiveness.
* The Department is committed to maintaining the highest levels of integrity and professionalism in all its operations.
* The Department believes that the police function operates most effectively when the organization and its operations are marked by stability, continuity, and consistency.

authorities and can at any given moment be called upon to make a life-and-death decision...It would seem to be reasonable to expect that police officers maintain a high moral standard [and avoid circumstances]...that would alter their ability to make a sound decision at any given moment [Police Executive Research Forum, 1986:1].

A police officer is a public official with a particular unique moral obligation not to violate the law (Lowenthal, 1981). This seems a simple concept. It can, however, place a police officer in a dilemma. A socio-cultural dichotomy exists. Even though it is unacceptable for any person to violate the law, it seems even more discrepant when a police officer does so, regardless of whether the violation carries little social condemnation. Does the officer compromise his/her integrity for violating minor laws? Are ethical standards abrogated by this behavior? Certainly, the answers to these questions must be examined from the differing perspectives of social/public expectations, legal mandates, administrative guidelines, ethical constraints of the occupation, and moral beliefs held by the individual officer.

The problems imposed on officers with these prescriptions of integrity contribute to ethical inconsistencies in the practice of policing. Through socialization, a person learns that certain behaviors (e.g., speeding, drinking in public, cheating on taxes) while unlawful, are not inherently wrong (i.e., the so-called mala prohibita offenses). Violations of such laws frequently bring inconvenience, sometimes embarrassment, but seldom serious condemnation. However, when that person becomes a sworn officer, the standards of behavior change and all facets of that person's behavior are expected to reach a "hyper-caliber" of integrity. This is a social reality that many police officers may begrudgingly recognize but do not readily accept.

"The belief that police employees must be more circumspect in their off-duty hours than other workers is a major element in the majority of [labor] arbitration cases...[In one case] the city argued for higher standards for police functionaries: the City has [this] responsibility to the citizenry..." [Marmo, 1986:106]. According to Marmo, not only is the argument that police employees can be held to higher standards of off-duty behavior frequently raised by police administrators, "it is uniformly accepted by arbitrators" [1986:107]. He goes on to note that...

As has long been the case in the private sector, arbitrators have held that police administrators have the right to discipline police personnel for their off-duty behavior when it has an adverse impact on the department that employs them. In fact, because of the sensitive nature of police work and its susceptibility to adverse publicity, police personnel are held to higher standards of off-duty behavior than workers in other types of employment [1986:110].

# THE FACTORS OF PUBLIC OPINION

Overall, the public has a fairly high opinion of the police. They feel law enforcement officers are honest, concerned, faithful to duty, have a high level of integrity, perform their job in the best interests of society, do not abuse their authority, and are fair in enforcement of laws (c.f., McGarrell and Flanagan, 1985; Radelet, 1986). These opinions can be influenced, however, by scandal, misconduct, or even unflattering publicity about the police department. "A direct relationship exists between the publicity given police employees' off-duty behavior and the adverse impact on management; that is, the greater the amount of publicity, the greater the chance the department will be perceived in a negative light" [Marmo, 1986:107].

Public opinion of the police is also influenced by behaviors which bring into question matter of police integrity. In McAllen, Texas, vivid videotapes of several instances wherein police officers used unjustified physical force on prisoners were broadcast on local television stations as well as on the network news. During the time of the initial broadcasts, public opinion of the police dropped significantly and the police department was the subject of significant ridicule. In Philadelphia, when the house occupied by the radical MOVE group was confronted by police in an attempt to apprehend the members, resulting in 11 deaths and 61 destroyed homes in the neighborhood, the police department experienced significant condemnation even though some of the critical decisions were apparently made by city officials not in the police command structure. The drug-running scandals in New York's 77th Precinct left the New York Police Department at a significant center of distrust—almost fear—from the perspective of many citizens. Dallas recently has seen an unusually high number of shootings by police officers with most of the victims being black. The publicity surrounding the incidents has set off significant controversy and public calls to investigate and control the police department. Confessions by Miami police officers of participation in a violent drug ring have brought criticism of the department's selection, supervision, and control.

While these represent a summary of significant problems in various departments, the point to note is that each of these incidents focused on police impropriety, or the allegation of same, and were publicized nationally. Not only did the publicity influence citizens' attitudes toward the police in the respective cities, national opinion was directed at the police departments and their cities concerning the environment of impropriety. Questions have been raised about the departments' "loss of control" in these agencies as well as the character of the officers.

Although public support for the police is generally high, it is of a fragile nature. Because of the stock we place in our constitutional rights and democratic freedoms, the public retains concerns about police authority and its abuse. When there are reports of officers involved in misconduct, the department's image can become tainted and public support can wain. With decreased support, a plethora of problems can arise ranging from budget issues, competency, and the capability of the police to effectively perform their tasks.

# POLICY IMPLICATIONS

This chapter has addressed a wide variety of issues associated with police integrity and off-duty behavior. Importantly, these two factors are intricately linked together. Dimensions of ethics, values, laws, and labor arbitrations have been addressed to illustrate the many variables implicit with this administrative dilemma. It has been demonstrated that precedent clearly exists for both requiring higher standards of behavior for police officers and outlining some forms of conduct expectations for off-duty officers. As a result, the following policy-related actions are recommended to enhance administrative control on matters of off-duty conduct and standards of integrity.

1. The department should affirmatively articulate its position that a higher standard of conduct and integrity applies to sworn police officers than to non-sworn citizens. Such a policy statement should be supported by a clear definition of the concept and citation of supporting literature to show the logic of the department's position.
2. If the department has expectations of behavior for off-duty officers, those expectations should be specified in written policy and procedures. Included in such an order should be the distinction, if any, for the officer when he/she is outside of the employing jurisdiction. Regardless of the department's position on this issue, it should be detailed in written policy. If the department expects officers to take official action as necessary when off duty, the department must also be prepared to compensate the officer and afford all protections and privileges it would to an officer who acts on duty.
3. Consistent with the concept of professionalism and standards of ethical conduct, all police officers have the obligation—on or off duty—to report to Internal Affairs (or similar appropriate channels) any wrongdoing by officers. Wrongdoing includes both the violation of criminal laws and departmental rules. As with other recommendations, this obligation must be written and incorporated in the department's policies and procedures.
4. If the police department is going to subscribe to the Law Enforcement Code of Ethics and/or Canons of Police Ethics, the standards should be *formally* adopted as part of the agency's policies.

5. Departments which have a contract with a collective bargaining unit should attempt to get contractual provisions in the agreement which address: (a) the expected higher standard of integrity for officers; (b) off-duty responsibilities of officers; and (c) a position on special off-duty conduct.
6. If departments have not articulated a clear set of value statements, it should be done to effectively inform employees and the public of the department's philosophical and operational standards (Carter and Stephens, 1988).

While the policy recommendations have been written specifically with sworn officers in mind, administrators must also consider what policies should be applicable to civilian employees. With increased civilianization in police departments, one finds non-sworn personnel in a wide variety of positions with varying degrees of responsibility. It is unrealistic (and perhaps unjustifiable) to apply the same policies and rules to a civilian mechanic in the police department's garage that would be applied to a civilian intelligence analyst. As such, departmental policy on issues of conduct and integrity will most likely need to be selectively applied to civilian positions based on logically deduced criteria.

Once new policies, procedures, and rules are developed they must be effectively communicated to all appropriate personnel. This includes not only distributing the information to employees but also ensuring that all aspects of the new directives are understood. Communications should include, at the minimum, dissemination of the written directives and discussion of the policies during training sessions. It is important to recognize that for the integrity and conduct directives to have an impact—either directly on behavior or collaterally through court or grievance hearings—the *rationale* for the directives, the *communication* of the directives, and the *enforcement* of the directives must be demonstrated on a day-to-day basis.

# REFERENCES

Blumberg, A.S. and E. Niederhoffer (eds.) (1985). *The Ambivalent Force, 3rd ed.* New York: Holt, Rinehart, and Winston.

*Calvert v. Pontiac* 288 Mich 401 (1939).

Carter, D.L. and D.W. Stephens. (1988). *Drug Abuse by Police Officers: An Analysis of Critical Police Issues.* Springfield, IL: Charles C Thomas, Publisher.

Durkheim, E. (1958). *Professional Ethics and Civic Morals.* Translated by C. Brookfield. Glencoe, IL: The Free Press.

Elliston, F.A. (1985). "Police, Privacy, and the Double Standard." In F.A. Elliston and M. Feldberg (eds.) *Moral Issues in Police Work.* Totowa, NJ: Rowan and Allenheld, Publishers.

Felkenes, G.T. (1984). "Attitudes of Police Officers Toward Their Professional Ethics." *Journal of Criminal Justice.* Vol. 12:211-230.

Houston (Texas) Police Department. (undated). *Statement of Philosophy and Values.*

International Association of Chiefs of Police (IACP) (1957). *Canons of Police Ethics.* Gaithersburg, MD.

International Association of Chiefs of Police (IACP) (1957). *Law Enforcement Code of Ethics.* Gaithersburg, MD.

Lowenthal, M.A. (1981). "Police Professionalism—Law and Ethics." *Journal of Contemporary Criminal Justice.* (2:1) page numbers missing.

Madison (WI) Police Department, (1986). Newsletter: *Office of the Chief.* Vol. 14, No. 8 (December 23).

Marmo, M. (1986). "Off-Duty Behavior by Police: Arbitrators Determine if On-the-Job Discipline is Appropriate." *Journal of Police Science and Administration.*

McGarrell, E.F. and T. Flanagan (eds.) (1985). *Sourcebook of Criminal Justice Statistics.* Washington, DC: Bureau of Justice Statistics.

Michigan State Police. (undated). *Statement of Values, Mission, and Goals.* Unpublished administrative document.

Newport News, Virginia Police Department. (undated). *Statement of Values.* Unpublished administrative document.

*Parker v. Levy,* 417 U.S. 733 (1974).

Police Executive Research Forum. (1986). *Task Force Report on Police Drug Use.* Washington, DC: (unpublished).

Radelet, L.A. (1986). *The Police and the Community. 4th Edition.* New York: MacMillan Publishing Company.

*Royal v. Ecorse Police and Fire Commission,* 75 N.W.2d 841 (1956).

*Thompson v. City of Appleton,* 366 N.W.2d 326 (1985).

# STUDY QUESTIONS

1. What is meant by a "higher standard of integrity" for police officers? What effect does that have on issues such as training, supervision, and off-duty behavior?

2. What controversies are associated with police officers taking official police action while they are off duty? What is your opinion about these controversies?

3. *Argument 1 on Ethics:* A Code of Ethics is nothing but a collection of emotional words espousing principles which sound good but are vague and lack substance.
   *Argument 2 on Ethics:* A Code of Ethics provides a conceptual foundation for what police responsibilities ought to be and how police services ought to be provided. It is up to the police organization to provide meaning to the ethics.
   There are logical components to each argument. Discuss the critical elements of each.

4. Carefully reread the values of either the Houston or the Newport News Police Department. Assume you are a new patrol officer and are given these values. You are told, "These values guide everything you do as a police officer." Describe, within this context, what the values mean to you.

5. Given the policy recommendations for ethics, values, and a higher standard of integrity, think of the police department in your hometown. Would the chief implement any or all of these recommendations? Why or why not? What characteristics of the chief, department, and community would facilitate or hinder implementation of these recommendations?

# 4

# PEER GROUP SUPPORT FOR POLICE OCCUPATIONAL DEVIANCE*

## Thomas Barker

Within the past few years there has been a great deal of interest in police corruption. In addition to journalistic accounts, several ex-officers have described their deviant exploits (Schecter and Phillips, 1973; Barrett, 1973). Large-scale investigations into corrupt police behavior have occurred in Chicago, Indianapolis, New York City, and Philadelphia. This interest has been accompanied by urgent calls for scientific research into the causes and prevention of corruption (Criminal Justice Newsletter, 1972; National Advisory Commission on Criminal Justice Standards and Goals, 1973; Law Enforcement Council, 1974). The first annual symposium of the American Academy for Professional Law Enforcement was entirely devoted to "Corruption and Its Management."

A review of the literature reveals no reliable research on the subject. Works which could be classified as scientific research lack operational definitions, valid data sources, or both. A widely quoted work, Stoddard (1968), used one knowledgeable informant as a data source and contains numerous errors of fact and interpretation (see Barker, 1976). The area is still clouded by few, if any, theories, a large number of popular definitions, and very little empirical research.

The author believes that one of the reasons for the lack of research in this area is the lack of theoretical frames of reference to guide such research endeavors. The purpose of this paper is to suggest a frame of reference which may guide research and stimulate discussion.

## FRAME OF REFERENCE

Although there are few specific theories of police corruption, there have been two recurring themes used to account for its occurrence. The first, and what has been the most often used by police administrators and laypersons, is the "myth" of the "rotten apple."

According to this theory which bordered an official Department doctrine, any policeman found to be corrupt must promptly be denounced

* Reprinted from *Criminology*, Vol. 15, No. 3 (November 1977). Reprinted with permission of Sage Publications, Inc.

as a rotten apple, in an otherwise clean barrel. It must never be admitted that his individual corruption may be symptomatic of underlying disease [Knapp Commission, 1973:6].

The "rotten apples" are either weak individuals who have slipped through the elaborate screening process of most police departments and succumbed to the temptations inherent in police work, or deviant individuals who continue their deviant practices in an environment which provides them ample opportunity. Investigations have shown little support for this explanation (Knapp Commission, 1973). Patrick Murphy (1973:72), president of The Police Foundation and former police commissioner of New York City, states:

The "rotten apple" theory won't work any longer. Corrupt police officers are not natural born criminals, nor morally wicked men, constitutionally different from their honest colleagues. The task of corruption control is to examine the barrel, not just the apples—the organization, not just the individuals in it, because corrupt police are made, not born.

In dealing with police corruption, one has a subject population which is supposedly free of deviant sophistication upon entry into the occupation. Most, but not all, police organizations have elaborate background examinations which would eliminate prospective members with prior deviant experiences. The New York City Police Department, the scene of one of the most extensive police corruption exposés in recent history, accepts only 9 percent to 15 percent of all applicants (Symonds, 1970).

The "rotten apple" theme is best seen as an impression management or "normalization of deviance" technique rather than an explanation of police corrupt behavior (see Lemert, 1967). The initial reaction to police administrators, applying the label "rotten apple" or "rogue cop" to publicly exposed officers, is an attempt to "normalize" or invent plausible excuses and explanations for deviant conduct. Even those who use this technique often recognize the futility of this political rhetoric.

A second theme, more in line with sociological theory, is a functional explanation of police corruption. That is, police corruption is the latent result of society's attempts to execute unenforceable "victimless" crime laws. This has been the most popular sociological explanation and appears in the writings of most sociologists who mention this topic (Schur, 1969; Manning, 1974). However, this explanation does not encompass many patterns of police corrupt behavior that have no direct relationship to so-called "victimless crimes," e.g., accepting gratuities from businessmen, opportunistic theft, fixing traffic tickets, burglaries, and robberies. A functional explanation may explain some but not all patterns of corruption.

# OCCUPATIONAL DEVIANCE

Clinard and Quinney (1967) have suggested that Sutherland's concept of "white collar crime" be expanded to include all criminal violations which occur in the course of occupational activity. Occupational crimes are occupational violations by "normal" persons during the course of occupational activity and are related to employment (Robin, 1974). However, even this concept is too narrow for the study of occupational deviance. Many deviant acts committed during the course of one's occupational activity are deviant (violations of norms) but are not necessarily criminal, e.g., some violations of professional ethics by doctors, dentists, lawyers, politicians; the presentation of false data by college professors and researchers (cf. Bryant, 1974); and other work norm violations (Snizek, 1974). These activities violate accepted occupational norms but not codified laws.

A broadening of Robin's definition of occupational crime to cover occupational deviance, i.e., deviant behavior (criminal and noncriminal) committed during the course of "normal" work activities, will provide a framework for a study of police corruption. A definition of occupational deviance should encompass violations of any or all the following normative systems: criminal acts which are directly related to employment, violations of occupationally prescribed ethical standards, and violations of work rules and regulations. In addition, for a violation to be considered an act of corruption, the police officer must receive or expect to receive some material reward or gain. Any definition of police corruption requires some external referent, but this external reference system need not be confined to legal violations. Any proscribed act which involves the misuse of the officer's official position for actual or expected material reward or gain is police corruption.

Most occupations provide its members with three elements which are important to an understanding of occupational deviance: (1) opportunity structure and its accompanying techniques of rule violations, (2) socialization through occupational experiences, and (3) reinforcement and encouragement from the occupational peer group, i.e., group support for certain rule violation.

Every work specialty houses a unique opportunity for pathological behavior, and both the formal and informal system may tend to motivate and facilitate the actualizing of this opportunity structure. Finally, the occupational subculture provides indoctrination and socialization as well as reinforcement and reward for such deviant patterns, rendering them seemingly relevant and functional as well as sanctioned [Bryant, 1974:94].

## OPPORTUNITY STRUCTURE IN THE POLICE

The occupational setting and its attendant opportunity structure is a signifi-cant issue in the matter of corrupt police behavior. The occupational structure provides the police officer with more than ample opportunity for a wide range of deviant activities. The police come into contact with a melange of deviant actors during their normal work routine, under conditions of little or no supervision.

Many of these deviant individuals are willing to pay considerable sums to avoid arrest. A "black Mafia" narcotics kingpin was arrested in New York City for offering two police officers a $130,000 bribe to ignore two pistols found in his car. He had $133,000 in cash on him when he was arrested (*Atlanta Journal,* 1974). Members of a Chicago gambling syndicate offered a newly elected Dallas sheriff $40,000 a month for protection for their illicit operations (Leonard and More, 1974:429). Unfortunately, police officers operating alone and unobserved may be placed in a position to accept more money than they make in a year's salary (Knapp Commission, 1973). There are extreme examples, but sooner or later every police officer will probably be offered a payoff or bribe to ignore some violation, a fact not overlooked by some police officers.

In the area of so-called "victimless crimes," the police officer is placed in a very untenable position. He has a great deal of discretionary power in what are primarily police-invoked actions, i.e., whatever action is taken comes about through his own initiative. He must also act as a mediator between those elements of society who want to engage in these activities and those who would wish to see them suppressed. It is very possible that many forms of police corruption in the area of vice enforcement may be the working of institutionalized arrangements in order to maintain community peace. To enforce unwanted and unsupported laws may be more disruptive to the community than to allow them to operate in a regulated fashion.

Their position as regulators of vice activities presents the police with the oppor-tunity to "go on the pad," collect a "steady note," or "collect the rent." That is, police officers may collect systematic and regular payoffs from illegal operators.

During routine investigative duties, officers have the opportunity to "take" items from burglary scenes and unsecured businesses. In their security checks, they are expected to find burglarized buildings, unlocked doors, and open win-dows. Upon finding them it is part of their occupational duties to enter the business and look for the possible burglary suspects. They also have the oppor-tunity to look for the owner's "stash" (money hidden in the business by the owner) on the pretext of looking for a name and number to call and notify of a disturbance at the business. Corrupt officers can rifle the cash register, pick up change and currency lying on the floor, or take merchandise.

In a Southern city with a population of over 300,000, a police officer told me:

Well, we found this one safe job, and called for a backup car to help us search the building. There was change lying all over the floor, but when those two guys' [backup car] left you would've thought someone had vacuumed the place.

One captain said that it helps if a police officer is a little dishonest when he is making security checks.

I've never seen an effective policeman who was completely honest. To be an effective officer a man has to be part "rabbit." If he is honest, he does not understand what he sees when a man is in a business [referring to a burglary as a business].

The police officer has numerous occasions to engage in other forms of occupational deviance unrelated to material reward or gain. He is required to testify in court as part of his duties, and he may lie or distort the truth in order to insure a conviction (see Younger, 1967; Chevigny, 1969; Comment, 1971). Some acts of perjury are related to corruption, e.g., an officer agrees to leave out certain pertinent facts or misrepresent material elements of an arrest in order to "fix" a criminal prosecution. But not all acts of police perjury are the result of police venality; the largest percentage probably occur through the overzealous and misguided efforts of well-intentioned officers who believe that "good" crime control requires some misrepresentation of the facts. In this case, the organizational ends—convictions—becomes more important than the means to attain them. The nature of police duties, working alone or in pairs beyond the eyes of any immediate supervisor, presents the police officer with situations to engage in other work-related deviance such as brutality, sleeping on duty, drinking on duty, and illicit sex on duty (cf. Reiss, 1972).

This occupational opportunity structure also varies by placement in the organizational structure. The "street cop" may have a limited range of corruption opportunities, e.g., traffic offenders, business burglaries, or street "scores." The plainclothes officer has a limited but more lucrative range of opportunities. Specialized detective divisions have a demarcated set of opportunities, according to the specific deviant actors with whom they come into contact. The organizational placement of police supervisors provides them with the opportunity to get a "piece of the action" from all their subordinates or "sell" their occupational prerogatives, e.g., days off, work assignments.

# SOCIALIZATION THROUGH OCCUPATIONAL EXPERIENCES

A typical police organization represents a form of social organization in which a continuing collectivity of individuals shares a significant activity (police duties); the individuals have a history of continuing interaction based on that activity (clannishness); they acquire a major portion of their identity from the closeness of this interaction (police solidarity); and they share special norms and values with a particular argot. In short, most police organizations possess the qualities of a subculture (Skolnick, 1966; Strecher, 1967).

As Skolnick (1966) points out, a recurring theme in the sociology of occupations is the effect of man's work on his outlook of the world. The American police are socially isolated from the society and community they serve and draw a substantial number of friends from their police group. They have little social participation in outside organizations, such as church, voluntary, and civic organizations. Because of social isolation and withdrawal into their own group for support and approval, the police officer becomes subjected to intense peer group influence and control. The peer group can set up and maintain effective subcultural mechanisms of informal control through occupational socialization, including prescribed deviant conduct.

The occupational socialization of the rookie officer takes place in two stages, rookie school and training by older men on the job. The temporal order is not the same in all departments; the new man may work in the field for some time before attending rookie school or he may receive all his training from the members of the department with no rookie school.

Even if the neophyte officer should be sent to the academy before he begins actual police duties, the work group remains his main source of occupational socialization. One source estimates that 85 percent of American police officers have received the major portion of their occupational training via on-the-job training by fellow officers (Leonard and More, 1974). Most formal training at the academies is generally considered irrelevant and useless by police officers. The real training of recruits occurs in the street under the tutelage of veterans and street-wise officers. This training promotes norms and behavior patterns ignored or repudiated by academy instructors. (Van Maanen, 1974).

Savitz (1971) longitudinally tested recruits at three different time periods and found that they became more permissive toward corrupt police conduct and approximated the values of experienced officers as they progressed in the work group. The recruits began to favor less severe punishments for taking a $10 bribe not to issue a traffic ticket or for stealing liquor from a guarded store.

A traditional pattern of most police training is for experienced patrolmen to train the rookie officer. The traditional promotion system is advancement from within the department. These structural patterns appear to be contributing factors in corruption scandals which have become common in certain American police departments (cf. Sherman, 1974). Once patterns of corrupt conduct become entrenched in a police organization, they may be passed from one generation of officers to the next through occupational socialization.

TABLE 4.1. QUESTION: IN YOUR OPINION HOW OFTEN DO YOU THINK POLICEMEN IN YOUR DEPARTMENT WOULD REPORT ANOTHER POLICEMAN FOR THE FOLLOWING ACTS?

| CORRUPT PATTERNS | RESPONSES | | | | | | | |
|---|---|---|---|---|---|---|---|---|
| | Always | | Sometimes | | Rarely | | Never | |
| | N | % | N | % | N | % | N | % |
| CORRUPTION OF AUTHORITY | | | | | | | | |
| Free Meals | 1 | ( 2) | 9 | (21) | 14 | (33) | 19 | (44) |
| Services or Discounts | 4 | ( 9) | 13 | (30) | 13 | (30) | 13 | (30) |
| Liquor | 8 | (19) | 13 | (30) | 16 | (37) | 6 | (14) |
| KICKBACKS | | | | | | | | |
| Money | 19 | (44) | 11 | (26) | 8 | (19) | 5 | (12) |
| Goods & Services | 11 | (26) | 14 | (33) | 11 | (26) | 7 | (16) |
| OPPORTUNISTIC THEFTS | | | | | | | | |
| Victims | 33 | (77) | 7 | (16) | — | (—) | 3 | ( 7) |
| Burglary or Unlocked | 25 | (58) | 11 | (26) | 4 | ( 9) | 3 | ( 7) |
| Buildings | 25 | (58) | 11 | (26) | 4 | ( 9) | 3 | ( 7) |
| SHAKEDOWNS | | | | | | | | |
| Criminals | 30 | (70) | 10 | (23) | 1 | ( 2) | 2 | ( 5) |
| PROTECTION OF ILLEGAL ACTIVITIES | | | | | | | | |
| Vice Operators | 32 | (74) | 6 | (14) | 1 | ( 2) | 4 | ( 9) |
| Businessmen | 34 | (79) | 5 | (12) | 1 | ( 2) | 3 | ( 7) |
| TRAFFIC FIX | 32 | (74) | 6 | (14) | 1 | ( 2) | 4 | ( 9) |
| MISDEMEANOR FIX | 21 | (49) | 11 | (26) | 6 | (14) | 5 | (12) |
| FELONY FIX | 37 | (86) | 1 | ( 2) | 1 | ( 2) | 4 | ( 9) |
| DIRECT CRIMINAL ACTIVITIES | | | | | | | | |
| Burglary | 34 | (79) | 5 | (12) | 1 | ( 2) | 3 | ( 7) |
| Robbery | 38 | (88) | 1 | ( 2) | — | (—) | 4 | ( 9) |
| INTERNAL PAYOFFS | | | | | | | | |
| Off-days, etc. | 18 | (42) | 13 | (30) | 7 | (16) | 5 | (12) |
| Work assignments | 20 | (47) | 9 | (21) | 9 | (21) | 5 | (12) |

N = 43

# GROUP SUPPORT FOR RULE VIOLATIONS

Matza states that the major contribution of sociology to the understanding of deviance consists of two fundamental insights: "First, persistent deviance typically is not a solitary enterprise; rather it best flourishes when it receives *group support*. Second, deviance typically is not an individual or group innovation, rather it has a history in particular locales" (Matza, 1964:63, emphasis added). In many police departments one finds two factors: group support for certain deviant practices and long histories of corrupt activities.

Many patterns of police deviance, including certain forms of corruption, are examples of what Schur terms "forms of approved deviance in organizational settings," i.e., deviant behavior which does not reflect unfavorably on the individual's overall identity (Schur, 1971:25). These forms of "approved deviance" are supported by the group in the sense that they are not defined as deviant and actors who engage in them run little risk of exposure and sanction.

In an investigation of deviance in one medium-sized police department, I found that the perceived extent of ten patterns of corrupt behavior varied inversely with the perceived deviance of each pattern (Barker, 1976). In this same police department there was a wide variation in "risk" or possibility of being reported for corrupt activities (Table 4.1).

All variants of corruption of authority, i.e., the receipt of free meals, services or discounts and liquor, were perceived to invoke little risk of sanction. These are seldom reported because the group does not perceive them as forms of corruption. Free meals and services or discounts are "fringe benefits" of the job or occupation. Nonetheless they violate departmental rules and regulations and prescribed ethical conduct for police officers (such as the Code of Ethics for Police Officers adopted by the International Association of Chiefs of Police) and involve a material reward or gain. The policeman has placed himself in a compromising situation whereby one or both parties to the act may expect some favorable treatment in the present or in the future.

The "risk" for an officer who engages in kickbacks (receiving goods, services, or money for referring business to towing companies, ambulances, or garages) depends on the nature of the material reward or gain. The subjects felt that money kickbacks would be reported more often than those involving goods and services. A large majority (77%) of the subjects reported that an officer who takes something of value from a victim (opportunistic thefts) would be turned in by his colleagues. However, opportunistic thefts from a burglary scene or an unlocked building were not as likely to be reported. Only 58 percent of the officers believed this form of opportunistic thefts would be reported every time.

Officers who engage in shakedowns of criminals and accepted payoffs from vice operators and businessmen who operate outside the law (Corrupt Patterns 4 and 5) were likely to be reported. Over 70 percent of the subjects believed that a policeman who engaged in any of these acts would be reported. All forms of the "fix" involved a great amount of risk for the corrupt actor, except the "fixing" of misdemeanor court cases. Only 49 percent of the subjects believed that an officer who "fixed" a misdemeanor case would be reported every time.

Direct criminal activities such as burglaries and robberies committed by police officers are "dirty money" patterns of corruption. The majority of the subjects believed that policemen who engaged in this form of corruption would be reported every time. Nevertheless, seven of the subjects believed that these corrupt activities would never be reported.

Internal payoffs, the sale of days off, holiday, and desirable work assignments, were medium-risk forms of corruption. Over 40 percent of the men believed these activities would be reported. A higher percentage did not believe internal payoffs would invariably be reported, as superior officers are most likely to be "selling" days off and work assignments.

Various social definitions of corrupt behavior exist in this police organization. Numerous writers on the subject have suggested that peer group support for corruption depends on a group distinction between "clean" and "dirty" money forms of corrupt behavior. There has been little or no empirical evidence to support this hypothesis. It would appear that the presence or absence of a human victim, the nature of the material gain, i.e., whether it is goods and services, money or liquor, the identity of the corrupters, and the corrupted, and the social situation are important variables in assessing the risk potential and reinforcement received from the police peer group.

## SUMMARY

The police occupation per se provides its members with numerous opportunities for corrupt acts and other forms of deviance. In some police departments there is a social setting where this inherent occupational structure is combined with peer group support and tolerance for certain patterns of corruption. The peer group indoctrinates and socializes the rookie into patterns of acceptable corrupt activities, sanctions deviations outside these boundaries, and sanctions officers, who do not engage in any corrupt acts. The peer group can also discipline officers who report or attempt to report fellow officers.

It may well be that all occupations offer a basis for deviance, i.e., an occupation structure, and peer group support. Police corruption is not a peculiar form of deviant conduct. It shares common characteristics with other forms and patterns of occupational deviance.

## Notes

1   Expansion of the eight types of police corruption which appeared in Barker and Roebuck's (1973) typology.

2   This research was conducted in a Southern city of over 25,000 population located east of the Mississippi River with a majority white population and a sizable minority of non-white inhabitants.

# REFERENCES

*Atlanta Journal* (1974). "Alleged Drug King Pin Arrested on Bribe Charge." December 20.

Barker, T. (1976). "Peer Group Support for Occupational Deviance in Police Agencies." Ph.D. dissertation, Mississippi State University.

Barker, T. and J. Roebuck (1973). *An Empirical Typology of Police Corruption*. Springfield, IL: Charles C Thomas.

Barrett, J.K. (1973). "Inside the Mob's Smut Racket." *Reader's Digest* (November):128-133.

Bryant, C.D. (1974). *Deviant Behavior: Occupational and Organizational Bases*. Chicago: Rand McNally.

Chevigny, P. (1969). *Police Abuses in New York City*. New York: Holt, Rinehart & Winston.

Clinard, M.B. and R. Quinney (1967). *Criminal Behavior Systems*. New York: Holt, Rinehart & Winston.

Comment (1971). "Police Perjury in Narcotics 'Dropsy Cases': A New Credibility Gap." *Georgetown Law Journal* (November):507-523.

*Criminal Justice Newsletter* (1972). "Top Administrators Cite Urgent Need for Research on Causes of Police Corruption." 3 (December):193-194.

Knapp Commission (1973). The Knapp Commission Report on Police Corruption. New York: George Braziller.

Law Enforcement Council (1974). "Official Corruption." *Crime and Delinquency* 20 (January):15-19.

Lemert, E.M. (1967). *Human Deviance, Social Problems and Social Control*. Englewood Cliffs, NJ: Prentice-Hall.

Leonard, V.A. and H.W. More (1974). *Police Organization and Management*. Mineola, NY: Foundation Press.

Manning, P.K. (1974). "The Police Mandate, Strategies, and Appearances." In R. Quinney (ed.) *Criminal Justice in America: A Critical Understanding*. Boston: Little, Brown.

Matza, D. (1964). *Delinquency and Drift*. New York: John Wiley.

Murphy, P.V. (1973). "Police Corruption." *Police Chief* (December):36-72.

National Advisory Commission on Criminal Justice Standards and Goals (1973). *Police*. Washington, DC: U.S. Government Printing Office.

Reiss, A.J., Jr. (1972) *The Police and the Public*. New Haven, CT: Yale University Press.

Robin, G.D. (1974). "White Collar Crime and Employee Theft." *Crime and Delinquency* 20:251-263.

Savitz, L. (1971) "The Dimensions of Police Loyalty," In Harlan Hahn (ed.) *Police in Urban Society.* Beverly Hills, CA: Sage.

Schecter, L. and W. Phillips (1973). *On the Pad.* New York: G.P. Putnam.

Schur, E.M. (1971). *Labeling Deviant Behavior.* New York: Harper & Row.

Schur, E.M. (1969). *Our Criminal Society: The Social and Legal Sources of Crime in America.* Englewood Cliffs, NJ: Prentice-Hall.

Sherman, L.W. (1974). *Police Corruption: A Sociological Perspective.* Garden City, NY: Doubleday.

Skolnick, J.H. (1966). *Justice Without Trial: Law Enforcement in Democratic Society.* New York: John Wiley.

Snizek, W.E. (1974). "Deviant Behavior Among Blue-Collar Workers-Employees: Work-Norm Violation in the Factory." In C.D. Bryant (ed.) *Deviant Behavior: Occupational and Organizational Bases.* Chicago: Rand McNally.

Stoddard, E.R. (1968). "The Informal Code of Police Deviancy: A Group Approach to "Blue-Coat Crime." *Journal of Criminal Law, Criminology and Police Science* 59 (June):201-213.

Strecher, W.C. (1967). "When Subcultures Meet: Police-Negro Relations," In Sheldon Yefsky (ed.) *Science and Technology in Law Enforcement.* Chicago: Thompson.

Symonds, M. (1970). "Emotional Hazards of Police Work," In A. Niederhoffer and A.S. Blumberg (eds.) *The Ambivalent Force: Perspectives on the Police.* Waltham, MA: Xerox Publishing Co.

Van Maanen, J. (1974). "Working the Street: A Developmental View of Police Behavior." In Herbert Jacob (ed.) *The Potential for Reform of Criminal Justice.* Beverly Hills, CA: Sage.

Younger, I. (1967). "The Perjury Routine." *Nation* (May):596-597.

# STUDY QUESTIONS

1. The term rotten "rotten apples" has been used to account for police corruption. Who are the "rotten apples"? What are the problems associated with this explanation?

2. Is police corruption the result of society's efforts to execute unenforceable "victimless" crime laws?

3. What are the three elements which are important to an understanding of occupational deviance?

4. What are the two stages of police occupational socialization? Supposedly, where does the "real" training of police officers occur?

# PART II: OCCUPATIONAL DEVIANCE

# 5

# THE TOUCHABLES: VICE AND POLICE CORRUPTION IN THE 1980s*

## John Dombrink

## THE RECENT WAVE OF POLICE CORRUPTION

A federal investigation that resulted in the conviction of 31 Philadelphia police officers *(Philadelphia Inquirer)* referred to the city as a "petri dish for corruption,"[1] and described the elements that made Philadelphia one of the leading examples of systemic police corruption in recent years. A hierarchical and lucrative system of payoffs from pimps, video gambling machine purveyors, and numbers operators cut through several layers of the police force, extending as far as the second-in-command of the entire city.[2] Through a series of federal investigations and prosecutorial efforts that netted several high-ranking police officers, some of whom turned states's evidence and broke what the chief prosecutor called the conspiracy of silence, the Philadelphia situation was brought to the forefront in a country which had experienced several significant police scandals in recent years. As the chief prosecutor explained, "[t]he message has been sent that officers cannot trust anyone to insulate them from the consequences of their wrongdoing."[3]

In other major American cities, corruption episodes were also coming to the attention of authorities. In New York City, several members of the 77th Precinct were indicted after they were suspected of extorting money from crack dealers.[4] In Boston, officers were convicted of activities including extorting payoffs from vice purveyors.[5] In San Francisco, an initiation ceremony for a rookie police officer that included the services of a prostitute was among several key events that forced that city to reexamine some of the controls it maintained over its police force.[6] In Miami, where the onslaught of drug importation in the last decade has inexorably changed the nature of the community to one reminiscent of the Wild West, a ring

*Reprinted from *Law and Contemporary Problems,* Vol. 51, No. 1 (Winter, 1988), Pages 201-232. Reprinted with permission of *Law and Contemporary Problems.*

of police officers was tried for running a drug distribution enterprise.[7]

In many ways, the forms the examples noted above took were either predictable or routine. For instance, while the Philadelphia example was noteworthy for the extent of its operation and the success of the prosecutorial team in gaining cooperation from insiders,[8] the extortion schemes themselves were fairly traditional forms of shakedowns from that frequent victim, the illegal gambler. Amidst the third wave of legalization of gambling in this country, which saw the approval of casinos in one state,[9] horse racing in several states,[10] and lotteries in many others,[11] the meaning of the Philadelphia example is difficult to discern. We are thrown back to the insights of Gardiner, who found in Wincanton the apparent contradiction among the residents there who were tolerant of illegal gambling, but alarmed and disapproving toward the police corruption that ensued from the implementation of such a policy of tolerance.[12]

In Miami and New York City, the cocaine-related cases, coming at a time when the country has devoted significant financial and emotional resources to curtailing the flow of illicit drugs into the country, are of great import.[13] The five cases, Philadelphia, New York City, Miami, Boston, and San Francisco, taken together represent a sample of the types of police corruption issues related to vice that have developed in the past decade. They have done so against a backdrop of increased gambling legalization,[14] increased use of cocaine and debate over its decriminalization,[15] a prostitute rights movement, bitter debate of the abortion laws,[17] discussion of pornography and its effects,[18] and increased use of marijuana and heroin.[19] Moreover, these examples have happened at the same time as a number of changes in the operation of police departments,[20] and as interventions in police departments to prevent and discover police corruption[21] have been spawned.

For virtually the entire existence of the urban American police force, situations involving vice and its control have presented opportunities for corruption and posed a challenge to police administrators who hoped to limit their officers' misconduct without alienating the officers' loyalties.[22] Vice creates many police problems, not only those which are corruption related. Resource allocation is naturally complicated by the need to respond to disorderly situations or other complaints.[23] Misconduct as serious as perjury can be undertaken in vice circumstances to circumvent procedural due process in situations which are otherwise serving organizational goals.[24] Vice control combines the often critical mandate for order maintenance functions of policing with the law seriousness assigned most vice offenses.[25] That sort of conflict is rarely found in other activities. Police, like other bureaucratic actors, are naturally concerned with achievement of their performance criteria. The clearance rate of vice arrests (the percentage of successful prosecutions or arrests) is too small either to please administrators or to assuage the concerns of a public threatened by the perception of high and increasing crime rates.

The ambivalence of vice control, a confusion created by the contradictory messages American citizens send to their police, has created several persistent moral, legal, and organizational dilemmas for American police departments.[26] If the police were to pursue policies of total enforcement, the work could consume the available resources of police agencies, preventing them from devoting even minimal effort to the policing of more serious crimes and the processing of mundane citizen complaints. Moreover, as Gardiner and others have shown, while corruption and vice feed on each other, Americans have shown a strong dislike for one while tolerating the other.[27] At a time when vice is perceived as rising, and when the expense of both traditional and innovative policing strategies is significant, especially in fiscally strained, vice-impacted urban centers, new events and situations have amplified these concerns, created complicated dilemmas, and generally added to the complexity of vice control.

Studies analyzing the role of corruption in effecting organizational reform indicate that, despite the substantial attention which scandals attract, the conditions and costs of reforming corrupt police departments for any meaningful length of time are so great that the mere fact of scandal is not enough to ensure subsequent reform.[28] Nonetheless, the lull in American police corruption after the well-publicized Knapp Commission report[29] and the Special Investigations Division scandal[30] seemed to represent the resolution of endemic problems associated with vice and police corruption. Coming at the end point of this lull, however, the series of scandals in five major American police departments called into question the effectiveness of existing internal organizational controls as well as external monitoring processes. Despite commitment of extensive federal law enforcement resources and the "moral equivalent of war" applied to the control of illicit drugs, the persistence of vice presented continued opportunities for wrongdoing.[31] Moreover, the form and opportunities for corruption shifted.

Nine years ago, the trend toward legalization of vice appeared as though it would have a profound effect on society, and scholars suggested a variety of rationales and a number of models for legal regulation and control of various forms of vice.[32] In the intervening years, however, a great impact on society and the legal system by vice-related issues has occurred, but arguably more in the nature of confounding and contradictory effects. Marijuana causes little concern, but government agencies reward agents for building marijuana cases.[33] Heroin is considered serious, and efforts to control street-level dealing seem to have an effect on the heroin market.[34] Prostitution is usually assigned low priority for policing, but the disorderly aspects of it sometimes make for public uproar. Legal gambling has grown dramatically over the past decade, yet other forms of gambling are resisted, due to possible problems.[35] Nowhere is this combination of mixed messages and mixed results of more significance than in the ability of police departments to effectively deploy strategies of corruption control at the same time as they pursue crime-fighting techniques. In fact, some of the reforms aimed at deterring police corruption, such as rotating police in their precinct assignments, are directly at odds with some of the premises of the resurgence of community-based policing norms. How the events of the last decade and the policing challenges of the next decade have been affected by vice development will be examined below.

## THE CHANGING PATTERNS OF VICE

During the 1960s, many prominent legal scholars argued against the wasteful use of the crime-fighting resources in enforcing virtually unenforceable laws in the area of vice.[36] From Packer's admonition to guard against exceeding the limits of the criminal sanction[37] to Kadish's[38] and Allen's[39] discussion of the unique properties of enforcement at the fringes of the criminal law, various legal scholars rallied against the use of the criminal sanction to legislate morality. Some followed Mill's notion that state intervention in such areas was not compelled,[40] while others, such as Packer[41] and Skolnick,[42] espoused the view that the impracticality of such laws was of paramount concern.

Cocaine's passage from a rarely used, elitist, and little-understood drug in the early 1970s to a more widely used substance by 1988 has brought to the foreground many complex and contradictory factors. As late as 1985, Americans responding to an American Broadcasting Company (ABC) poll, overwhelmingly (92% to 6%) rejected the notion of making possession of small amounts of cocaine for personal use legal.[43] Yet, cocaine use was the fastest growing illegal drug use during this period.[44] One has to go back ten years to find a time when fewer Americans favored either legalizing the use of marijuana or removing criminal sanctions on its possession.[45] At the same time, six or seven respondents to the ABC poll thought that "[d]rug abuse will never be stopped because a large number of Americans will continue to want drugs and be willing to pay lots of money for them."[46]

The generational patterns of familiarity and use, and the inability of Americans to decide whether cocaine is in fact a soft or hard drug, have created a stratified response to policy issues in this area.[47] While the polls cited above may indicate otherwise, the perception of cocaine has been increasingly separated from the stigma attached to heroin. Naturally, some of the disreputability of a drug is a result of the status of the average user. Cocaine has long been billed as an affluent drug,[48] a feature which has gained it some positive status but also provides as obstacle against widespread social acceptance. In any case, its use more closely parallels that of marijuana, rather than heroin, and thus it has avoided some of the traps associated with the latter.

At the same time, as patterns of drug perceptions were changing, the number of legal abortions grew annually, and even conservative groups were in favor of the liberalized abortion laws established by *Roe v. Wade*.[49] Gay-rights groups had been successful in advancing the passage of more than 50 state, county, and local ordinances prohibiting discrimination on the basis of sexual orientation.[50] In addition, gay and lesbian activists in several large American cities had become articulate political actors and effective political constituencies.[51] Furthermore, the growth in legal gambling has taken place against a curious situation regarding illegal gambling prevention. The federation of gambling control[52] in the 1970s reduced many of the temptations related to local responsibility for policing, but has not reduced police perception of links between illegal gambling and organized crime.[53] Vice has become at once more politicized, more subsumed under expectations of civil rights, more commercialized, more available to ordinary Americans, and essentially more ambivalent over the past decade.

In Skolnick's words, ever-present public ambivalence has been reinforced.[54] Measures to reduce or control police corruption are needed for many reasons. For one thing, the reaction of citizens to police and their performance and legitimacy may be predicated upon their perception of police corruption. To the extent that citizens, particularly in high-crime, vice-impacted areas, think less of their police force, civic cooperation might be reduced on more serious investigations. This conundrum will be examined in the five case studies below.

## Miami

"Miami Vice" may be a stylized and sensationalized television show, but the scenes portrayed have their basis in the reality of the past decade's drug wars. While the police in "Miami Vice" are generally noble and full of integrity, the reality in Miami has often been otherwise. In numerous examples, federal, state, and local law enforcement officers have fallen prey to the lure of drug-related payoffs.[55] The temptations are ever present and sizeable. As one high-ranking police officer observed, "[i]t's not unusual for a police officer to stop a car in a routine traffic violation and find $20,000 in cash."[56] The price of a kilogram of cocaine is almost the same as a Miami police officer's annual salary.[57]

As "Miami Vice," numerous news shows, and a spate of new journalistic accounts have emphasized in recent years, Miami has become the illicit drug capital of the United States.[58] The responsibility of policing such an area has fallen primarily on the shoulders of federal interagency task forces, but has also extended over the local police forces in the South Florida region. In the last decade, a number of law enforcement officers at all levels have been convicted of misconduct related to drug business.[59] According to one report, 100 of the 1060 Miami police officers have been, or currently are being, investigated on corruption-related matters, and officials are predicting that as many as 200 officers may face investigation.[60]

In Miami, the indictment of seven officers, known as the River Cops or the Enterprise, revealed that they had started by stealing drugs from motorists stopped for traffic violations and worked their way up to major rip-offs.[61] Informants would reveal the location of million-dollar loads of cocaine, and the police officers would steal the drugs instead of arresting the dealers.[62] They were indicted, but the jury deadlocked in their first trial. After that, a new series of indictments has targeted 20 officers, including the first group of defendants.[63] Six of the 20 were fugitives from justice in August 1987.

The Miami River Police Case is presumably not the end of the corruption probe, nor the only instance of finding police gone bad. Recently, in Miami, an FBI agent pleaded guilty to accepting cocaine kickbacks,[64] and three Miami police officers were each charged with three counts of first-degree murder for their roles in a drug execution.[65] Authorities have yet to catch the person(s) who stole $150,000 from the safe at the headquarters office of the Miami police vice squad, as well as the thief of a quarter of a ton of marijuana from a supposedly secure place in the Miami Police Department Compound.[66] In February 1986, a police officer in nearby North Bay Village was arrested for allegedly selling protection to FBI agents posing as drug dealers.[67]

To fight the corruption in South Florida, an FBI corruption squad has been in operation for several years. Federal initiative in this matter follows a series of failed state investigations into Miami area police corruption.[68] One group is working on corruption in local zoning processes, including one case where an officer is accused of racketeering, bribery, and conspiracy to murder.[69] In all, 26 agents are assigned to corruption. Several are Spanish-speaking agents who have worked on police corruption cases in other cities. Across town, IRS agents are tracking the assets of suspect police officers and filling in the financial gaps of suspects in a variety of corruption investigations.[70] Another group of federal agents is investigating prominent Miami businessmen suspected of corrupting police with gifts and money.[71] A swelling intelligence base is adding to the driving force of these investigations. When the corruption unit began in 1983, very little information was available on the web of relationships that facilitate corruption in Dade County; the body of knowledge about how things work in Miami has grown significantly. The FBI and other agencies are thus able to target entire networks of corruption. A team of agents and prosecutors can react effectively to the informant or witness who comes forward with a story about a bribe paid for a zoning decision or a shakedown by a crooked cop.

Some of the issues generated by the Miami scandal have been the influence of youthfulness among police officers and attempts to achieve racial diversity in the police force amid rapid expansion. At the same time, the Miami Police Department was described as "overwhelmingly young and inexperienced."[72] Moreover, the police force had grown from 650 officers in 1980 to 1033 officers in 1985. One reason for the growth was the heavy influx of Cuban refugees to Miami in 1980, the year of the Mariel boatlift from Cuba. That event led to the resettlement of 100,000 Cubans, many with criminal records or other antisocial histories.[73] Promoted by the Liberty City uprising of the early 1980s, among other influences, Miami police began to rapidly absorb many new recruits from minority groups.[74] Later, when the River Police Scandal unfolded, and all the suspects were either black or Latino, one police administrator noted, "[a] lot of people resistant to affirmative action are using the arrests of Hispanic officers as a subterfuge...[to attack minority hiring programs.]"[75]

The Miami River Police case will probably come to trial again in 1989. Temptations related to the enormous drug traffic remain, and the unique demands of policing a biracial city continue to pose challenges for the coming decade.[76] How the Miami police rebound from the River Police case will depend on larger efforts of drug interdiction, and site-specific issues of recruiting from and policing a culturally diverse community.

## Philadelphia

The unprecedented federal prosecutions of systemic corruption in the Philadelphia Police Department, including convictions of more than 30 officers, revealed a deep-rooted structure, primarily centered on gambling-related misconduct, that reached as high as the second-in-command in the police department.[77] Far from an isolated example, the Philadelphia cases revealed sophisticated networks of corruption grafted onto the police command structure itself. According to federal prosecutor Howard Klein, who personally tried 22 of the convicted police officers, "I think we provided the depth and prevalence of corruption at the department, and this led to the city to reexamine the department and begin an extensive reform to prevent the recurrence of institutionalized corruption."[78] The creation of a stronger anti-corruption mechanism was a recommendation of the Report of the Philadelphia Police Study Task Force,[79] headed by Professor Gerald Caplan.[80] The report, issued in March 1987, characterized the Philadelphia Police Department as "unfocused, unmanaged, under-trained, underequipped and unaccountable.[81] The report attributed the sorry state of the Philadelphia Police Department to a combination of community neglect and management failure. In a particularly trenchant summary, the Caplan report concluded that, "[t]he dead hand of past traditions guides the department rather than the challenge of the future. A history of favoritism, corruption and brutality hangs over it."[82]

The public response to police corruption and performance generally, as measured by a poll for the Philadelphia Police Study Task Force in 1986,[83] indicated that the Task Force's assessment had to take into account a curious and often contradictory approach by Philadelphia residents to their police. Seventy percent of city residents responding to a poll taken for the Philadelphia Police Study Task

Force rated the Philadelphia police as doing a good or excellent job overall. One apparent reason was that the force, the largest force per capita of America's ten largest cities, responded to over three million calls for service in 1985, an average of nearly two calls per resident.[84] A majority of residents had a high regard for the police profession, but at the same time felt that Philadelphia police were underenforcing some types of laws, especially in the areas of drugs and prostitution. Fully 69 percent of the respondents thought that the law on drugs is underenforced, 56 percent thought laws on prostitution were so treated, and 49 percent considered gambling laws underenforced.[85] Eighty-one percent of residents describe their police as being honest, but roughly half thought the police to be discourteous.[86] By far, the most striking results were related to how Philadelphia residents felt their police were rated regarding illegal and nonprofessional behavior. Almost half of the respondents felt that Philadelphia police engaged in some form of illegal or unprofessional behavior sometimes or often, including a remarkable 32 percent who believed the police used illegal drugs while on duty.[87]

One of the Philadelphia Police Department's significant attempts to redress the corruption problems was to appoint Philadelphia-based United States Secret Service official Kevin Tucker as the Philadelphia Police Chief in January 1986. Part of Tucker's attraction lies in his status as an outsider. Unlike many of his predecessors and other possible commissioner candidates, Tucker had little personal or professional incentive to protect corruption within the department, and he was not in debt to any of the ranks below him. Tucker initiated a number of actions directed against corruption, some soon after his appointment. He established review boards to depoliticize promotions and transfers within the police department.[88] He also shifted the assignments of the top police commanders and reassigned hundreds of mid-level commanders.[89] The new commissioner ordered the department to begin a field associates program, using new recruits to report incidents of police corruption they might witness.[90] Tucker also reestablished foot patrols in neglected neighborhoods to restore the bond between communities and police.[91] To reduce police abuse of citizens, Tucker issued guidelines for the use of night sticks and ordered that the Internal Affairs Division ("IAD") investigate all instances where a citizen is injured by police.[92] Tucker also increased the budget for outside training by 400 percent.[93]

The history of police corruption in Philadelphia can trace its dubious roots back almost to the very beginning of the police department.[94] Ward leaders exerted their corrupt influence on all the police districts in their areas, and the mayor exercised his corrupting influence over the entire police force.[95] The police were pawns that the politicians tried to control and use to advance their own interests. With the prevalence of corruption, official probes soon began. The first inquiry into police misconduct was in 1928. A county grand jury claimed that officers were taking as much as $2 million a year to protect vice.[96] This grand jury found numerous officers, including detectives, captains, and inspectors, "unfit" to serve.[97] Less than nine years later in 1937, another grand jury found that, not only had corruption not been eliminated, but it had actually grown and become more systematic and ingrained.[98] Vice had flourished between the grand jury investigations.[99] The grand jury concluded that corruption touched all aspects of the police department.[100] Corruption functioned in the internal dynamics of the force, extending from promotions to transfers. Corruption was no longer confined to the streets.

Compared with federal prosecutors, whose record of thirty-one convictions in 36 federal district court cases between 1983 and 1986 was formidable, local prosecutors had fared less well historically with police corruption cases in the Pennsylvania courts.[101] In the 1950s, several indictments against police were quashed, and seven police officers tried for accepting gambling bribes were acquitted.[102] In 1971, then Commissioner Joseph O'Neill, Mayor Frank Rizzo, and District Attorney Arlen Spector promoted the need for self-policing and blamed the current cases on the actions of a few rotten apples.[103] After the *Philadelphia Inquirer* published a series of articles asserting that the Philadelphia police were accepting payoffs to protect gambling operations, Pennsylvania Governor Milton Shapp ordered an independent investigation of police corruption by the Pennsylvania Crime Commission.[104] The Crime Commission report concluded that history of the Philadelphia Police Department revealed a clear cut trend: Corruption was widespread and continuing, and the department was unable or unwilling to control it.[105] Although a special prosecutor followed up on the report with the indictment of nine officers, only three were convicted, and the case against the highest ranking senior officer in the group was thrown out of court.[106] A later study by Watergate Counsel Sam Dash attributed the special prosecutor's problem to the unwillingness of the Philadelphia Police Commissioner to provide the special prosecutor with police records or to suspend officers indicted by his grand jury.[107]

The present investigation of police corruption which began in 1981 has proven to be different than previous investigations. The scope of the investigation has been wider, and convictions with strict sentences have been the rule rather than the exception.[108] The current investigation of the Philadelphia Police Department began as a result of a complaint filed with the FBI by Donald Hersing, the owner of a house of prostitution.[109]

By far, the predominant police corruption-related activity in Philadelphia has been illegal gambling. Beginning in the late 1970s,[110] vending machine companies began buying video poker machines and placing them in bars and taverns in Philadelphia. A patron who played the games would win free games by beating the programmed odds and would be paid off in cash for the free games won, with the bar owner and the vendor splitting equally the profits from the machine.[111]

The illegal gambling use of the machines made the machines subject to seizure and the bar owners or bartenders subject to arrest. The defendants and their co-conspirators used the threat of arrest and seizure to extort money from the vendors. At times, a machine was seized or bartender arrested to instigate contact with a vendor and to emphasize the necessity of paying the police for protection.[112]

This initial investigation of some vice officers led to a citywide probe of police taking payoffs to protect vice.[113] FBI wiretaps revealed the extent and depth of police corruption in the department.[114] Vice officers, detectives, a lieutenant, and an inspector all were implicated in this extortion scheme by the FBI wiretaps. In previous investigations, officers were implicated by other officers, but in this investigation, officers implicated themselves on tape recordings.

As the Philadelphia federal prosecutors noted, the government's evidence introduced at the trial of several officers, including Deputy Commissioner James Martin, established that the defendants used the Philadelphia Police Department to conduct a pattern of racketeering activity,[115] as defined by the federal RICO statute.[116] Martin had been Inspector for the Northwest Division, one of nine in the city, from July 1982 to November 1983. In January 1984, he became Deputy Commissioner of the Philadelphia Police Department. The evidence presented at his trial showed that, upon becoming Inspector of the Northwest Division, he received protection money for poker machines and numbers operations from his vice lieutenants, receiving $10,000 a month until he was promoted.[117]

In the midst of this secret investigation, newly elected Mayor Wilson Goode appointed a new Police Commissioner, Gregor J. Sambor, Tucker's predecessor. In one of his first major decisions, the new Commissioner consolidated the functions of those officers enforcing vice laws into a new Major Investigations Division.[118] Until his appointment, vice enforcement operated on tiered levels of responsibility.[119] Uniformed patrol officers, plainclothes police assigned to district captains and inspectors, and vice officers all enforced vice laws.[120] The reasoning behind the tiered levels of responsibility was to make the results of payoffs unpredictable as well as expensive.[121] The costliness and unpredictability of payoffs would force criminals to refuse to pay, and thus the police would enforce the laws.

Sambor made the commander of the Major Investigations Division directly accountable to Deputy Commissioner Martin.[122] Martin and his co-conspirators planned to use the unit to operate a citywide, not just division-wide or precinct-wide, extortion ring.[123] All vice operations would pay the officers in their district, and the officers would then give Martin a percentage of the money.[124] Before Martin could put his plan fully into motion, the FBI identified most of the conspirators, and the grand jury started to hand down indictments.[125] Thirty-one police officers and officials, including Deputy Commissioner Martin, were convicted.[126] The significance of the trials was not the news of police corruption. The news was that not just lower-ranking officers were indicted.[127] Four lieutenants, a captain, an inspector, a Chief Inspector, and the Deputy Commissioner all were charged with various crimes.[128] The convictions of these men and the other officers destroyed the "rotten apple" explanation.[129] Corruption was shown to be far-reaching and associated with all ranks.

In addition to the Philadelphia Task Force, the Citizens' Crime Commission of Delaware Valley has also made several conclusions and recommendations for the Philadelphia Police Department.[130] One conclusion they draw is that the higher ranks must be intolerant of corruption.[131] Tucker's tenure has been a welcome event in this regard. The Commission also suggests that the "rotten apple" theory of corruption has been abandoned, to the extent that the theory only reinforces the code of silence and acts against systematic reform of the police department.[132]

The Philadelphia Police Department has implemented some of the Citizens' Crime Commission recommendations: requirements of full financial disclosure for all candidates for command-level promotions; limited tenure in specialized vice and narcotics units; prosecution of all involved in corruption including officers, officials, and citizens; lenient treatment of officers cooperating with official investigations in regard to their own misconduct; arousal of public concern; establishment of field associates; and, finally, establishment of proactive instead of reactive probes of possible corruption.[133] The department is working on implementing two other recommendations.[134] The first recommendation is the establishment of a system to reward technical specialization independent of the promotion process.[135] Often excellence in that particular field is rewarded by promotion. Many times these promotions remove the officer from precisely the area where his or her expertise lies. The second recommendation that is likely to be implemented is a plan to distribute vice intelligence so that the Major Investigations Division, Ethics Accountability Division, and/or Internal Affairs Division are all apprised of the investigation.[136] Monitoring of vice operations is critical in reducing police corruption. When officers know they are being watched, they are less likely to misbehave.

The many recommendations of the Philadelphia Police Study Task Force, which include drug testing, the institution of mechanisms to transform police managers from narrow supervisors to more effective decisionmakers, civilization, more community policing techniques, and enhanced training, all are directed at institutional reforms which will make the police more responsible for controlling and preventing corruption.[137]

The efficacy (or lack thereof) of prosecution as a deterrence strategy was highlighted by the argument of Philadelphia law enforcement officials who indicated that real reform depended less on the prosecution than on the organizational changes Tucker had introduced and the commitment of his eventual successors to maintain them.[138] If political ties among city hall, the police, the district attorney's office, and the courts reasserted themselves, less aggressive prosecution of police might result.[139]

The ability of the Philadelphia Police Department to institutionalize anti-corruption sentiment and control capabilities will be tested after the initial vigilance of the Tucker administration dies down. Whether this city, with its checkered history of police malfeasance, will adopt new approaches will be a major national test of the efficacy of police reform.

## New York City

With over 27,000 officers, New York City by far enjoys the largest police department in the country,[140] charged with the protection of a diverse population of over seven million.[141] The task of policing New York City has long been a demanding one, and the history of police corruption in New York City has deep roots, including periodic assessments of a desired corruption control mechanism. The early 1970s saw the revelations of Detective Frank Serpico,[142] the study by the Knapp Commission,[143] and the corruption episodes of the elite Special Investigation Unit detailed in *The Prince of the City*.[144]

With the exposure of some crack-related corruption events in the mid-1980s,[145] New York City was once again thrust into the spotlight, amid acrimonious disputes between rank-and-file officers and the police commissioner. The recent New York City police corruption problems took place against the largest increase in serious crime (5 percent) in five years, including a 14 percent increase in murder from 1985 to 1986.[146] In the revelations to date, including trial testimony by one officer against another,[147] allegations of entrapment,[148] and the suicide of one implicated officer,[149] evidence indicates that New York City Police Department (NYPD) officers in a remote precinct regularly stole or accepted drugs and money from marijuana and crack dealers.[150] After having been disciplined for a departmental infraction, one implicated officer had been transferred to the "dead end" precinct from the narcotics division a few years prior, thus exposing the limitations of internal disciplinary action against police officers.[151]

When New York City Commissioner Benjamin Ward responded to the scandal by ordering a rotation plan including 20 percent of all officers, the Police Benevolent Association countered with a work slowdown among other means and caused Ward to rescind the action.[152] The largest percentage of official complaints regarding police behavior received by the NYPD in 1985 (22 percent) concerned narcotics.[153] The 644 narcotics-related complaints were 36 percent more than in 1984.[154] "Two-thirds of the increase in narcotics complaints between 1984 and 1985 involved allegations of drug use by members of the service and alleged protection of drug dealers."[155] In 1985, New York officers with less than five years of experience constituted 45 percent of the police force but were responsible for 89 percent of the drug charges and 72 percent of the complaints received by the Civilian Complaint Review Board (CCRB).[156] Such overrepresentation, however, could be explained by the fact that younger officers comprise 75 percent of the street patrol force or that newer police officers are more frequently assigned to front-line operations, such as lower Manhattan's "Operation Pressure Point."[157] Moreover, city police officers called drug use their primary corruption problem in 1986.[158] For the first time, the NYPD's annual corruption assessment survey[159] found growing concern among commanders over the possibility of drug abuse by off-duty officers. Even the many advances made by the NYPD, as far as instituting mechanisms for corruption control, were being questioned.[160] More recent probes found that management controls within the NYPD were inadequate for the early identification and disposition of those individuals with a propensity toward misconduct.[161]

The police scandals paled alongside three major upperworld and underworld crime prosecutions in the mid-1980s. The highest levels of the borough party machinery were prosecuted for municipal corruption, including payoffs in the city's parking violations bureau.[162]At the same time, another unit of the federal prosecutor's office was focusing on insider trading schemes on Wall Street, resulting in a flurry of criminal prosecutions and fines.[163] By no means the least of the three scandals was the trial of leaders of the five New York organized crime families in the celebrated "Commission case."[164]

The Knapp Commission was created in the early 1970s by then Mayor John Lindsay, as a result of the publicity generated by renegade detective Frank Serpico.[165] After failing to get any support or action from his superiors in the department, Serpico went to the *New York Times* with a story outlining police corruption.[166] The resulting publicity forced Lindsay to appoint Whitman Knapp, a Wall Street attorney, to head an independent commission to look into the matter.[167] After months of hearings, investigation, and deliberation, the commission found institutionalized, widespread corruption in the NYPD.[168] They further determined that there was organized protection of vice by the NYPD.[169] In fact, according to the report, the climate of the department is inhospitable to attempts to uncover acts of corruption, and protective of those who are corrupt.[170]

The Knapp Commission recommended that commanders must be held accountable for their subordinates' actions, that commanders were to prepare periodic reports on the key sites and situations that could breed corruption, and that field officers of the internal affairs division were to be created at all precincts, and were to be staffed by undercover informants in each precinct.[171] The police department in New York responded to the Knapp-era scandal by taking several courses of action: decentralizing authority and responsibility, reducing the autonomy of the detective branch, setting new standards of accountability for senior officers, instigating proactive investigatory procedures for police deviance, altering certain aspects of enforcement, rotating personnel, and emphasizing integrity in training.[172]

With those ideas in mind, Commissioner Patrick Murphy was appointed to clean up the department. Murphy was a no-nonsense ex-NYPD officer who was passionate in his hatred of corruption.[173] Murphy used the Knapp findings as a battle cry to revamp the department completely. "There were massive transfers to senior officers, rotation of policemen in sensitive areas, and...[a severe reduction of] the autonomy of the detective branch."[174] A new policy of accountability and decentralization was instituted. Murphy told 180 commanders that he would hold each of them personally responsible for any misconduct within the ranks at any level of command.[175] Murphy revamped the internal investigatory system, which up to that point seemed "deliberately designed not to work,"[176] by sponsoring proactive internal affairs projects with "integrity tests on field associates."[177] Unit commanders were unaware of the identity of those field associates.[178] Murphy also attempted to alter the "opportunity structure" for corruption by "virtually ending enforcement of gambling and Sabbath laws, by providing policemen with sufficient funds to pay informants, and by starting a campaign to arrest those citizens offering bribes."[179] By using political, legal, and press support, Murphy was successful in reducing the corruption problem to a very "minimal level."[180] Murphy's biggest contribution, however, possibly was his development and deployment of those proactive means for the prevention of corruption. Those programs marked a change in the focus of anti-corruption efforts. Murphy tried to avoid corruption before it started, rather than waiting for it to become a problem again. His success was commendable. In a number of informal police interviews by the criminologist, Maurice Punch, conducted in 1980 and 1981, members of the NYPD spoke of the "revolution" put into place by Murphy.[183] In his 1978 book, *Scandal and Reform,* criminologist Lawrence Sherman wrote, "from all indicators the most recent episode of scandal and reform in the NYPD has reduced police corruption to a very minimal level.[182] Four years later the *New York Times* stated that "[t]he whole climate of the department has been reversed since Knapp."[183]

As early as 1973, however, just one year after the Knapp Commission released its findings, a corruption profile conducted by the Intelligence Section of the Internal Affairs Department found that while some traditional forms of graft had diminished, other forms of corruption (such as theft from suspects and impounded cars and the use of prostitute services under the threat of arrest) were on the increase in certain precincts.[184] Despite the gains made by Commissioner Murphy, corruption in the NYPD was far from over.

In the years immediately after Knapp, lapses of resurgent corruptive practices occurred in the NYPD. In addition to the Special Investigative Division *Prince of the City* Scandal,[185] in 1981, 1983, and 1985, small episodes of localized corruption (some related to bribes from club owners) took place in selected precincts.[186]

In 1986, however, a major scandal in a Brooklyn precinct erupted which embraced the police commissioner, the Police Benevolent Association (PBA), and the Mayor's Office. Thirteen Officers from the 77th Precinct in the Bedford-Stuyvesant area were indicted on various charges including stealing and selling drugs.[187] The group of officers included some who had been transferred to the 77th Precinct because there were disciplinary problems at other locales. Some were 18-year veterans of the NYPD.[188] The major source of temptation was from drug dealers, their cash revenues, and even their illicit substances.[189] The officers who were involved in the activities offered many rationalizations for their acts: they were harassing drug dealers and the criminal justice system would not do anything anyway; they were robbing criminals or "lowlife," they were not law-abiding citizens; and they were displacing crime from their precinct.[190]

Some observers found a reassuring aspect in the 77th Precinct scandal: through the use of the Internal Affairs Department, the city police responded well to investigation of the charges of corruption.[191] One immediate response from the Police Commissioner was frequent reassignment of patrol officers to prevent entrenchment of corruptive practices and influences.[192] In response, the PBA encouraged work slowdown which demonstrated the rank and file's resistance to the Commissioner's plan.[193] The slowdown caused the Commissioner to delay his plan.[194] Some hoped the scandal would direct police attention to itself and would result in better policing and better police/community relations.[195]

According to the 1987 Zucotti Report,[196] New York was also suffering from a severe supervisory crisis. This crisis was caused by several factors: "long-term vacancies for the position of sergeant, the inexperience of many new supervisors, the absence of an effective system of performance evaluation, inadequate training and the distinct supervisory needs of a young police force."[197] The report concluded:

> The net result has been a tendency to move authority and responsibility upward within the ranks, thereby diminishing the stature of the sergeant as a key actor at the first line of supervision. A companion result is that less responsibility and accountability is delegated to those whose like supervision is essential for the prevention of misconduct.[198]

Furthermore, the panel found that the NYPD lacked an effective program of field in-service to reinforce what was initially learned at the Academy.[199]

As perhaps the most studied American police department, the NYPD's recent corruption episodes echo the concern that illegal drug use and sales in the 1980s pose new and more serious temptations for corruption. Corruption issues will remain a salient topic of contention in the more general discussion of management relations and policing strategies.

## Boston

Boston, like the other four cities described at length in this article, is not a stranger to municipal corruption. Professor Herman Goldstein, responding to reports of recent Boston police scandal, noted that "[c]orruption has been part of the culture in Boston for a long time…It's more accurate to view these things as the ebb and flow of officialdom's willingness" to investigate corruption.[200] In recent years, however, the trial of Boston mob boss, Geraldo Anguillo, brought the issue to public attention. During the trial, willful police blindness to illegal gambling and loansharking operations associated with Anguillo's organization were uncovered.[201] The scandal was the most serious since 1976, when the Special Investigations Unit charged that the Department was rife with corruption and incompetence.[202]

In Boston, one complication when dealing with police corruption is that Boston police officers are official agents of the Boston Licensing Board and possess power to inspect bars for compliance with liquor regulations.[203] Thus, another key elements in the Anguillo scandal was the existence of off-duty police detail programs which permitted police officers to work after hours in privately owned businesses, including such licensable facilities as bars or restaurants.[204] After a noted shakedown episode caused publicity in the mid-1970s,[205] Police Commissioner Robert J. diGrazia prohibited the off-duty details, but they slowly reemerged through restaurants and grocery stores.[206] Still, some changes have been made to limit the temptations for informal or illegal agreements. While the Boston Police Department does not keep track of which police officers work off-duty details or how often they do so, the officers are at least now paid by check instead of by cash, as was the case in the past.[207] Accusations of harassment and vigilante activity by members of the Boston Police Department were made.[208]

In Boston, three theories of the origins of the recent complaints regarding police corruption have emerged. One maintains that the owner of a gay bar took the tale of police shakedowns to the FBI after he grew tired of paying off police officers.[209] Another version has the FBI, working from similar information, using implicated police officers to collect evidence by placing body wires on them to record conversations with confederates.[210] A third version holds that a rising number of complaints led ranking Boston police officers to engage in greater departmental investigation efforts.[211]

In October 1986, a pair of top-ranking federal officials appeared with Police Commissioner Francis M. Roache to announce that a grand jury was hearing evidence about allegations of widespread corruption in the Boston Police Department.[212] The investigation, which had been going on for five years, focused on patterns of corruption involving top administrators, not just rank-and-file officers.[213]

Certain distinct stations were targeted as centers of police misconduct, in particular involving protecting criminal activities at bars and other licensed premises in return for cash and favors.[214] The General Investigations Units and the district stations of Dorchester, Roxbury, West Roxbury, and Downtown began to be investigated.[215] Investigators were trying to determine if officers on paid details at private clubs took payoffs and intercepted violation reports so that no punitive action was taken against the license holder.

Records on personnel, paid detail assignments, licensed premise inspections, and incident reports of criminal violations at licensed premises, some dating back ten years, were seized from the four district stations.[216] The grand jury also subpoenaed voluminous records at two city hall agencies that oversee liquor and entertainment licenses.[217] Records of the Mayor's office of Consumer and Licensing Affairs, which regulates entertainment permits for such things as peepshows, jukeboxes, and video games, were subpoenaed as well,[218]

Boston Police Commissioner Roache and Mayor Flynn have been cooperating with the investigation fully. Flynn said, "They made it very clear to me that very serious problems with corruption existed in the Boston Police Department. We have participated fully in an intensive investigation. You will begin to see the result in the coming weeks and months."[219] Roache pledged his full support to the investigation after being told of its purpose "regardless of wherever and to whomever the investigation may lead."[220] Former Commissioner Joseph Jordan (Commissioner, 1976-1985), however, was never told about the investigation even though the probe was underway during his time in office.[221] Jordan was indirectly linked to the alleged payment of bribes to more than 50 city officers for overlooking under-the-counter sales of illegal drugs.[222] Jordan denied the accusation.

Instances of police corruption uncovered in Boston involve many illegal activities, charges of illegal shakedowns, bribes, drug trading, vice operations, and harassment have cast the greatest blow to the morale and reputation of the Boston Police Department. For example, in the fall of 1986, convicted copshooter and drug dealer Jesse Waters became a federal witness in exchange for protection by federal prosecutors.[223] Another recent string of allegations involved Boston police officers taking bribes for overlooking violations of liquor license laws at bars.[224] Several bar owners describe situations where officers threatened to site bar owners for liquor license violations if they did not pay off the officer.[225]

One bar owner explained, "[s]imply put, if you owned a bar in Boston, sooner or later you paid someone for protection."[226] Special circumstances would exacerbate this arrangement. If someone was caught with drugs on the bar's premises, the threat to a bar's license could be significant. The most vulnerable bars were gay bars.[227] One former club owner informed the *Boston Globe* that he did not believe that gay establishments were approached because they might violate the laws, but because owners of gay clubs are forced to pay just to stay in operation.[228] Rumors even maintained that some liquor licenses in the city were owned by city police.[229] Eventually, seven Boston police officers were indicted under the RICO statute for obtaining kickbacks from Boston restaurants and nightclubs.[230]

## San Francisco

The city of San Francisco has weathered decades of political conflict resulting from the diversity of the city's population, no more so than in recent years when Bohemians, hippies, commune members, activist groups, gay and lesbian communities, and various influxes of immigrants have made San Francisco a unique melting pot. The drug culture of the 1960s and the gambling dens of Chinatown have grown along with the prostitution in the hotel district in this most Eastern of West Coast cities. Since police are conservative and dominated by an Irish-American tradition, they have been thrown into even more conflict with the diverse lifestyles and groups. The 1978 assassination of a liberal mayor and gay city/county supervisor showed the cleavages, some vice-related, existing below the cheerful facade of this popular tourist destination.[231]

After a police recruit graduation dinner in 1985, a bashful recruit was handcuffed to a chair, where a prostitute was brought in to perform oral sex on him.[232] Of the many officers present, several of whom were recruits, not one person reported this episode known as the Rathskellar incident.[233] The internal investigation of the incident was hampered by the traditional code of silence. Chief Cornelius Murphy recommended harsh penalties for all of the officers involved and circulated a code of ethics paper.[234] Eventually, he recommended the firing of two recruits, two veterans, and two sergeants.[235] As a result of that incident and a series of others, 10 of 21 captains were reassigned to new divisions.[236]

The number of reports of police brutality had increased,[237] and three San Francisco police officers were tried and cleared of charges that they kidnapped and beat a local Chinese gang member.[238] The rate of complaints exceeded that of the more drug-plagued city of Oakland and the much larger city of Los Angeles, prompting concern by Mayor Dianne Feinstein.[239] In response to the mayor's questioning, the deputy police chief claimed that the difference reflected the different reporting methods among cities and San Francisco's willingness to process complaints.[240] He also pointed to the job maturity issue, noting that, as in New York, 50 percent of San Francisco's officers had less than five years of experience.[241] Chief Murphy pointed to the youthfulness of the police force, noting that they lacked discipline and military experience.[242]

While the officers were technically better than their predecessors, Murphy noted that they lacked street sense.[243] Murphy developed a two-tiered system of intervention to deal with corruption which included the addition of situational ethics problem-solving courses in the academy curriculum and participation by officers in peer group sessions on ethics.[244] Department-wide, day-to-day accountability and a drive to strengthen the chain of command within the department were introduced.[245]

A San Francisco Police spokesman has explained that the San Francisco system, in which nine district stations cover the city/county, has been the basis for a form of team policing, though it is not pure team policing.[246] Every police officer has a personnel evaluation program folder, which is retained at the workplace and maintained by a sergeant in charge.[247] Weekly reviews of each officer are held, and praise, as well as counsel, is used to indicate the department's evaluation of the officer. According to the San Francisco Police Department (SFPD), this has been a very promising intervention.[248] In effect, the system provides immediate supervisors for everyone, at low expense. All new sergeants are instructed in the supervisory system, and over time existing sergeants will be instructed. Two changes have been made in the police academy and training routines.[249] At the academy, a two-hour class on ethics and professionalism is taught in the first week. San Francisco has gone beyond the state standards dictated by the Police Officers Standards Training (POST) system and mandated more hours of ongoing education and training. SFPD has sought to provide an example by sanctioning officers at the top of the system, as well as at lower levels.[250] The city has enhanced its field training officer system, in the belief that more officers learn from the peer group level than from teachers.[251] One police lieutenant, however, indicated that the problems evidenced by the Rathskellar recruit incident would not be cured by these measures and mandated a different supervisory posture.[252]

On another front of the vice effort, the gay-bashing issue has led to several changes in the way in which the Department approaches that visible and politically active minority community.[253] At various stations, ongoing community relations have been furthered by police bringing in local gay and lesbian community leaders for "gripe sessions," which have been very valuable in reducing the distance between the police and the community.[254] At the same time, the community relations department employs an openly gay officer as liaison to the gay and lesbian community. At the Police Academy, sensitivity training has been introduced. One week is spent discussing the minority communities in the city. One day is scheduled each for blacks, Asians, and gays, a seemingly brief time but an improvement over prior efforts. While some problems are encountered when policing the rougher gay bars in the city, the police department has made strides since the riots caused by the relatively light sentence that was handed to former supervisor and police officer Dan White, the killer of the liberal mayor and gay supervisor.[255]

# CONCLUSION

For many years, criminologists have identified a host of factors which generate or maintain corruption, as well as defining possible bases for legal and institutional mechanisms to prevent, discover, or punish such corruption.[256] Changes in American approaches to vice in the last decade have altered the parameters of police corruption control.

For instance, Goldstein observed, "Corruption thrives best in poorly run organizations where lines of authority are vague and supervision is minimal.[257] Kornblum identified several obstacles to compliance which included lack of knowledge of how to do so, competing external incentives, and conflicting organizational goals.[258] To Sherman, three elements of internal administration are important in controlling corruption: increased internal accountability as led by an active and committed chief, the strengthening of front-line supervision over both the work time and work products of subordinates, and the implementation of a program of positive discipline which rewards integrity and abolishes those formal procedures which inadvertently encourage corruption.[259] While informal procedures such as interdepartmental transfers were used more often than formal procedures, Punch explains that internal disciplinary procedures are slow, cumbersome, inadequately staffed, and are "hindered by the perceived illegitimacy of a vast array of petty and out-of-date discipline regulations."[260]

Whereas anti-corruption measures must be realistic, manageable, and continually reinforced to be successful, the importance of civilian review is questionable.[261] Experience in several cities indicates that civilian review is less likely than police internal review to find officers guilty of misconduct and is more lenient in its disciplinary recommendations when it does find officers guilty.[262] Others argue that in instances where police themselves gather, assemble, present, interpret, and then judge the facts related to misconduct complaints, few serious complaints are likely to be sustained.[263] In contrast, Goldstein points out that no civilian board can exert the kinds of immediate and day-to-day influences on officers' street performance that are traditionally the responsibilities of the chief.[264] In fact, close supervision seems to have a negative, rather than a positive, effect on policing.[265] Increasing the number of supervisors relative to patrol officers, without making other changes, may be very costly and of little significance.

Consequently police organizations which wish to reduce incidents of corruption in the face of a constant level of vice face several dilemmas. First, a longstanding debate exists between those who advocate further decriminalization of vice, even legalization in some instances,[266] and others who believe that the disorder caused by tolerance of vice can lead to the furthering of more serious crime.[267] Second, the issue of centralizing vice patrol responsibility as opposed to decentralizing it continues to cause debate, and proponents of either side can cite information supporting the reasonableness of embracing either approach.[268] Similarly, a third issue, which might be termed a specialist versus generalist debate parallels a disagreement on that theme regarding policing as a whole.[269] Namely, are police who specialize in vice control more effective or efficient, independent of their corruptability, than police who encounter vice as one item in the course of their enforcement duties? The fourth issue is the conflict between autonomy and supervision.[270] This is particularly meaningful when the topic of community policing arises and beat integrity conflicts with the rotation of police personnel to prevent entrenchment of corruption.

The problems of drug use and drug-related police corruption have grown since the time when the Knapp Commission could identify drug-related corruption as "dirty" graft.[271] The crack phenomenon, however short-lived or exaggerated, has brought police in certain cities into more contact with street sales of cocaine, at the same time as cocaine use has spread throughout middle-class society. New York police officials now identify use of drugs by police as their foremost corruption problem rather than other misconduct associated with the profits from drug-related enterprises.[272] This has naturally added a new dimension to the corruption problems related to drugs. What is the implication of the possibility that a free line of cocaine from a friend may have replaced the free cup of coffee as the most important precipitating event on the slippery slope toward corruption.

The official reaction to cocaine use by police officers, certainly reasonable because of the drug's illegal nature, may have created vulnerabilities to corruption. By official treatment of cocaine use as a deviant category, police officials may unintentionally open the door for rationalization of accepting money from drug dealers. If cocaine use was treated more like alcohol issues, intermediate steps of corruption may be removed. The lesson of overdramatizing the marijuana use issue is still fresh in many memories. The campaign against drugs may cause problems when individual officers use cocaine on occasion or know others who use it recreationally.

Another illegal drug, heroin, continues to confound anti-corruption efforts. The success of lower-end heroin market enforcement complicates matters. Because local police, often young and relatively new on the force, have more opportunities for selective enforcement and because they have difficulty in seeing their efforts as equal in importance to making major cases against large-scale dealers, they may be open to corruptive influence. At the same time, endemic problems from the use of informants in drug control raise complicating factors for street police.[273]

Ironically, some of the corruption revelations may be explained as a result of a historically specific combination of two cohort-related phenomena: the willingness to blow the whistle and demand integrity in government and the problems of certain kinds of drug use opening the way to corrupt careers. A police officer who is 22 years old in 1987 was in first grade when *Roe v. Wade*[274] was decided and the Watergate break-in took place. He was in the early years of elementary school when the Democratic party included marijuana decriminalization in the platform debates.[275]

On a more symbolic level, the unwillingness of individual police officers, or some police departments, to acknowledge the legitimacy of gays and lesbians, even after the enactment of specifically designed anti-discrimination ordinances,[276] can cause police to subject gay bars to shakedowns differentially. In each of the five cities examined, gay rights ordinances have been offered, gay or AIDS victimization issues have been central, and some amount of police issues related to gay bars have surfaced.

Gambling, traditionally the quintessential "clean graft," has changed dramatically in the past decade, as several states have approved lotteries or pari-mutuel wagering.[277] At the same time, the ambivalence of the public and of officials to illegal gambling has increased.[278] Certainly, more research needs to be done to determine the actual relationship of illegal gambling to organized crime. Most parties to the debate are generally interested parties,[279] and a neutral data base would help informed decision-making in that area. Earlier findings, showing that police perceive the seriousness of illegal gambling as a product of organized crime's role in it, and that many police favor the legalization of gambling, are dated.[280] Reuter's data from New York City, challenging the "Kefauver orthodoxy" of illegal gambling as important and lucrative for major organized crime groups,[281] could be extended to other cities. The President's Commission on Organized Crime[282] collected data from local law enforcement agencies which indicate the continued allegiance to such an orthodoxy. These data do not aid in any widescale attempt to embrace legalization as the leading alternative to the current level of illegal gambling prevention.[283] More research also needs to be done to examine the competitiveness of state-run gambling with illegal forms. Many have suggested that legal counterparts cannot effectively compete, because the illegal forms offer more credit, hours, phones, and wagers.[284]

The Wilson and Kelling argument on "broken windows," and the effect or disorder on crime, challenges policing priorities that are informed by prosecutorial policies or by citizen response to seriousness measures.[285] Their rationale for giving attention to offenses of relatively low seriousness because such offenses can encourage more serious crimes offers another complication in an effort to reduce the ambivalence related to vice.[286]

On the control side, deterrence and discovery issues related to preventing corruption may be effectively separated. Deterrance may limit the effectiveness of other policing mandates, but may nonetheless be less expensive than employing full observation, reporting, and discovery mechanisms. The deployment of the latter may affect morale enough to encourage cynicism, possibly contributing to receptiveness to corruption.

Some responses that emanate from the rank and file would have greater weight, but might also be limited by street officers' beliefs that corruption publicity and control is a political reaction to a media problem.[287] Where corruption is less than systemic but still tacitly condoned through a code of silence, it may be susceptible to efforts to train and preach against it, something short of "[j]ust say 'No' to corruption opportunities."

The momentum of the government undercover sting operations, like ABSCAM, after faltering, may have gathered steam in recent years with municipal corruption investigations in New York City, Chicago, Philadelphia, and elsewhere, especially after the initiation of the Iran-Contra investigation and hearings.[288] A phenomenon like the post-Watergate emphasis on institutional integrity may emerge. To the extent that federal prosecutors, as outsiders, are able to act more effectively than their local counterparts, they are likely to be the creators of scandal. They tend towards an overreliance upon prosecution and its deterrent capacity and are less suited to suggest and implement institutional reforms.[289]

Another federal-local police cooperation issue is relatively new. The issue is a product of federal regulations which allow for the sharing of forfeited criminal assets with contributing local police agencies.[290] How much local partnership efforts in the asset forfeiture area increase local police participation in drug control efforts of a previously exclusively federal nature will be instructive in determining whether increase or decrease in corruption opportunities results. More contact with drug dealers might lead to an increase in corruption. Conversely, less frustration on the part of local police with perception of their status as junior actors in the drug wars could decrease corruption. In addition, more careful oversight by other cooperative federal agencies could reduce corruption.

Gardiner's "Wincanton" findings remain valuable because they pointed to the contradiction of high tolerance of illegal activity (gambling) and low tolerance of police corruption.[291] In Philadelphia, the survey conducted for the Philadelphia Police Study Task Force found that the public thought highly of the police, yet also thought that the police might succumb to corruption and underenforcement in vice areas.[292] This response to corruption revelation is entirely appropriate in a city with a high crime rate, fiscal problems, and a generally high level of police delivery of services.

An emphasis on reducing corruption might deter effective and preferable policing of major crimes in a number of ways. It might make police wary of any contacts with potential informants or witnesses who are involved in vice, limit the aggressiveness of successful police who are both corruption-prone and courageous in their other policing efforts,[293] or make police officers fear that their partners are field associates, thus reducing trust and exposing both police and citizens to increased danger.

Field associates programs have been controversial. Anthony Bouza, former New York Police Department Commander, has called the field associates program the "'most effective tool for controlling a police department.'"[294] In contrast, Phil Caruso, the President of the New York Police Department Police Benevolent Association, claims "'[t]his kind of spying within the ranks is very demoralizing and casts an aura of suspicion on your brother officer.'...You don't know who you can trust and who you can't trust.''[295] Representatives of the Philadelphia Fraternal Order of Police have complained that officers who are not part of the program might be unduly ostracized. They also suggested that veterans would assume that any recruit coming out of the academy is a field associate and would treat that recruit accordingly. " 'It virtually seals the fate of the rookies...Ninety-five percent of the rookies who hit the street will not be field associates,...but they are all going to get a frosty reception.'''[296] According to this view, rookies, who must normally contend with a potentially hostile or indifferent environment, could suffer added strain which could lead to poor socialization, increased danger to police, and less effective policing overall.

Finally, the demands of community-based policing complicate the police patrol organization which attempts to prevent rootedness of corruption in individual units or geographical areas. This conflict caused New York Police Commissioner Ward to back down from plans to rotate police officers on a regular basis to prevent the entrenchment of corruption.[297]

Skolnick's and Bayley's suggestions about the appropriateness of various forms of policing strategies and their deployment in specific communities indicate that no conclusions can be easily applied to any of the five cities mentioned, or any other particular city, for that matter.[298] They believe that policing will probably be more effective to the extent it relies on a mix of strategies appropriate to each neighborhood rather than relying on the single complaint strategy as the primary approach for all neighborhoods.[299] Further, they argue that community police commanders should be given the authority to conduct informal experiments with different strategies to determine the optimal fit between the unique characteristics of the community and the mixture of policing techniques.[300] As community-oriented policing programs expand, the need for responsiveness among police organizations becomes a key factor in the ability of contemporary police departments to accommodate changes in crime, disorder, funding, and policing techniques in the 1980s.[301]

In a less instrumental sense, police corruption control represents a range of strategies aimed at installing professionalism, high morale, and commitment to innovation in police organizations. As John Kaplan points out, the very police organizations that may be revealed as corrupt are also typified by a level of organizational ossification that limits the introduction of innovative policing strategies and the elevation of officials who are not protective of the corruption and rigidity of the existing order.[302] Police-community relations and citizen respect for police are adversely affected by police corruption. The events of the past decade have further confounded the ambivalence surrounding the policing of vice. New situations, new cohort attitudes, new policing demands, and more decriminalization have muddied the waters in the vice enforcement area. With this ambivalence of innovative policing strategies, yet another powerful reason for societal resolution of the legal treatment of vice has been created.

# Notes

1   Lopez, "The Good Guys in This Town," *Philadelphia Inquirer,* Nov. 28, 1986, at B1, col. 1.

2   Klein, *Fighting Corruption in the Philadelphia Police Department: The Death Knell of the 'Conspiracy of Silence,'* 60 Temple L. Q. 103 (1987).

3   *Id.* at 115.

4   *N.Y. Times,* Sept. 26, 1986, at B1, col. 1; M. McAlary, *Buddy Boys: When Good Cops Go Bad* (1987).

5   Doherty, "Vest Found Guilty on 2 Perjury Counts," *Boston Globe,* Oct. 7, 1986, at 1, col. 2.

6   Interview with David Ambrose, San Francisco Police Department Public Affairs Officer (Apr. 27, 1987).

7   *L.A. Times,* Jan. 22, 1987, at 114, col. 1.

8   Klein, supra note 2, at 115.

9   J. Dombrink & W. Thompson, *The Last Resort: Success and Failure in Campaigns for Casinos* (forthcoming).

10   *Id.*

11   *Id.*

12   J. Gardiner, *The Politics of Corruption: Organized Crime in An American City* 55 (1970).

13   J. Dombrink & J. Meeker, *Criminal Capital: Making Organized Crime Unprofitable* (forthcoming).

14   V. Abt, J. Smith & E. Christiansen, *The Business of Risk: Commercial Gambling in Mainstream America* 193 (1985).

15   L. Grinspoon & J. Bakalar, *Cocaine: A Drug and Its Social Evolution* (1985).

16   R. Weitzer, "Immoral Crusade: The Prostitutes' Rights Movement in the United States" (1987) (unpublished manuscript).

17   K. Luker, *Abortion and the Politics of Motherhood* (1984).

18   E. Donnerstin, D. Linz & S. Penrod, *The Question of Pornography: Research Findings and Policy Implications* (1987).

19   E. Schur, *The Politics of Deviance: Stigma Contests and The Uses of Power* (1980).

20   J. Skolnick & D. Bayley, *The New Blue Line: Police Innovation in Six American Cities* (1986).

21   See generally A. Kornblum, *The Moral Hazards: Police Strategy for Honest and Ethical Behavior* (1976); M. Punch, *Conduct Unbecoming: The Social Construction of Police Deviance and Control* (1985); L. Sherman, *Scandal and Reform: Controlling Police Corruption* (1978).

22   Skolnick, *Police: Vice Squad, in Encyclopedia of Crime and Justice* 1148, 1151-53 (S. Kadish ed. 1983).

23   See J. Wilson, *Varieties of Police Behavior* 83-139 (1968).

24   M. Punch, supra note 21, at 13-14.

25   *Bureau of Justice Statistics, Report to the Nation on Crime and Justice:* The Data 4, 5 (1984).

26   Skolnick, *The Social Transformation of Vice, Law & Contemporary Problems,* Winter 1988, at 9.

27   J. Gardiner, supra note 12, at 55-56.

28   L. Sherman, supra note 21, at 242-63.

29   *The Knapp Commission Report on Police Corruption* (1973).

30   M. Punch, supra note 21, at 25-27.

31   See generally Reuter, *Quantity Illusions and Paradoxes of Drug Interdiction: Federal Intervention into Vice Policy, Law & Contemporary Problems,* Winter 1988, at 233; M. Kleiman, *Drug Enforcement and Organized Crime: Current Knowledge and Research Prospects* (1985) (unpublished manuscript prepared for symposium sponsored by Northwest Policy Studies Center, Dulles International Airport, Virginia, Sept. 25-26, 1986); Kleiman & Reuter, Risks and Prices: "An Economic Analysis of Drug Enforcement," 7 *Crime & Justice* 289 (1986).

32   See e.g., J. Kaplan, *Marijuana: The New Prohibition* (1970); J. Skolnick, *House of Cards: The Legalization and Control of Casino Gambling* (1978) Skolnick & Dombrink, "The Legalization of Deviance," 16 Criminology 193, 198-206 (1978).

33   M. Kleiman, "Allocating Federal Drug Enforcement Resources: The Case of Marijuana 179" (1985) (unpublished doctoral dissertation, John F. Kennedy School of Government, Harvard Univ.).

34   J. Kaplan, *The Hardest Drug: Heroin and Public Policy* 79, 83 (1983); see also *Street-Level Drug Enforcement* (National Institute of Justice video crime film series 1986).

35   J. Dombrink & W. Thompson, "Riding the Crest of the Third Wave: Illegal and Legal Gambling Policies in America" (1985) (unpublished manuscript prepared for the President's Commission on Organized Crime).

36   See infra notes 37-39.

37    H. Packer, *The Limits of the Criminal Sanction* 250 (1968).

38    Kadish, *The Crisis of Overcriminalization*, 374 Annals 157, 164-65 (1967).

39    F. Allen, *The Borderland of Criminal Justice: Essays in Law and Criminology* 7-9 (1964).

40    J. Mill, *On Liberty* 100 (C. Shields ed. 11th printing 1956) (1st ed. 1859).

41    H. Packer, supra note 37, at 261-69.

42    Skolnick, *Coercion to Virtue: The Enforcement of Morals,* 41 S. Cal. L. Rev. 588, 632 91966).

43    ABC News/*Washington Post* Poll, May 1985.

44    J. Polich, P. Ellickson, P. Reuter & J. Kahan, *Strategies for Controlling Adolescent Drug Use* 33 (1984). The misidentification of cocaine as a narcotic and its identification as a dangerous drug has persisted from the early twentieth century, even though widespread use might somewhat mollify this notion. L. Grinspoon & J. Bakalar, supra note 15, at 211-237. The emergence of crack as a more volatile concoction of cocaine reinforced this idea in the mid-1980s. Kerr, *Use of Crack; The Future, New York Times,* Sept. 1, 1986, at 25, col. 5. Moreover, cocaine is considered more a recreational drug than one likely for medicalization. L. Grinspoon & J. Bakalar, supra note 15, at 238-67.

45    The Gallup Poll, June 20, 1985.

46    ABC News/*Washington Post* Poll, supra note 43.

47    L. Grinspoon & J. Bakalar, supra note 15, at 211-37.

48    *Id.* at 58-63.

49    *Roe v. Wade,* 410 U.S. 113 (1973).

50    Meeker, Dombrink & Geis, "State Law and Local Ordinances in California Barring Discrimination on the Basis of Sexual Orientation," 10 *U. Dayton L. Rev.* 745, 756 (1985).

51    D. Altman, *The Homosexualization of America: The Americanization of the Homosexual* 109-45 (1982).

52    P. Reuter, *Disorganized Crime: The Economics of the Visible Hand* 177-81 (1983).

53    Pratter & Fowler, *Police Perceptions about Gambling Enforcement: A National Survey of Law Enforcement Agencies, in Gambling in America,* at 461, 464, app. 1 (1976) (Report of the Commission on the Review of the National Policy Toward Gambling); J. Meeker & J. Dombrink, *Bookies and Bosses: Illegal Gambling and Legalization Efforts* 86 (1988) (proceedings of the Seventh International Conference on Gambling and Risk-Taking).

54    Skolnick, supra note 26, at 12.

55   Stanford, "Drugs and the Law," 470 *Rolling Stone* 64 (Mar. 27, 1986).

56   Nordheimer, "Police Corruption Plaguing Florida," *New York Times*, Aug. 3, 1986, at 19, col. 1.

57   Peterson, "Miami Virtue, or Vice?" *Washington Post,* Jan. 12, 1986, at A1, col. 4.

58   Rothchild, "Crime Stoppers Notebook," 470 *Rolling Stone* 61 (Mar. 27, 1986).

59   Volsky, "Wide Miami Inquiry into Police Is Seen," *New York Times*, Dec. 13, 1987, at 29, col. 1. According to the U.S. Attorney for the Southern District of Florida, Leon Kellner, "The Miami Police Department has an extraordinarily serious problem, equal or surpassing anything I've seen anywhere. Unfortunately, our probe is mushrooming and we could end up with the largest police corruption case in United States' history." *Id.*

60   *Id.*

61   Bearak, "Miami Seeking Answers and Police Trial Unfolds," *Los Angeles Times,* Oct. 6, 1986, at 4, col. 1.

62   *Id.*

63   Volsky, supra note 59.

64   Stanford, supra note 55, at 66.

65   *Id.*

66   *Id.*

67   *Id.*

68   McGee & Leen, "Feds Assault High-Level Corruption in S. Florida," *Miami Herald,* Nov. 16, 1986, at 1A, col. 1.

69   *Id.*

70   *Id.*

71   *Id.*

72   Ingwerson, "Miami Grapples with Allegations of Police Corruption," *Christian Science Monitor,* Jan. 13, 1986, at 1, col. 2.

73   See generally D. Rieff, *Going to Miami* (1987); T. Allman, *Miami: City of the Future* (1987).

74   Nordheimer, "Miami Police Scandal Raising Questions on Minority Recruits," *New York Times*, Jan. 9, 1986, at 10, col. 1.

75   *Id.* at col. 3.

76   D. Rieff, supra note 73.

77   U.S. Government Sentencing Memorandum, *United States v. Martin,* No. 84-00106 (E.D. Pa. Sept. 21, 1984).

78   Interview with Howard Klein, former federal prosecutor, Philadelphia (Mar. 19, 1987).

79   Philadelphia Police Study Task Force, *Philadelphia and Its Police: Toward a New Partnership* (1987).

80   Professor of Law, George Washington University Law School.

81   Philadelphia Police Study Task Force, supra note 79, at 16.

82   *Id.* at 17.

83   *Id.* at 16-17.

84   *Id.* at 21-23.

85   *Id.* at 168.

86   *Id.* at 169.

87   *Id.* at 170.

88   Hepp, "Tucker Casts a New Image for Police," *Philadelphia Inquirer,* Jan. 5, 1987, at BO1, col. 1.

89   *Id.*

90   *Id.*

91   *Id.*

92   *Id.*

93   *Id.*

94   Citizens' Crime Commission of Delaware Valley, *Vice Enforcement and Corruption in the Philadelphia Police Department* 8 (1985).

95   *Id.*

96   *Id.*

97   *Id.*

98   *Id.*

99   *Id.*

100  *Id.*

101  Heidorn, "A Tough Challenge Faces Tucker: Cleaning House, Inside Out," *Philadelphia Inquirer,* Oct. 21, 1986, at BO6, col. 1.

102    *Id.*

103    *Id.*

104    *Id.*

105    Pennsylvania Crime Commission, *A Decade of Organized Crime: 1980 Report* at x-xi (1980).

106    Heidorn, supra note 101.

107    *Id.*

108    Klein, supra note 2, at 114.

109    Citizens' Crime Commission of Delaware Valley, supra note 94, at 14.

110    Klein, supra note 2, at 108.

111    *Id.* at 108.

112    See Government Sentencing Memorandum, supra note 77, at 4.

113    Klein, supra note 2, at 111.

114    *Id.* at 114.

115    *United States v. DePeri,* 778 F. 2d 963 (3d Cir. 1985).

116    18 U.S.C. §§ 1961-1968 (1982).

117    Klein, supra note 2, at 112.

118    Hepp, "Police Chief Shifts Supervision of Ethics Division," *Philadelphia Inquirer,* Jan. 7, 1987, at BO6, col. 5.

119    Citizens' Crime Commission of Delaware Valley, supra note 94, at 15.

120    *Id.* at 15. Police officers testifying at the trials of other officers told how easy it was to take money. One officer described how the tiered level of enforcement was easily circumvented by corrupt police so that they could accept payoffs. This officer said that in order to ensure protection, all he had to do was get in touch with the "cronies in other divisions." Interview with Howard Klein, supra note 78.

121    Citizens' Crime Commission of Delaware Valley, supra note 94, at 16.

122    *Id.*

123    *Id.* at 17.

124    *Id.*

125    See interview with Howard Klein, supra note 78.

126    Lounsberry, "Crime Fighter Regretfully Says Goodbye," *Philadelphia Inquirer*, Jan. 17, 1987, at BO1, col. 1.

127    Klein, supra note 2, at 111, 112.

128    *Id.* at 114.

129    Citizens' Crime Commission of Delaware Valley, supra note 94, at 18.

130    *Id.* at 23-32.

131    *Id.* at 23. Interview with Ian Lennox, Executive Director, Citizens' Crime Commission of Delaware Valley in Philadelphia (Mar. 19, 1987).

132    Citizens' Crime Commission of Delaware Valley, supra note 94, at 18.

133    Interview by Angelo Duplantier, University of California-Irvine student, with Ian Lennox, Executive Director, Citizens' Crime Commission of Delaware Valley (Jan. 21, 1987); Angelo Duplantier, "Too Much Brotherly Love in the Philadelphia Police Department" (unpublished student paper, Mar. 20, 1987) (Program in Social Ecology, University of California, Irvine).

134    *Id.*

135    Citizens' Crime Commission of Delaware Valley, supra note 97, at 23.

136    *Id.* at 28.

137    Philadelphia Police Study Task Force, supra note 79, at 153-63.

138    Interview with Gerald M. Caplan, Professor of Law, George Washington University Law School (Mar. 17, 1987).

139    Interview with Howard Klein, supra note 78.

140    *1988 Information Please Almanac* 798 (41st ed. 1988).

141    *Id.* at 764.

142    P. Maas, *Serpico* (1973).

143    See Knapp Commission Report, supra note 29.

144    R. Daley, *Prince of the City* 25-27 (1978).

145    Purdum, "12 from Brooklyn Precinct Arraigned on Broad Range of Charges," *New York Times*, Nov. 7, 1986, at 15, col. 2.

146    Purdum, "Serious Crimes in New York City Rise 5%, First Increase in 5 Years," *New York Times*, Mar. 20, 1987, at A1, col. 1.

147    Buder, "Officer Tells Why He Decided to Inform on Others," *New York Times*, May 7, 1987, at B8, col. 4.

148    Shipp, "An Inquiry or a Trap?" *New York Times*, Sept. 27, 1986, at 12, col. 1.

[149]   Purdum, "Missing Indicted Officer Found Dead in Motel," *New York Times*, Nov. 8, 1986, at 1, col. 2.

[150]   M. McAlary, "Buddy Boys," supra note 4.

[151]   "Officer in Graft Trial Called Naive by Lawyer," *New York Times*, Apr. 28, 1987, at A29, col. 3.

[152]   Purdum, "Ward Says Slowdown by Officers Has Worsened and May be Illegal," *New York Times*, Nov. 13, 1986, at A1, col. 3.

[153]   2 New York City Mayor's Advisory Committee on Police Management and Personnel Policy 171 (1987) [hereinafter *Mayor's Advisory Report*].

[154]   *Id.*

[155]   *Id.*

[156]   *Id.* at 23.

[157]   *Id.* at 24.

[158]   *Id.*

[159]   Kerr, "Officers Facing Drug Charges Call 11 Others Cocaine Users," *New York Times*, Mar. 19, 1986, at B1, col. 4.

[160]   Purdum, "Suspensions Stir Accountability Issue," *New York Times,* Sept. 24, 1986, at B4, col. 4.

[161]   1 *Mayor's Advisory Report,* supra note 153, at 7.

[163]   Kilborn, "U.S. Said to Issue Subpoenas Linked to Boesky Trading," *New York Times,* Nov. 17, 1986, at 1. col. 1.

[164]   Lubasch, "Mob's Ruling 'Commission' to Go on Trial in New York," *New York Times,* Nov. 17, 1986, at 1, col. 1.

[165]   See Knapp Commission Report, supra note 29.

[166]   P. Maas, supra note 142.

[167]   Knapp Commission Report, supra note 29.

[168]   *Id.* at 1.

[169]   *Id.* at 2.

[170]   *Id.* at 5-7.

[171]   *Id.* at 16-34.

[172]   See M. Punch, supra note 21, at 27-28; see also B. Gelb, *Varnished Brass: The Decade After Serpico* (1983).

173  See P. Murphy & T. Plate, *Commissioner* 167 (1977).

174  M. Punch, supra note 21, at 27.

175  P. Murphy & T. Plate, supra note 173, at 239.

176  *Id.* at 217-54.

177  *Id.* at 237.

178  *Id.*

179  M. Punch, supra note 21, at 28; see also John F. Kennedy School of Government, Harvard University, The Knapp Commission and Patrick Murphy 182 (1977).

180  M. Punch, supra note 21, at 28.

181  *Id.*

182  L. Sherman, supra note 21, at xxix.

183  Farber, "Decade After Knapp Inquiry, A Sense of Revolution Pervades Police Force," *New York Times*, Nov. 29, 1982, at B1, col. 1. "But as a widespread and organized thing, as something that was once accepted, that's gone. The whole climate of the department has been reversed since Knapp." *Id.*

184  M. Punch, supra note 21, at 28.

185  See R. Daley, supra note 144.

186  "Police Corruption: A Look at History," *New York Times*, Sept. 24, 1986, at 84, col. 5.

187  Purdum, "12 from Brooklyn Precinct Arraigned on Broad Range of Charges," *New York Times*, Nov. 7, 1986, at 15, col. 2.

188  Purdum, "Officer Admits Guilt in Sale of Cocaine," *New York Times*, Mar. 11, 1987, at B1, col. 6.

189  M. McAlary, supra note 4; "Drug Influx a Strain on the Best," *New York Times*, Sept. 2, 196, at B1, col. 1.

190  M. McAlary, supra note 4, at 171.

191  "The Cops Caught the Crooked Cops," *New York Times*, Sept. 26, 1986, at A34, col. 1 (editorial). One of the more controversial issues involved in the 77th Precinct scandal was the use of some police officers to wear recording devices, or "wires" on their bodies, or otherwise provide testimony against their fellow officers, thus piercing the traditional "blue wall" of police silence and solidarity amid investigation of corruption charges. See M. McAlary, supra note 4, at 230-51; see also Purdum, supra note 187.

192  Boorstin, "Ward, Defending Transfers, Calls Some Officers 'Bandits,'"*New York Times*, Nov. 10, 1986, at B1, col. 2.

193   Purdum, "Anticorruption Moves Set Off Slowdown by Police," *New York Times*, Nov. 11, 1986, at 14, col. 3.

194   Purdum, "Ward Agrees to Delay His Precinct Transfer Plan," *New York Times*, Nov. 14, 1986, at 1, col. 1.

195   Smothers, "In Drug-Wracked 77th Precinct, Police Suspensions Draw Varied Reactions," *New York Times*, Sept. 25, 1986, at B4, col. 1.

196   2 Mayor's Advisory Report, supra note 153, at 7.

197   *Id.*

198   *Id.* at 7-8.

199   *Id.* at 84.

200   Larmer, "Indictments Rock Bay State Police," *The Christian Science Monitor*, Aug. 1, 1986, at 3, col. 4.

201   Merry, "Simmering Boston Police-Corruption Changes Boil Over Again," *The Christian Science Monitor*, Oct. 27, 1986, at 5, col. 1.

202   Birtwell, "Another Shot at Hub Police," *Boston Herald*, Oct. 23, 1986, at 7, col. 1.

203   Alters & Paz-Martinez, "Charges Leveled of Illegal Payoffs to Boston Police," *Boston Globe*, Dec. 21, 1986, at 33, col. 1.

204   *Id.*

205   *Id.*

206   *Id.*

207   *Id.*

208   Birtwell, supra note 202.

209   Paz-Martinez, "Many Theories on Cause for Payoff Probe," *Boston Globe*, Dec. 21, 1986, at 53, col. 1.

210   *Id.*

211   *Id.*

212   Cullen & Connolly, "Records Seized in Probe of Hub Police," *Boston Globe*, Oct. 23, 1986, col. 6.

213   *Id.*

214   Fehrnstrom, Murphy & Mooney, "Massive Fed Probe of Police," *Boston Herald*, Oct. 23, 1986, at 1, col. 2.

215   *Id.*

216 *Id.*

217 *Id.*

218 *Id.*

219 *Id.*

220 *Id.*

221 *Id.*

222 Cullen & Connolly, supra note 212.

223 Waters was the star witness in the case against Boston Police detective George Vest, who was convicted on two counts of perjury when he denied receiving cash from Waters in return for allowing Waters to sell marijuana over the counter at his Roxbury variety store. Vest was convicted of lying to a federal grand jury. In the second count, Vest was convicted of lying when he denied acting as the middleman in a bribery scheme to fix a court case. Waters testified he paid bribes to more than 50 police officers, including former Commissioner Jordan, to protect his drug dealing business. All those named by Waters denied receiving any payoffs. Vest testified that he paid 10 percent of his $18,000-a-week income from his stores to police officers in bribes for protection. He said he gave the money out in brown paper bags. Besides protection, Waters said police provided him with advance information about raids and told him when his store would be under surveillance. Doherty, supra note 5.

224 Criminal Indictment in *United States v. Boylan,* No. A.87-345 (D. Mass. Nov. 9, 1987); 7 "Indicted in Case on Boston Police," *New York Times,* Nov. 11, 1987, at A28, col. 4.

225 Cullen & Malone, "Kickback Probe is Widespread," *Boston Globe,* Oct. 24, 1986, at 1, col. 6.

226 Paz-Martinez, "Ex-bar Owner: Police Solicited $500 'Tip,'" *Boston Globe,* Dec. 21, 1986, at 54, col. 4.

227 Alters & Paz-Martinez, supra note 203.

228 *Id.*

229 Paz-Martinez, "700-900 Hub Liquor Citations Issued Yearly," *Boston Globe,* Dec. 21, 1986, at 53, col. 1.

230 See Indictment, supra note 224.

231 W. Hinckle, Gayslayer (1985); F. Fitzgerald, *Cities on a Hill: A Journey Through Contemporary American Cultures* (1986).

232 Chung & Magagnini, "Sex Probe Must Allow Legal Counsel for Cops," *San Francisco Chronicle,* May 5, 1984, at 1, col. 2.

[233]   Hughes, "Chief Orders Ethics Talks for Police," *San Francisco Sunday Examiner and Chronicle,* June 10, 1984, at 1, col. 2.

[234]   *Id.*

[235]   Chung & Leary, "Murphy Livid," *San Francisco Chronicle,* May 3, 1984, at 1, col. 4.

[236]   "Officers Reassigned in Coast Police Scandal," *New York Times*, Sept. 9, 1984, at 31, col. 1.

[237]   Wallace, "Big Rise in Complaints Against Police in San Francisco," *San Francisco Chronicle,* May 25, 1984, at 1, col. 6.

[238]   *San Francisco Chronicle,* July 24, 1984, at 4, col. 1.

[239]   Wallace, "Feinstein Calls for Meeting on Police Department," *San Francisco Chronicle,* May 25, 1984, at 1, col. 1.

[240]   *Id.*

[241]   *Id.*

[242]   Wallace, supra note 237.

[243]   Hughes, supra note 233.

[244]   *Id.*

[245]   *Id.*

[246]   Interview with David Ambrose, supra note 6.

[247]   *Id.*

[248]   *Id.*

[249]   *Id.*

[250]   Interview with Lieutenant Dan Carlson, San Francisco Police Department (Apr. 10, 1987).

[251]   *Id.*

[252]   *Id.*

[253]   Hinckle, "Cop Makes it Safer for Gays," *San Francisco Chronicle,* Oct. 1, 1984, at 6, col. 1.

[254]   Interview with Dan Carlson, supra note 250.

[255]   *Id.*

[256]   See generally L. Sherman, supra note 21; M. Punch, supra note 21.

[257]   H. Goldstein, *Policing a Free Society* 210 (1977).

[258]  A. Kornblum, supra note 21, at 5.

[259]  Sherman, supra note 21, at 5.

[260]  M. Punch, supra note 21, at 198.

[261]  2 Mayor's Advisory Report, supra note 153.

[262]  See generally Hudson, Police Review Boards and Police Accountability, 36 *Law & Contemporary Problems*. 515 (1971) (studies of New York City and Philadelphia).

[263]  Schwartz, *Reaching Systemic Police Abuses—The Need for Civilian Investigation of Misconduct: A Response to Wayne Kersteller, in Police Leadership in America: Crisis and Opportunity* 187 (W. Geller ed. 1985).

[264]  H. Goldstein, supra note 257, at 174.

[265]  Kerstetter, "Who Disciplines the Police? Who Should?" in *Police Leadership in America,* supra note 263, at 149.

[266]  See generally E. Schur, supra note 19; Kadish, supra note 38; F. Allen, supra note 39.

[267]  See generally Wilson & Kelling, "Broken Windows," *Atlantic Monthly,* March, 1982, at 34.

[268]  J. Skolnick & D. Bayley, supra note 20, at 214-29.

[269]  See, e.g., *id.* at 121-22.

[270]  Skolnick, supra note 22, at 1151.

[271]  The Knapp Commission Report on Police Corruption, supra note 29, at 91-115.

[272]  2 Mayor's Advisory Report, supra note 153, at 24.

[273]  J. Skolnick, supra note 22, at 1150-51; P. Reuter, supra note 52, at 194-97; see also M. Moore, *Buy and Bust* 126 (1977).

[274]  *Roe v. Wade,* 410 U.S. 113 (1973).

[275]  P. Anderson, *High in America* 5 (1981).

[276]  Meeker, Dombrink & Geis, supra note 50, at 756.

[277]  J. Rosecrance, *Gambling Without Guilt* 4-5 (1988).

[278]  See J. Meeker & J. Dombrink, supra note 53, at 3.

[279]  *Id.* at 8.

[280]  Pratter & Fowler, supra note 53.

[281]  P. Reuter, supra note 52, at 181-87.

[282]  J. Meeker & J. Dombrink, supra note 53, at 2.

[283]   *Id.* at 96.

[284]   Wilson & Kelling, supra note 267.

[285]   Bureau of Justice Statistics, U.S. Department of Justice, *Report to the Nation on Crime and Justice* 4-5 (Oct. 1983).

[286]   J. Meeker & J. Dombrink, supra note 53, at 96; see generally Skolnick, supra note 26.

[287]   M. Punch, supra note 21, at 200.

[288]   G. Caplan, ABSCAM Ethics: Moral Issues and Deception in Law Enforcement (1983); President's Special Review Board, The Tower Commission Report (1987).

[289]   Ruff, "Federal Prosecution of Local Corruption: A Case Study in the Making of Law Enforcement Policy," 65 *Georgetown L.J.* 1171, 1171-72 (1977).

[290]   U.S. Department of Justice, Asset Forfeiture Office, Criminal Division, Department of Justice Forfeiture Manual 127-28 (1987).

[291]   J. Gardiner, supra note 12, at 56.

[292]   Philadelphia Police Study Task Force, supra note 79, at 164, 168-71.

[293]   M. Punch, supra note 21, at 204.

[294]   Hepp, "Police Spying on Police: Quiet and Controversial," *Philadelphia Inquirer,* Aug. 11, 1986, at BO1, col. 2.

[295]   *Id.*

[296]   *Id.*

[297]   See Purdum, supra note 187.

[298]   J. Skolnick & D. Bayley, supra note 20, 210-29.

[299]   *Id.*

[300]   *Id.*

[301]   *Id.*

[302]   Comments of John Kaplan, Professor of Law, Stanford University, at Law and Contemporary Problems Symposium on Vice at Duke Law School, Durham, North Carolina (June 5-6, 1987).

# Study Questions

1. What factors have predominantly characterized the "recent wave" of police corruption in the United States?

2. Enforcement of "vice" laws has changed in the past decade as a result of notable changes in society. Describe those changes which have affected police vice enforcement activities. Have the police been responsive to those changes or have they attempted to utilize traditional enforcement tactics?

3. In the cities discussed in this chapter, what common factors emerged in officer corruption?

4. Choose any one of the cities discussed in the chapter and describe how you would deal with the corruption problem. What actions would you take?

5. What was the most shocking or surprising aspect of police corruption you discovered in this chapter? Why were you surprised?

# 6

# AN OVERVIEW OF ISSUES CONCERNING POLICE OFFICER DRUG USE*

## David L. Carter and Darrel W. Stephens

Abuse of drugs (other than alcohol) by police officers has received considerable attention in recent years. This problem has made headlines in cities across the nation where police drug use has manifested itself in ways that attracted media attention. While the extent of the actual problem is unknown, the implications of drug abuse by police officers are such that, even if they are half the levels reported for the general population, a serious problem exists.

In many cases where police departments have discovered drug use by officers, the problem has often been dealt with through either termination/resignation by the officer; departmental disciplinary processes; collective bargaining unit arbitration; or referral to Employee Assistance Programs. These actions often are motivated by the desire to dispose of the problem as quickly and quietly as possible. Unfortunately, a full understanding of the policy issues involved frequently does not exist. Although the police have been addressing the drug problem on a case by case basis for some time, it has only been in the past two or three years that the issue of abuse by the police has been the subject of open discussion.

Many departments have recognized the problems associated with alcohol abuse and have learned to treat it more effectively. However, abuse of substances other than alcohol present an entirely different dimension. Officers, for example, may be committing a felony through possession of the substance, not to mention the potential for disaster to citizen safety if an officer is under the influence of drugs while in the performance of official duty.

The problem of police substance abuse is complicated by embarrassment, emotional issues, political dynamics, questions of liability, concerns about police competence, and the personal trauma for those involved. Because of these factors, both empirical data and anecdotal evidence is difficult to obtain. In an effort to be comprehensive in the treatment of this area, the authors have relied heavily on personal contacts to learn about the extent of the problems—notably those resolved through informal means. Consequently, the sources of some of the information and incidents discussed must remain confidential.

---

*This chapter was written expressly for inclusion in this book.*

# NATURE OF THE PROBLEM

While no published research exists to specifically document the extent of substance abuse by police officers, it is reasonable to assume that the problem is more extensive than we may want to admit. Like the proverbial iceberg, it appears only a small portion of the problem is actually visible.

The author's research indicates that drug-related problems among law enforcement personnel have at least two dimensions. The first is a strong impression that incidents of police corruption associated with drug trafficking either by law enforcement officers or through the assistance of police is increasing. The second is that some police officers use drugs simply as a recreational activity.

## Drugs and Corruption

Goldstein defines corruption as the "misuse of authority by a police officer in a manner designed to produce personal gain for the officer or for others" [1987:188]. The research on corruption illustrates how this problem can take on many forms. Its genesis is usually found in a series of minor acts of misconduct which may be tacitly condoned and grow into a pervasive pattern of actions for personal gain.

Even in cases where an officer's intent to use drugs is simply for recreational purposes, it is clearly recognized that the potential for corruption exists. An officer must obtain the drug which means that there is some contact with a pusher or intermediary. The transaction opens the door to corruption in that once the officer's identity is discovered, the pusher will have a lever that may be used to press for favors or information from the officer. From another perspective, the officer who steals drugs from users, traffickers, or the police property room with the intent to either use the drugs or sell them is also corrupt.

More serious, however, is the overt trafficking of drugs by police officers as indicated by the publicized investigations in New York and Miami, as well as the lesser known cases in a number of other cities. In these cases the drugs typically have been obtained from either (1) shakedowns and confiscations of drugs from people on the street or (2) thefts of drugs from police property rooms. [NOTE: For a detailed case study of the problem see (Daly, 1986).]

A graphic experience by a college student illustrates this problem:

Some friends and I went to [a city] to go to a Heart concert. We had parked the car and were walking across the lot toward the arena's entrance, when this [name of city] cop *in uniform* [emphasis added] walked up to us and asked us if we wanted to buy any dope. We couldn't believe it! He not only surprised us with that, he scared us.

What do you do when a cop with his gun and all tries to sell you some dope? We didn't know if this was a set up, if he was just trying to pick up some fast cash, how he would act if we said no, or if this guy was crazy. We just got out of there fast...We didn't report him because we were afraid and figured nobody would believe us anyway...How do you know if the cop you're reporting this to is not getting a cut of the drug money? [Statement of a male university student (1986)].

We must recognize that a tragic phenomenon is emerging in American policing with a new generation of police corruption associated with the drug trade. Police department internal investigations and criminal indictments occurring across the country are all too prominent to suggest that this is not a major problem for the police. The "bottom line" of this problem appears to be the large quantity of money involved. As one Drug Enforcement Administration official commented...

The money involved [in drug trafficking] is hard to comprehend. Think of it: An agent [or officer] sees the opportunity to make a score of cash, either through a bribe or a ripoff, that involves more money than that agent may make in a year, five years, hell, maybe a lifetime. I hate to say it, but you've got to admit that you can understand how an agent could go on the take [Confidential statement of a Drug Enforcement Administration official (1986)].

Officers who appear to be most susceptible to corruption are those working in jurisdictions where the drug trade, notably as a trafficking distribution center, is particularly pervasive. For example, state and federal investigations of drug corruption in the Miami Police Department are expected to involve one in ten officers in the 1,000 officer department. Florida Department of Law Enforcement Commissioner Robert Dempsey, commenting on the Miami drug corruption stated...

It had to come somewhere along the line...[I]t happened unfortunately in the city of Miami, which is the heart of the drug trafficking area. Given the amount of money involved there, and the fact that drug traffickers act almost with impunity, it was inevitable that eventually some policemen would become involved and corrupted by it [*Law Enforcement News* [LEN], December 8, 1987:6].

The consistent theme of officer drug corruption is the influence of large amounts of money—money of proportions not experienced in past incidents of police corruption in this country. Unfortunately, a growing symptom of the problem is increased violence by officers associated with drug corruption as seen both in New York and Miami (Daly, 1986; *LEN,* December 8, 1987). Currently, far too little is known about drug corruption and the police. It is clear, however, the problem exists and it is serious. What is less clear at this point is the most effective ways for police administrators to identify the presence of this type of corruption in order to resolve the problem.

## Recreational Use

A more significant issue than corruption at the current time is recreational drug use by police officers. It is more significant, in the author's view, because of the greater numbers of officers apparently involved in this form of use. Further, more pervasive use may be indicative of a greater potential for corruption. What complicates the problem further is the attitude expressed by some officers that "what I do on my off-duty time is my own business." This makes it even more difficult to identify officers using drugs on a recreational basis.

"Recreational" use of drugs is a somewhat broad characterization. Admittedly, it is a term which may not be completely inclusive of all drug use, particularly in cases of addiction. What is included in this category is drug use that does not involve corruption and where use was initially a product of the desire to experience the expected exhilaration, psychoactive effects, and/or mood changes associated with drug use. Under this definition, drug use may include both on-duty and off-duty use as long as corruption is not involved.

It is difficult to identify the recreational user because drug use is generally a private activity because of its unlawful nature. This is particularly true with police officers. Substance abusers will typically do so only in seclusion or within the confines of a strictly limited, consenting social group. This selective use combined with the officers' knowledge of investigative techniques and the general lack of any form of drug detection programs for employees in police departments, makes detecting substance abusers a very difficult task.

Just as in the general population, drug use in law enforcement can be seen as a sociocultural phenomenon. That is, with increased acceptance—or at least tolerance—over the years of selected drug usage by society, the negative "moral" impact of drug usage decreases. In this vein, one must remember that many of today's police officers grew up in a social environment where drug use was simply not uncommon. It was not limited to persons who were criminals or on the periphery of crime, but was used by middle- and upper-class persons and as a social activity in college life. Former Justice Department official and President Reagan's former Supreme Court nominee, Judge Ginsburg, exemplified this in his admission that he smoked marijuana when he was a Harvard law professor. Drug use has also been a routine source of material by comedians and a regular part of many popular movies which further contributes to its commonality.

In this regard, the generally increased drug usage in society may have an influence similar to that of peer pressure for acceptability in a defined upwardly mobile social group. Similarly, one may also infer that drug usage is learned behavior as influenced by one's social group as described by Dull's (1983) research on differential association and adult drug use. This is reinforced by the social acceptability of marijuana and cocaine usage as illustrated in the entertainment media where it has been exhibited and discussed as acceptable behavior in many "progressive social circles."

Simply put, it appears that abusing officers use drugs for social reasons and to experience the euphoria of the drug. A related reason deals with the more primal instincts of "danger and excitement" associated with participating in illicit activities. That is, there is a so-called "rush" produced simply by participating in prohibited conduct.

## On-Duty Drug Use

The extent of on-duty drug use by officers is simply not known. An intuitive assumption is that some on-duty use occurs, however, it is not extensive. When it does occur, the potential ramifications are widespread. The most serious are that the officer may use deadly force or be involved in a traffic accident while under the influence. Other effects of use include poor judgment in the performance of official duties, misfeasant or nonfeasant behavior, having a negative influence on co-workers, and having a negative influence on community relations.

In one case of on-duty drug use, a patrol officer in one of the nation's largest municipal police departments was discovered by accident to be using cocaine on duty. During the internal affairs investigation the officer admitted he had regularly used cocaine on duty for a little over a year. One would assume that the officer's behavior while under the influence would be a signal to co-workers that the officer was "high." However, the officer stated that after each time he "snorted" cocaine he would "chase" it with whiskey. He knew co-workers would "cover" for him if they thought he was an alcoholic, therefore, he masked the cocaine's behavioral influences with the odor of alcohol. This experience, which provides insight into the occupational culture of policing, serves as evidence of how substance abuse during working hours can occur without being discovered.

On-duty drug use can also occur if the problem becomes systemic within the work group. In one moderate-sized, mid-western city about 30 officers were identified as being involved in a "user's ring" (not all of whom used drugs on duty). The drug use became so pervasive and widespread that there was tolerance for its use even on duty. While some officers in the group did not like the on-duty use, they would not inform on those who used drugs while working because of the strong implication they would be discovered as a drug user, albeit during off-duty hours. One could conclude from this experience that in light of the systemic and subcultural variables, if off-duty use becomes prevalent, then the likelihood of on-duty use appears to increase among officers involved.

In perhaps the only study of the subject, Kraska and Kappeler (1987) serendipitously discovered on-duty use during the course of working on another project at a police department of about 50 officers in the southwestern United States. During the course of their work with the department, Kraska and Kappeler were befriended by a number of officers and accepted into their social group which lead to the discovery of the problem. Through the use of "unstructured self-report interviews, departmental records, and researcher observations,... [they found that] 20 percent of the officers in the department used marijuana while on duty twice a month or more" [1987:21]. Another four percent had used marijuana at least once while on duty. Furthermore, ten percent of the officers reported they had used non-prescribed control substances (defined in the study as including hallucinogenics, stimulants, or barbituates) while on duty. (This may not be an additional ten percent; it may include some of the marijuana users.) Most of the officers involved in on-duty drug use were between the ages of 21-38 and had been on the job 3-10 years.

Despite some methodological limitations of the study discussed by Kraska and Kappeler, the findings are sound—and somewhat surprising. One may hope that the high incidence of on-duty drug use found in this study was an exceptional occurrence. If not, the problem may be greater than we believe. Furthermore, when one envisions the on-duty drug use problem, there is a tendency to conclude it would be a problem found only in the nation's larger police agencies. This study, and the experience of the authors, suggests that may not be the case.

These illustrations show that on-duty drug use does occur at least to some extent. It is also reasonable to assume that those agencies which have had more serious drug-related problems, such as corruption, have also experienced on-duty drug use by officers. A police administrator must assume the potential for on-duty drug use exists and steps must be taken to address the problem.

## Drugs of Choice by Police Officers

In cases where drug abuse has been documented, there are indications that officers have a "drug of choice." Not surprisingly, marijuana appears to be the most commonly used drug. This may be because of its comparatively minor addictive and limited long-term effects, the ease of obtaining it, its comparatively low cost, and importantly, the lesser social stigma associated with the use of marijuana when compared with other drugs.

Cocaine use is clearly the second most frequently used drug and appears to be fairly prevalent. The best explanation of this seems to be its availability and prevalent use in the general society. Findings in an internal investigation in Detroit of officers using drugs were very surprising. The drug of choice in this series of cases among Detroit officer-users was "crack." The reasons given by the officers (during the course of *Garrity* interviews) were that the drug was very inexpensive and could be obtained easily without going to the same dealer. The officers reasoned that if they could get a drug by going to different dealers, they were less likely to be discovered and the likelihood for being blackmailed by a dealer was significantly reduced.

Finally, there is some evidence of abuse of non-prescribed or falsely prescribed pharmaceutical substances. Amphetamines and barbituates fall into this category typically where officers have used the drugs as a way of coping with various personal problems. In some cases, stimulants have been used to help keep officers "alert" (or awake) when they have been working excessive hours in a second job. This form of substance abuse appears to have different dynamics than the marijuana or cocaine use. As such, the disposition of officers abusing these drugs *may* warrant some degree of benevolence in the administrative remedy of the problem.

There are no indications of a significant problem with synthetic hallucinogenic drugs or heroin. (The most common of all substances abused by police officers is alcohol. The obvious difference in dealing with the problem is the fact that alcohol is not a controlled substance.)

## Substance Abuse as a Job-Related Condition

In cases of recreational drug abuse by police officers, there are two primary arguments that officers (or their attorneys) may pose as causal factors for use: stress and job assignment.

With respect to stress, it has been proposed that police drug use may be a product of job stress. Those who advance the argument state that because of the high levels of stress in law enforcement some officers have resorted to drug use as a coping mechanism. The authors do not agree. In fact, the opposite situation could conceivably occur. That is, an officer who is abusing substances could possibly experience more stress since the discovery of this behavior is likely to result in disciplinary action or termination.

If stress was, in fact, a major causal factor in drug abuse among police officers, then it is likely that significant levels of use would have surfaced in the last 15 years and that such use would be more obvious. Moreover, in cases where drug-abusing officers have been disciplined, plea bargained, and/or arbitrated, the evidence suggests that job stress was not a facet of the drug abuse. Nevertheless, no empirical support has been found either for or against the drug/stress hypothesis in police work.

The second job-related issue is that substance abuse may be a product of job assignment. Some argue that officers who are working in an undercover capacity with frequent or ongoing exposure to narcotics and drugs may become socialized into the "drug culture." That is, constant interaction with the drug environment reduces the negative socio-moral implications of drug usage and concomitantly reinforces both the frequency and permissibility of drug usage.

Again, no research is available to substantiate or disclaim this argument. There have been instances (e.g., Newport News, Virginia) where narcotics officers have been found to be abusing drugs both on and off duty. There have also been cases where job assignment has been ruled by the courts to be a factor in alcoholism. Particularly in the case of narcotic officer drug use, it may conceivably be argued that occupational socialization contributed to the abuse. The implications for this are: (1) preventive procedures should be developed for high risk assignments to help avoid (or at least minimize) this potential problem, and (2) procedures should be established to fairly deal with officers who may have abused substances as a result of socialization. These decisions are very difficult and the literature provides little direction because of the relative contemporary nature of the problem.

## POLICY ISSUES FOR POLICE EMPLOYEE DRUG CONTROL

For police departments to effectively address officer substance abuse through policy, there are three central issues which must be addressed; Identifying the drug user, disposition of the drug user, and dealing with the police union/Police Officer Association (POA). Critical decisions must be made before any internal drug control program can be promulgated. The following discussions highlight some of the issues involved in these areas.

### Identifying the Drug User

Various issues surface in the philosophy, legal standards, and approaches to identifying police drug users. At the outset, screening police applicants is a critical first step in dealing with the substance abuse problem among employees. Whether the screening is done by urinalysis, background investigation, polygraph, or a combination of these, the point to note is that the best way to deal with the problem is by minimizing its potential to occur. It is unrealistic in today's society to expect police applicants have not experimented with drugs. The pervasiveness of drugs in our society among the age groups from which the police normally recruit indicates this will be a problem for some time. Departments in the Washington, DC metropolitan area, for example, have reported that as many as 75 percent of the applicants in recent years have experimented with drugs. Police departments are using different standards for applicants who have used drugs. The general rule appears to be that if the applicant has only used marijuana, that he/she did not use the drug "extensively," and if the applicant has not used the drug for a given time period (normally from six months to a year), then the applicant is acceptable. The central issue in identifying users, however, concerns personnel already in the police ranks.

*Informant Information.* One source for identifying users is through the use of complaints and informant information. Sources in this category may include suspicious officers, citizens observing "unusual" officer behavior, rumors in "the grapevine," and statements of persons arrested for drugs particularly when there is a conflict with the officer's statement. While there is a tendency for the department to want to deny this information, especially when it comes from outside the agency, it should not be ignored. In one case with which the authors are familiar, follow-up on an overheard conversation between a narcotics officer and another individual resulted in the discovery of a major drug abuse and corruption problem as a unit. A degree of skepticism is reasonable. However, information should not be dismissed simply because the complaint may come from a "criminal" or someone else outside of the department.

*Supervision.* Supervisory observations are important sources for identifying drug users. To be effective, supervisors must be trained to be cognizant of indicators which point to a potential drug abuse problem. Without the appropriate training, it is difficult for the supervisor to identify the substance abuser. Several reasons support this contention: (1) The supervisor might mistake drug symptoms for other symptoms such as alcoholism, illness, or stress; (2) the employee will make every effort to hide the drug symptoms/indicators; and (3) there is a tendency for the police supervisor to not want to believe subordinates are drug users.

*Polygraph.* Some agencies, in the course of drug use investigations, have relied on the polygraph. For the polygraph to be used there must first be other indicators of drug use to serve as the grounds for further investigation. The polygraph's value as a means of user identification is limited by the evidentiary restrictions found in court rules and arbitration evidentiary procedures. In addition, the polygraph cannot conclusively determine the presence of drugs as can a forensic analysis of blood or urine. In sum, the polygraph should not be used as the initial screening mechanism to determine if an officer is abusing drugs. If used in any form, it should only be relied upon as an added investigatory tool as it would be used in any other form of internal investigation.

*Self-Reports.* One means of user identification often overlooked is the self-report. There are different reasons why an officer may report his/her substance abuse. Among these reasons are: (1) The officer may feel the drug use is "getting out of control"—too much time is spent on financing, obtaining, and using drugs; (2) the officer feels substances are ruining his/her life; (3) the officer may feel drugs are pulling him/her toward corruption or some other compromising situation; or (4) the officer may feel his/her drug use is about to be discovered and hopes that self-reporting the problem, before being "charged" with it, will mitigate any penalty. Should these different motives for the self-report affect the types of severity of disposition the officer receives? The answer to this question lies largely in the management philosophy of the chief with influence from the prevailing community standards. Regardless of the disposition alternatives, policy should be established so that the department's actions can be a product of planning, rather than an unplanned reaction to the problem.

*Drug Testing.* The most effective and most controversial method of identifying drug users is through forensic drug testing. A great deal of debate on the forensic reliability of drug testing can be found in both the scientific literature and media. While analysis for drugs can be performed on both blood and urine, urinalysis is the most common methodology. For this discussion, it is sufficient to note that the scientific literature is quite clear that the forensic processes of analysis using confirmatory drug testing by the gas chromatograph/mass spectrometer (GC/MS) can identify the presence of specific drugs in urine samples. Moreover, such urinalysis will stand the scrutiny of evidentiary hearings both in court and union arbitration hearings. Issues that can be raised related to the analytic processes are related to quality control at the laboratory, chain of custody of the sample, technician expertise, instrumentation, "cut-off" levels for determination of a substance's presence, and the reporting of results. These are all potential weak links in the overall urine-testing process. It should also be noted that the forensic process can only confirm the presence of drugs—it cannot determine the amount of the substance used, the time frame associated with the drug use, nor can it draw conclusions about the degree of "intoxication" or psychoactive effect.

Beyond the forensic issues, there are important policy decisions related to employee drug testing. A primary issue is the legal parameters of drug-testing programs. While no unequivocal precedents exist that are applicable to all agencies, some clear trends have begun to emerge. In general, it appears that if a department established mandatory drug testing for all tenured employees, the courts may rule the program, by virtue of the Fourth Amendment, unconstitutional. If, however, the testing program was "limited" and applicable only to those persons wherein the test was a *bona fide* compelling interest for the job, then the courts may look more favorably on the program (e.g., testing officers assigned to narcotics division, VIP security details, etc.) Drug testing police applicants; testing as part of a regularly scheduled medical examination; regular urinalysis of probationary police officers who are informed of such a program; and testing prior to promotion or reassignment are most likely to be supported by the courts. Similarly, an officer that freely and voluntarily provides a sample for urinalysis, does not appear to present a Fourth Amendment problem. It is still unclear whether proper consent is inferred through a ratified union contract agreeing to a random drug-testing program. Obviously, any drug-testing program should be conceptually developed then thoroughly reviewed by legal counsel prior to implementation.

A sensitive issue in a drug-testing program is the chain of custody. An important aspect of this issue is whether there should be a witness to the collection of the urine sample in order to ensure the sample is not false or "bootleg." Those arguing in support of the sample witness maintain that without this procedure, the reliability of the sample can be challenged. (Some cases of false samples have been documented in the media such as in Washington, D.C.) Those against witnessing the sample argue that human dignity must be maintained. Requiring a witness is regarded as a degrading experience. Other chain of custody issues that apply to criminal evidence going to a laboratory apply here as well.

The Police Executive Research Forum (PERF), in an attempt to better understand the concerns of the police executives on drug testing, surveyed its member police chiefs on a variety of police drug use issues. Among the findings associated with drug testing were (Carter and Stephens, 1988):

*87.7%   Supported drug testing if reasonable grounds existed to suspect an officer was using drugs
*76.4%   Favored drug screening of police applicants
*66.1%   Favored regular drug testing of officers during the probationary period
*64.7%   Favored random screening of officers in "sensitive" assignments
*50.5%   Favored a mandatory universal random drug-screening program
*42.6%   Favored the drug testing of officers after they had been involved in a "serious incident"

It is safe to say that all chiefs of police desired to have a drug-free workplace, however, they differed on their standards and approaches to deal with the issue. In a debate on drug testing, Houston Police Chief Lee Brown argued in support of mandatory drug testing, stating that an aggressive program is the best possible deterrent against drug use. Conversely, Kansas City Police Chief Larry Joiner argued against such programs. His rationale was that after recruiting, testing, investigating, selecting, training, and supervising police officers, departments should presume officers are drug-free unless evidence is presented otherwise to show reasonable cause exists to believe an officer is using drugs. At that point, drug tests should be administered.

The lack of clear guidance from court cases and labor arbitrations, coupled with the diversity of police chief opinions, is important evidence to show there remains a significant amount of planning and experimentation needed to resolve the dilemmas of the drug-testing issue.

## Disposition of Drug-Abusing Employees

Just as identifying drug users presents a number of difficult policy decisions, so does the disposition of drug-abusing officers. The problem cannot be easily resolved with the "fire 'em" approach. As in most management decisions, there are aggravating and mitigating circumstances which should be addressed in the planning and research process before policy is established. The debate on disposition centers, on whether officers abusing drugs should simply be punished through termination, or whether attempts should be made to rehabilitate them. Although most chiefs currently favor termination, once again there is no clear definitive answer. Nevertheless, some important criteria are presented for consideration.

*Termination and Discipline Short of Termination.* When police departments began discovering substance abuse among police officers, the initial reaction was to terminate the officer. However, in some cases—notably union departments—the agency found that they did not have proper policy, procedures, or rules to support this decision (particularly when no criminal charges had been filed.) The nature and severity of discipline may be dependent on factors such as whether use was on or off duty, the type of substance used, factors on the job which may have contributed to the drug use, the officer's service and personnel record and aggravating or mitigating factors unique to the individual officer.

In making policy on discipline for drug use, agencies may also consider the investment that has been made in recruitment, selection, and training of the officer. As a management decision, the investment should be realistically balanced with the harm done to the organization and the ability of the officer to perform the job. When discipline is used as a disposition alternative, the agency must promulgate formal written policy, procedures, and rules to help ensure officers are aware of the departments expectations.

*Rehabilitation.* Some police departments have explored a rehabilitation alternative for substance-abusing personnel. Those in support of rehabilitation base their argument on the department's investment in the officer, the possibility that the job may have contributed to the problem, a recognition that drug use is a social problem not limited to policing, and the organizational obligation to the employee (notably in organizations subscribing to the so-called "Theory Z" management philosophy).

At the outset, it must be recognized that rehabilitation should only be an option to deal with substance abuse—it is a part of the discipline process. This option carries with it many important policy questions that a police administrator must carefully evaluate and answer. Among the more critical questions are:

*To whom would the program be open? All officers? Only those self-reporting a drug problem? Only marijuana users? Only those *using* drugs, not dealing? How will past misconduct for actions *other* than drug use be considered?

*What will the department's position be if the officer subsequently uses drugs after the rehabilitation? Is the subsequent use the "failure" of the program or the failure of the officer?

*What are the criteria to be evaluated in a rehabilitation program to determine if the officer is "fit for duty"? Will the department have any input to determine if the rehabilitation has been accomplished or is this solely a therapeutic/treatment decision?

*Who pays for the rehabilitation program? Police department? Officer? Union? Standard health insurance? Special insurance policy?

*Do any unique liability problems arise for the officer or department if an officer who has admitted drug use and has gone through a rehabilitation program returns to a law enforcement position? (i.e., Can the department be deemed negligent if it retains an officer who has admitted drug use?)

*Will there be any credibility problems for the officer in criminal trials if the defense counsel learns that the officer testifying in a criminal case (particularly a drug case) was an admitted drug abuser who has gone through a rehabilitation program?

There are no easy answers to these questions. The manner in which the police administrator addresses these issues will be dependent on social, political, economic, and ideological variables. Clearly, implementation of a rehabilitation program, or at the least an Employee Assistance Program for drugs, requires significant thought and planning.

*Criminal Prosecution.* A final disposition alternative obviously tied to discipline, is criminal prosecution. Like other criminal offenses, all aspects of police officer drug use must be examined. Does sufficient evidence exist? Would a case of this type be pursued if it were not an officer? Will the presence of drugs in urine support a criminal charge? Is the case for possession only, or are sales involved? What is the likely impact of prosecution on the individual and the department? For possession of small amounts of use, departmental sanctions may be sufficient punishment. However, for sales it seems that every effort should be made to prosecute the officer to the full extent of the law.

## Union Issues

On the matter of substance abuse, labor leaders and police administrators agree that they both want a drug-free workplace. However, Police Officer Associations (POAs) have emphasized two important points: (1) They do not want a drug-free workplace at the expense of employee rights, and (2) they want employee drug use policies to support the rehabilitation model.

The central issue is employee rights—the interpretation upon which labor and management disagree. For example, both agree that internal investigations should incorporate minimal due process rights, however, they disagree as to what specific rights are included in the "minimal due process" standard. The union sentiment was summarized by one Fraternal Order of Police (FOP) national official speaking to a group of police managers: "If you're going to get one of our members, you've got to get him *right*" (emphasis in original), (Possumato, 1987).

A major issue in the employee rights arena is drug testing. POAs have been outspoken critics of drug-testing programs generally arguing that drug testing of tenured employees violates their rights and improperly sets them apart (on a Fourth Amendment basis) from other citizens. According to Possumato, (1987) POA's view drug-testing programs, *per se*, as being a disciplinary action, not a preventive program. The logic used is that drug testing is a Napoleonic approach tantamount to a presumption of guilt until the officer "proves" his/her innocence through a negative drug test.

On the matter of testing, unions support testing police applicants, drug tests as part of personnel physical examinations (although not enthusiastically), "for cause" testing, and drug screening prior to assignment to a "sensitive" position (although the definition of a "sensitive position" is a source of debate). There are conflicting union opinions about the testing of probationary officers. In general, if a probationer is not covered by a contract/collective bargaining agreement, the union will not argue against drug testing.

Union representatives have generally not supported testing after incidents such as an accident or shooting. They argue, it taints the officer and there are no grounds to believe the officer used drugs simply because of involvement in an incident of this nature. Without question, most unions vehemently oppose random drug-testing programs although some notable exceptions have occurred (such as in Hawaii).

With respect to the disposition of drug-abusing officers, unions tend to support discipline, even termination, of an officer who is dealing drugs or involved in corruption. However, for "minor users" the POAs strongly support the rehabilitation model. In this regard, two major components of the union argument are: (1) The policing occupation contributed to the drug use as a result of stress and occupational socialization, and (2) the organization has an obligation to its employees.

To state the obvious, union and management must establish a dialogue on their defenses to meet the mutual goal of a drug-free workplace. Both must have empathy for each other's advocacy responsibilities and be willing to resolve differences for the betterment of the department and the community.

# CONCLUSION

Recently it was reported that some 400 drug cases will be dropped in the District of Columbia because Metropolitan Police officers may have been involved in the theft of drugs and money during drug arrests (*USA Today*, 1987:3A). In Flint, Michigan a police sergeant who pled guilty on a misdemeanor drug possession charge after a plea bargain and was initially fired, was ordered reinstated by a labor arbitrator "...because procedural irregularities denied [the officer] his due process rights and fair treatment..." [Flint Journal, 1987:A-3]. An officer on leave from the Pontiac, Michigan Police Department who refused to take a drug test before returning to duty was finally allowed to return to work without the test because the drug screening was not a matter of policy and there was not reason to suspect the officer had been using drugs (*MAP*, 1987:5-7). A Florida Deputy Sheriff who had been decertified for "gross misconduct" by the Criminal Justice Standards and Training Commission because he had admitted using marijuana two years before had his case reversed. The Florida Court of Appeals held that the act did not amount to gross misconduct as required by the Florida decertification statute, *McClung v. Criminal Justice Standards and Training Commission* 458 So. 2d. 887 (Fla. App. 5 Dist. 1984).

These cases were variously aggravated because the agencies did not fully understand the nature of the drug problem nor did they have adequate planning, policy, or supervision to specifically address drug use.

How serious is the problem in law enforcement? As noted previously, the anecdotal evidence clearly shows its presence, however, the actual number of cases simply cannot be accurately measured. The authors believe that assessing the severity of police drug use should not be entirely a quantitative exercise. Given the responsibilities of the police it should take on a qualitative perspective as well. In this regard, Wistosky argues that...

> ...the dimensions of illegal drug use in the workplace are small in comparison to those of alcohol abuse, so that universal drug testing is radically disproportionate to the scope of the problem [1987:764].

In law enforcement the "small numbers" do not address the appropriate issues. Police departments must consider the implications of officer drug use on public confidence. They must also consider the impact on performance, the integrity of criminal cases, the potential for officer corruption, citizen and officer safety, and the ever-present departmental liability. Officers who use excessive force, steal, or violate other organizational rules also typically represent a small portion of the sworn personnel in a given department. Despite this, the "small proportion" argument is not presented as a factor which should mitigate the department's sanctions against the involved officer(s). Drug use should be no different.

Any internal drug control program must have a disciplinary element, however, the program must be fundamentally fair and consistent with the standards of due process. As observed by Richard Koehler (1986), the New York Police Department Chief of Personnel, the objective of personnel drug programs is prevention, not punishment. Policies prohibiting drug use and prescribing sanctions for violations should be viewed primarily as a preventive tool with invocation of the disciplinary process as a secondary role when prevention does not occur. Philosophically, when this approach is taken, the program presumes the innocence of officers rather than the guilt on the matter of drug use. Moreover, when the drug control program is viewed by management as a preventive mechanism, there will likely be reduced anxiety and less animosity among the officers.

Officers have a more positive outlook when the department states the program is preventive; a message is sent to the employees that the agency is concerned about their health and safety. Furthermore, a preventive (presumption of innocence) program reinforces departmental trust in the officers and does not make accusations about misconduct unless there are grounds for allegation. This approach contributes to a collegial feeling between managers and line officers.

Anxiety among personnel will be particularly prevalent in conjunction with drug-testing programs. One reason for this is that drug testing—notably mandatory random testing—gives the officer a feeling of lost control. That is, one must submit to the test or face disciplinary action. This is a difficult situation for anyone to accept—especially police officers who are trained and expected to respect citizens' rights. Random mandatory testing causes the officers to feel their rights must be forfeited in order to stay employed.

Anxiety is also heightened with mandatory testing because the officer is receiving a message from management, intended or not, of organizational mistrust. This is further aggravated when procedures require that a urine sample must be witnessed. In those cases where an officer is required to submit to a drug test simply because of a change of rank or reclassification, then the sample witness adds "insult to injury." Police managers clearly have difficult decisions to make on these issues some of which will inevitably cause resentment in some personnel.

Drug testing will also contribute to anxiety because of the fear—unfounded or not—that the forensic process of analyzing the samples may be flawed. With the recent increased use of drug testing, there has been a wide impact on the reputations and careers of the people effected. Concerns range from the fear that prescriptions or over-the-counter drugs will produce positive tests to beliefs that samples will be mixed or analysis will be improperly performed.

Drug testing will remain a controversial element of any internal drug control program. Abrams observed that...

There is a serious question whether a mandatory and universal drug-testing policy is advisable. The success of the strategy turns on two assumptions: the risk of discovery will deter drug use and the use of the tests will rid the workplace only of dangerous or non-productive workers. Both assumptions are questionable...the strategy becomes one of roulette, where the innocent have as much to fear from the process as the guilty [1987:3].

Because of the limited direction afforded to administrators on police officer drug abuse, the first step in planning for an effective drug control program is to look back. Policies and procedures related to misconduct need to be assessed, the nature of the drug problem within the agency must be analyzed, and mistakes from the past must be scrutinized. One must be particularly cognizant of omissions, applicability, comprehensiveness, fairness, clarity, propriety, and functionality of the policies and procedures as related to their goal.

Once police managers understand the current status of the problem, they must then decide the desired policy and status they hope to have. This projection must be realistic, legal, and functional. Therefore, a drug control program must be the product of critical introspection and consideration of what is best for the total organization and community. The administrator must minimize personal bias on the issue in order to establish the best program for the agency.

In cases where voids exist, the department must create comprehensive directives to address drug testing, discipline, treatment, training and drug education, and any other aspects of the department's drug program. Perhaps the weakest link in police departments' internal drug control programs has been employee training. As is frequently the case when "new" problems surface, organizations find themselves in a reactive posture dealing with the problem. In law enforcement, as internal drug abuse became more evident, many agencies immediately turned to drug-testing programs and began to invoke rigid disciplinary sanctions without thorough examination of the alternatives.

Training, on the other hand, is a proactive measure designed to make the employee more informed and to prevent the problem. Police departments should incorporate the problem. Police departments should incorporate preventive training programs to inform officers of the potential for drug abuse and the department's policy responses to such use.

In dealing with units wherein personnel have consistent contact with drugs and the drug environment, the department should explore both special training and policy needs. This is a critical area where police departments have continued problems. Too often it is assumed that everything is going well. The "if it ain't broke, don't fix it" point of view persists. Administrators need to look back at past problems and current practices in an attempt to identify any weaknesses in procedures. Once accomplished, plans need to be developed to ensure these weaknesses have been addressed. For example, the chain of custody of drug evidence in criminal cases needs to be assessed for security and accountability.

This should be done periodically from the point of seizure, through laboratory analysis and storage, to presentation of the evidence in court. In vice and narcotics units procedures relating to the protection of officers from allegations of drug use must be imposed. Similarly, control procedures need to be implemented in those units to assist supervisors in the detection of an officer who may be using drugs. Obviously, the greater the contact with drugs, the higher the probability of abuse, hence the need for special policies. These policies need to be carefully constructed to ensure they do not lose sight of the narcotics' unit objectives. The authors believe a unit can be effective, if not more so, with carefully prepared and implemented policies.

In all matters of drug policy, procedures, and rules the department should have directives reviewed by legal counsel. Concerns need to focus on administrative law, labor law, criminal law, and issues of liability. These address a wide range of factors and can become extraordinarily complex—even conflicting. Good legal guidance on these matters is very important. Nevertheless, care must be taken by the police administrator to ensure the practical application of policy. What is best for lawyers and administrators is not always the most effective approach.

A final factor which must be stressed is the need for effective communications between management and the line officers. A major responsibility of supervisory and management personnel is to communicate clearly the importance of maintaining a drug-free workplace. Similarly, the rationale for the department's approach to the problem must be clearly explained. Furthermore, management must listen to line officers and consider their input in policy development. Effective communication can alleviate conflict when rules are enforced and policies are debated.

The police administrator must keep the issue of officer drug use in perspective. Organizational denial must be avoided and police administrators must recognize the problem can and does exist in police departments of all sizes. At the same time, administrators must avoid paranoia about a feared pervasiveness of drug abuse among personnel. It is incumbent on the police administrators to be proactive, while making informed, judicious decisions. The problem may not be totally eliminated, but it can certainly be effectively managed.

# Notes

[1] The information in this chapter is based on the research conducted by the authors for *Drug Use by Police Officers: An Analysis of Critical Policy Issues,* Springfield: IL, Charles C Thomas, Publisher (1988). While this chapter touches on a broad range of issues, each issue is examined by the book in significant detail.

[2] In eight *Garrity* sworn statements of Flint, Michigan police officers who had been charged with conspiracy to possess controlled substances and subsequently entered pleas for simple possession, the officers freely admitted using marijuana and/or cocaine and steadfastly maintained their position that off-duty behavior was their own business and they had no law enforcement responsibilities during this time.

[3] There is some precedence for this in other forms of police/constituent interaction such as gambling, prostitution, and minor forms of corruption. (c.f., Barker and Carter, 1986).

[4] For greater detail on the legal aspects of drug testing, see Carter and Stephens, 1988; Higginbotham, 1987; Higginbotham; 1986a; and Higginbotham, 1986b.

[5] For greater details on the chain of custody see Carter and Stephens, 1988; McEwen, et al., 1986

# REFERENCES

Abrams, R.I. (1987). "Wishful Thinking and Public Policy." *International Drug Report.* 28:7 (p.3).

Barker, T. and O. Carter (eds.) (1986). *Police Deviance.* Cincinnati: Anderson Publishing Co.

Carter, D.L. and D.W. Stephens (eds.) (1988). *Drug Abuse by Police Officers: An Analysis of Critical Policy Issues.* Springfield, IL: Charles C Thomas, Publisher.

Daly, M. (1986). "The Crack in the Shield." *New York Magazine.* (December 8) pp. 51-59.

Denenberg, T.S. and R.V. Denenberg (1987). "Drug Testing From the Arbitrator's Perspective." *Nova Law Review.* 11:2 (pp. 371-414).

Dull, T.R. (1983). "Friends' Use and Adult Drug and Drinking Behavior: A Further Test of Differential Association." *Journal of Criminal Law and Criminology.* 74(4):1608-1619.

Elkouri, F. and E.A. Elkouri (1985). *How Arbitration Works. 4th ed.* Washington: Bureau of National Affairs.

*The Flint Journal.* "City Delays Reinstating Fired Officer." (July 7, 1987), p. A3.

Gates, D.F. and G.H. Kleinknicht (1987). "One Side and the Other—Random Drug Testing." *The Police Chief.* (April):pp. 16-17.

Goldstein, H. (1977). *Policing a Free Society.* Cambridge, MA: Ballinger Publishing Co.

Higgenbotham, J. (1986a). "Urinalysis Drug Testing Programs in Law Enforcement (Part I)." *FBI Law Enforcement Bulletin.* (October)55:10.

Higgenbotham, J. (1986b). "Urinalysis Drug Testing Programs in Law Enforcement (Part II)." *FBI Law Enforcement Bulletin.* (November) 55:11.

Higgenbotham, J. (1987). "Urinalysis Drug Testing Programs in Law Enforcement (Conclusion)." *FBI Law Enforcement Bulletin.* (January) 56:1.

Koehler, R.J. (1986). Chief of Personnel, New York City Police Department. Comments at conference on "Substance Abuse: The Dilemma of Law Enforcement," John Jay College of Criminal Justice. New York, NY. (May 30, 1986).

Koehler, R.J. (1985). *Drug and Narcotic Screening of Police Personnel.* Unpublished mimeographed report of the New York City Police Department.

Kraska, P.B. and V.E. Kappeler. (1987). *A Theoretical and Descriptive Examination of Police On-Duty Drug Use.* A paper presented at the 1987 annual meeting of the American Society of Criminology, Montreal, Quebec, Canada.

*Lansing (MI) State Journal.* "Profits Reaped on Selling 'Clean' Urine for Drug Testing." (January 4, 1987), p. 3A.

*Law Enforcement News.* "Police Narcotics Lab Chemist Fired for Cocaine Theft." (January 13, 1987), p. 2.

*Law Enforcement News.* "Police Personnel Suspended in Drug Theft Investigation." (December 9, 1986), p. 2.

Marmo, M. (1986). "Off-Duty Behavior by Police: Arbitrators Determine if On-the-Job Discipline is Appropriate." *Journal of Police Science and Administration.* (14:2) pp. 102-111.

McEwen, J.T., B. Manili, and E. Connors. (1986). "Employee Drug Testing Policies in Police Departments." *NIJ Research in Brief.* Washington, DC: National Institute of Justice.

Michigan Association of Police. (1987). "A Roundup of Other MAP 'Battles' in Pontiac." *News n' Views.* (Issue 1) pp. 5-7.

Ostrov, E. (1985). *Validation of Police Officer Recruit Candidates' Self-Reported Drug Use on the Inwald Personality Inventory Drug Scale.* Paper presented at the mid-year meeting of the American Psychology Law Society.

*The Police Chief.* (1986). "IACP Announces Drug Testing Policy." (October) pp. 24-26.

Police Executive Research Forum. (1986). Task Force Report on Police Drug Use. Washington, DC: (Unpublished).

Possumato, T. (1987). "Labor-Management Issues: The Union Point of View on Drug Testing." Presentation at the Police Executive Research Forum Program, *Police Drug Abuse and Testing: Issues and Information.* Arlington, VA (April 9-10).

Shortreed, S. (1987). Sergeant of Internal Affairs, Detroit Police Department. Commenting on experiences and graduate study research of other police agencies on criminal law violations by police officers.

*USA Today.* "Drug Cases Dropped." (September 17, 1987), p. 3A.

Walsh, J.M. and R.L. Hanks. (1986). *Employee Drug Screening.* Washington: National Institute on Drug Abuse.

Wisotsky, S. (1987). "The Ideology of Drug Testing." *Nova Law Review.* 11:2 (pp. 763-778).

# STUDY QUESTIONS

1.  You are a rookie patrol officer invited to a party that is predominantly police officers and their spouses or dates. At the party you notice a few police officers (all off duty) and others are openly smoking marijuana and no one really seems to notice or care. What would you think? What would you do? Why would you choose that course of action? What decisions do you face? What are your options? What factors/forces would affect your decision(s)? Be realistic in your response.

2.  As noted in the chapter, an ongoing dilemma in dealing with drug-abusing police officers is whether officers should be rehabilitated. There are compelling arguments on both sides of the issue. What is your opinion? What factors do you feel are most important in your position? Why? Could you make an exception? Why or why not?

3.  In looking at the "drugs of choice" by police officers, what surprised you the most? Why?

4.  The Detroit Police Department, as a result of widespread drug use by officers, developed an "Amnesty Program" for a limited time. Under the program, officers who had used marijuana or cocaine since becoming a police officer, could admit that use to the department and *not* be subjected to any discipline. Rather, the officer had to admit him/herself to a departmentally accepted drug treatment program. Those who admitted cocaine use were placed on non-punitive unpaid suspension during the course of the rehabilitation. Officers admitting only marijuana use remained on duty as full-service police officers but were reassigned (the new assignment could be to any position, but was generally in patrol). What is your opinion of this program? What are the advantages and disadvantages? If you were chief, would you implement this program? Explain your response.

5.  Many people including judges, political officials, business leaders, physicians, pilots, and professors have admitted to some degree of marijuana use. There is little social condemnation for people who smoke marijuana and, in fact, marijuana is portrayed in the entertainment media in a wide range of casual situations. In light of this, do you feel police officers who smoke marijuana off duty should be subjected to discipline by the police department? Justify your response.

# 7

# AN EMPIRICAL STUDY OF POLICE DEVIANCE OTHER THAN CORRUPTION*

## Thomas Barker

The empirical study of police deviance, i.e., rule or norm violating behavior, has been a neglected area of concern. Social scientists and police administrators have conducted few, if any, systematic factual studies on this phenomena. Numerous works on police misconduct have appeared in the literature, but the vast majority of these accounts have been value-laden exposés written by muckraking journalists and exposed police officers.

Social scientists in the past either have been denied access to most police organizations or have been reluctant to approach police administrators. Therefore, whatever research that was conducted on this "touchy" topic was done surreptitiously and without the knowledge and consent of high police officials. The usual method of scientific study was for a research to locate an informant(s) within the department and have him (them) give an account of the deviant exploits of their fellow officers. Stoddard's classical study of police deviance used one ex-officer who had been charged, convicted, and imprisoned on charges of grand larceny and robbery. Stoddard also claimed that "standard sociological research methods were ineffective in this type of investigation."[1] This may no longer be true.

One can identify several reasons why the police have had (and still have) cause to fear research in the area of police deviance. The publication of research findings without the proper guarantees of anonymity for subjects and department could damage the department's reputation and lead to a "shake-up" of the entire organization and dismissal of all who cooperate. Research by an outside agent could disrupt departmental investigations and drive deviant, especially corrupt, officers underground. Police administrators know that the whole organization can be permanently damaged by an unethical researcher more interested in sensationalism and muckraking than in the advancement of scientific knowledge. Nevertheless, some police administrators concerned with the general understanding of police deviance and its control are beginning to reluctantly grant permission for this type of research.[2]

The purpose of this chapter is to report on the findings of one such study

*Reprinted from *Journal of Police Science and Administration*. Vol. 6, No. 3 (1978), pp. 264-272. Reprinted with permission of the International Association of Chiefs of Police.

conducted by this author. Specifically, the chapter will identify five patterns of police deviance which are not directly linked to police corruption. That is, they do not involve any monetary reward or gain. The article will also present data on these patterns of police deviance gathered in one medium-sized police organization.

## THEORETICAL ORIENTATION

The author believes that the patterns of police deviance to be discussed are all examples of occupational deviance. *Occupational deviance* is deviant behavior— criminal, and noncriminal—committed during the course of "normal" work activities. Specifically, occupational deviance is defined as all deviant acts, i.e., rule violations, which occur during the course of occupational activity and are related to employment.[3] Most occupations provide their members with three elements which are important to an understanding of occupational deviance:

1. Opportunity structure and its accompanying techniques of rule violations
2. Socialization through occupational experiences
3. Reinforcement and encouragement from the occupational peer group, i.e., group support for certain rule violations.[4]

The police occupation structure is no exception. The police occupational peer group can indoctrinate and socialize the rookie into patterns of police deviance;[5] reinforce certain patterns of deviance within informal boundaries determined by the peer group, e.g., distinctions between "clean" and "dirty" money forms of corruption;[6] and censure deviance outside these boundaries. To deviate from the group's definition is to be a criminal,[7] and the "subculture" can censure attempts to report to other officers.

The specific patterns of police occupational or work-related deviance can and do take a variety of forms: criminality, corruption, ethical and work norm violations. These forms of behavior are not always mutually exclusive, but all of these acts violate at least one of three normative standards: criminal laws, departmental rules and regulations, or ethical police standards. Police rule violations—that is, police deviance—may vary, then, from transgressions or prescribed ethical conduct to engagement in criminal activities.

## POLICE OCCUPATIONAL DEVIANCE OTHER THAN CORRUPTION

### Police Perjury

A police officer commits perjury whenever he lies or deliberately misrepresents the truth while under oath. The officer is required as a part of his work duties to testify in court; therefore, his occupation provides him with numerous opportunities for this form of deviance. The perjured statement may be a means to effect an act of corruption; for example, an officer agrees to leave out certain pertinent facts or misrepresents material elements of an arrest in order to "fix" a criminal prosecution. Other acts of perjury are unrelated to corruption; that is, they do not involve any monetary reward or gain.

The police officer is always under constant pressure to be efficient or productive, much like an industrial worker.[8] But unlike the industrial worker, whose efficiency and productivity can be measured by a tangible finished product, the officer is determined to be efficient or productive by such intangible criteria as the number of arrests he makes or the number of convictions he obtains. Police organizations may set up some "norm" or informal quota system to insure an acceptable level of efficiency.[9] Informal quota systems are especially prevalent in areas of proactive police work related to vice. This type of pressure places the officer in a very untenable position. On one side—the police organization—he is pressured to produce, and on the other side—the courts—he is pressured to operate within the law. He is also in the intolerable position of being ultimately responsible for his own measure of efficiency. This organizational and occupational pressure can create a situation where certain acts of perjury are tolerated and accepted by the police peer group.

Narcotics "dropsy" evidence is a star example of police accommodation to this organizational dilemma. "Narcotics 'dropsy testimony' occurs when a police officer testifies that a defendant abandoned a quantity of narcotics by dropping it on the ground. The officer will allege that he saw the narcotics and then arrested the defendant for illegal possession."[10] Perjured testimony in this case is believed necessary to circumvent the exclusionary rule imposed in *Mapp v. Ohio*.

Police perjury is also possible in the issuance of search warrants. In order to obtain a search warrant, the officer must swear under oath that he has investigated the situation or information and has probable cause to execute a search. But it is not always possible to thoroughly investigate every situation, and "reliable" informants are not always as reliable as the officer claims. Therefore, the "honest" policeman must perjure himself to the judge. The ironic part of the whole matter is the fact that everyone who participates in this legal charade may know that the officer is lying or "bending" the truth.

> Everyone involved—the policeman, his sergeant and lieutenant, the captain who approves it, and the judge who grants him the warrant—knows that the policeman is perjuring himself...[11]

Unfortunately, increased legal restrictions often have the unintended consequence of increasing police perjury, particularly when the officer or his peer group decide that the ends of convictions and arrests are more important than the means to attain them. For example, this author has been told by a number of police officers that it is not necessary to give the *Miranda* warning prior to questioning; it is only necessary to say that one has done so in court.

All acts of police perjury are not the result of police venality; the largest percentage probably occurs through the overzealous and misguided efforts of well-intentioned officers who believe that "good" crime control requires some misrepresentation of the facts. Perjury to insure convictions is a form of administratively and occupationally induced deviance; i.e., the unethical behavior is based on the officer's perception of what is expected by his fellow workers and supervisors.[12]

## Police Brutality

The charge of police brutality is one of the most frequent citizen complaints made against individual officers and police organizations. Police brutality is also an ambiguous term used to cover a variety of police practices. When a citizen charges police brutality, he may be referring to a number of actions:

1. Profane and abusive language
2. Commands to move or get home
3. Field stops and searches
4. Threats
5. Prodding with a nightstick or approaching with a pistol
6. The actual use of physical force[13]

Although any of the above acts may at times be illegal and unethical, only the unreasonable and unnecessary use of physical force is actually police brutality. One can argue that the terms *unreasonable* and *unnecessary* are also ambiguous terms and depend on the circumstances involved, but instances of police brutality can and do occur for a variety of reasons. And it is possible for police perjury and police brutality to arise out of the same situation. An officer may commit an act of brutality and lie on the stand to prevent the possibility of a lawsuit or departmental charges.[14]

The police occupation provides the individual police officer with numerous opportunities for police brutality. Instruments of force and violence are a necessary part of the officer's occupational equipment. The police officer may need them to effect an arrest or defend himself, and society recognizes that the use of force is part of the policeman's legal mandate. Unfortunately, some officers go beyond their legal mandate and use unreasonable and unnecessary force to accomplish legal and nonlegal ends.

There are a number of possible reasons why an officer might engage in acts of brutality.[15] He might be the pathological personality who enjoys physically abusing and hurting others, and he has become a police officer because of the potential opportunities for violence. Every experienced police officer has probably come in contact with such individuals in his career. These violent men are a small minority of the police occupation; but, unfortunately, they do exist. Some instances of police brutality are also the result of fear with the officer overreacting to what are, or what he perceives to be, potentially dangerous situations. These individuals believe that physical force is an absolute necessity in the "street jungle." In other instances, this use of unnecessary physical force is the result of verbal abuse and provocation. Demonstrators have often tried (and been successful) to provoke officers into the use of force. A police officer does not have the legal right to strike an individual who has insulted him or called him a profane name, but sometimes the officer may be pushed beyond endurance. Actually, an officer who reacts to such abuse and provocation has compounded his problems because he will probably have to perjure himself in court to protect his job.

The use of unnecessary and unreasonable force can occur for any of the above-mentioned reasons, but the largest percentage of all acts of police brutality are the result of occupational socialization and peer group support. The police peer group may define the excessive use of force as acceptable in certain circumstances; such as to command respect from an unruly prisoner, to obtain information, to punish certain classes of deviants (sex criminals, hardened criminals) or classes of perceived deviants ("hippies," radicals, hillbillies, punk kids, etc.). Those individuals who actually resist arrest are particularly vulnerable targets of police brutality. The author has been told by some police officers that any force short of actually killing the subject is acceptable whenever an individual resists arrest.

When someone resists arrest you have to teach him a lesson. You have to. He may kill the next policeman who tries to arrest him. My sergeant says that there is no resisting unless the man goes to the hospital. So we send them [resisters] to the hospital.[16]

## Sex On Duty

The police officer comes into contact with a number of females during the routine patrol duties. These contacts occur under conditions that provide numerous opportunities for illicit sex. The women and the officers are frequently alone, and supervision of the officer on patrol is usually minimal. Officers working late-night shifts have the added cover of darkness and little traffic on the road. The officer also has the opportunity to stop a number of women coming home after a night of drinking. An intoxicated female may decide that her sexual favors are a small price to pay in order to avoid an arrest for driving while intoxicated. Other "promiscuous" women may use sex to avoid the inconvenience of a traffic citation. Sooner or later, every police officer will probably be propositioned while on patrol. This fact was impressed on the author when he first became a police officer and was given the following caution:

> There are three things that ruin most police officers, money, women, and liquor. As long as you stay away from them, you will make a good cop.[17]

Also, a veteran officer gave the rookie author the following advice:

> Never stop a woman unless you have plenty of witnesses. It is a good way to keep your job and your marriage.

The woman may also be coerced into the act by a "rogue" officer, but on numerous occasions the woman is a more than willing partner. Some women have a great deal to gain from sex with a policeman; for example, prostitutes, barmaids, and other female employees of establishments who operate on the fringe or outside the law. There are also a number of women who are attracted to the uniform or the aura of the occupation. Some of this latter group commit minor traffic violations as a ruse to see if the policeman is interested in illicit sex. Police officers soon learn the names of women in their district or city who just "love" the police. These women may make the rounds of the entire district or city. Several years ago a major sex scandal occurred in the Memphis, Tennessee, Police Department; as many as 200 police officers were alleged to have been involved with one 19-year-old divorcee. She would wave at the police officers, get them to stop, and then have sex with them.[18] After a lengthy investigation, police officers were suspended and four others reprimanded.[19]

## Sleeping On Duty

Sleeping while at work probably occurs in all occupations where workers engage in late-night shift work under minimal supervision, such as night watchmen, factory workers, and the military. But this form of occupational deviance may be especially prevalent in police work, especially on the last shift. The police car is sometimes referred to as a "traveling bedroom" because of the amount of sleeping and sex which takes place in the car. Included in the police argot are such terms as "hole" or "coop" where the sleeping takes place.

> A "hole"—a place into which a [police officer] can disappear in the middle of the night and sleep in safety and comfort. A hole can be anything from a back room in a store to which a cop has a key, to an all-night theater.[20]

Several social scientists, while conducting research on police activities, have actually observed police officers sleeping on duty.[21] One of these researchers observed officers sleeping in every district in all three cities studied, but found sleeping on duty to be most prevalent in areas where field supervision was lax.[22]

The nature of the occupation has some influence on the amount of sleeping on duty. The most obvious influence is the fact that police operations take place 24 hours a day, and the rest of society operates during daylight hours. Therefore, it takes a great deal of adjustment on the part of nightworkers to accomplish what are routine day activities. The officer also has to cope with a criminal justice system that is daytime-oriented. His court appearances are scheduled during the day, and it is not unusual for an officer to spend an entire day in court following a tour of duty and then have to return to duty the same night. In addition, night tours of duty are extremely dull and monotonous with usually only security checks to perform. When lack of sleep during the day and dull and monotonous duties at night are combined with minimal, nonexistent, or poor supervision, a certain amount of sleeping becomes inviting.

Certain off-duty activities engaged in by the officer may also force the officer to catch up on his sleep at work. The police officer who moonlights during the day in order to provide his family with a decent or increased standard of living soon finds it hard to stay awake at night. Many police officers who attend college during the day either study or sleep in a "hole." Finally, some police officers sleep in their cars for the same reason that clerks sleep in the stockroom; they are alienated from their work roles.[23]

## Drinking On Duty

One of the most serious violations of departmental rules and regulations a police officer can commit is drinking while on duty. The officer who drinks on duty presents a grave threat to citizens and his fellow officers. He is armed and usually in command of a powerful police car, and mistakes made by an intoxicated policeman can cause serious injuries to citizens and police officers. Nonetheless, some police officers do drink while on duty. Reiss and his colleagues observed 50 different police officers drinking on duty in the three cities they studied.[24] Rubinstein in his participant-observation study of the Philadelphia Police Department also observed officers drinking on duty, and he believes that one of the reasons why alcoholism can be a serious problem among policemen is the endless opportunities they have to drink while on duty.[25]

As with sleeping on duty, drinking on duty can also be a symptom of alienation from their work roles. In addition, the officer who drinks on duty could have a serious drinking problem which manifests itself on and off duty. Finally, drinking on duty may also be the result of boredom, monotony, and opportunity combined with lax or ineffectual supervision.

The remainder of this article will concern itself with the extent and peer group support for the five patterns of police deviance in the South City Police Department.

## RESEARCH SITE AND SAMPLE

South City is a southern city of over 25,000 population located east of the Mississippi River with a majority white population and a sizable minority of nonwhite inhabitants. There are 50 members of the South City Police Department, including two radio dispatchers and three jailers.

The researcher, after several informal contacts, received permission to administer a questionnaire to the members of the South City Police Department.[26] The questionnaire was designed to measure the perceived extent and support for each of the patterns of police deviance which might exist in the South City Police Department.

The researcher appeared at two police roll calls and personally administered the questionnaire to all but seven of the South City officers. The seven remaining subjects were either off duty or on vacation. Seven questionnaires and self-addressed envelopes were left with a cooperative superior officer for these men. Six of the questionnaires were returned, and all but one were usable. This resulted in 43 questionnaires out of a population of 45 subjects.[27]

## MEASUREMENTS OF PERCEIVED EXTENT

The actual extent of police deviance in South City is unknown and probably unknowable; and, to complicate matters, South City has no official records on police deviance. Therefore, the only measurements remaining were direct observation or some indirect measurement. Any form of participant observation was ruled out because the writer had neither the time, resources, nor desire to become a police officer again. Consequently, it was decided to use an indirect measure of the extent of police deviance. Each subject was asked to make a judgment as to what percentage of the men in his department engage or have engaged in each of the five patterns of police deviance. This indirect manner was the added advantage of not putting the subjects on "the spot" by asking him to report on his own behavior or identifying any other member of his department. The perceived extent of each deviant pattern was operationally defined as the average percentage for the total respondents Sigma %/N.

## MEASUREMENT OF PERCEIVED SUPPORT

Perceived peer support for each pattern of police deviance was measured in two ways. First, each subject was asked his opinion concerning the "wrongness" or perceived deviance for each pattern of police deviance which was operationally defined as the man for the total respondents Sigma X/N.

This scale measures the social definition of police deviance in the South City Police Department. Deviance is usually a continuum. There are very few forms of deviant conduct perceived by members of most groups as a black and white dichotomy, with the possible exception being such morally objectionable forms of behavior as in-group murder and incest. Therefore, it was expected that most patterns of deviant police behavior would receive a perceived deviance score somewhere between 0-9.

The second method of measuring peer group support was to ask each subject to give his opinion as to how often a policeman in his department would report another policeman for engaging in the various forms of behavior. Choices were *every time, sometimes, rarely,* and *never.* The extent of police deviance should vary inversely with the risk or fear of sanction which exists in the police organization. Police officers presented with the opportunity for deviant acts who believe that such behavior is not considered "wrong" by their peer group and who further believe that such behavior will not be reported are probably more likely to engage in such behavior.

## RESULTS

### Perceived Extent

Concerning police brutality, each respondent was asked to give his opinion on what percentage of the men use or have used excessive force on a prisoner. Although we have indicated that police brutality may be an ambiguous term, any excessive force on a prisoner is clearly police brutality. The sample believed almost 40 percent (39.19%) of the members of the South City Police Department engage in or had engaged in this form of police deviance.

When asked the percentage of men who lie or have lied in court—a clear case of police perjury—the perceived extent was almost 23 percent (22.95%). This perceived extent of the three remaining forms of police deviance ranged from a little over 8 percent to nearly 40 percent: drinking on duty, 8.05 percent; sex on duty, 31.84 percent; and sleeping on duty, 39.58 percent (Table 7.1).

### Perceived Support

The first measurement of support was the perceived "deviance" or "wrongness" for each deviant pattern. The perceived deviance score for the use of excessive force on a prisoner (police brutality) was a mean of 6.72, which is the lowest of any of the patterns. The remaining perceived deviance scores are: 8.58, lying in court (policy perjury); 7.42, sex on duty; 8.72, drinking on duty; and 7.95, sleeping on duty. Table 7.2 presents the perceived extent and perceived scores for each of the deviant patterns.

## TABLE 7.1

### PERCEIVED EXTENT OF POLICE
### OCCUPATIONAL DEVIANCE
### IN SOUTH CITY

| Deviant Pattern | Perceived Extent (Percentage) |
|---|---|
| Police brutality (excessive force on prisoner) | 39.19 |
| Police perjury (lying in court) | 22.95 |
| Sex on duty | 31.84 |
| Drinking on duty | 8.05 |
| Sleeping on duty | 39.58 |

## TABLE 7.2

### PERCEIVED EXTENT AND
### PERCEIVED DEVIANCE SCORES
### (RANKED ON EXTENT)

| Deviant Pattern | Perceived Extent | Perceived Deviance |
|---|---|---|
| Sleeping on duty | 39.58 | 7.95 |
| Police brutality | 39.19 | 6.72 |
| Sex on duty | 31.84 | 7.49 |
| Police perjury | 22.95 | 8.58 |
| Drinking on duty | 8.05 | 8.72 |

NOTE: There is a high inverse association between perceived extent and perceived deviance, r—.79, which is significant at the .05 level.

The second measure of support comes when each subject was asked how often a policeman in their department would report another officer for the five patterns of police deviance.

---

### TABLE 7.3

#### QUESTION: HOW OFTEN WOULD A POLICEMAN IN YOUR DEPARTMENT REPORT ANOTHER POLICEMAN FOR THESE KINDS OF ACTS?

| DEVIANT PATTERN | RESPONSES | | | |
| --- | --- | --- | --- | --- |
| | Always | Sometimes | Rarely | Never |
| Sleeping on duty ................ | 6 (14%) | 21 (49%) | 10 (23%) | 6 (14%) |
| Police brutality (excessive force) ... | 5 (12%) | 18 (42%) | 16 (37%) | 4 (9%) |
| Sex on duty ................... | 8 (19%) | 11 (26%) | 15 (35%) | 9 (21%) |
| Police perjury ................. | 12 (28%) | 8 (19%) | 12 (28%) | 11 (26%) |
| Drinking on duty .............. | 24 (56%) | 14 (33%) | 1 (2%) | 4 (9%) |

N = 43

---

(Table 7.3). Thirty-seven percent said sleeping on duty would be rarely or never reported. Forty-nine percent said this behavior would be reported sometimes and 14 percent said a police officer who slept on duty would be reported every time. An even higher percentage (46%) reported that a policeman in South City would rarely or never report a fellow officer for the use of excessive force (police brutality). Forty-two percent reported that this form of brutality would be reported sometimes, and 12 percent checked every time. It is ironic that sleeping on duty is perceived to involve more risk of sanction than police brutality.

Illicit sex while on duty is perceived to involve more risk than brutality or sleeping on duty. Nineteen percent of the subjects believe that this would be reported every time. Nonetheless, 56 percent believe that this form of police deviance would be never or rarely reported, and 26 percent believe sex on duty would be reported sometimes. A police officer who commits perjury in court does so with little risk of being reported. Seventy-three percent said that he would be reported sometimes (19 percent), rarely (28 percent), or never (26 percent). But this form of police deviance involves more risk than brutality and sex and sleeping on duty. Twenty-eight percent believe that perjury would be reported every time.

Drinking on duty is perceived to involve the greatest amount of risk. Fifty-six percent of the subjects believe that a police officer in South City who drinks on duty will be reported. Even so, 11 percent reported that an officer who drinks on duty will rarely or never be reported.

## SUMMARY

The purpose of this study was to identify patterns of police occupational deviance other than corruption and test for their existence in a real world setting.

We have tried to develop the thesis that all forms of police deviance, i.e., rule or norm violating, are examples of occupational deviance which vary according to opportunity structure and group support.

In the particular police organization studied, one finds that the perceived extent of each pattern of police deviance did, in fact, vary inversely with the group support as measured through the perceived "wrongness" and risk which existed in the police organization. The extent of each deviant pattern was almost a direct function of how "wrong" the police peer group perceived the act and the perception of how often the men thought it would be reported. These findings have very practical aspects for the police administrators in South City and in other police organizations where the same situation exists. Police administrators can exert some control over the opportunity structure through increased supervision. The author in his dealings with the South City Police Department got the impression that field supervision was indeed very lax. Furthermore, police administrators who understand the importance of the peer group in facilitating acts of misconduct can use the peer group to discourage these same acts.

In conclusion, the author believes that the study of police deviance can add to the general body of knowledge concerning all forms of deviant behavior and can be of significant practical use to police administrators and others concerned with police professionalization. As more and more police officers "go off to school," we should expect scholarly and unbiased accounts of police deviant behavior to appear in the literature. The author hopes that this work can stimulate more research into the understanding of the phenomenon. In order to manage and control police misconduct, we must have a greater understanding of its varieties and complexities.

# Notes

1    E.R. Stoddard, "The 'Informal Code' of Police Deviance: A Group Approach to 'Blue Coat'," *Journal of Criminal Law, Criminology and Police Science,* 59 (June 1968):201-213.

2    See B. Cohen, *The Police Internal Administration of Justice in New York City* (1970); J. Rubinstein, *City Police* (1973).

3    This definition is a modification of a definition of occupational crime which appeared in G.D. Robin, "White Collar Crime and Employee Theft," *Crime and Delinquency,* 20(3) (1974):251-263. Robin gave this definition under the heading of occupational deviance, but he failed to draw the distinction between deviant behavior which is criminal and deviant behavior which is deviant but not criminal.

4    C.D. Bryant, *Deviant Behavior: Occupational and Organizational Bases* (1974).

5    See Stoddard; W.A. Westley, *Violence and the Police* (1971); J.H. McNamara, "Uncertainties in Police Work: The Relevance of Police Recruits' Background and Training," in D.J. Bordua (ed.), *The Police: Six Sociological Essays* (1967), 163-252.

6    See T. Barker and J. Roebuck, *An Empirical Typology of Police Corruption* (1973).

7    A.J. Reiss, Jr., *The Police and the Public* (1972).

8    J.H. Skolnick, *Justice Without Trial: Law Enforcement in a Democratic Society* (1966).

9    J.H. Skolnick; Rubinstein, note 2 at 50; D.M. Peterson, "Informal Norms and Police Practice: The Traffic Ticket Quota System," *Sociology and Social Research,* 55(3) (April 1971): 354-362.

10    "Comment, Police Perjury in Narcotics 'Dropsy Cases:' A New Credibility Gap," *Georgetown Law Journal* (November 1971): 507-523.

11    Rubinstein, note 2 at 385.

12    See A.K. Kornblum, *The Moral Hazards* (1976).

13    A.J. Reiss, Jr., "Police-Brutality—Answers to Key Questions," *Trans-Action,* 5 (July-August 1969), 15-16.

14    P. Chevigny, *Police Power: Police Abuses in New York City* (1969).

15    L.A. Radelet, *The Police and the Community* (1973).

16    Comments of a veteran police officer.

17    Remarks of a police captain.

18    D. Stone, "Teen-Ager Tells of Sex Activities with Police," *Birmingham News*, November 5, 1973.

19    M. Hanna, "Charlotte Episode is 'Closed'," *Commercial Appeal* (December 15, 1973).

20    J.F. Ahern, *Police in Trouble* (1972), 10. (Mr. Ahern is an ex-police officer who spent 14 years with the New Haven, Connecticut, Police Department. He worked his way up from patrolman to chief of police before leaving to become director of the Insurance Crime Prevention Institute in Westport, Connecticut.

21    Reiss, note 7; Rubinstein.

22    Reiss, note 7, 164-166.

23    T. Denber, R. Callender, and D.L. Thompson, "The Policeman as Alienated Laborer," *Journal of Police Science and Administration,* 3(3) (September 1975):251-258.

24    Reiss, note 7 at 165 (Table 35).

25    Rubinstein, note 2 at 421.

26    The ongoing shift commander graciously consented to call in the offgoing shift in order to administer the questionnaire to two shifts at one time.

27    The decision was made not to administer the questionnaire to the dispatchers and jailers as they have no arrest powers and are never on the street. Any information they could supply on deviant activities would be based on hearsay and conjecture.

# Study Questions

1. What are the reasons why a police officer might commit perjury or misrepresent the truth under oath?

2. The author proposes that police perjury and brutality often arise out of the same situation. Under what circumstances does this occur?

3. The author suggests that there are a number of possible reasons why an officer might engage in brutality. What are they? Which might explain the largest percentage of all acts of police brutality?

4. Why does the author suggest that sleeping on duty is more prevalent in police work than in other occupations?

5. Why is drinking on duty one of the most serious violations a police officer can commit?

# 8

# SEXUAL MISCONDUCT
# BY POLICE OFFICERS*

## Allen D. Sapp

This chapter discusses sexually motivated actions and behavior by police officers as a form of police misconduct. The discussion is presented as a preliminary analysis of a complex phenomenon. There is no attempt to discuss cause or any of the multiple relationships that are involved. An attempt is made to provide a preliminary categorization of police sexual misconduct behaviors as a heuristic device to further research in this area.

The literature on police misconduct has, until recently, focused primarily upon corruption and graft (see, for example, Barker and Roebuck, 1974; Goldstein, 1975; Lundman, 1980; Meyer, 1976; Sherman, 1974; among others). The research into police misconduct has examined police corruption from a variety of perspectives and theoretical and empirical approaches. Recently, some researchers are turning their attention to forms of misconduct outside the areas of corruption (see, for example, Barker, 1978; Carter, 1985; Kevlin, 1986; Shearing, 1981). This chapter examines an area of police misconduct that is often hidden and rarely discussed.

## RESEARCH METHODOLOGY

This report is part of a study that began in 1981 and has continued since then. The data for this study was obtained from lengthy interviews with police officers and police supervisors in several large, metropolitan municipal police departments in seven states. Additional input came from conversations with hundreds of municipal and state police officers and former police officers. A number of deputy sheriffs were also interviewed.

The lengthy interviews, some lasting as long as five hours, were conducted in private, often in the home or office of the subject. Many of the conversations took place in patrol cars or in station houses. Wherever possible, the anecdotal material was verified. The research followed basic research methods for participant-observer research as suggested by Polsky (1967). It is problematic whether the findings can be generalized to other law enforcement personnel and departments.

---

*This chapter was written expressly for inclusion in this book.*

The sample used in this study is small and there is no way of determining whether or not the sample is representative of the larger population.

Generalization of the findings is further limited by the inclusion of anecodotal evidence as well as self-reports. Some of the interviewees reported anecdotes of activities related to the study that the interviewee had had from others, not necessarily from the perpetrator. Anecdotal evidence is particularly susceptible to exaggeration and modification. Self-reports are also subject to a variety of biases, distortions, and subject to the vagaries of memory.

## POLICE SEXUAL MISCONDUCT

Police officers are in a unique position and have numerous opportunities to sexually harass citizens. Perhaps no other occupation presents the opportunities for sexual misconduct as does law enforcement. The basis for the police opportunity is a combination of police authority and constant contact with members of society. Additionally, contacts between male law enforcement officers and female citizens often take place in relative isolation. Thus, the combination of isolated contacts between male police officers and female citizens in conjunction with the authority of the police officer creates the opportunities for sexual harassment and misconduct.

Certainly, all police officers, even most law enforcement officers, do not use the opportunities to sexually harass citizens. However, enough do take the opportunity to create a problem worthy of study. While it is true that female law enforcement officers also have opportunities to sexually harass male citizens, such opportunities are much less frequent and the harassment much less likely to occur. Similarly, opportunities for sexual harassment of citizens of the same sex as the officer also may occur. However, this discussion will be limited to male police officer and female citizen forms of sexual harassment. Sexually motivated harassment of females by police officers takes a variety of forms ranging from non-sexual contacts to sexual shakedowns and demands for sexual services. It is probably more correctly stated to term the behaviors as sexually motivated behaviors since many of the types of activities are not overtly sexual in nature. Seven categories of police sexually motivated or sexual harassment behaviors are suggested:

1. Non-sexual contacts that are sexually motivated
2. Voyeuristic contacts
3. Contacts with crime victims
4. Contacts with offenders
5. Contacts with juvenile females
6. Sexual shakedowns
7. Citizen-initiated sexual contacts.

Each of these seven categories is discussed in some detail below.

*Non-Sexual Contact.* This category of sexual harassment involves behaviors that are best described as sexually motivated without direct sexual actions or inferences. These behaviors may not be recognized by the female citizen and she may not be aware of the underlying motivations of the officer. Nevertheless, the behaviors qualify as a form of sexual harassment. Essentially, the behaviors in this category are forms of officer-initiated contacts with female citizens without legal basis or probable cause. The motivation of the officer is to get a closer look at the female or to gain information about her.

The invalid traffic stop to check out the female driver and/or passengers is a common form of sexually motivated behavior.

> Sure! I see a good-looking chick driving around by herself or even a couple of foxes together, I pull them over and check them out. You can always claim a stoplight isn't working or something like that. Most people are so shook up when you stop them and they don't question what you tell them. You'd be surprised how many times I end up with a phone number or an invitation to stop by. I've been invited to some wild parties, too. I always write down the chick's name, address and license number and sometimes I see her again somewhere or maybe see her on the street and stop her for a chat and that leads to some action. Lots of times it sure doesn't lead anywhere but you'd be surprised how much action I get just from stopping chicks. (Interview: Patrolman, Traffic Squad, Medium Municipal Department.)

Similar activity involves running a vehicle license check through the computer to obtain the driver's name and address. Officers may also stop a female on foot under one pretense or another in order to obtain information or to initiate a conversation. These latter forms of contact may also be followed up by the officer in more direct sexual contacts.

These non-sexual contacts rarely lead to citizen complaints. Either the contact is a single occurrence, soon forgotten, or it develops into mutual social meetings and further social contacts. Only when repeated illegal stops are made is the citizen likely to complain. An officer in a midwestern city was recently disciplined after several women complained of being stopped several times for no apparent cause. The officer had no explanation for his behavior other than "just checking them out."

One dispatcher in a large sheriff's department noted that: "you could make a pretty good living betting that every stop Deputy B. makes involves a woman driver." A review of automobile license checks at one medium-sized municipal police department indicated that one officer checked female drivers 82 percent of all license checks he made in a two-week period. Less than three percent of his license checks were followed by a vehicle stop. Another officer's vehicle license checks over the same two-week period reflected 73 percent female drivers. Both were identified by other officers as "likely to check out the ladies."

*Voyeuristic Contacts.* Some officers spend varying amounts of time engaged in voyeuristic behaviors while on duty. The officers spend this time seeking opportunities to view unsuspecting women partially clad or nude. Other officers seek out parked cars in "lovers lane" in hopes of observing sexual activities by the occupants of the cars.

> I'll never forget my first night on the street after the Academy. I was all fired up to go out and fight crime. I was assigned to a twelve-year veteran for on the street training. As soon as we left the station, he drove over to a side street behind the college dorms and parked in the middle of the block. He even had a pocket-type telescope in his briefcase and proceeded to check out the dorm windows while telling me all about the college girls he had seen. He pointed out two windows that were usually "good hunting." After checking the dorms for 15-20 minutes, he drove over into a residential area to show me three houses where "on a good night, you'll get an eyeful." Around two o'clock, he drove into another patrol district and into a parking lot to check the windows in an apartment building where "several barmaids and go-go dancers live." He said it was a "waste of time to get there before two o'clock because they don't get home before then." I rode with him for two months and he spent most of every shift looking for women undressing in front of windows. (Interview: Patrolman, Patrol Division, Large Municipal Department).

Officers who spend their time looking for windows to view are rarely noted by the citizens who may be the target of their peeping. Women who discover the patrol car on the street are likely to blame themselves for leaving the curtains open or the blinds undrawn rather than to complain. As long as the officer responds to his service calls and does not leave the patrol vehicle to carry out his voyeuristic activities, he is unlikely to be caught and reported. Even if the officer is caught in a yard or behind a house, he can always claim to be checking out a call about a prowler.

More overt voyeurism is practiced by some officers who leave their cars and walk quietly to check parked cars in lovers' lane areas. These officers seek to observe and interrupt couples engaged in sexual activities in the parked automobiles.

Joe P. and I used to hit the local parking places where the high school and college kids go to make out every weekend. Friday and Saturday nights were the best. Lots of times we sneaked up and watched the kids. You wouldn't believe some of the things we saw! [Several sexually graphic examples deleted.] Some of the girls would just really take their time getting their clothes back on like they enjoyed having us watch them. We never took anybody in—just made them get dressed while we watched and moved them on. We did arrest a couple of [homosexual males] once when we caught them. (Interview: Sergeant, Patrol Division, Large Municipal Department.)

Officers engaged in overt voyeuristic activities similar to those discussed above are rarely the subject of a complaint since the citizens being harassed are engaged in illicit activities and would likely be embarrassed to file a complaint. Unless other officers complain or unless the officer goes beyond voyeurism, the offending officer usually is not detected.

The first two classifications dealt with citizen-police contacts with police initiation of the contact. The next category is one where the potential victim of sexual harassment contacts the police. The authority of the police becomes a major factor in such contacts.

*Contacts With Crime Victims.* Victims of crime are particularly susceptible to sexual harassment by police officers. The victims are often emotionally upset and turn to the police for support and assistance. The officer is at the scene at the request of the citizen, who is fully aware of the authority of the police officer. A wide variety of sexually motivated misbehaviors may occur.

Unnecessary callbacks to the residence of female victims are one of the most common forms of police misconduct.

When you drop in a few times to check on the victim or to tell her that you are still working on her case, you kind of establish a connection there. She will offer a cup of coffee or a drink. When one of them offers a drink, I usually tell them I can't drink on duty but I'll take a rain check. I get invited back a lot after hours and that sometimes leads to something. You can't do this with everyone, but if you pick them carefully, it gets me a lot of action. (Interview: Detective, Burglary Squad, Large Municipal Department.)

Sex crime victims are also susceptible to sexual harassment by officers. Some of the harassment is unintentional and results from a lack of sensitivity and knowledge on the part of the officer. Victims of sex crimes should be interviewed by well-trained officers who are knowledgeable of the psychological needs of sex-victims. When an officer questions victims of sex offenses beyond the depth of details needed for investigation purposes, the questioning becomes a form of sexual harassment.

Many victims of rape and sexual assault have complained of being raped again by the criminal justice system. This "second rape" often starts with questioning by insensitive officers who insist on graphic details and who ask judgmental questions. Some officers have insisted on examining the victim for signs of physical injury which may involve partial disrobing by the victim. Such forms of questioning and examination are unnecessary and constitute a form of sexual harassment.

Two officers were fired by a sheriff's department in a southern state for unnecessary bodily contact with accident victims. The officers were accused of fondling or touching the breasts and genitals of accident victims on two separate occasions. Behavior of this type is likely to be reported unless the victim is unconscious. Other officers who observe such behavior may also be a source of reporting.

*Contacts With Offenders.* Police officers have relatively frequent opportunities for sexual harassment and sexual contact with offenders. Offenders are not only aware of the authority of the officer but are also in a position where their complaints may be disregarded or played down.

> You bet I get (sex) once in a while by some broad who I arrest. Lots of times you can just hint that if you are taken care of, you could forget about what they did. One of the department stores here doesn't like to prosecute, but they always call us when they catch a shoplifter. Usually, we just talk to them and warn them and let them go. If it's a decent looking woman, sometimes I'll offer to take her home and make my pitch. Some of the snooty, high class broads turn on real quick if they think their friends and the old man doesn't have to find out about their shoplifting. I never mess around with any of the kids, but I know a couple of guys who made out with a couple of high school girls they caught on a B and E. (Detective, Theft Squad, Large Municipal Department.)

In addition to sexual demands placed on offenders, officers may also sexually harass female offenders by conducting body searches, frisks, and pat downs. Although departmental rules and regulations require the female suspects be frisked and searched by female officers or jail matrons, officers in the field often feel justified in making a pat down for weapons. Offenders who resist arrest may also become involved in unnecessary bodily contact. One state police officer stated: "Whenever a female starts to hassle or fight me, I just grab a [breast] and twist. That quiets them down quick."

Officials of a large metropolitan county in a midwestern state have been the subject of a civil rights suit over body searches and strip searches by officers of a different sex than the offenders. Although most all of the cases cited have involved female officers strip searching offenders returning from work release programs, apparently there is a possibility for male officers to conduct similar searches for female offenders. As a result, the county has agreed to avoid opposite sex strip searches whenever possible. Interestingly, the county justified its actions by reference to a previous civil suit that resulted in a court order requiring the county to assign identical duties to male and female corrections officers.

Offenders who are in detention are in a position where sexual harassment behaviors can take place with relative impunity. Most jails are not constructed to provide privacy for any inmates. Female inmates often can be seen in their cells, showers, toilets, or during searches by jail matrons. Some officers apparently seek out opportunities to observe females in various degrees of undress.

> Look at the women? Hell, you can't help but look at the women in here. The showers don't have any doors on them and you can't always wait until the showers are empty to go into the cell block. Some of the women try to show their bodies off to you, too. We don't have air conditioning and when the weather is hot, they lay around their cells with just underwear or even buck naked most of the time. I see so many naked women that after a while you just don't even notice it anymore. Now once in a while, we get a really built one in and the guys will make it a point to catch her in the shower or dressing, but most of these we get are really pigs, not worth looking at. (Sheriff's Detention Officer, Large Sheriff's Department.)

Female inmates in smaller jails particularly are sometimes exposed to sexual demands by their guardians. In many small jails, only one or two officers are on duty during the evening hours and their behavior is largely unsupervised. A number of cases of sexual assaults on jail inmates have been documented in recent years. Recently, a former sheriff in a border state was indicted on 15 counts of rape and sodomy where the victims were inmates in his jail. At the time of the latest indictments, he was serving a sentence in a federal prison for earlier conviction based on similar behavior. While a number of officers interviewed for this study indicated they were aware of such things happening, none were willing to admit to such activities.

> Over in a county west of here, they tell me that a sheriff will sometimes grab a hooker working one of the truck stops or the rest areas on the Interstate (highway) over there and keep her in jail over the weekend. He works out some kinda deal where he turns them loose

without any charges or anything and they put out for the sheriff and the deputies that might be interested. I've heard this from several officers and I believe it's true. Now I don't go for that kind of stuff at all. Seems to me that the sheriff over there is really asking for trouble over this kind of thing. It is different if some woman in the jail wants to have a party or whatever with some of the deputies or the sheriff but to go out and arrest one and then make the deal is too much. (Patrolman, working as jailer at Medium Municipal Jail.)

*Contacts With Juvenile Females.* Younger females may also be the subject of sexual harassment by police officers. Runaways, truants, and delinquents are in a position similar to that of adult offenders in relation to police authority and lack of credibility. Juvenile females may be highly impressionable and easily influenced by the police officer. They are much less likely to be "street-wise" and to understand the limits of police authority and proper police behavior. A former juvenile squad sergeant in Louisiana was the subject of a recent television program after he failed to appear for trial on charges that he sexually molested a 12-year-old girl that he was "counseling" after earlier abuse by someone else.

Several of the officers interviewed for this chapter were aware of sexual contact between officers and underage females but all declined to discuss details or to have their comments recorded. In a Texas city, an officer assigned to a junior high school as a school liaison officer was fired after disclosure of his sexual involvement with several female students. Of the officers interviewed for this study, none admitted to having such contact themselves. This may be the rarest of the various forms of sexual misconduct because of the possible penalties.

*Sexual Shakedowns.* Demanding sexual service from prostitutes, homosexuals, or other citizens involved in illegal or illicit activities is perhaps the most severe of all of the forms of sexual harassment. Actual sexual activities are involved with an unwilling citizen who yields solely on the basis of the police authority to arrest and prosecute.

I know several dozen guys who have worked vice in the ten years I've been assigned to the vice squad. I believe everyone of them has gone beyond the rules on sex with prostitutes. You see, when you are assigned to the prostitute detail, you have to get the female subject to offer specific sexual acts and then state a price for those sex acts. Once you have that, you have a case and are supposed to identify and arrest. Sometimes the officer goes ahead and has the sex and then makes the arrest and files a report saying he followed the procedures. If the whore claims otherwise, no one believes her anyway since they think she is just trying to get her case tossed out. Have I ever done that? Well, I'm not saying I did but I've been in this business ten years so you draw your own conclusion. Everyone I know does it at one time or another. The prostitute squad isn't the only way vice officers get action. I've been offered, and I'm not saying I took up the offers, understand, but I've been offered sexual services from barmaids, gamblers, narcotic addicts and dealers, and damn near every other kind of case you run into. Most of those cases are just between you and the suspect and they will do almost anything to avoid the arrest. Guys that would never even consider taking money will take (oral sex or intercourse) from a good-looking woman. I don't know if the guys who are oversexed get assigned to vice or if being exposed to so much of it makes the vice squad oversexed, but it seems to me there is more going on in vice than anywhere else. (Vice Squad Sergeant, Large Municipal Department.)

Police officers who exchange preferential treatment for sexual favors are not limited to those with the vice squad. Officers on traffic details, patrol, or other investigative squads may also offer differential treatment in exchange for sexual services.

When I first went on patrol, I was surprised to hear some of the other officers talking about the sex they got on duty or as a result of on duty calls. Seems like everyone talked about it. I really didn't have any offers or even really think about it until I was assigned to a one-man car and one night I stopped a female subject for running a traffic light. She was really first class and the way she acted I just kind of hinted that maybe we could reach an understanding and she picked right up on it. Well, she had enough moving violations that another one could take her license and I guess she didn't want that to happen. Anyway, I met her later that night and had a wild session. I called her again a few days later and she wouldn't even talk to me. Yeah, I've had a few similar type experiences since but I'm real careful. It really isn't worth it if you get caught. There is plenty of opportunities without pressuring someone or taking a chance on someone filing on you. (Patrol Officer, Patrol Division, Medium Municipal Department.)

I worked traffic for a couple of years in (another city) before I quit and came here. I tell you, it was a rare night when I didn't get the batted eyes and tears and the "officer, I'll do anything" routine. My zone was close to the college and lots of the college girls were afraid that their old man would take their cars away, I guess, if they got tickets. We used to refer to traffic duty around the college as "fox hunting." It was quite an experience but after a while you get tired of it. Some of them would

really give you a come-on and then later when it got right down to the
nitty-gritty they wanted to back out or play kids games. You know,
petting and no serious sex. One guy was supposed to meet one girl after
the shift and when he showed up, her boyfriend came along. Man, that
kind of stuff is weird and too risky. Naw, I didn't take up very many of
them on the offers. I guess you could say that a couple of times I let it be
known that maybe we could negotiate, but most always they made the
offers. (Former Traffic Officer. Medium Municipal Department.)

Officers engaged in various forms of sexual shakedowns are engaged in
activities that clearly are illegal and subject to severe penalties. While sexual
shakedowns of prostitutes may be less risky, shakedowns of other citizens could
easily become the subject of complaints.

*Citizen-Initiated Sexual Contacts.* Some sexual contacts between law
enforcement officers and female citizens are initiated by citizens rather than by
the police officer. It is a rare police department that does not have stories about
"police groupies," females, often young, who are attracted sexually to the uniform, weapons, or power of the police officer. Officers in many departments have
been disciplined and/or dismissed for participating in sexual activities with
"groupies."

Another form of citizen-initiated sexual contact is the call from lonely or
mentally disturbed women who seek attention and affection from an officer. Most
law enforcement officers are familiar with these service calls when a citizen calls
for an officer and has no real reason for doing so other than to have someone with
whom to talk. Some women offer sex in exchange for the officer's time and
attention. Officers who participate in the offered sexual services often are dealing
with a person who needs other forms of professional attention. These citizens may
become well-known throughout the department.

We have several of the women who will call once or twice a week,
always late at night to report a prowler or an attempted break-in or some
other reason. We have to dispatch an officer when we get calls like that
but everyone knows the addresses now and we warn our officers to
avoid any situation where they would be compromised. We have orders
to the dispatchers to always send a two-man unit or else send two units.
These women are sick in my opinion because all they want when the
officers get there is to talk and have the officers stay for a while. Some
of them will offer sex or money or whatever just to keep the officers
around for a while. I don't think we have any of our troops engaging in
sex with any of these that we know about. Everyone knows what is
going on when we get a call from them. I'm sure they aren't the only

ones around and maybe there are others I don't know about. I guess some of the officers might not recognize that these subjects are sick but I don't know. (Captain, Patrol Division, Large Municipal Department.)

There are three or maybe four addresses here in town that everyone knows when a car is dispatched that it's another call from one of the "lonely hearts" club. Everyone laughs but no one really wants the call because every time you make one of those runs everyone kids about whether you took care of the lady and so forth. You know, some guys never seem to know when an old joke is enough. You know what I mean? They just keep it up and no one is going to mess around with those women even though one of them is pretty young and fairly good-looking. She always answers the door in a nightgown that is nearly see-through and is scared or pretends to be so scared that she wants you to stay for a while. I answered one call, not one of the known addresses, and the woman just had a towel around her and she claimed someone was trying to get into her window while she was taking a shower. Well, when we looked the place over, the bathroom wasn't wet, the bed had been slept in and this was three o'clock in the morning. She just got lonely and wanted a man. I'll admit, she looked pretty good in that towel and she wasn't real careful, you know, about keeping it closed up and all. If I was there by myself I might of been tempted. My partner and I laughed about it but I think he got a little turned on too. No one talks much about it but I'm sure other calls like that happen. The brass really stresses the known addresses and we have all been warned about them. They don't know about others though. (Patrolman in Captain's division—see above.)

A third type of sexual contact initiated by the citizen is the offer of sexual services in return for favors, preferential treatment, or additional protection. This form of sexual contact is differentiated from officer-initiated contacts by the citizen making the offer without any prior indication from the officer that such an offer might be considered. Obviously, law enforcement officers who accept such offers in exchange for favors or preferential treatment are engaged in illegal use of police authority.

Even though most police officers do not misuse their authority or take advantage of the numerous opportunities for sexual harassment of female citizens, some do and the result is that exploitation of citizens by law enforcement officers lessens the respect for the department involved and all other law enforcement agencies and officers. Control of officers who sexually harass citizens is extremely difficult to achieve but is a task that should receive attention from police administrators.

# PRESCRIPTION TO CONTROL SEXUAL HARASSMENT

Sexual misconduct and sexual harassment of female citizens by male law enforcement officers can be reduced or eliminated only by a concerted effort of police administrators and supervisors. Apathy towards sexual misconduct and harassment must be reduced, both on the part of police officials and the general public. As long as the "boys will be boys" attitude prevails, sexual harassment will not receive the attention it deserves.

Sexual harassment and sexual misconduct as part of law enforcement must not be acceptable in any law enforcement agency. This problem is similar to many others; by accepting some level of misconduct, the department invites such conduct. Only when administrators and supervisors make it clear to every member of the department that sexual misconduct and sexual harassment will not be tolerated in any form or any degree is the behavior likely to decrease. Police officers should be educated about sexual misconduct and its effect upon the department and the public.

The secrecy surrounding sexual harassment and other forms of police misconduct must be removed. As long as misconduct of any type is hidden and thus largely invisible, the misconduct will continue. If the general public and the police officers are fully aware of the appropriate limits on police contacts with female citizens, the shroud of secrecy is torn and the misconduct is identified.

Once police misconduct involving sexual harassment or sexually motivated behavior and activities is identified, appropriate disciplinary action must be taken. The disciplinary action should be fair, firm, and appropriate for the degree and type of misconduct. Dismissal and/or criminal charges are certainly within the range of appropriate responses to some of the more serious forms of sexual harassment and misconduct. On a broader scale, sexual misconduct in all occupations will not be eliminated until such time as we make basic changes in society and in our views of sex roles.

# REFERENCES

Barker, T. and J.B. Roebuck (1974). *An Empirical Typology of Police Corruption: A Study in Organizational Deviance.* Springfield, IL: Charles C Thomas.

Barker, T. (1978). "An Empirical Study of Police Deviance Other than Corruption." *Journal of Police Science and Administration.* Vol. 6 No. 3, 264-272.

Carter, D.L. (1985). "Police Brutality: A Model for Definition, Perspective, and Control." In Blumberg and Niederhoffer (eds.) *The Ambivalent Force: Perspectives on the Police, 3rd Edition),* New York: Holt, Rinehart, and Winston.

Goldstein, H. (1975). *Police Corruption: A Perspective on Its Nature and Control.* Washington, DC: Police Foundation.

Kevlin, T.A. (1986). "Police Corruption and Prostitution in the United States: The Historical Background." *Journal of Police and Criminal Psychology,* Vol. 2, No. 2:24-38.

Lundman, R.J. (ed.). *Police Behavior.* New York: Oxford University Press.

Meyer, J.C., Jr. (1976). "Definitional and Etiological Issues in Police Corruption: Assessment and Synthesis of Completing Perspectives." *Journal of Police Science and Administration,* 4:46-55.

Polsky, N. (1967). *Hustlers, Beats, and Others.* Chicago, IL: Aldine Publishing. (See Chapter 3, pp. 117-149 particularly).

Shearing, C.D. (ed.). (1981). *Organizational Police Deviance: Its Structure and Control.* Toronto, Canada: Butterworth and Company.

Sherman, L.W. (ed.). (1974). *Police Corruption: A Sociological Perspective.* New York: Doubleday and Company.

Simpson, A.E. (1977). *The Literature of Police Corruption.* Volume 1, "A Guide to Bibliography and Theory," New York: John Jay Press.

# Study Questions

1.  Why are law enforcement occupations inherently susceptible to opportunities for sexual harassment?

2.  What is the distinction, if any, between sexual harassment and sexually motivated behavior?

3.  Are non-sexual contacts initiated by the law enforcement officer always apparent to the victim? Why or why not? When is the victim most likely to complain?

4.  Why is a police officer unlikely to be caught when engaging in voyeuristic activities?

5.  Why do some victims of rape and sexual assault claim to have been "raped again" by the criminal justice system?

6.  Why do some citizens willingly exchange sexual favors in exchange for preferential treatment by police officers?

7.  How can we eliminate sexual misconduct and sexual harassment by police officers?

# 9

# POLICE LIES AND PERJURY: A MOTIVATION-BASED TAXONOMY*

## Thomas Barker and David L. Carter

Lying and other deceptive practices are an integral part of the police officer's working environment. At first blush, one's reaction to this statement might be rather forthright. Police officers should not lie. *If you can't trust your local police, who can you trust?* However, as with most issues, the matter is not that simple.

We are all aware that police officers create false identities for undercover operations. We know that they make false promises to hostage takers and kidnappers. We also know officers will strain the truth in order to spare the feelings of a crime victim and his/her loved ones. Police officers are trained to lie and be deceptive in these law enforcement practices. They are also trained to use techniques of interrogation which require deception and even outright lying.

Police officers learn much of this in the police academy, where they are also warned about the impropriety of perjury and the need to record all incidents fully and accurately in all official reports. The recruit learns that all rules and regulations must be obeyed. He/she learns of the danger of lying to internal affairs or a supervisor. The recruit is told to be truthful in his dealings with the non-criminal element of the public in that mutual trust is an important element in police community relations. Once the recruit leaves the academy—and some departments where officers work in the field before attending rookie school—the officer soon learns from his/her peers that police lying is the norm under certain circumstances.

Our purpose is to discuss the patterns of lying which might occur in a police organization, the circumstances under which they occur and the possible consequences of police lying.

## TAXONOMY OF POLICE LIES

### Accepted Lying

Certain forms of police lying and/or deception are an accepted part of the police officers working environment. The lies told in this category are accepted by

*This chapter was written expressly for inclusion in this book.*

the police organization because they fulfill a defined police purpose. Administrators and individual police officers believe that certain lies are necessary to control crime and to "arrest the guilty." In these instances, the organization will freely admit the intent to lie and define the acts as a legitimate policing strategy. On face value, most would agree with the police that lies in this category are acceptable and necessary. However, a troubling and difficult question is "to what extent, if at all, is it *proper* for law enforcement officials to employ trickery and deceit as part of their law enforcement practices (Skolnick, 1982, italics added)?" As we shall see, the answer to this question is not so easy. Acceptable lies may be very functional for the police but are they always proper, moral, ethical, and legal?

The most readily apparent patterns of "accepted" police lying are the deceptive practices that law enforcement officers believe are necessary to perform undercover operations or detect other forms of secret and consensual crimes. Police officers engaged in these activities must not only conceal their true identity but they must talk, act, and dress out of character, fabricating all kinds of stories in order to perform these duties. One could hardly imagine that FBI Special Agent Joseph Pistone could have operated for six years in the Mafia without the substantial number of lies that he had to tell (Pistone, 1987). However, the overwhelming majority of the undercover operations are neither as fascinating nor as dangerous as working six years with the Mafia or other organized crime groups. The most common police undercover operations occur in routine vice operations dealing with prostitution, bootlegging, gambling, narcotics, bribery of public officials (e.g., ABSCAM, MILAB, BRILAB) and sting operations.

These deceptive practices in undercover operations are not only acceptable to the law enforcement community but considered necessary for undercover operations to be effective. Nevertheless, such activities are not without problems. The "Dirty Harry" problem in police work raises the question as to what extent morally good police practices warrant or justify ethically, politically, or legally suspect means to achieve law enforcement objectives (Klockars, 1980). Marx also raises the issue that many of the tactics used by law enforcement officers in such recent undercover operations as ABSCAM, MILAB, BRILAB, police-run fencing or sting operations and anti-crime decoy squads may have lost sight of "the profound difference between carrying out an investigation to determine if a suspect is, in fact, breaking the law, and carrying it out to determine if an individual can be induced to break the law (Marx, 1985:106)." One congressman involved in the ABSCAM case refused the first offer of a cash bribe only later to accept the money after federal agents, concluding that he was an alcoholic, gave him liquor (Marx, 1985:104).

Encouraging the commission of a crime may be a legally accepted police practice when the officer acts as a willing victim or his/her actions facilitate the commission of a crime which was going to be committed in the first place.

However, it is possible for "encouragement" to lead the suspect to raise the defense of entrapment. According to *Black's Law Dictionary* entrapment is "the act of officers or agents of the government in inducing a person to commit a crime not contemplated by him, for the purpose of instituting a criminal prosecution against him (277)." For the defense of entrapment to prevail the defendant must show that the officer or his/her agent has gone beyond providing the encouragement and opportunity for the commission of a crime and through trickery, fraud, or other deception has induced the suspect to commit a crime. This defense is raised far more times than it is successful because the current legal criteria to determine entrapment is what is known as the "subjective test."

In the subjective test the predisposition of the offender, rather than the objective methods of the police, is the key factor in determining entrapment (Skolnick, 1982; Marx, 1985; Stitt and James, 1985). This makes it extremely difficult for a defendant with a criminal record to claim that he/she would not have committed the crime except for the actions of the officer. The "objective test" of entrapment raised by a minority of the Supreme Court has focused on the nature of the police conduct rather than the predisposition of the offender (Stitt and James, 1985). For example, the objective test probably would examine whether the production of crack by a police organization for use in undercover drug arrests is proper and legal. According to an Associated Press story, the Broward County Florida Sheriff's Department, not having enough crack to supply undercover officers, has started manufacturing their own crack. The sheriff's department chemist has made at least $20,000 worth of the illegal substance. Local defense attorneys have raised the issue of entrapment. In fact, one public defender stated:

> I think there's something sick about this whole system where the police make the product, sell the product and arrest people for buying the product (*Birmingham Post-Herald,* April 19, 1989:B2).

The issue of deception aside, this practice raises a number of ethical and legal issues concerning police practices. At what point do we draw the line to make a police undercover operation convincing?

In addition to the accepted practices of lying and deception required for undercover operations, members of the police community often believe that it is proper to lie to the media or the public when it is necessary to protect the innocent, protect the image of the department, or calm the public in crisis situations. The department's official policy may be one of openness and candor when dealing with the media. However, as a practical matter, members of the department may deny the existence of an investigation or "plant" erroneous information to protect an ongoing investigation (i.e., disinformation). The untimely revelation of facts may alert the suspects and drive them underground or cause them to cease their illegal activities. Nevertheless, one could argue that public exposure of certain criminal activities or the possibility of them might decrease the risk of injury to persons or property. This issue was raised in the recent terrorist bombing of PanAm Flight 103 over Lockerbie, Scotland. What was the best course of action? Tell the public of all threats against airliners—most of which were unfounded—and create fear? Or keep all threats confidential and hope that airline and government officials effectively deal with the threats?

In some crimes, such as kidnapping, the publication of accurate information, or any information at all, might lead to the murder of the victim. Therefore, under these circumstances, police administrators might view lies told to protect the victim as perfectly acceptable and necessary.

Police administrators are well aware of the possibility that the entire organization may be labeled deviant because of the deviant acts of its members. The "rotten apple" theory of police corruption has often been used as an impression management technique by police administrators who are aware of this possibility (Barker, 1977). It is easier to explain police deviance as a result of individual aberrations than to admit the possibility of systemic problems and invite public scrutiny. However, candor and public scrutiny may be the best way to insure that corruption and other forms of police deviance do not occur or continue in an organization (see Cooper and Belair, 1978).

Thus, accepted lies are those which the organization views as having a viable role in police operations. The criteria for the lie to be accepted are:

*It must be in furtherance of a legitimate organizational purpose.

*There must be a clear relationship between the need to deceive and the accomplishment of an organizational purpose.

*The nature of the deception must be one wherein officers and the management structure acknowledge that deception will better serve the public interest than the truth.

*The ethical standing of the deception and the issues of law appear to be collateral concerns.

## Tolerated Lying

A second category of police lies are those which are recognized as "lies" by the police organization but are tolerated as "necessary evils." Police administrators will admit to deception or "not exactly telling the whole truth" when confronted with the facts. These types of situational or "white" lies are truly in the gray area of propriety and the police can provide logical rationales for their use. When viewed from an ethical standpoint they may be "wrong," but from the police perspective they are necessary (i.e., tolerated) to achieve organizational objectives or deal with what Goldstein has termed the basic problems of police work (Goldstein, 1977:9).

The basic problems of police work arise from the mythology surrounding police work; e.g., statutes usually require and the public expects the police to enforce all the laws all the time, the public holds the police responsible for preventing crime and apprehending all criminals, the public views the police as being capable of handling all emergencies, etc. (Goldstein, 1977). Most police administrators will not publicly admit that they do not have the resources, the training or the authority to do some of the duties that the public expects. In fact, many police administrators and police officers lacking the education and insight into police work would be hard pressed to explain police work, particularly discretionary decision-making, to outside groups. Therefore they resort to lies and deception to support police practices.

Police administrators often deny that their departments practice anything less than full enforcement of all laws rather than attempt to explain the basis for police discretionary decisions and selective enforcement. We continually attempt to deal with social problems through the use of criminal sanctions and law enforcement personnel. Mandatory sentencing for all offenders committing certain felony and misdemeanor offenses is often seen as a panacea for these offenses. For example, in recent years many politically active groups such as Mothers Against Drunk Drivers (MADD) had pressured legislators for stronger laws with mandatory enforcement in drunk driving cases. However, their sentiment in cases not involving accidents may not be shared by the general public (Formby and Smykla, 1984) or the police. One can only speculate as to the number of discretionary decisions still being made by police officers in DUI offenses in departments where full enforcement is the official policy. One of the authors learned of an individual who had two DUI offenses reduced and asked a police supervisor about it.

> *Barker:* The chief has said that all DUI suspects are charged and those over the legal blood alcohol level never have the charge reduced. In fact, he said this at a MADD meeting. Yet, I heard that [      ] had two DUI offenses reduced.

> *Supervisor:* That is true Tom. However, [      ] is helping us with some drug cases. MADD may not understand but they do not have to make drug busts.

The point of note is that the police, in response to political pressure, make a policy on DUI cases and vow that the policy will be followed. However, in this case, that vow was broken. The police made a discretionary judgment that the assistance of the DUI offender in drug investigations was of greater importance than a DUI prosecution. Thus, this policy deviation was tantamount to a lie to the MADD membership—a lie tolerated by the police department.

The public also expects the police to handle any disorderly or emergency situations. The American public believes that one of the methods for handling any problem is "calling the cops" (Bittner, 1972). However, in many of these order-maintenance situations the police do not have the authority, resources or training to deal with the problem. They often face a situation "where something must be done now" yet an arrest is not legally possible or would be more disruptive. The officer is forced to reach into a bag of tricks for a method of dealing with the crisis. Lying to the suspects or the complainants is often that method. For example, police officers may tell noisy teenagers to move along or be arrested when the officers have neither the intention nor legal basis for an arrest. They often tell complainants that they will follow up on their complaint or turn it over to the proper agency when they have no intention of doing it. The police see these lies as a way of handling "nuisance work" that keeps them from doing "real police work" or as a way of dealing with a problem beyond their means. In these cases, the lie is used as a tool of expediency—arguably an abuse of police discretion but one which is tolerated.

In domestic disturbances police officers face volatile situations where the necessary conditions for an arrest often are not present. Frequently there is a misdemeanor where the officer does not have a warrant, an offense has not been committed in his/her presence, and the incident occurred in a private residence. However, the officer may feel that something must be done. Consequently, the officer may lie and threaten to arrest one or both combatants, or take one of the parties out to the street or the patrol car to discuss the incident and arrest them for disorderly conduct or public intoxication when they reach public property. Another option is to make an arrest appear legal. Obviously, the latter strategy will not be a tolerated pattern of lying. It would fall into the pattern of deviant lying to be discussed later.

Officers soon learn that the interrogation stage of an arrest is an area where certain lies are tolerated and even taught to police officers. The now-famous *Miranda v. Arizona* case decided by the U.S. Supreme Court in 1966 quoted excerpts from Inbau and Reid's *Criminal Interrogation and Confession* text to show that the police used deception and psychologically coercive methods in their interrogation of suspects (George 1966:155-266). The latest edition of this same text gives examples of deceptive and lying practices for...skilled interrogators to engage in (Inbau, Reid, Buckley, 1986).

As an illustration of these techniques, the reader is told that the interrogator should put forth a facade of sincerity so convincingly that "moisture may actually appear in his eyes" (p. 52). Another recommended effective practice of deception is that the interrogator have a *simulated* evidence case folder on hand during the course of the interrogation if an actual case file does not exist (p. 54). The interrogator may also make inferences such as a large number of investigators are working on the case and drew the same evidentiary conclusion about the suspect's guilt, even if, in reality, the interrogator is the only person working the case (p. 85). The inference is that the case against the suspect is strong because of the number of people involved in the investigation and the consequent weight of the evidence.

One particularly troublesome piece of advice for interviewing rape suspects is that:

> Where circumstances permit, the suggestion might be offered that the rape victim had acted like she might have been a prostitute and that the suspect had assumed she was a willing partner. In fact, the interrogator may even say that the police knew she had engaged in prostitution on other occasions...(p. 109).

As a final illustration, the book notes that an effective means to interrogate multiple suspects of a crime is "playing one offender against the other." In this regard it is suggested that the "interrogator may merely intimate to one offender that the other has confessed, or else the interrogator *may actually tell the offender so*" (emphasis added, p. 132).

It is difficult to say whether or not these tolerated forms of lying are "wrong"—many investigators would argue that they are not really "lies" but good interrogation techniques. One could also argue that the ends justifies the means as long as the actions of the officers are not illegal. However, one can hypothesize that deception in one context increases the probability of deception in other contexts (c.f., Skolnick, 1982: Stitt and James, 1985). As a veteran police officer told one of the authors while they were discussing ways to convince a suspect to agree to a consent search...

*Barker:* That sure sounds like telling a lot of lies.

*Officer:* It is not police lying; it is an art. After all, the criminal has constitutional protection. He can lie through his teeth. Why not us? What is fair is fair.

This attitude, which is borne in the frustrations of many officers, sets a dangerous precedent for attitudes related to civil liberties. When law enforcement officers begin to tolerate lies because it serves their ends—regardless of constitutional and ethical implications of those lies—then fundamental elements of civil rights are threatened.

## Deviant Police Lying

The last example raises the possibility of the third category of policy lying—deviant lies. After all, "he (the suspect) can lie through his teeth. Why not us?" Deviant police lies are those which violate substantive or procedural law and/or police department rules and regulations. The deviant lies which violate substantive or procedural law are improper and should not be permitted. However, organization members (including supervisors), and other actors in the criminal justice system are often aware of their occurrence. Noted defense attorney Alan Dershowitz states that police lying is well known by actors in the criminal justice system. He clearly illustrates these as the "Rules of the Justice Game." In part, the rules include:

Rule IV:    Almost all police lie about whether they violated the Constitution in order to convict guilty defendants.

Rule V:     All prosecutors, judges, and defense attorneys are aware of Rule IV.

Rule VI:    Many prosecutors implicitly encourage police to lie about whether they violated the Constitution in order to convict guilty defendants.

Rule VII:   All judges are aware of Rule VI.

Rule VIII:  Most trial judges pretend to believe police officers who they know are lying.

Rule IX:    All appellate judges are aware of Rule VIII, yet many pretend to believe the trial judges who pretend to believe the lying police officers. (Dershowitz, 1983: xxi-xxii).

This may be an extreme position. However, other criminal defense attorneys believe that the police will lie in court. In fact, one study concluded that "the possibility of police perjury is a part of the working reality of criminal defense attorneys" (Kittel, 1986:20). Fifty-seven percent of the 277 attorneys surveyed in this study believed that police perjury takes place very often or often (Kittel, 1986:16). Police officers themselves have reported that they believe their fellow officers will lie in court (Barker, 1978). An English barrister believes that police officers have perjured themselves on an average of three out of ten trials (Wolchover, 1986).

As part of the research for this chapter, one of the authors asked an Internal Affairs (IA) investigator of a major U.S. police department about officer lying:

*Carter:* During the course of IA investigations, do you detect officers lying to you?

*IA Investigator:* Yes, all the time. They'll lie about anything, everything.

*Carter:* Why is that?

*IA Investigator:* To tell me what I want to hear. To help them get out of trouble. To make themselves feel better—rationalizing I guess. They're so used to lying on the job, I guess it becomes second nature.

An analysis of deviant lies reveals that the intent of the officer in telling deviant lies may be either in support of perceived legitimate goals, or illegitimate goals.

## Deviant Lies in Support of Perceived Legitimate Goals

The deviant lies told by the officer to achieve perceived legitimate goals usually occur to put criminals in jail, prevent crime, and perform various other policing responsibilities. The police officer believes that because of his/her unique experiences in dealing with criminals and the public he/she knows the guilt or innocence of those they arrest (Manning, 1978). Frequently, officers feel this way independently of any legal standards. However, the final determination of guilt or innocence is in the judicial process. The officer(s), convinced that the suspect is factually guilty of the offense, may believe that necessary elements of legal guilt are lacking, e.g., no probable cause for a "stop," no *Miranda* warning, not enough narcotics for a felony offense, etc. Therefore, the officer feels that he/she must supply the missing elements. One police officer told one of the authors that it is often necessary to "fluff up the evidence" to get a search warrant or insure conviction. The officer will attest to facts, statements, or evidence which never occurred or occurred in a different fashion. Obviously when he/she does this under oath, perjury has then been committed. Once a matter of record, the perjury must continue for the officer to avoid facing disciplinary action and even criminal prosecution.

Charges were dropped in a case against an accused cop killer and three Boston police officers were suspended with pay pending a perjury investigation. The perjury involved a Boston detective who "invented" an informant. The detective maintained that the informant gave critical information which was cited in the affidavit for a search warrant (*New York Times,* 1989:K9). The "no knock" search warrant's execution led to the death of a Boston detective. Similarly, the officer(s) who lies in these instances must employ creative writing skills in official reports to ensure that the written chronology of events are consistent with criminal procedures regardless of what actually occurred.

These lies are rationalized by the officer because they are necessary to ensure that criminals do not get off on technicalities. A central reason for these deviant lies is officer frustration. There is frustration with the criminal justice system because of the inability of courts and corrections to handle large caseloads. Frustration with routinized practices of plea negotiations and intricate criminal procedures which the officer may not fully understand. The officer sees the victims of crimes and has difficulty in reconciling the harm done to them with the wide array of due process protections afforded to defendants. Nevertheless, the officer has fallen into "the avenging angel syndrome" where the end justifies the means. The officer can easily rationalize lying and perjury to accomplish what is perceived to be the right thing. The officer's views are short-sighted and provincial. There is no recognition that such behavior is a threat to civil liberties and that perjury is as fundamentally improper as the criminal behavior of the accused.

## Deviant Lies in Support of Illegitimate Goals

Lies in this category are told to effect an act of corruption or to protect the officer from organizational discipline or civil and/or criminal liability. Deviant lies may be manifest in police perjury as the officer misrepresents material elements of an arrest or search in order to "fix" a criminal prosecution for a monetary reward. Lying and/or perjury in court is an absolute necessity in departments where corrupt acts occur on a regular basis. Sooner or later every police officer who engages in corrupt acts or observes corrupt acts on the part of other officers will face the possibility of having to lie under oath to protect him/herself or fellow officers. Skolnick has suggested that perjury and corruption are both systematic forms of police deviance which occur for the same sort of reason: "Police know that other police are on the take and police know that other police are perjuring themselves" (Skolnick, 1982:42).

It is also possible that other forms of police deviance will lead to deviant lying. For example, the officer who commits an act of police brutality may have to lie on the report to his/her supervisor and during testimony to avoid the possibility of criminal sanction, a civil lawsuit, or department charges. The officer who has sex on duty, sleeps or drinks on duty may have to lie to a supervisor or internal affairs to avoid department discipline. The officer who causes an injury or death to a suspect which is not strictly according to law or police policy may have to lie to protect himself or his fellow officers from criminal and/or civil liability.

As an illustration, one of the authors assisted a police department which was under a federal court injunction related to an extensive number of civil rights violations for excessive force and harassment. During one series of inquiries, the following conversation occurred:

> *Carter:* Did you ever talk to other accused officers before giving your deposition in these cases?

> *Officer:* Of course. [NOTE: The tone of the response was almost incredulous.]

> *Carter:* Would you discuss the facts of the allegation?

> *Officer:* Sure. We had to be sure our stories were straight.

The implications from these statements and the continued conversations were clear: Officers were willing to lie during the sworn deposition to protect themselves and others. They would swear to the truth of facts which were plainly manufactured for their protection. Moreover, their remorse was not that they lied, but that they got caught in misconduct. Similarly, a police chief in West Virginia recently told a federal judge he lied to investigators in order to cover up for four officers accused of beating handcuffed prisoners (*Law Enforcement News,* March 15, 1989, p. 2). Again, the illegitimate goal of "protection" surfaces as a motive for lying.

The typical police bureaucracy is a complex organization with a myriad of rules and regulations. The informal organization, including many supervisors, overlooks these rules until someone decides to "nail someone." Given the plethora of rules and regulations in most large urban police departments it is virtually impossible to work a shift without violating one. It may be common practice to eat a free meal, leave one's beat for personal reasons, not wear one's hat when out of the car, to live outside the city limits, etc. All of these acts may be forbidden by a policy, rule, or regulation. When a supervisor decides to discipline an officer for violating one of these acts, the officer, and often fellow officers, may resort to lies to protect themselves and each other. After all, such "minor" lies are inherent in the "Blue Code." Manning observes that rule enforcement by police supervisors represents a mock bureaucracy where ritualistic and punitive enforcement is applied after the fact (Manning, 1978). The consequences of these seemingly understandable lies can be disastrous when discovered. The officer(s) may be suspended, reduced in rank, or dismissed. The same organization where members routinely engage in acceptable, tolerated, and deviant lying practices can take on a very moralistic attitude when it discovers that one of its own has told a lie to avoid internal discipline. Nevertheless, the lies told in these examples are told in support of the illegitimate goal of avoiding departmental discipline.

# CONCLUSION

The effects of lying, even those which are acceptable or tolerated, are multi-fold. Lies can and do create distrust within the organization. When the public learns members of the police department lie or engage in deceptive practices, this can undermine citizen confidence in the police. As we have seen, some police lies violate citizen's civil rights and others are told to cover up civil rights violations. Police lying contributes to police misconduct and corruption and undermines the organization's discipline system. Furthermore, deviant police lies undermine the effectiveness of the criminal justice system. What should the organization do to deal with the reality of police lies? An important first step is to establish a meaningful code of ethics and value statements for the organization. Importantly, this should go beyond the development of documents. The operational and managerial levels of the police department must know that the code of ethics and value statements are guides to police moral and ethical behavior. There should never become another set of rules and procedures to be used when necessary to "nail someone." Once ethics and values are embodied, it is essential to develop a support structure consisting of directives, training, and supervision. This will create a moral environment throughout the organization and establish parameters of acceptable behavior giving notice to employees about management.

# REFERENCES

Barker, T. (1978). "An Empirical Study of Police Deviance Other Than Corruption," *Journal of Police Science and Administration* (6:3): 264-272.

_____ (1977). "Peer Group Support for Police Occupational Deviance," *Criminology* (15:3): 353-366.

Bittner, E. (1971). *The Functions of the Police in Modern Society,* Washington, DC: U.S. Government Printing Office.

*Birmingham Post-Herald* (1988). "Sheriff's Chemist Makes Crack," April 19: B2.

Black, H.C. (1983). *Black's Law Dictionary,* Abridged Fifth Edition. St. Paul, MN: West Publishing Co.

Cooper, G.R. and R.R. Belair (1978). *Privacy and Security of Criminal History Information: Privacy and the Media.* U.S. Department of Justice. Washington, DC: U.S. Government Printing Office.

Dershowitz, A.M. (1983). *The Best Defense,* New York: Vintage Books.

Formby, W.A. and J.O. Smykla (1984). "Attitudes and Perception Toward Drinking and Driving: A Simulation of Citizen Awareness." *Journal of Police Science and Administration* (12:4): 379-384.

George, J.B. (1966). *Constitutional Limitations on Evidence in Criminal Cases.* Ann Arbor, Michigan: Institute of Continuing Legal Education.

Goldstein, H. (1977). *Policing A Free Society.* Cambridge, MA: Ballinger Publishing Company.

Inbau, F.E., J.E. Reid and J.P. Buckley (1986). *Criminal Interrogation and Confessions, 3rd Ed.,* Baltimore, MD: Williams and Wilkins.

Kittel, N.G. (1986). "Police Perjury: Criminal Defense Attorneys' Perspective," *American Journal of Criminal Justice* (XI:1) (Fall): 11-22.

Klockars, C.B. (1980). "The Dirty Harry Problem," *The Annals,* 452 (November): 33-47.

*Law Enforcement News* (1989). March 15: 2.

Manning, P.K. (1978). "Lying Secrecy and Social Control." In P.K. Manning and John Van Maanen (Eds.) *Policing: A View from The Street,* Santa Monica, CA: Goodyear Publishing Co. 238-255.

Marx, G.T. (1985). "Who Really Gets Stung? Some Issues Raised By The New Police Undercover Work." In Elliston, F.A. and M. Feldberg (Eds.) *Moral Issues in Police Work.* Totowa, NJ: Rowan and Allanheld.

*New York Times* (1989). "Dead Officer, Dropped Charges: A Scandal in Boston," March 20: K9.

Pistone, J.D. (1987). *Donnie Brasco: My Undercover Life in the Mafia.* New York, NY: Nail Books.

Skolnick, J. (1982). "Deception By Police," *Criminal Justice Ethics,* 1(2), (Summer/Fall): 40-54.

Stitt, B.G. and G.G. James (1985). "Entrapment An Ethical Analysis" in Elliston, F.A. and M. Feldberg (Eds.) *Moral Issues in Police Work.* Totowa, NJ: Rowman and Allanheld.

Wolchover, D. (1986). "Police Perjury in London." *New Law Journal* (Feb.): 180-184.

## Study Questions

1. Before you read this chapter, did you think that police officers lied? What was the basis for your opinion? How has the material in this chapter changed your opinion?

2. What did you find as the most surprising aspect of police officer lying presented in this chapter? Why did you find this surprising?

3. Do you think that any police officer lying should be "tolerated" as described in this chapter? Why or why not?

4. What is your personal opinion about deviant lies in support of legitimate goals? Can you empathize with the officers' rationale? Could you ever justify a police officer lying in order to prosecute a known dangerous criminal?

5. Assume you are a police officer just off probation riding with a veteran officer of 20 years on the department. During your shift you witness the veteran officer strike a criminal suspect a few times in order to get the criminal "to talk." The suspect says he's going to file a complaint. The veteran officer says to you, "Here's the story we tell internal affairs. You know how cops have got to stick together on things like this." Would you tell the investigators what you saw? Why or why not? How do you think you would feel during the internal investigation?

# 10

# DECEPTION BY POLICE*

## Jerome H. Skolnick

The ideal of legality implies that those convicted of crimes will not only be factually guilty but legally guilty. A political commitment to legality is, after all, what distinguishes democratic governments from totalitarian. Yet for every ideal, there seems to be a practical challenge. The ideal of right to bail is challenged by the reality of the criminal's dangerousness, the presumption of innocence by the reality of factual guilt, the right to counsel by the triviality of certain offenses, or the difficulties of providing counsel to those who have just been informed of their privilege against self-incrimination. Hard and fast rules limiting police conduct may challenge common sense, while the absence of such rules may invite arbitrary and abusive conduct. This paper discusses one of the most troubling and difficult questions pertaining to the ideal of legality: To what extent, if at all, is it proper for law enforcement officials to employ trickery and deceit as part of their law enforcement practices?[1]

Whatever the answer to that question—if, indeed an answer can be formulated—it has to be measured against a hard reality of the criminal justice system. That reality is that deception is to detection as pouncing is to a cat. As we shall see, that is why it is so difficult both to control deceptive practices of detectives and to prescribe long-term measures to guarantee control.

A seminal, thought-provoking attempt has been made in Sissela Bok's important book on lying (Bok, 1978). Bok does not deal explicitly with deception by detectives, as she does with deception by social scientists. However, she does refer to certain police practices in what must be regarded as the central chapter of her book—that on justification of deception, where she introduces standards for backing away from Kantian categorical imperative.[2] Essentially, she argues for combining two standards for justifiable deception, insisting, first on a *public* offering of justification for a lie and, second on having the justification offered to an audience of *reasonable persons*. The chapter goes on to develop these notions in creative and original ways, but does not fully develop the implications of her guidelines for the detecting process. I would like to offer some observations, which have been stimulated by her analysis, about the detecting process itself.

*Reprinted from *Criminal Justice Ethics* 1 (2), Summer/Fall 1982:40-54.

# THE NORMATIVE CONTEXT OF DETECTING

Detecting occurs in the context of fluid moral constraints that are circum-scribed by a tradition of due process of law, by ever-changing and not altogether clear interpretations of individual rights offered by the courts, and by the social organization of policing that develops its own moral norms and constraints. Finally, this amalgam of normative prescription is set within the context of an adversary system of justice.

If all that sounds complicated and confusing, it is. It suggests that, because of the multiple contexts of police action, there are unstable, even contradictory, norms. Is detecting to be considered akin to a poker game, where the players understand that deception is part of the game? It surely is not like the doctor-client, or even the social scientist-subject relationship. The detective is not treat-ing the subject, nor is the detective merely observing.

The detective deceives in order to establish grounds for convicting and punishing. The detecting process is informed and controlled by notions of fairness and dignity, but these notions, as embodied by law, are often unclear both in outcome and justification. The law often, but not always, supports police decep-tion. The law permits the detective to pose as a consumer or purveyor of vice,[3] but does not allow the policeman to employ certain ruses to gain entry without a search warrant,[4] or to obtain a search warrant with a false affidavit.[5] The police subculture—the workday normative order of police—permits, and sometimes demands, deception of courts, prosecutors, defense attorneys, and defendants but rarely, if ever, allows for deception of fellow policemen.[6] Police thus work within a severe, but often agonizingly contradictory, moral order which demands certain kinds of fidelities and insists upon other kinds of betrayals. The police milieu is normatively contradictory, almost to the point of being schizophrenic. Norms regarding deception, written and implied, abound in this moral order.

# THE STAGES OF DETECTING

Deception occurs at three stages of the detecting process: investigation, interrogation, and testimony. If we place these three stages within the framework of a broad portrait of the moral cognition of the policeman, we observe that the acceptability of deception varies inversely with the level of the criminal process. Thus, deception is most acceptable to police—as it is to the courts—at the investigation stage, less acceptable during interrogation, and least acceptable in the courtroom.

If we inquire as to why that should be, the answer seems fairly obvious. Each stage is related to a set of increasingly stringent normative constraints. Courtroom testimony is given under oath, and is supposed to be the truth, the whole truth, and nothing but the truth. Nobody is supposed to lie in a courtroom. When a policeman lies in court, he may be able to justify his deception on the basis of an alternative set of normative judgments (assuming that he is acting as a prosecution witness and is not himself the defendant), but he is still aware that courtroom lying violates the basic norms of the system he is sworn to uphold. Nevertheless, police do lie in the courtroom, particularly when they believe that judicial interpretations of constitutional limits on police practices are ill conceived or overly constraining in that they interfere with the policeman's ability to do his or her job as the police subculture defines it.

I shall argue in this paper that courtroom lying is justified within the police culture by the same sort of necessity rationale that courts have permitted police to employ at the investigative stage: The end justifies the means. Within an adversary system of criminal justice, governed by due process rules for obtaining evidence, the policeman will thus lie to get at the truth. The contradiction may be surprising, but it is sometimes inevitable in an adversary system of justice where police perceive procedural due process norms and legal requirements as inconsistent obstacles to truth and the meting out of just deserts for the commission of crime.

## Testimonial Deception

As I have indicated, it is difficult to prove a causal relationship between permissible investigative and interrogatory deception and testimonial deception. Police freely admit to deceiving suspects and defendants (Skolnick, 1975). They do not admit to perjury, much less to the rationalization of perjury.

### TABLE 10.1
### NEW YORK CITY POLICE OFFICERS' ALLEGATIONS REGARDING DISCOVERY OF EVIDENCE IN MISDEMEANOR NARCOTICS OFFENSES, 1960-1962

| HOW EVIDENCE FOUND | PERCENT OF ARRESTS | | |
|---|---|---|---|
| | Six-month Period | | |
| | Before *Mapp* | After *Mapp* | Difference |
| I. Narcotics Bureau | | | |
| (a) Hidden on person | 35 | 3 | 32 |
| (b) Dropped or thrown to ground | 17 | 43 | + 26 |
| II. Uniform | | | |
| (a) Hidden on person | 31 | 9 | 22 |
| (b) Dropped or thrown to ground | 14 | 21 | + 7 |
| III. Plainclothes | | | |
| (a) Hidden on person | 24 | 4 | − 20 |
| (b) Dropped or thrown to ground | 11 | 17 | + 6 |

Original source: Comment, "Effect of *Mapp v. Ohio* on Police Search and Seizure Practices in Narcotics Cases." *Col. J. Law & Social Problems* 4 (1968:94).

There is evidence, however, of the acceptability of perjury as a means to the end of conviction. The evidence is limited and fragmentary and is certainly not dispositive. However, the evidence does suggest not only that a policeman will perjure himself—no surprise there—but that perjury, like corruption, does not lend itself to "rotten apple" explanations.[7] Perjury, I would suggest, like corruption, is systematic, and for much the same sort of reason—police know that other police are on the take, and police know that other police are perjuring themselves. The following two items of evidence suggest that perjury represents a subcultural norm rather than an individual aberration.

Scholarly evidence of testimonial lying was revealed in a study conducted by Columbia law students in which they analyzed the effect of *Mapp v. Ohio*[8] on police practices in New York City. In *Mapp*, the Supreme Court held that the federal exclusionary rule in search-and-seizure cases was binding on the states. New York was the only large state that had not previously adopted the exclusionary rule as a matter of state law. (The exclusionary rule, of course, suppresses at trial evidence that was illegally obtained—usually in violation of the Fourth Amendment.) The students analyzed the evidentiary grounds for arrest and subsequent disposition of misdemeanor narcotics cases before and after the *Mapp* decision. Based on officers' accounts of the evidence for the arrest (see Table 10.1), the student authors concluded that:

> ...uniform police have been fabricating grounds of arrest in narcotics cases in order to circumvent the requirements of *Mapp*. Without knowledge of the results of this study, the two Criminal Courts judges and the two Assistant District Attorneys interviewed doubted that a substantial reform of police practices had occurred since *Mapp*. Rather, they believe that police officers are fabricating evidence to avoid *Mapp*.[9]

Such lies came to be known as "dropsy" testimony since the police testified that those charged with drug possession were now dropping illicit drugs on the ground rather than keeping them where they were. Prior to *Mapp*, evidence obtained from unlawful searches of the person was admissible, even when illegally obtained. New York State was governed by the famous 1926 dictum of Judge Cardozo, who, while he was on the bench of the New York Court of Appeals, had dismissed the federal rule with the observation that under it "the criminal is to go free because the constable had blundered."[10] Obviously, the New York police had not been blundering prior to *Mapp*. Instead, they simply and routinely ignored the requirements to the Fourth Amendment.

In a more popular account, Robert Daley's fascinating *Prince of the City,* the former New York Deputy Police Commissioner writes of a surveillance showing that, on the one hand, defendants were guilty of hijacking television sets, and, on the other, the cops were stealing some of the hijacked sets. The evidence was obtained through a legal wiretap. The detectives erased that part of the tape proving that the precinct cops had stolen some of the sets. Daley writes, "Tomorrow they would deny the erasure under oath...It was the type of perjury that detectives...committed all the time in the interest of putting bad people in jail." (Daley, 1978).

The point here is not whether to deplore the police violations of the Fourth Amendment or the lying of police in the testimonial context; rather, it is to understand how police who engage in it themselves come to justify it, so that moral prescriptions might be given a better chance of being persuasive to police who do not find them compelling in practice.

The policeman lies because lying becomes a routine way of managing legal impediments—whether to protect fellow officers or to compensate for what he views as limitations the courts have placed on his capacity to deal with criminals. He lies because he is skeptical of a system that suppresses truth in the interest of the criminal. Moreover, the law permits the policeman to lie at the investigative stage, when he is not entirely convinced that the suspect is a criminal, but forbids lying about *procedures* at the testimonial stage, when the policeman is certain of the guilt of the accused. Thus, the policeman characteristically measures the short-term disutility of the act of suppressing evidence, not the long-term utility of due process of law for protecting and enhancing the dignity of the citizen who is being investigated by the state.

I quote at this point from a passage in *Justice Without Trial* which recent discussions with police persuade me is still essentially valid:

> The policeman...operates as one whose aim is to legitimize the evidence pertaining to the case, rather than as a jurist whose goal is to analyze the sufficiency of the evidence based on case law...

> The policeman respects the necessity for "complying" with the arrest laws. His "compliance," however, may take the form of post hoc manipulation of the facts rather than before-the-fact behavior. Again, this generalization does not apply in all cases. Where the policeman feels capable of literal compliance (as in the conditions provided by the "big case"), he does comply. But when he sees the case law as a hindrance to his primary task of apprehending criminals, he usually attempts to construct the appearance of compliance, rather than allowing the offender to escape apprehension. (Skolnick, 1975).

As I stated earlier, I am not aware of an ethical theory that would condone perjured testimony. Bok's standards for justifying deception would provide a useful guideline here, because the lying policeman would be required to justify courtroom perjury before a relevant public. This is precisely the sort of test I think

Bok had in mind. Although police might justify perjury to each other over drinks after work, or in the corridors of the locker room, I can scarcely imagine any policeman willing to justify such conduct in a public setting—unless he was perhaps on a television talk show wearing a mask and wig. But any hesitation on the part of an officer to testify could be caused by fear of a perjury charge, not by moral scruples about lying in courtroom situations where criminals might go free.

## Investigative Deception

Let us examine more closely the rationale for lying at the investigative stage. Here, police are permitted by the courts to engage in trickery and deception and are trained to do so by the police organization. One might properly conclude, from examining police practices that have been subjected to the highest appellate review, that the police are authoritatively encouraged to lie.[11]

Detectives, for example, are trained to use informers or to act themselves as informers or agent provocateurs when the criminal activity under investigation involves possession or sale of contraband. The contraband itself does not much matter. From an enforcement perspective, the problems involved in apprehending those who sell counterfeit money are almost identical to those involved in trapping dealers of illegal drugs. Years ago, when I studied a vice squad intensively, the squad was asked to help the United States Secret Service in apprehending a counterfeiting ring. They were asked because vice squads are especially experienced in law enforcement practices involving use of informants, deception, security of information, and, most generally, the apprehension of offenders whose criminality is proven by the possession for sale of illegal materials. A similar point can be made with respect to burglary enforcement. Victims (or police) rarely observe burglars in action. In fact, burglars are usually apprehended when detectives are able to employ a decoy or an informer who tells them that so-and-so is in possession of stolen goods.

The line between acceptable and unacceptable deception in such enforcement patterns is the line between so-called entrapment and acceptable police conduct. How does the law presently define entrapment? From my reading, the definition is hazy, murky, unclear. Two approaches are employed in legal writing about entrapment. One, the subjective approach, focuses upon the background, character, and intention of the defendant. Was he or she the sort of person who would have been predisposed to have committed the crime, even without the participation of the government official or agent? The objective test, by contrast, sets its sights on the nature of governmental participation. Justice Frankfurter, concurring in *Sherman v. United States*, presented the objective test as follows: "The crucial question, not easy to answer, to which the court must direct itself is whether police conduct revealed in the particular cases falls below standards, to which common feelings respond, for the proper use of governmental power."[12] More recently, *United States v. Russell*, Justice Rehnquist wrote the majority opinion affirming the prevailing rule—the subjective test—in a case where an undercover agent from the Federal Bureau of Narcotics and Dangerous Drugs told the suspect that he represented an organization that was interested in controlling the manufacture and distribution of methamphetamine.[13] The narcotics agent offered to supply Russell with a chemical that was an essential, hard-to-find ingredient in the manufacture of methamphetamine in return for half of the drug produced. The agent told Russell that he had to be shown a sample of the drug in the laboratory where it was produced before he would go through with the deal.

Russell showed him the laboratory and told the agent he and others had been making the drug for quite some time. The agent left and returned to the laboratory with the necessary chemical and watched while the suspects produced the drug. The narcotics agent did not actively participate in the manufacturing of the drug but he was courteous and helpful to those who did. When a suspect dropped some aluminum foil on the floor, it was testified, the narcotics agent picked it up and put it into the cooker.

The majority of the court held that Russell was not "entrapped" because he had been an active participant in an illegal drug manufacturing enterprise that began before the government agent appeared on the scene and continued after the government agent left the scene. Russell was not an "unwary innocent," but rather, an "unwary criminal." The subjective test, in short, permits police to engage in deceptive practices provided that the deception catches a wolf rather than a lamb.[14]

The objective test, focusing on the activities of the government, seems to suggest a more high-minded vision of the limits of police deception. By a high-minded vision, I mean to suggest one which conceives of significant limitations on police conduct in the interest of maintaining a civilized or moral constabulary. For example, a civilized police officer should not be permitted to torture a suspect in order to obtain a confession, even if it should turn out that the tortured party was an unwary criminal, that is, even if torture should produce the truth.[15] Nor, to cite a real case, would an officer be permitted to pump the stomach of a suspected narcotics dealer to show that the pills he had just swallowed contained morphine, even if that is exactly what the pills did contain.[16]

However, the objective test may lose its objectivity when it relies on such concepts as "common feelings" or the "conscience of the community" (Rossum, 1978). Although these concepts seem to imply enduring qualities or values, one could also argue that such concepts are variables. "Common feelings" might allow for far more latitude in police practices in a "high fear of crime" period than in a "low fear" period. Some might argue that values should be tested in the crucible of experience, and that flexibility is itself a virtue. The trouble is that one person's flexibility may be interpreted as another's lack of principle.

Moreover, "common feelings" may not be informative when we consider particular examples. I am reminded of a passage in Arthur Schlesinger's biography of Robert Kennedy, where Schlesinger tries to resolve the issue of whether Kennedy really knew about FBI wiretapping when he was Attorney General. Schlesinger relates a conversation between J. Edgar Hoover and Kennedy, where Hoover tells Kennedy that he had the situation "covered" (Schlesinger, 1978). According to Schlesinger, Hoover felt that he had thus informed Kennedy of the wiretap, while Kennedy took the term "cover" to mean that a secret government informant had worked his way into the suspect's entourage.

Assuming for the purposes of argument that Kennedy did not know about the wiretapping, by what principle is a wiretap or electronic bug to be considered less morally acceptable than a secret informant?[17] A wiretap or bug clearly invades expectations of privacy. But wiretaps and bugs enjoy two advantages over secret informants. First, the evidence they report as to what the defendant did or did not say is trustworthy. Second, and perhaps more important, a bug cannot encourage lawbreaking: it can neither advocate nor condone such conduct. It is not clear to the author how an objective standard would distinguish between the two, and it is genuinely puzzling as to why informants are usually thought to be morally acceptable, while bugs are not. Indeed, an argument could be made that when the government attempts to modify dispositions (by employing secret informants who worm their way into the confidence of suspects, for example), that this is more violative of human dignity than the involuntary extraction of evidence from the body, even through stomach pumping. At least one whose stomach is being pumped can identify his adversary, while the secret informant "messes with the mind," as it were.

In any event, for the purpose of a more general argument, it is enough to acknowledge that both legal tests of entrapment—objective and subjective— permit police to employ an enormous amount of routine deception, although the prevailing subjective test permits even more. Even in the dissenting opinion in *Russell*, Justice Stewart, supporting the objective test, writes that "the government's use of undercover activity, strategy, or deception is [not] necessarily unlawful. Indeed, many crimes, especially so-called victimless crimes, could not be otherwise detected.[18] In short, police are routinely permitted and advised to employ deceptive techniques and strategies in the investigative process. The police may in the real world deal mostly with wolves—and in the eyes of the courts the wolf might be wearing the clothing of either a congressman or a cocaine dealer.

Judicial permissiveness regarding investigative deception suggests how difficult it would be to defend a Kantian imperative against lying even in the abstract and how impossible it would be for any such defense to be accepted by courts, police, and the public. I shall conclude this discussion of investigative deception by suggesting a hypothesis: Judicial acceptance of deception in the investigation process enhances moral acceptance of deception by detectives in the interrogatory and testimonial stages of criminal investigation, and thus increases the probability of its occurrence.

This hypothesis does not suggest that every detective who deceives also perjures himself. It does suggest that deception in one context increases the probability of deception in the other. This hypothesis cannot be tested, and therefore may not hold. It cannot be tested because a true test would require an environmental design where we could manipulate the independent variable (authoritative permission to employ investigative trickery) and measure the dependent variable (courtroom perjury by police). Since we can neither manipulate the former nor measure the latter, the hypothesis, however plausible, must remain speculative.

## Interrogatory Deception

In the remainder of this chapter, I shall assume that the previously mentioned hypothesis is plausible and organize discussion around it. Thus, let us turn our attention to deception and interrogation—and here I shall confine my remarks to in-custody interrogation, although I recognize that the line between *custody* and *precustody* is unclear, and that the one between *conversation* and *interrogation* is also unclear. For the present, I simply want to make a historical reference to the in-custody interrogation problem which *Miranda v. Arizona,* decided in 1966, sought to resolve.[19] The holding of *Miranda* has now become so familiar as to be part of American folklore. The case held that the arrested person must be informed of his or her right to remain silent, must be warned that any statement he or she does make may be used as evidence, and must be told that he or she has the right to the presence of an attorney. The accused should also be informed that an attorney will be provided if he or she cannot afford one. The court also held that the government has a "heavy burden" to prove that a waiver of such rights was made voluntarily, knowingly, and intelligently.[20]

The *Miranda* decision was the evolutionary outcome of the Supreme Court's response to the admission, in state and federal courts, of confessions which, in the early part of the century, were based on overt torture, later, on covert torture (the third degree), and later still on deception and psychological intimidation. Overt torture is exemplified by the facts in *Brown v. Mississippi* where black defendants were beaten and whipped until they confessed. By 1936, the Supreme Court could no longer overlook the glaring fact that a confession so elicited was deemed admissible by the Supreme Court of the State of Mississippi.

But punitive in-custody interrogation was, of course, not confined to the South. The 1931 Wickersham Commission reported numerous instances of covert torture in many cities between 1920 and 1930.[21] The chief distinction between covert and overt torture is not in the severity of pain induced, but in its deniability. The Mississippi sheriffs did not deny whipping their black suspects. They were brutal, but truthful. By contrast, the third degree classically involved deniable coercion: starving suspects, keeping them awake day and night, confining them in pitch-black airless rooms, or administering beatings with instruments which left few, if any, marks. For example, a suspect might be hit over the head with a blackjack (though a telephone book would be placed between the blackjack and the head), or he might be hit with a rubber hose (Hopkins, 1931, 1972).

Other types of in-custody interrogation might evoke forms of torture even more terrifying, but also more deniable. Detectives in one police department reportedly hanged suspects from their heels outside windows of tall buildings to induce confessions. Others simply required that defendants stand erect and be forbidden use of bathroom facilities. The dramatic impact of the sadism of the third degree[22] has tended to obscure the fact that, in using it, the police necessarily condoned systematic deception in the courts, as well as torture of suspects. Thus, not only did the police subculture's norms of the period permit station house physical punishment of those whom the police might have felt deserved it, these norms also condoned wholesale perjury—disregard of the moral authority of the courts and of the oaths taken in them.[23]

*Miranda* overruled *Crooker v. California* and *Cicenia v. LaGay*[25] both of which were cases where the accused asked to see a lawyer after he agreed to be interrogated. In Cicenia's case, not only did he ask to see a lawyer, but his lawyer, who had arrived at the police station, had asked to see his client. *Miranda* might well be interpreted as a case where the Supreme Court was concerned not only with whether a confession was coerced—that had long been a concern of the courts—but whether the right of the accused not to be coerced was being effectuated properly in the context of the adversary system. The dissenters in *Crooker*—Douglas, Warren, Black, and Brennan—took a strong position on the right to counsel at the pretrial stage, arguing:

> The right to have counsel at the pre-trial stage is often necessary to give meaning and protection to the right to be heard at the trial itself. It may also be necessary as a restraint on the coercive power of the police.[26]...No matter how well educated, and how well trained in the law an accused may be, he is surely in need of legal advice once he is arrested for an offense that may exact his life.[27]...The demands of our civilization expressed in the due process clause require that the accused who wants a counsel should have one at any time after the moment of arrest.[28]

The dissent also wrote that "the third degree flourishes only in secrecy."[29] It is quite clear, I think, that Justices Warren, Douglas, Black, and Brennan (and later Fortas, with whom they were to form a majority in *Miranda*) simply did not trust police to behave noncoercively when they had a suspect in custody; only counsel, they believed, would constrain police.

Ironically, compelling evidence for the view that police custody is inherently coercive was elicited from a 1962 book by professional police interrogators Fred E. Inbau and John E. Reid, titled *Criminal Interrogation and Confessions*. This book was a revision and enlargement of the second half of Inbau and Reid's earlier book, *Lie Detection and Criminal Investigation* (Inbau and Reid, 1953). The book is replete with suggestions for coercive and deceptive methods of interrogation, which the authors clearly considered necessary and proper for police conducting an investigation. Inbau and Reid were not advocates of the third degree. On the contrary, their book, seen in historical context, was a reformist document, representing a kind of dialectical synthesis between the polarities of third degree violence and civil liberties for protection of human dignity. Such a synthesis would have been progressive in the 1930s.

The benchmark test employed by Inbau and Reid was: "Although both 'fair' and 'unfair' interrogation practices are permissible, nothing shall be done or said to the subject that will be apt to make an innocent person confess." (Inbau and Reid, 1962). A more philosophically-based and sophisticated version of the Inbau and Reid position (and a more modern one) is Joseph Grano's "mental freedom" test of voluntariness. It is an objective test, asking "whether a person of ordinary firmness, innocent or guilty, having the defendant's age, physical condition, and relevant mental abnormalities (but not otherwise having the defendant's personality traits, temperament, intelligence, or social background), and strongly preferring not to confess, would find the interrogation pressures overbearing." (Grano, 1979). What might these pressures be?

It is worthwhile, I think, to quote substantially from the *Miranda* decision itself, partly to understand the impact Inbau and Reid's books had on the courts, and partly to understand what sorts of police trickery might or might not be regarded as coercive. Justice Warren wrote:

> The officers are told by the manuals that the "principle psychological factor contributing to a successful interrogation is privacy—being alone with the person under interrogation." The efficacy of this tactic has been explained as follows:

> If at all practicable, the interrogation should take place in the investigator's office or at least in a room of his choice. The subject should be deprived of every psychological advantage. In his own home he may be confident, indignant, or recalcitrant. He is more keenly aware of his rights and more reluctant to tell his indiscretions or criminal behavior within the walls of his home. Moreover his family and other friends are

nearby, their presence lending moral support. In his office, the investigator possesses all the advantages. The atmosphere suggests the invincibility of the forces of the law.

To highlight the isolation and unfamiliar surroundings, the manuals instruct the police to display an air of confidence in the suspect's guilt and from outward appearance to maintain only an interest in confirming certain details. The guilt of the subject is to be posted as a fact. The interrogator should direct his comments toward the reasons why the subject committed the act, rather than court failure by asking the subject whether he did it. Like other men, perhaps the subject has had a bad family life, had an unhappy childhood, had too much to drink, had an unrequited desire for women. The officers are instructed to minimize the moral seriousness of the offense, to cast blame on the victim or on society. These tactics are designed to put the subject in a psychological state where his story is but an elaboration of what the police purport to know already—that he is guilty. Explanations to the contrary are dismissed and discouraged.

The texts thus stress that the major qualities an interrogator should possess are patience and perseverance.[30]

The manuals also suggest that suspects be offered legal excuses for their actions, says the *Miranda* Court. The interrogator is instructed to tell the suspect something like:

Joe, you probably didn't go out looking for this fellow with the purpose of shooting him. My guess is, however, that you expected something from him and that's why you carried a gun—for your own protection. You knew him for what he was, no good. Then when you met him he probably started using foul, abusive language and he gave some indication that he was about to pull a gun on you, and that's when you had to act to save your own life. That's about it, isn't it, Joe?[31]

If the suspect does not respond to the understanding interrogator, notes the Court, another investigator is brought in—Mutt, the tough guy who plays against Jeff's nice guy role.

In this technique, two agents are employed. Mutt, the relentless investigator, who knows the subject is guilty and is not going to waste any time. He's sent a dozen men away for this crime and he's going to send the subject away for the full term. Jeff, on the other hand, is obviously a kindhearted man. He has a family himself. He has a brother who was involved in a little scrape like this. He disapproves of Mutt and his tactics and will arrange to get him off the case if the subject will cooperate. He can't hold Mutt off for very long. The subject would be wise to make a quick decision. The technique is applied by having both investigators present while Mutt acts out his role. Jeff may stand by quietly and demur at some of Mutt's tactics. When Jeff makes his plea for cooperation, Mutt is not present.[32]

Although *Miranda* is generally interpreted as focusing on the inherently coercive aspects of custodial interrogation, it should be noted that interrogatory tactics employ both deception and coercion. It is questionable whether custodial interrogation would be effective without deception. Indeed, deception appears to serve as custodial interrogation's functional alternative to physical coercion. Hence, deception and the inherent coercion of custody are inescapably related in modern interrogation.

    *Miranda* generated enormous controversy. Studies were conducted by scholars and law reviews to try to demonstrate the impact of *Miranda*.[33] (It would be interesting to conduct a new round of studies to see if the findings of the older ones still hold.) Basically, the studies came to much the same conclusion: The *Miranda* warning did not appreciably reduce the amount of talking that a suspect would do, nor did *Miranda* significantly help suspects in making free and informed choices about whether to talk. A nice statement of how *Miranda* warnings could be rendered ineffectual, written by an author of the *Yale Law Journal's* study of *Miranda's* impact, appeared in the *Yale Alumni Magazine* in 1968.

Even when detectives informed suspects of their rights without undercutting devices, the advice was often defused by implying that the suspect had better not exercise his rights, or by delivering the statement in a formalized, bureaucratic tone to indicate that the remarks were simply a routine, meaningless legalism. Instinctively, perhaps, detectives tended to create a sense of unreality about the *Miranda* warnings by bringing the flow of conversation to a halt with the statement, "...and now I am going to inform you of your rights." Afterwards, they would solemnly intone: "Now you have been warned of your rights," then immediately shift into a conversational tone to ask, "Now would you like to tell me what happened?" By and large the detectives regarded advising the suspect of his rights as an artificial imposition on the natural flow of the interrogation.[34]

    *Miranda* also generated a substantial law review literature—some might say an industry—because the United States Supreme Court has been unwilling to set the only standard that would eliminate practically all the *Miranda* problems. That standard would be: Once the Miranda warnings are given, the accused is also given a lawyer who explains the implications of the warning.[35]

The privilege against self-incrimination existed before *Miranda*. The *Miranda* rule essentially argues that, as part of due process, the government should not be permitted to make its case on the basis of the defendant's ignorance. Defendants *must* be informed of their rights. If we accept *Miranda* and take it seriously, we also must acknowledge that suspects do not—across the board—possess the legal acumen to waive their *Miranda* rights. In the late 1960s, at least persons of "ordinary firmness" interpreted—or misinterpreted—their *Miranda* rights in such a way so as not to exercise them. From the perspective of those who would like to see *Miranda* overturned, that might not be a problem. But it also suggests that the average suspect, however "ordinarily firm," is not legally competent.

Those who *are* legally competent (lawyers) will routinely advise suspects to maintain silence. The continuing debate over *Miranda* reflects an ambivalence over enforcing the rule that the values expressed by the *Miranda* majority seem to call for: There can be no confession without a genuinely *voluntary* and knowledgeable waiver, exercised after consultation with a lawyer. The *Crooker* minority was unquestionably correct in its assessment that people cannot fully understand the implications of legal warnings—offered, after all, in the rather coercive situation of arrest—without legal consultation. We apparently still prefer to offer the government an edge based on the defendant's ignorance. Knowledgeable defendant's will remain silent. The ignorant will talk.

Grano's "ordinary firmness" test necessarily implies overruling *Miranda*. His test, which is oriented to crime control, would surely result in far more admissible evidence than a genuinely voluntary, lawyer-advised waiver would. The present *Miranda* rule lies somewhere in between. Perhaps we tolerate *Miranda* because on the whole we have learned that it does not matter very much. Pressures of in-custody interrogation are such that, apparently, most suspects will talk despite the *Miranda* warning. In any event, most confessions are elicited in cases where there is a victim, where the confession is not the only evidence, and where the suspect is willing to plead guilty to a lesser offense.

Besides, once the suspect begins to talk, the very techniques the court sought to avoid are probably permissible. When a policeman says, in the kindliest of tones, "Look Joe, it will be better for you to confess," he is of course essentially deceiving the suspect into believing that he is the suspect's friend rather than his adversary.

In a recent article, Welsh S. White has argued that certain interrogation tactics are, nevertheless, likely to risk depriving the suspect of his constitutional rights.[36] Accordingly, White believes that the court should prohibit, via per se exclusions, "police conduct that is likely to render a resulting confession involuntary or to undermine the effect of required *Miranda* warnings or a suspect's independent right to an attorney.[37] What would some of these prohibitions be? One would be against deceiving a suspect about whether an interrogation was taking place, as in *Massiah v. United States*.[38] There, after indictment, one confederate, Colson, agreed to cooperate with the government, and deceptively interrogated his accomplice, Massiah. The resulting incriminatory statements were held inadmissible as a violation of the Sixth Amendment right to counsel. White argues that this right should be triggered at the point of arrest.

He also argues that statements elicited from "jail plants" should be prohibited, on grounds that someone who is experiencing the pressures of confinement is more likely to confide in a police agent.[39] Slightly different forms of trickery, which White also advocates prohibiting, are police misrepresentations of the seriousness of the offense or police use of threats or promises for confessing.

Finally, White argues for prohibition of "father figure" trickery, where a police officer falsely acts like a friend or counselor rather than an adversary. White offers as one example the famous Connecticut murder case, *State v. Reilly*, where the principle interrogating officer manipulated an 18-year-old into falsely confessing that he murdered his mother.[40] White treats the case primarily as an example of the officer pretending to be a father figure. White's discussion, however, omits entirely what two books about the case point to as the real culprit—the use of the polygraph during the interrogation of Reilly, who confessed after being told by the "father figure" that a machine, which could read his mind, had indicated that he actually was the murderer (Connery, 1977; Barthel, 1976).

## THE POLYGRAPH AS A DECEPTIVE DEVICE

Inbau and Reid were not only advocates of deceptive interrogation; they were also proponents and developers of polygraph examination techniques. The polygraph is an instrument which measures changes in blood pressure, pulse, respiration, and perspiration. Detection of lies via the examination of physical change is actually a throwback to early forms of trial by ordeal. There are reports of a deception test used by Hindus based on the observation that fear may inhibit the secretion of saliva (Lykken, 1981b). To test credibility, an accused was given rice to chew. If he could spit it out, he was considered innocent; but if it stuck to his gums, he was judged guilty. Until 1895, however, nobody had ever used a measuring device to detect deception. In that year, the Italian criminologist Cesare Lombroso used a combination of blood pressure and pulse readings to investigate crime. Before the First World War, others experimented with blood pressure and respiratory recordings. John A. Larson, perhaps the most scholarly of the Chicago-Berkeley group which sought to advance the "science" of lie detection, built an instrument in 1921 which he called a "polygraph"; it combined all three measures—blood pressure, pulse, and respiration. His junior collaborator, Leonard Keeler, added galvanic skin response to the list. Contemporary lie detector machines basically employ all these measures, although there were some other technical improvements as well. For example, integrated circuits and other components reduce the margin of error in measurement.

According to a survey conducted by the *New York Times* in 1980, the lie detector is widely used by law enforcement groups:

> The Federal Bureau of Investigation conducted 1990 polygraph examinations in 1979, an increase of about 800 from 1978. The number of polygraph examinations administered by the Army, Navy, Marines and Air Force increased by 18 percent in two years, from 5710 to 6751. Polygraphs are finding a steadily growing market among state and local law enforcement agencies, litigants in civil cases and private retailers, who use the device to screen job applicants and combat pilferage. (Pear, 1980).

It is understandable, but distressing, that the use of the polygraph should be increasing. It is distressing because the validity of polygraph results is flawed by fundamental theoretical problems, not by technical ones. The increase in use is understandable because even though the polygraph is not a dispositive truth-finding device, it is nevertheless an effective instrument of social control.

In the past, one problem of polygraph examination was imprecision of measurement. Thus, the machine recorded blood pressure, but there was a question as to whether it recorded blood pressure accurately. There is no doubt that imprecision of measurement was a problem in the past, but the problems with the lie detection process itself were far more fundamental and serious. These problems stem from the inadequacy of the theory behind lie detection. That theory involves the following premises: The act of lying leads to conscious conflict; conflict induces *fear* or *anxiety;* and these emotions are accompanied by measurable and interpretable physiological changes (Skolnick, 1961).

However, the assumptions of the theory are questionable. The act of lying does not always lead to conscious conflict. Some witnesses believe their own stories, even when they are false. Even when witnesses know they are lying, they may not experience much fear. Or, innocent witnesses may experience fear and anxiety just by being asked threatening questions. All this depends on witnesses' individual personalities, social backgrounds, what they are testifying to, and to whom they are testifying. Polygraph examiners acknowledge that subjects must "believe in" the lie detector.

Even if witnesses do experience fear and anxiety, these emotions may not consistently be expressed as changes in bodily response. If all bodily responses rose and fell exactly with emotional states, the responses would have a precise relationship to each other. But that is not the case. Bodily responses do not vary regularly either with each other or with emotional states. If they did, only a unigraph, not a polygraph, would be required. Four imprecise measures are not more accurate than one precise measure.

Since the relations among lying, conflict, emotion, and bodily responses are so fuzzy, the accuracy of the lie detector is not comparable to that of, say, blood tests or X-rays. It is unlikely that a dozen lie detector examiners would consistently reach the same conclusions regarding truth or falsity if they depended only on the squiggles produced by a polygraph.

So why is the use of lie detectors sharply increasing? The fact that the polygraph is not reliable does not mean it is ineffective as a social control instrument. Crime suspects may confess when questioned by a skilled interrogator. When a suspect is strapped into what he or she would view as a technologically foolproof "lie detector," the coercive power of the interrogator is heightened. The interrogator is not an adversary, but an objective scientific observer. Even those suspicious of father figures may embrace the trappings of science.

Job applicants, in particular, are effectively "screened" with a lie detector. Consider the following lines of questioning. First, softballs: Is your name John Jones? Are you 36 years old? Were you born in New York City? Then, hardballs: Have you ever done anything you are ashamed of? Have you ever stolen anything? Have you ever known anyone who has stolen anything? Who? Have you ever engaged in homosexual acts? And so forth. This sort of questioning may well produce results.

There are thus two quite different empirical issues regarding the polygraph. Is it highly accurate, like X-rays and blood tests? The answer is no. Is it effective in eliciting information from subjects who believe in it? The answer is yes. Whether the lie detector ought to be used by police—or by employers—is ultimately an ethical question. Should we allow deceptive, intrusive, yet nonviolent methods of interrogation in various institutions of a free society? Different people will have different answers to that question. But at least we should ask the right questions when considering the role of the so-called lie detector in American society.

The ethical problem is even more complicated because some who employ the lie detector actually believe that it detects lies, while others use it primarily as a technique of psychological intimidation. The police sergeant who told Peter Reilly that "this machine will read your mind" and then falsely persuaded Reilly that he had killed his own mother, thus eliciting from Reilly a critical but untrue confession, may himself have believed that the polygraph detects lies. Did the sergeant also believe that the lie detector reads the mind?

The lie detector is symbolically scientific, and its technologically sophisticated trappings commend it to the most thoughtful and professional segments of the policing community. Thus, police use the polygraph because they believe in it. Yet the technique's results can convict innocent people, where old-fashioned techniques of deception would not. An instance of this, the case of F.B. Fay, is reported by psychophysiologist David T. Lykken (Lykken, 1981a). Fay was asked by a police polygraphist in Toledo in 1978, "Did you kill Fred?" and "Before age twenty-four did you ever think about doing anyone bodily harm to get revenge?"

It was assumed that, if Fay were innocent of Fred's murder, the second or "control" question would frighten Fay more, and that this would, in turn, "dampen" his autonomic reaction to the first or "relevant" question. Unfortunately for Fay, he responded more strongly on the "relevant" questions. The examiner, therefore, testified that Fay's denials were deceptive, and he was found guilty of murder and sentenced to prison for life. In October 1980, the actual killers were identified, and Fay was released after serving two and a half years.

In sum, then, we have to educate the law enforcement community as to the realistic limits of the polygraph. This will be difficult, partly because there is, as has been noted here, considerable controversy over use of the polygraph, and partly because, for the reasons I have already suggested, it is a uniquely valuable tool of interrogation. I myself have no hesitancy in stating where I stand on the use of the instrument. I would argue against its use—first, because the false claims for its accuracy permit the highest degree of nonviolent coercion, and second, because cool nonreactors (sociopaths, skilled con men, the mildly self-drugged) can beat the test. Finally, if one of the important reasons for the *Miranda* rule is the inherent coerciveness of police interrogation, then how much more coercive is an interrogation by a questioner who is armed with a deceptively scientific instrument that can "read the mind?"

## CONCLUSION

I have tried in this chapter to offer several observations about deception in the detecting process. First, I have suggested that detecting is a process moving from investigation, often through interrogation, to testimony. Police are offered considerable latitude by the courts during the investigation stage. This latitude to deceive, I have argued, carries over into the interrogation and testimonial stages as a subculturally supported norm. I have suggested that there is an underlying reason for this. When detectives deceive suspects in the course of criminal investigations or interrogations, they typically are not seeking to promote their own self-interest (as a detective would if he had lied about accepting bribes). On the contrary, the sort of deception employed to trap a narcotics dealer or dealer in stolen goods, or to elicit a confession from a murderer or rapist, is used for the public interest. The detective—and here I am speaking of the professional detective who explicitly condemns the use of physical violence but accepts employing psychological intimidation during interrogation—is also interested in eliciting truth. This results, I have suggested, in a paradox. The end of *truth* justifies for the modern detective the means of *lying*. Deception usually occurs in the interest of obtaining truth.

Both the detective and the civil libertarian, I have suggested, employ a utilitarian calculus. In so doing, each reveals the obvious limitations of such a calculus for resolving major issues of public policy. The detective measures the costs of the act of lying against the benefits to the crime victim and the general public. The civil libertarian is also concerned with the public interest but measures it in terms of rules protecting the long-range interests of all citizens in a system of governance, as opposed to the shorter range interests of punishing perpetrators.

The law reflects the tension between due process and crime control imperatives by establishing different—and inconsistent—standards for investigation and interrogation. At the investigative stage, the law's subjective test of entrapment comes perilously close to tests like Inbau and Reid's "innocent person" or Grano's more sophisticated "mental freedom" test: Both permit deceptive and coercive interrogation against wolves but not lambs.

Is there a moral justification for distinguishing between governmental deception at the investigative stage and at the interrogation stage? One could approach this issue by asking: What would be the rule of law regarding police deception in a moral society? It seems clear that in a moral society, authorities such as police would not be permitted to employ tactics that are generally regarded as immoral against those suspected, or accused of a crime.

Indeed, we already have such rules: Police are not permitted to coerce a suspect physically. The police may, however, subject suspects to psychological coercion provided they consent to be interrogated. Unreliability is one reason we prohibit the admission of evidence obtained from physically coerced confessions. But we could have a rule distinguishing between a pure mea culpa confession and one which produces material evidence, such as a gun or a body. We do not have such rules partly because we deplore physically coercive tactics even when used against the guilty; we also do not have them because we fear that physical coercion would become a routine aspect of police interrogation. Physical coercion is clearly indistinguishable from deceit and trickery, and few of us would, really, I suspect, choose to be smashed in the face with a rifle butt, or hung from a high window, rather than be betrayed by a friend who is actually and secretly a police informant gathering incriminating evidence.

The more difficult question is whether deception—which we accept at the investigative stage—is as morally offensive as psychological coercion. Recall that earlier I discussed the distinction between gathering information by a secret informant and gathering it by electronic eavesdropping. I suggested there that I could not see any principle by which one was, on balance, worse than the other, even though we can perceive different sorts of objections to each. The wiretap or bug clearly invades privacy, while the secret informant invades both privacy—in some ways more, in some ways less, than electronic eavesdropping—and personality. Not only is the secret informant privy to actions and conversations one would never consent to have had overheard; the secret informant also modified personality by deliberately attempting to impair judgment. The wiretap is, in social science jargon, an "unobtrusive measurer." By contrast, the informant necessarily produces a reaction—speech, behavior—on the part of the observed, and may prove influential in determining that reaction.

If there is a distinction between investigative and interrogatory trickery and deceit, it has to be based on situational ethics, the morality of practical necessity. Practically speaking, it is impossible to enforce consensual crime statutes— bribery, drug dealing, prostitution—without employing deception. This need for deception may not be as clear at the interrogation stage. Often, evidence can be produced independently of confessions, and occasionally, false confessions are elicited.

However, confessions may also be a practical necessity in many cases, particularly when dealing with the most serious sorts of criminals, such as murderers, rapists, and kidnappers. Miranda himself, it may be recalled, had confessed to the forcible kidnapping and rape of a 19-year-old woman. Why should situational ethics permit lying to a drug dealer but forbid in-custody conversational questioning of a forcible rapist? That question can be answered on historical and constitutional grounds, but it is hard to see how to make consistent common sense out of it.

I cannot here reconcile such inconsistencies, nor am I writing to lobby the Supreme Court. But I would like to conclude by suggesting that apparent inconsistency makes law look more like a game than a rational system for enforcing justice. Because of this appearance of inconsistency, police are not likely to take the state rules of the game seriously and are encouraged to operate by their own codes, including those which affirm the necessity for lying wherever it seems justified by the ends.

# Notes

1    See generally, Welsh S. White, "Police Trickery in Inducing Confessions," *University of Pennsylvania Law Review* 127 (1979): 581-629; Welsh S. White, "Interrogation without Questions: *Rhode Island v. Innis* and *United States v. Henry*," *Mich. L. Rev.* 78 (1980): 1209-51.

2    See Sissela Bok, *Lying: Moral Choice in Public and Private Life,* discussion in Chapter VII, "Justification," of the group decision to deceive the public. Bok says it is based on the shared belief that the group's norms are good, and that any means used to achieve group ends would therefore also be good (p. 97). See also the discussion of unmarked police cars as justifiable deception because the practice is publicized, while entrapment is not deemed justifiable unless the public agrees this is proper police behavior (pp. 98-99).

3    See, generally, Gary Marx, "Undercover Cops: Creative Policing or Constitutional Threat?" *Civil Liberties Review* 4 (July/August 1977): 34-44.

4    *United States v. Ressler,* 536 F. 2d 208 (1976), and list of cases cited in the body of that opinion.

5    6 *Franks v. Delaware,* 98 S. Ct. 2674 (1979).

6    As to "code of honor" regarding deception, see Lawrence W. Sherman, *Scandal and Reform: Controlling Police Corruption* (Berkeley and Los Angeles: University of California, 1978), pp. 46-67. As to existence of police subculture, see Ellwyn R. Stoddard, "A Group Approach to Blue-Coat Crime," in *Police Corruption: A Sociological Perspective,* ed. Lawrence W. Sherman (Garden City, NY: Doubleday, Anchor Books, 1974), pp. 277-304.

7    The Knapp Commission Report, City of New York Commission to Investigate Allegations of Police Corruption and the City's Anti-Corruption Procedures (New York, 1972), discussed in Sherman, *Scandal and Reform,* p. 160.

8    *Mapp v. Ohio,* 367 U.S. 643 (1961).

9    Quoted and discussed in Dallin Oaks, "Studying the Exclusionary Rule in Search and Seizure," *University of Chicago Law Review* 37 (1970): 665-757.

10    *People v. Defore,* 242 N.Y. 13 (1926).

11    For a discussion of institutional support for trying to cover up misuse of force charges, see Paul Chevigny, *Police Power* (New York: Pantheon, 1969), p. 139. For case law and discussion of trickery and deception at the investigative stage, see Yale Kamisar, *Police Interrogation and Confessions* (Ann Arbor: University of Michigan Press, 1980).

12    *Sherman v. United States,* 356 U.S. 369 (1958).

13    *United States v. Russell,* 411 U.S. 423 (1973).

14    Welsh S. White, "Policy Trickery."

15    *Brown v. Mississippi,* 297 U.S. 278 (1936).

16    *Rochin v. California,* 342 U.S. 165 (1952).

17    Provisions for issuing a warrant to wiretap are stringent. The rule is that wiretaps may be conducted only after a warrant has been issued. Title III of 18 U.S.C. "2510-20 prescribes a careful procedure for obtaining a warrant to use electronic surveillance, and the federal law preempts state law on this subject. By contrast, an informant paid by the DEA, for example, may freely roam about southwestern Florida, working his way into any corner of the drug subculture, without specific judicial authorization. See Stuart Penn, "The Informer," *Wall Street Journal,* 10 May 1982.

18    *United States v. Russell,* 411 U.S. 423 (1973).

19    *Miranda v. Arizona,* 384 U.S. 486 (1966).

20    *Lego v. Twomey,* 404 U.S. 477 (1972) (Voluntariness must be proven by a preponderance of evidence).

21    *Report on Lawlessness in Law Enforcement,* National Commission on Law Observance and Enforcement (Washington, DC: U.S. Government Printing Office, 1931).

22    A list of such tactics is found in the Wickersham Report; see note 27.

23    Modern commentators claim that the most outrageous examples of the third degree tactics are no longer employed in American police departments. See Robert M. Fogelson, *Big City Police* (Cambridge, MA: Harvard University Press, 1977), p. 302.

24    *Crooker v. California,* 357 U.S. 433 (1958).

25    *Cicenia v. LaGay,* 357 U.S. 504 (1958).

26    *Crooker v. California,* 357 U.S. 433, 433 (1958).

27    *Ibid.,* p. 446.

28    *Ibid.,* p. 448.

29    *Ibid.,* p. 443.

30    *Miranda v. Arizona,* 384 U.S. 436, 449-50 (1966), citing Charles O'Hara, *Fundamentals of Criminal Investigation* (Springfield, IL: Charles C Thomas Publishing Co., 1956), p. 99.

31    *Ibid.,* pp. 451-52, citing Inbau and Reid, *Criminal Interrogation and Confessions,* p. 40.

32    *Ibid.,* p. 452, citing O'Hara, *Fundamentals,* p. 104, and Inbau and Reid, *Criminal Interrogation,* pp. 58-59.

33    Project, "Interrogations in New Haven: The Impact of Miranda," *Yale Law Journal* 76 (1967): 1519-1648; Richard H. Seeburger and R. Stanton Wettick, Jr., "Miranda in Pittsburgh—A Statistical Study," *University of Pittsburgh Law Review* 29 (1967): 1-26; Cyril D. Robinson, "Police and Prosecutor Practices and Attitudes Relating to Interrogation," *Duke Law Journal* 1968:425-524.

34    Richard E. Ayers, "Confessions and the Court," *Yale Alumni Magazine* (December, 1968): 18, 20. Cited in Yale Kamisar, Wayne R. LaFave, and Jerold H. Israel, *Modern Criminal Procedure: Cases, Comments, Questions,* 5th ed. (St. Paul, MN: West Publishing Co., 1980), p. 632.

35    John Baldwin and Michael McConville, "Police Interrogation and the Right to See a Solicitor," *Criminal Law Review* 1979: 145-152; Welsh S. White, "Police Trickery."

36    Welsh S. White, "Police Trickery," p. 586.

37    Welsh S. White, "Police Trickery," p. 599-600.

38    *Massiah v. United States,* 377 U.S. 201 (1964).

39    *United States v. Henry,* 100 S. Ct. 2183 (1980).

40    *State v. Reilly,* No. 5285 (Conn. Super. Ct. Apr. 12, 1974), vacated 32 Conn. supp. 349, 355 A.2d 324 (Super. Ct. 1976).

# REFERENCES

Barthel, J. (1976). *A Death in Canaan*. New York: E.P. Dutton.

Bok, Sissela (1978). *Lying: Moral Choice in Public and Private Life*. New York: Pantheon.

Connery, D.S. (1977). *Guilty Until Proven Innocent*. New York: G. P. Putnam's Sons.

Daley, R. (1978). *Prince of the City: The True Story of a Cop Who Knew Too Much*. Boston: Houghton-Mifflin Co.

Grano, J. (1979). "Voluntariness, Free Will, and the Law of Confessions." *Virginia Law Review* 65:906.

Hopkins, E.J. (1972). *Our Lawless Police: A Study of the Unlawful Enforcement of the Law*. New York: Da Capo Press.

Inbau, F.E. and J.E. Reid (1962). *Criminal Interrogation and Confessions*. Baltimore: Williams and Wilkins Co.

Lykken, D.T. (1981a). "Review: The Art and Science of the Polygraph Technique." *Contemporary Psychology* 26:480.

Lykken, D.T. (1981b). *A Tremor in the Blood: Uses and Abuses of the Lie Detector*. New York: McGraw-Hill Book Co.

Pear, R. (1980). "As Use of the Polygraph Grows, Suspects and Lawyers Swear." *New York Times*, July 13.

Rossum, R.A. (1978). "Entrapment Defense and the Teaching of Political Responsibility: The Supreme Court as Republican Schoolmaster." *American Journal of Criminal Law* 6:287-306.

Schlesinger, A.M., Jr. (1978). *Robert Kennedy and His Times*. Boston: Houghton-Mifflin.

Skolnick, J. (1975). *Justice Without Trial. 2nd ed*. New York: Wiley and Sons.

Skolnick, J. (1961). "Scientific Theory and Scientific Evidence: An Analysis of Lie Detection." *Yale Law Journal* 70:699.

# Study Questions

1.  The author suggests that deception occurs at three stages of the detecting process. What are the stages? Is deception equally acceptable at each stage?

2.  What are the legal tests for entrapment?

3.  What is the relationship between judicial acceptance of deception and the probability of its occurrence.

4.  What does the author say is the fundamental problem with the polygraph?

5.  The author is against the use of the polygraph. Why?

# PART III: ABUSE OF AUTHORITY

# 11

# THEORETICAL DIMENSIONS IN THE ABUSE OF AUTHORITY BY POLICE OFFICERS*

## David L. Carter

The use of force by police officers is of interest both practically and theoretically. From the operational perspective it is important to understand the use of force in order to maintain the sanctity of legal mandates as well as to establish a firm base of organizational control. Theoretically it is of interest to conceptualize the interactive nature of multiple behavioral systems. In turn, this may lead to greater understanding of human motivations which, after scientific verification, can be applied to practical conditions. In the case of policing, integration of theory and practice regarding the use of force can provide a more judicious and effective law enforcement organization which can boast greater community support.

In a previous work (Carter, 1985) the writer proposed a causal model to explain the abuse of authority by police. The model, developed a posteriori from an empirical study of police officers, attempted to explain the conditions under which police officers used excessive force. Moreover, the model proposed organizational mechanisms to control such behavior. While this approach served as a genesis at the practical level, the author perceived the need to focus the model at the theoretical level for purposes of scientific assessment. Thus, the current work is directed toward this end.

Initially the author focused on the term "police brutality" and found it was not operational for purposes of scientific inquiry. The problem begins with one's initial impression that "brutality" is a physically injurious act toward a citizen by a police officer. However, this is frequently not the case. Thus, for scientific causal analysis one must not measure the product (i.e., brutality) but evaluate the

*Reprinted from *Police Studies,* Vol. 7, No. 4 (Winter 1984), pp. 224-236. Reprinted with Permission of *Police Studies.*

precipitive behavior (i.e., causal factors). Deductively, however, these concepts must be examined at an even more fundamental level.

For example, the excessive use of force, while illegitimate, is not necessarily injurious. A police officer who maliciously tightens an arrestee's handcuffs too tight in order to inflict punitive discomfort would be "brutalizing" the arrestee. Conversely, an officer who must legitimately use his/her baton as that amount of force necessary to effect an arrest, would not be "brutalizing" the arrestee even if injury occurred. The significant point to note is that the visual impression of these incidents would be quite different, with the term "brutality" failing to accurately describe either.

Previous research has recognized the definitional problem inherent in the term "brutality." As noted by Reiss (1968:11)

> what citizens mean by police brutality covers the full range of police practices...[It can include] any practice that degrades their status, that restricts their freedom, that annoys or harasses them, or that uses physical force that is frequently seen as unnecessary or unwarranted.

Brutality has been alternately classified as the use of excessive force, name-calling, sarcasm, ridicule, and disrespect (President's Commission, 1967). The United States Commission on Civil Rights (1961) was equally vague when it defined brutality as "a violation of due process" (p. 25) and later, in the same report, as "the unnecessary use of violence to enforce mores of segregation, to punish, and to coerce confessions" (p. 28). Whereas the former Civil Rights Commission definition is broad and includes nonviolent and unintentional acts, the latter definition is restricted to violent, specific-intent acts. Friedrich (1980) implies the use of force is any forceful activity by the police, either legitimate or illegitimate, which produces physical or emotional injury. Kania and Mackey (1977) take somewhat of a different approach by defining "excessive force" as violence of a degree that is more than justified to effect a legitimate police function. They go further by postulating that:

> "police brutality" is also excessive violence, of a more extreme degree, and includes violence used by police which does not support a legitimate police function. Force and violence are not synonymous. Force implies the exertion of power to compel or restrain the behavior of others...[while violence] refers to the use of manual restraints, blows, and weapons (Kania and Mackey, 1977:29).

Each of these definitions is descriptive of the police brutality/excessive force/violence phenomenon; however, they share two common delimitations. First, they do not adequately address the peripheral behavior that is improper but short of being excessive. Second, the definitions are not sufficiently narrow to permit measurability. While the measurement of many aspects of human behavior is going to require some qualitative interpretation, the noted delimitations remain a significant problem for empirical assessment of the phenomenon. If, in fact, brutality and its associated issues of force are going to be explained, the behaviors must be operationalized within a structured framework of logic. Moreover, the behavior must be examined within a systematic paradigm, not as an individual, autonomous occurrence.

This leads to a second problem traditionally associated with brutality research. Typically, the research parameters of brutality have been narrowly limited in a close time proximity to the actual incident. The current work significantly expands this concept into a theoretical framework. There are numerous facts currently available about the incidence of brutality; however, the broader view of interactive continuity afforded by a theory is lacking. The significance of this, as noted by Willis (1983:448), is that "[f]acts without theory, no matter how voluminous, lack meaning. Furthermore, a field of study cannot advance as a scientific discipline on facts alone."

The current work strengthens the author's original model by placing the construct into a more structured taxonomy of measurement, causation, and containment. This author, following the traditional view of scientific problem-solving, maintains that true empirical inquiry into the causal relationships of phenomena must begin with a theory. In classic terms a theory is a set of interrelated constructs, definitions, and propositions that set forth a systematic view of phenomena by specifying relations among variables with the purpose of explaining and predicting the phenomena (Kerlinger, 1973). The theoretical model—which formulates the elements of the theory into a framework which is a conceptual representation of reality—formulates the elements of the theory into a framework, which can be empirically tested in "the real world." If, after a series of replications, scientific testing supports the model one can then truly move into the realm of explanation. Therefore, if the phenomena can be explained based on the causal relationship among the model's variables, then corrective measures may be introduced to prevent the undesirable behavior.

The causal model proposed in this article examines police brutality from an "applied theory" perspective. That is, while the model follows the traditional theory construction process, it has pragmatic applications. Thus, while the initial stages of empirical assessment involve basic research the model's characteristics are also consistent with applied research principles.

In sum, the writer suggests a comprehensive theoretical approach to examine police brutality. The causal model includes a rhetorical argument which justifies the propositions and presents a parsimonious conceptual structure for assessment. The fundamental components of the model are: (1) operationalizing *brutality* through an abuse of authority typology, (2) presentation of a causal paradigm, and (3) identification of control mechanisms for abusive behavior. The theoretical model therefore permits the researcher to measure both the various behaviors and the differential behavioral products.

# THE ABUSE OF AUTHORITY TYPOLOGY

The typology treats brutality as a behavioral product of a broader systemic phenomenon wherein the officer exercises illegitimate (or abusive) authority. In such cases the officer's behavior is inconsistent with law, policy, or normative standards embodied in his/her defined responsibilities. A theoretical extension of this concept would logically maintain—somewhat similar to the social contract—that the officer also has a moral obligation of authoritative constraint beyond those dictated by law and policy. The author, however, maintains that this is a logical fallacy when explaining police behavior. One can envision circumstances wherein police officers may abuse their authority; however, it is done so with a sincere moral belief of propriety. When the behavior is rationalized on the premise that the end justifies the means, then this implies that the officer is acting in response to his/her personal and occupational socialization experiences as they interact with the practical circumstances of a police encounter. Therefore, the causal structure of this model is largely based on determinism although not in the truest ideological context (particularly with regard to behavioral containment).

Before illustrating how abused authority can be rationalized, one should first understand the author's meaning of "abuse of authority" as it applies to this model. The concept is defined as any action by a police officer without regard to motive, intent, or malice that tends to injure, insult, trespass upon human dignity, manifest feelings of inferiority, and/or violate an inherent legal right of a member of the police constituency (Carter, 1985). It is significant to note that abuse of authority (1) does not have to be an intentional act—it can also be reactive behavior, (2) it is not limited to a physically injurious act, and (3) there does not have to be a violation of any normative obligation.

For example, based on limited facts and an intuitive feeling learned from the officer's experience he/she may believe that a person is in possession of contraband. While the officer may not have a legal basis for searching the person, he/she may nonetheless conduct the search for the expressed purpose of seizing the contraband. The behavior may be rationalized by an ethically motivated belief that the end justifies the means. Pragmatically, the behavior may even be desirable. Nonetheless, the behavior constitutes an abuse of authority by the officer in that the standards of protection afforded through the Fourth Amendment have not been met.

The importance of this and similar situations for the model is that the intent or motive of the officer's abusive behavior is largely irrelevant. The significant conditions to document are the incidence of abuse, the nature of the abusive act, and a profile of contributory stressors experienced by the officers. Thus, the model does not evaluate the officer's perception of legitimacy in that these perceptions are only residual to the causal factors.

As noted previously, the theoretical model requires that incidents of abuse be categorized into a typology based on the nature and effect of abuse. Consistent with the principle of parsimony, the complexity of the typology has been minimized with each category factoring multiple types of similar behaviors under a singular classification. The tripartite typology consists of: (1) physical abuse/excessive force; (2) verbal/psychological abuse; and (3) legal abuse.

*Physical Abuse/Excessive Force.* Operationally, this classification includes (a) any officer behavior involving the use of more force than is necessary to effect an arrest or search; and/or (b) the wanton use of any degree of physical force against another by a police officer under the color of the officer's office. The key test is whether there was any physical force directly used against an individual with no distinction between injurious and noninjurious incidents under the proposition that the causal variables are the same.

*Verbal/Psychological Abuse.* These are incidents where police officers verbally assail, ridicule, or harass individuals and/or place persons who are under the actual or constructive dominion of the officer in a situation where the individual's esteem and/or self-image are threatened or diminished. Also included in this category is the threat of physical harm under the supposition that a threat is psychologically coercive and instills fear in the average person.[1] Given the fact that this form of abuse is not as visibly apparent as physical abuse, there are obvious methodological problems in measuring the phenomena.

*Legal Abuse/Violation of Civil Rights.* The writer maintains that this form of abuse occurs with greater frequency than the other categories. Legal abuse is defined as any violation of a person's Constitutional, federally protected, or state-protected rights. Although the individual may not suffer any apparent physical or psychological damage in the strictest sense, an abuse of authority has nonetheless occurred. In all cases of physical abuse, and many cases of verbal abuse, there will also be a legal violation. However, legal abuse can—and does—occur frequently without the other forms.

Each type of abuse has multiple independent variables which must be identified by a researcher who employs the model. The specific variables should be selected based on a particular agency's documented problems or perceived problems with abuse. The dependent variables (i.e., the specific abusive activities in each element of the typology) may differ between research populations with the model remaining intact. The reason for this is that the model is designed to explain contributory factors (i.e., independent variables including antecedent and intervening variables) in the abuse of authority, not types of abuse, per se. Hence, the typology is merely a mechanism to operationalize the "effect phenomena" to be measured.

A limitation to the typology is that classification of an incident requires a qualitative judgment of behavior. To be sure, some incidents can be classified with ease while the bulk of cases will most probably be debatable. This is a problem which has plagued social scientists consistently, given the fact that no operational definition can account for every nuance of human behavior. Thus, the lessons learned from scientific inquiry direct researchers to operationalize to the degree possible and support the inquiry with a valid and reliable methodology.

The fundamental thesis in this typology postulates that whenever a police officer exercises power by virtue of his/her office in a manner that is not consistent with law or policy, that officer has abused his/her legitimate authority. Given these parameters of behavior the model must now address the phenomena which precipitate the abuse. A causal paradigm has been developed which operationalizes factors that lead to abusive behavior. As in the case of the typology, the paradigm is constructed within the confines of traditional theory in order to establish consistency, hence predictability, of behavior.

# THE CAUSAL PARADIGM

Friedrich (1980, p. 85) observed that a plethora of hypotheses has been proposed to explain the use of force by police. Specifically he observed that:

> ...most studies have suffered from a narrow explanatory focus. They zero in on one factor or set of factors as crucial to explaining the use of force without recognizing that other factors may be involved. This creates two problems. First, without attention to other factors, it is difficult to have confidence that the relationships observed are genuine... Second, when only one factor or set of factors is examined, it is difficult to compare its effects to the effects of other factors to see how much of an effect it has relative to the others.

In his analysis of the literature Friedrich describes explanatory research on the use of force as focusing on one of three approaches: the individual, the situational, or the organizational.

> The individual approach tries to explain police use of force in terms of the characteristics of the officers...The situational approach seeks to account for police use of force by relating it to the specific characteristics of the situations in which police encounter citizens...The organizational approach sees the use of force as a product of the organizational setting, or some aspect of the setting within which it occurs (Friedrich, 1980, p. 84).

The paradigm proposed in this article attempts to avoid the narrow focus of explanation and concentrate on the more global issues. In statistical terms, this avenue is necessary in order to account for the variation contributing to the multiple incidents. Specifically, the paradigm includes (as causal variables) factors that transgress across the individual, situation, and organization. Furthermore, the causal phenomena proposed in this work treat elements of the Friedrich approach not as isolated causal variables but as interactive behavioral influences.

The paradigm is designed to explain both intentional and reactive abusive behavior. Intentional abuse is that which is overtly and consciously imposed by the officer. The decision to inflict the abuse is stimulated by the stressors discussed in the paradigm; however, there is some specific circumstance or act which provokes the officer's abusive behavior. For example, the officer's abuse may be motivated by revenge (e.g., physical abuse may be used against an individual who assaults a police officer, Friedrich's individual and situational approaches) or the desire to achieve a specified goal (e.g., legal abuse through an unlawful search with the intent to gather evidence for a conviction, situational approach). Regardless of the motivating force, the ultimate decision is influenced by the stressors.

Conversely, reactive abuse exists in response to stimuli or conditions without any overt, conscious decision to inflict the abuse. The reaction may be that of a conditioned response (e.g., an officer aggressively retaliates after being struck by a person, situational and individual approaches) or it may be the product of poor supervisory control (e.g., an officer improperly stops persons for investigative checks, organizational approach). Despite the nature of the reaction, the causal stressors influence the officer's decision-making ability, thereby precipitating the behavior.

An interesting concept that may be important in the causal structure of abuse is the police officer's "locus of control." This concept refers to a person's belief about the factors that shape their behaviors and, more generally, their lives. As proposed by Levenson (1981:17), the locus of control can be measured in three dimensions. "The I scale measures the extent to which people believe that they have control over their own lives...; the P scale deals with [the influence of] powerful others...; and the C scale is concerned with perceptions of chance control." One may postulate that if an officer's locus of control is internal (I scale) he/she may have a free-will orientation that influences that decision to abuse authority. Conversely, both the P and C scales are more deterministic. Perhaps even more interesting is the relation between the Friedrich categories and locus of control: I scale relating to the individual approach; P scale, the organizational approach; and the C scale for the situation. This concept is particularly congruent with the author's theoretical model under the assumption that the effect of stressors is going to be influenced by locus of control. Thus, the cumulative effect of stressors will be less pronounced on persons who perceive that they are in personal control of their lives and more evident in people who perceive that their life experiences occur as a matter of chance.

The causal paradigm is based on a concept of "cumulative interactive stressors." That is, there are a number of generic variables—stressors—which interact with a police officer's job performance, decision-making, and organizational membership. Stressors, as an individual phenomenon, do not "cause" dysfunctional behavior per se. They may, in fact, have functional benefits such as heightening alertness and making an individual more time-conscious.

Problems begin to rise, however, when multiple stressors begin to accumulate in an officer's faculties. If there is no legitimate release mechanism for the stress, an illegitimate means will surface. When this occurs, so does abuse. Once again, this illegitimate release mechanism may be of either an intentional or reactive nature and result in physical, verbal, or legal abuse.

The author has identified seven generic stressors, each of which may contribute to the abuse of authority. As the reader will note, the stressors encompass the critical elements embodied in the individual, situation, and organization. Thus, the paradigm may be viewed as a "grand theory" of causation.[2]

1. *Life-Threatening Stressors.* These are characterized by the embodiment of a constant potential of injury or death. A particularly important aspect of these stressors is the knowledge that violent acts against officers are intentional rather than accidental behaviors. Because the potential of a life-threatening situation is constant, the stressors are inherently cumulative.

2. *Social Isolation Stressors.* Included in this category are such factors as isolation and alienation from the community; differential socioeconomic status between the police and their constituency; authoritarianism; cynicism; and cultural distinction, prejudice, and discrimination.

3. *Organizational Stressors.* The author feels that this source of stress is particularly significant but too frequently overlooked (notably at the practical level). These stressors deal with all aspects of organizational life—both formal and informal. Specific stressors include: peer pressure, role models, performance measures for evaluation, upward mobility, policies and procedures (or the lack thereof leading to inconsistent and/or unacceptable behavior), job satisfaction, training, morale, inadequate supervision and administrative control, inadequate training, internal organizational jealousy (including "empire building"), management philosophy, the organizational structure, and leadership styles. Thus, simply being a member of an organization and trying to succeed can provide a significant amount of stress for the officer.

4. *Functional Stressors.* These are variables specifically related to the performance of assigned policing duties. Included in this category is role conflict; the use of discretion; knowledge of law and legal mandates; and decision-making

responsibilities such as the use of force, when to stop and question persons, and how to resolve domestic disputes. If an officer does not have a good understanding of his/her responsibilities and is ill-prepared to handle them, stress will increase.

5. *Personal Stressors.* These are stressors which have their primary origin in the officer's off-duty life, such as family problems or financial constraints. Particularly noteworthy in this grouping is marital discord, school or social problems of children, family illnesses, and associated personal or family crisis. The literature indicates that such stressors clearly influence an officer's on-duty personality, affecting both attitude and behavior.

6. *Physiological Stressors.* A change in one's physiology and general health may also affect one's decision-making capabilities, as well as one's tolerance of others' behavior. Fatigue from working off-duty jobs; the physiological impact of shift work (which interrupts the "body clock"); changes in physiological responses during critical incidents (i.e., getting "pumped up"); and illness or medical conditions are all examples of physiological stressors.

7. *Psychological Stressors.* Most of the stressors discussed above could also be classified in this category. However, the author maintains that certain stress variables have a significant direct impact on the inner self. For example, fear that is generated when an officer responds to a dangerous call can be a psychological stressor. The fear may be functional if the officer recognizes it as a warning mechanism and becomes more alert as a result. However, if the officer masks that fear and it becomes internalized, it can upset one's psychological balance. Other stress variables in this category include constant exposure to the worst side of humankind and the impact of resolving situations which are of a repulsive nature (e.g., homicides, child abuse, fatality traffic accidents, etc.). These situations can have a traumatic effect on oneself, particularly in their cumulative state. Such stressors may also develop into a psychological condition, such as depression or paranoia, which may, in turn, have a significant impact on the abuse of authority.

The stressors in this paradigm are not mutually exclusive. It is their interactive nature which lends support to the cumulative effect of being precipitators to abuse. The idea that stressors are cumulative in nature is of importance to note. As exposure to the stressors increases in both time and intensity without a control mechanism, the more the officer's self-control is eroded. The result is police behavior on an emotional rather than rational level.

The literature is replete with research and monographs on stress. These works examine stress generating from multiple sources and discuss the impact of stress on the psyche, interpersonal relationships, decision-making, job performance and a plethora of related issues. The empirical evidence indicates that stress does, in fact, influence the working persona of a police officer. However, as noted by Malloy and Mays (1983), externally valid empirical evidence that links policing to the effects of stress is more scarce than one may intuitively believe. Much of the literature on police stress is hypothetical in nature, relying on research from other occupational groups. The significance of this situation is to illustrate that specific research needs to be conducted on police populations to determine what stressors exist, the source of those stressors, and their effect.

Spielberger, et al. (1981) observed in their research—The Florida Police Stress Survey—that the sources of stress in police work are still unknown. Moreover, they found that although stress is present in police organizations the best way to control job-related stress is still debatable. In order to isolate the sources of stress in police work, Spielberger, et al. (1974), in one of the most frequently cited series of stress research reports, found that organizational stressors were a paramount source of stress in police officers. This is supported by Hillgren, et al. (1976:447), who found that "many sources of stress are not inherent in the job itself, but tend to originate from within the organization and its procedures."

Hillgren's research, while maintaining organizational stressors as a primary thesis, also found that functional stressors and social isolation stressors affected the performance of line personnel. These findings are supported by Eisenberg (1975) who suggests that the sources of stress are manifest in the organization, criminal justice system practices and characteristics, public practices and characteristics, and police work itself. This translates into the organizational, functional, social-isolation, and life-threatening stressors of this writer's model. Moreover, there is an implied cumulative interaction of those stressors from Eisenberg's research which lends further support to the theoretical model.

Stoddard (1977) discusses the "informal code of police deviancy" addressing personal relationships among police officers within the informal police organization. The impact of peer expectations and peer pressure is clearly illustrated in this work, which leads to a conceptual understanding of how functional and organizational stressors can influence police behavior with a specific relationship to abuse of authority. In support of this position Bittner (1970:67) discusses the closed communications system and informal standards characteristic of police organizations which, as Bittner observes, "preclude informing on even those officers who are violent and sadistic." [p. 67]. Perhaps this silence could be interpreted as condoning the abuse, thus establishing an illegitimate organizational norm which could contribute to more abuse.

Role conflict of police officers also appears to be a significant source of functional and psychological stress (Reiser, 1976). While police officers perceive their role to be that of the "crime fighter" and are socialized in this regard through training with reinforcement through community perceptions and mass media, the reality of the police officer's job is increasingly service-oriented. This point is accentuated particularly well, as related to functional stressors, by

Skolnick (1975) who observed the hypocrisy and associated role-conflict stress an officer experiences when enforcing laws which he/she may not subscribe to.

Any of these forms of stress may certainly affect the officer's psyche thus leading to psychological stress. However, psychological stressors can also take other forms. For example, Reiser (1976) notes that the threat of losing social control, threat to conscience, and fear of loss of control can be significant psychological stressors that affect officer behavior and decision-making ability. These stressors, if prolonged, may manifest themselves to the point of affecting one's physiological system. Such physiological stressors can result in increased heart rate, elevation of blood pressure, secretion of adrenaline and other hormones, and mobilization of glucose and fatty acids. If these conditions occur frequently and/ or under prolonged time periods they may lead to tissue damage and serious debilitating effects of the officer. These physiological conditions, even if not yet at the "serious" level, have been shown to affect an officer's behavior and general on-duty performance (Hageman, et al., 1979).

In light of the proposed causal model it is important to note Selye's (1978) observations that stress is a matter of perception. This perception is an interactive product of the officer's life experiences (i.e., socialization), job preparation (i.e., training), and expectations of others. This is further exemplified in Keller's (1978) research of police/citizen violence, wherein it was found that a police officer's lack of skill frequently precipitated violence. These findings reinforce Toch's (1970) research where it was found in more than half of the instances of assault against police officers that the behavior of the officer played a precipitating role. Thus, if stress is a social-psychological product of perception, the behavioral dynamics are implicit. When this behavioral profile is aggravated by a lack of skill and expressed in solicitous acts or deeds by an officer, the probability of abuse of authority is significantly increased.

The phenomenon is exacerbated when the stressors experienced by the officers accumulate in a manner described by Selye (1978) as the General Adaptation Syndrome (GAS). Selye proposes that the body adapts to stress in three stages: (1) alarm reaction, (2) resistance, and (3) exhaustion. The mental processes employed that attempt to resolve the stress become influenced and finally weakened at the exhaustion stage, detracting from one's ability to make sound, rational decisions. If stress is, in fact, cumulative as proposed by both this author and Greller (1982), then the trauma of the General Adaptation Syndrome will geometrically increase, thus further diminishing rational judgment and increasing the probability of abuse. If the most significant stressors in policing are emotional in nature (i.e., life-threatening and personal), as proposed by Selye, then one may conclude that the cumulative effect of the GAS may play an even more dramatic role.

Cumulative interaction of stressors is further illustrated in Reiser's (1976) observations that a police officer's fear of failure and responsibilities for the welfare of people seem to incur an excess risk of degenerative effects. Reiser goes on to note that "each individual has [his/her] own stress tolerance level which when unbalanced either by a stress overload or underload will lead to symptoms of distress" (p. 157). These findings not only lend support to the author's "cumulative interactive stressors" hypothesis but also suggest that with the knowledge of stressors some forms of control—or containment—can be developed. The literature suggests that programs can be established which control stressors at the individual and organizational levels (Burgin, 1978). Stress management programs involve both recognition of stressors and techniques to control the effect of stressors. Thus, it becomes incumbent for the organization to establish programs which control causal stressors in order to minimize the abuse of authority. In this regard the issues of stress control and abuse control become synonymous.

## STRATEGIES TO CONTAIN ABUSE

It is clear that if an individual has been wronged by the police there must be some form of remedial action taken. The most common remedies cited in the literature are civil litigation against the police and revised police complaint procedures. In the United States Commission on Civil Rights Reports *Law Enforcement* (1965), *Mexican Americans* (1970), and *Who is Guarding the Guardians?* (1981), the consistent remedial theme recommended by the Commission was civil and criminal litigation against the abusing officer for deprivation of civil rights. Similarly, each report stressed the need for citizen complaint procedures with an implied preference for civilian review.[3]

One cannot deny the necessity for these alternatives to maintain accountability for one's actions and, perhaps, to insure some degree of punishment is administered. As noted by Goldstein (1977:159), "If one looks objectively at the anguish, humiliation, loss of income, and physical suffering by those who have been wronged by the police...and who have unsuccessfully sought redress through established channels, one can appreciate the intensity of feelings that underlie demands for more effective control of police conduct." This writer, however, maintains that such remedies are too limited, perhaps even short-sighted. To be truly remedial one must also view the broader "victims"—society and the integrity of the system—and impose programs which have both retributive and preventive elements.

Following this line of thought, the author maintains that the idea of remedies alone is too narrow. A "remedy" implies corrective action for a past deed; however, this writer argues that a police organization should additionally take action to prevent future incidents of abuse. In consideration of this argument and the recognition that a singular activity will not forestall abusive acts, the author proposes the concept of differential containment strategies.

Differential containment strategies employ a probability model that is based on intrusive organizational activities devised to be remedial for current and past abusive acts as well as preventive of future abusive acts. The strategies are synergistic in nature, thereby providing a therapeutic approach to abuse which relies on organizational manipulation of the intrusive strategies.

Selected strategies address multiple organizational purposes thereby affecting abuse as an artifact of general management. Other strategies are designed to address specific abusive behavior. As illustrated in Figure 11.1 (which was originally prepared for Carter, 1985), the probability of abuse is omnipresent; however, the probability can be significantly limited if containment strategies are maximized, thereby reducing the cumulative interaction of stressors. Conversely, the probability of abuse increases when the differential containment strategies have experienced limited application.

From a theoretical approach, abuse has been operationalized with cause and effect relationships proposed. If the causal variables are known (i.e., the stressors) one may then establish a true theoretical framework for prevention and control. In this regard, the author presents a series of containment strategies in light of the previous discussion. These strategies are not collectively exhaustive nor are they necessarily new. The significances of the strategies are: (1) they are broad-based to address the total police control mandate; (2) they are presented specifically as containment activities in light of the causal stressors; and (3) they complete the elements of a true theoretical model on the abuse of police authority.

# DIFFERENTIAL CONTAINMENT STRATEGIES

*Personnel Selection.* In addition to traditional criteria, the selection of police officers should provide a greater focus on personality traits such as intelligence, humanity, honesty, stability, and reliability. People should be sought who are both capable of performing the required tasks and exercising ethical judgment in that performance.

*Training.* Both pre-service and in-service training should be increased in such areas as: the legal *process* (not just law), civil rights, social psychology, counseling, and service responsibilities of the police. Furthermore, there should be a decrease in the "technical crime-fighting" training of officers. The author's rationale for this position is: (1) Police officers should receive training which is more reflective of their actual duties (service/order maintenance) rather than their perceived (and probably overemphasized) responsibilities of "crime fighting." (2) The prevalence of "crime-fighting training" may contribute to a more punitive performance role model which affects officer behavior through a distorted perception of "just deserts" toward criminals.

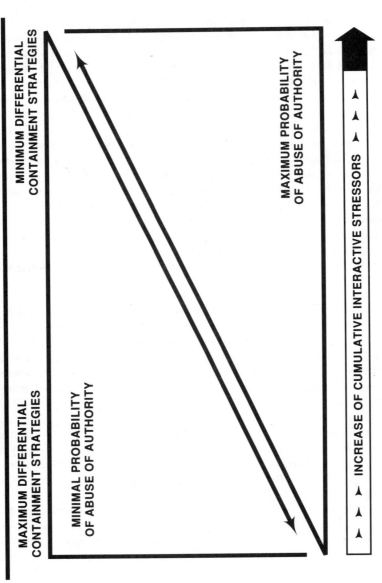

While continued development of training curricula is important, perhaps the most significant training issue is quality. Police agencies must ensure quality in: (1) the selection of trainers, (2) the types of training materials used, and (3) evaluation techniques of the training experience. The author has observed these quality-control limitations in agencies of various sizes. Police organizations must recognize that it is not the quality of training that must be increased but the substantive value of training. Moreover, if an officer's occupation socialization begins with marginal quality, one must expect that quality of job performance after training will also be marginal. Thus, training can be a significant influence on the officer's behavior. (Nota bene: This argument is consistent with the organizational approach and organizational/functional stressors.)

*Performance Evaluations.* This is one of the more difficult tasks to achieve objectively and accurately. Evaluations on traditional quantitative criteria of productivity are not truly indicative of police performance. Ideally, evaluations should be on qualitative variables addressing the service provided by officers. The use of unobtrusive measures would be the most utilitarian but difficult to instill in many police organizations. Similarly, validated forced choice or Behaviorally Anchored Performance Scales can provide important, reliable evaluative information (Whisenand, 1976). Qualitative evaluations are certainly more difficult than quantitative assessments; however, given the issue of reliability one must assume the effort is cost-beneficial.

*Open Complaint and Internal Investigation System.* If abuse is going to be controlled there must be an open system wherein citizens can make complaints. It is essential that a reliable mechanism exist for citizens to report improprieties in order for unacceptable behavior to be contained. This can also be an effective tool for evaluation by examining the nature of complaints and any trends in complaints. Evaluation can be at an individual level to identify officers that may need counseling, training, or some other form of intrusive activity to correct unacceptable behavior. Evaluation may also occur at the organizational level by identifying a pattern of complaints against officers. This may indicate a supervisory, control, training, or policy void that must be filled.

Regardless of the evaluative benefits of an open complaint and investigation system, one must be certain that the mechanism objectively investigates and adjudicates complaints.

*Public Information/Education.* A systematic method should be implemented which informs the public about the true dynamics of abuse of authority. Similarly, the public must be clearly informed of the complaint process. (At a minimum this process may establish empathy for the officers.) One may also hope that the information will contribute to some reduction of stressors and open communications between the police and the public. Generally, public opinion research indicates that the public is supportive of the police (Carter, 1983). Shedding the shroud of secrecy around the police and capitalizing on this support will decrease separatism and contribute to more productive and less conflictual performance.

*Trouble Shooting/Preventive Programs.* Internal programs should be developed which identify and treat potential (or existing) abusers. This writer maintains that the organization bear the responsibility for taking treatment action as well as punitive action. Under the premise that it is the organizational/work environment that generates a preponderance of the stressors one may conclude that the organization bears at least a moral responsibility to alleviate the stressors. If for no other reason, treatment of stressors can be a cost-beneficial investment for the department (e.g., reduces attrition, thus minimizing personnel costs; makes personnel more effective performers; etc.) and can serve to minimize the legal liabilities of officers and departments. Unfortunately, most police agencies tend exclusively to adopt a punishment mode for such individuals (which in some cases is certainly warranted) without consideration of a treatment mode.

*Policies, Procedures, and Organizational Control.* It is incumbent on the formal organization not only to promulgate rules for control of abuse but to also establish effective supervision of personnel to deal with the problem. Without clear organizational guidelines officers cannot know what is expected of them, nor will they have a firm base on which to rely for decision-making. Similarly, organizational control cannot be effectively achieved unless the officers are aware of possible sanctions which may be imposed for improper behavior.

## CONCLUSION

The development of any theory requires an initial proposition which must be critically examined and tested. As illustrated by Figure 11.2, the current paper has established a theoretical model based on interrelated constructs, operational definitions, and propositions. The next phase is to empirically assess the model in order to examine the proposed relationships and, in all probability, amend the model. Such evolution is the inherent nature of true scientific inquiry.

In viewing the model it should become apparent to the reader that the concept of abuse, the causal factors, and the remedies are all systemic. One should not examine each element of this paradigm as a separate entity. Rather, the constituents should be envisioned as a series of relationships that are reciprocal in nature.

The author has presented a comprehensive approach that defines "policy brutality," places the phenomena in perspective, and suggests methods for

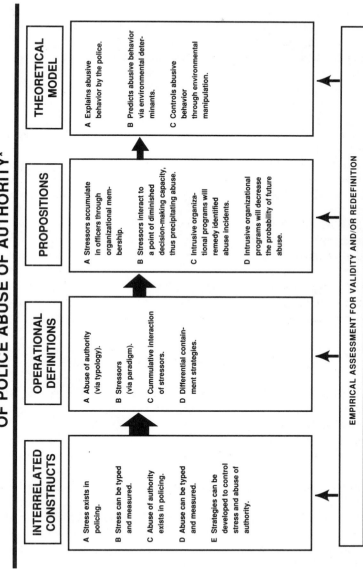

## SCHEMATIC OF A THEORETICAL MODEL OF POLICE ABUSE OF AUTHORITY*

**INTERRELATED CONSTRUCTS**

A Stress exists in policing.

B Stress can be typed and measured.

C Abuse of authority exists in policing.

D Abuse can be typed and measured.

E Strategies can be developed to control stress and abuse of authority.

**OPERATIONAL DEFINITIONS**

A Abuse of authority (via typology).

B Stressors (via paradigm).

C Cummulative interaction of stressors.

D Differential containment strategies.

**PROPOSITIONS**

A Stressors accumulate in officers through organizational membership.

B Stressors interact to a point of diminished decision-making capacity, thus precipitating abuse.

C Intrusive organizational programs will remedy identified abuse incidents.

D Intrusive organizational programs will decrease the probability of future abuse.

**THEORETICAL MODEL**

A Explains abusive behavior by the police.

B Predicts abusive behavior via environmental determinants.

C Controls abusive behavior through environmental manipulation.

EMPIRICAL ASSESSMENT FOR VALIDITY AND/OR REDEFINITION

*The author wishes to thank Dr. Abraham Blumberg of the University of Missouri-Kansas City for his comments and encouragement in the development of this model.

control. The model is not utopian, but a pragmatic avenue to understand how the frequency and intensity of abusive incidents can be minimized. In order for this objective to be realized there must be a commitment by the organization. This commitment involves re-thinking the police role as it specifically applies to the jurisdiction, conducting a critical organizational self-evaluation on efficiency and effectiveness variables, objectively establishing the true mission of the organization—not the perceived mission, and expressing a willingness to challenge traditionally-held beliefs and experiment with change.

## Notes

1   The idea of psychological coercion is closely akin to the concept of "police domi-
    nated atmosphere" the United States Supreme Court addressed in their opinion of
    *Miranda v. Arizona*, 383 U.S. 436, 86 S. Ct. 1602 (1966).

2   Descriptions of the stressors are taken from the author's original work on the theory
    (Carter, 1985) with only minor wording changes.

3   The courts also appear to have a strong penchant for civilian review as a mechanism to
    control police misconduct despite the rather dismal history of this approach. For a
    good overview of civilian review issues and a case study on civilian review see: Daniel
    K. Dearth, *The Court-Mandated Police Human Relations Committee: Its Reorgan-
    ization and Effect*. Paper presented to Academy of Criminal Justice Sciences Annual
    Meeting, San Antonio (1983).

# REFERENCES

Bittner, E. (1970). *The Function of the Police in Modern Society.* Washington, DC: U.S. Government Printing Office.

Burgin, A.L. (1978). "The Management of Stress in Policing." *The Police Chief* (April):14.

Carter, D.L. (1983). "Hispanic Attitudes Toward Crime and Justice in Texas." *Journal of Crime Justice* 11(3):213-227.

Carter, D.L. (1985). "Police Brutality: A Model for Definition, Perspective, and Control." In A. Niederhoffer and A. Blumberg (eds.) *The Ambivalent Force: Perspectives on the Police,* 3d ed. New York: Holt, Rinehart and Winston.

Eisenberg, T. (1975). "Labor-Management Relations and Psychological Stress—A View from the Bottom." *The Police Chief* (November):54-58.

Friedrich, R.J. (1980). "Police Use of Force: Individuals, Situations, and Organizations." *The Annals* (November):82-97.

Goldstein, H. (1977). *Policing in a Free Society.* Cambridge, MA: Ballinger Publishing Co.

Greller, M.M. (1982). "Police Stress: Taking a Department-wide Approach to Managing Stressors." *The Police Chief* (November):44-47.

Hageman, M.J. et al. (1979). "Coping with Stress." *The Police Chief* (February):24-28, 70.

Hillgren, J. et al. (1976). "Primary Stressors in Police Administration and Law Enforcement." *Journal of Police Science and Administration* 4(4):445-449.

Kania, R. and W.C. Mackey (1977). "Police Violence as a Function of Community Characteristics." *Criminology* 15:27-48.

Keller, P.A. (1978). "A Psychological View of the Police Officer Paradox." *The Police Chief* (April):24-25.

Kerlinger, F.N. (1973). *Foundations of Behavioral Research.* 2d ed., New York: Holt, Rinehart and Winston.

Kroes, W.H. et al. (1974). "Job Stress in Policemen." *Journal of Police Science and Administration* 2(2):145-155.

Levenson, H. (1981). "Differentiating Among Internality, Powerful Others and Chance." *Research with the Locus of Control Construct: Volume I.* New York: Academic Press.

Malloy, T.E. and G.L. Mays (1983). "The Police Stress Hypothesis: A Critical Evaluation." Paper presented at the Academy of Criminal Justice Sciences annual meeting. San Antonio, Texas. (Mimeographed).

President's Commission on Law Enforcement and Administration of Justice (1967). *Field Surveys, Volume 5: A National Survey of Police and Community Relations.* Washington, DC: U.S. Government Printing Office.

Reiser, M. (1976). "Stress, Distress and Adaptation in Police Work." *The Police Chief* (January):24-27.

Reiss, A.J. (1968). "Police Brutality—Answers to Key Questions." *Trans-Action* (July-August):10-19.

Selye, H. (1978). "The Stress of Police Work." *The Police Chronicle* (December):14.

Skolnick, J.H. (1975). "Why Police Behave the Way They Do." In J. Skolnick and T. Gray (eds.) *Police in America.* New York: Little, Brown and Company.

Spielberger, C. et al. (1981). *The Police Stress Survey: Sources of Stress in Law Enforcement.* Tampa, FL: University of South Florida.

Stoddard, E.R. (1977). "The Informal Code of Police Deviance: A Group Approach to 'Blue Coat Crime'." In D.B. Kennedy (ed.) *The Dysfunctional Alliance.* Cincinnati: Anderson Publishing Co.

Toch, H. (1970). "The Social Psychology of Violence." In E.I. Megargee and J.E. Hokanson (eds.) *The Dynamics of Aggression.* New York: Harper and Row.

United States Commission on Civil Rights (1961). *Justice.* Washington, DC: U.S. Government Printing Office.

United States Commission on Civil Rights (1964). *Law Enforcement: A Report on Equal Protection in the South.* Washington, DC: U.S. Government Printing Office.

United States Commission on Civil Rights (1970). *Mexican-Americans and the Administration of Justice in the Southwest.* Washington, DC: U.S. Government Printing Office.

United States Commission on Civil Rights (1981). *Who is Guarding the Guardians?* Washington, DC: U.S. Government Printing Office.

Whisenand, P.M. (1976). *Police Supervision: Theory and Practice.* 2d ed. Englewood Cliffs, NJ: Prentice-Hall, Inc.

Willis, C.L. (1983). "Criminal Justice Theory: A Case of Trained Incapacity?" *Journal of Criminal Justice* 11:447-458.

# Study Questions

1.  The term "brutality" is frequently used in the literature when referring to the excessive use of physical force by police officers. What are some of the inherent problems with the term "brutality" in the scientific investigation of the phenomenon?

2.  What is meant by police "abuse of authority"? How does the concept differ from "police violence" and "brutality" explanatory models?

3.  What are the fundamental concepts underlying the proposition of "cumulative interactive stressors?"

4.  The author proposes that police abuse of authority cannot be eliminated, but only "contained within the confines of a probability mode." What is meant by this statement and what are the implications for police management?

5.  How can training, personnel selection, and departmental policies minimize the occurrence of abuse of authority?

# 12

# POLICE USE OF DEADLY FORCE: EXPLORING SOME KEY ISSUES*

## Mark Blumberg

The United States is a society characterized by high rates of violent crime and easy citizen access to firearms. Because there are literally millions of handguns in circulation, it would be absurd to consider the possibility of disarming the police. Law enforcement personnel must be given adequate means to protect themselves and the general public from armed attack by criminals. However, the use of firearms by police officers raises a number of serious concerns which have increasingly received the attention of legal experts, police administrators, minority groups, social science researchers, and the public. Because law enforcement officers possess the ultimate power that any society can grant, the power to take life, and because this power is exercised without any judicial determination of guilt and without appellate review, it is clear that police use of deadly force raises a number of critical issues.

An unjustified killing by a police officer can result in a number of tragic consequences. Most important of all, a human life is needlessly lost. In addition, the officer may face termination from the department or in rare cases, criminal prosecution. The municipality may be forced to pay a large judgment as a result of a civil lawsuit. The reputation of the department may be tarnished and its relationship with the community can suffer irreparable harm. Finally, in some instances, the killing may trigger marches, protests, or even riots.

The serious consequences that may result when an officer makes the wrong decision have contributed to a proliferation of research studies dealing with the use of firearms by police officers. Many facets of this important question have been examined. This article explores six key concerns that have received a great deal of attention: 1) the "fleeing-felon" doctrine; 2) the impact of a more restrictive firearms policy; 3) the use of firearms by off-duty officers; 4) research measuring the frequency of police killings; 5) the relationship between officer characteristics and deadly force; and 6) whether blacks are over-represented as victims of police shootings because of racism on the part of law enforcement.

*This chapter was written expressly for inclusion in this book.

The author thanks Dr. James Fyfe for his ideas and contributions in the development of an earlier draft of this manuscript. Monica Weaver is also owed a debt of gratitude for her invaluable typing assistance.

# THE "FLEEING-FELON" DOCTRINE

Historically, American police officers have possessed enormous discretion regarding the use of deadly force. In addition to the right to use such force in self-defense (a right which is enjoyed by all citizens), police officers have also been granted, under the "fleeing-felon" doctrine, the right to use deadly force to apprehend any fleeing felony suspect who could not otherwise be captured. This doctrine evolved during the Middle-Ages in England and was transported to the 13 colonies. It later became the law in almost all of the United States. Although the "fleeing-felon" doctrine made sense at the time the "common-law" evolved, it is no longer an appropriate basis for public policy.

For one thing, all felonies were punishable by death in England during this period of time and courts did not devote as much attention as at present to safeguarding defendants' rights or to the presumption of innocence. Thus, if deadly force was used, the felon was merely receiving the same penalty that would be imposed after trial. Today, the situation is quite different. Very few felons are put to death.[1] In fact, as a result of the U.S. Supreme Court's ruling in *Coker v. Georgia*,[2] it is unlikely that a state could constitutionally execute an individual for any crime other than murder. Therefore, the common-law, as applied in twentieth-century America, no longer merely sanctions the use of deadly force for the purpose of apprehending a felon who is likely to be executed. It sanctions the use of deadly force to apprehend suspects who would be sent to prison if captured, or maybe even given probation.

The second reason that the fleeing-felon doctrine is no longer appropriate pertains to the nature of the felony/misdemeanor distinction. At common-law, only the most serious offenses were classified as felonies (e.g., murder, mayhem, arson, rape, etc.). Today, there are literally hundreds of felonies. Many of these are statutorily created offenses which are mala prohibita in nature and proscribe conduct that poses no physical danger to anybody (e.g., income tax evasion, possession of a substantial quantity of marijuana, shoplifting expensive items, etc.). Consequently, a rule which originally gave the authorities the right to use deadly force when necessary to apprehend the most dangerous criminals was transformed into a statute that allowed its use against a wide variety of individuals who did not present a demonstrable danger to either the police or the public.

The third distinction between the period in which the common-law developed and the present is that there was no communication between law-enforcement agencies in the former period. Therefore, felons who escaped were likely to remain at liberty forever. This is no longer true in many cases. Today, sophisticated computer networks give police departments the ability to instantaneously retrieve information on wanted criminal suspects from the FBI. Consequently, the choice is no longer to shoot at a fleeing felon or risk his permanent escape. In many cases, the choice is to use deadly force and perhaps kill the suspect in the process of apprehension or to let the individual escape and hopefully be apprehended at a later point in time.[3]

The fourth distinction between common-law times and the present also relates to changes in technology that have occurred. At the time that the "fleeing-felon" doctrine came into existence, there were no guns. Persons seeking to bring felons to justice were limited to the use of knives, swords, and other weapons that were effective only in hand-to-hand combat. With the invention of the handgun, the police were given the power through the fleeing-felon doctrine to stop individuals over a much greater distance, and at little risk to themselves.

Finally, it should be noted that felons had a greater incentive to resist arrest in common-law times. Because almost all felonies were punishable by death, suspects had every reason for using any method at their disposal to avoid capture. Under those circumstances, citizens (there were no municipal police agencies until the nineteenth-century) needed the legal right to use deadly force if necessary. Today, because very few felons are at risk of being executed, the incentive to escape at any cost is greatly reduced as well as the justification for allowing the police to use deadly force to effect capture.

Despite these criticisms, the fleeing-felon doctrine remained the law in all American jurisdictions until the 1960s. During this decade, many states began to change their statutes so that police officers no longer had unbridled discretion to shoot at all fleeing felons. Legislation generally followed one of two approaches in limiting the use of deadly force. The most common modification was to limit the use of deadly force to situations in which the police sought to apprehend individuals who have committed so-called forcible felonies. Such felonies are generally limited to the more serious offenses involving either violence or the threat of violence (e.g., robbery). By the early 1980s, 11 states had taken this approach (Wukitsch, 1983).

Another common approach was to adopt the legal guidelines suggested by the Model Penal Code[4] for the control of deadly force. Under the Model Penal Code, a police officer may use deadly force only when the arrest is for a felony that involved the use or threatened use of deadly force or when the officer believes that the suspect will cause death or serious bodily injury if not immediately apprehended. By the early 1980s, 10 states had adopted this approach (Wukitsch, 1983).

Despite these reforms, almost half of the states in 1985 still followed the common-law, fleeing-felon doctrine when the U.S. Supreme Court handed down its decision in *Tennessee v. Garner*.[5] In this case, the court ruled that the use of deadly force to apprehend a non-violent, fleeing-felon suspect violated the Fourth Amendment right to be protected against unreasonable searches and seizures. The rationale behind the Court's decision was that the use of deadly force to stop a fleeing suspect is a seizure within the scope of the Fourth Amendment. As such, these seizures must be reasonable and serve a legitimate law-enforcement purpose. Quoting from the *Amici Curiae* belief filed in the case by the Police Foundation,[6] the Court noted that "laws permitting police officers to use deadly force to apprehend unarmed, non-violent fleeing felony suspects actually do not protect citizens or law-enforcement officers, do not deter crime or alleviate problems caused by crime, and do not improve the crime-fighting ability of law-enforcement agencies" (p. 11). For these reasons, the use of deadly force under these circumstances is not reasonable and statutes still in effect which give police the legal right to use deadly force against non-violent, unarmed fleeing-felons were declared unconstitutional. The common-law fleeing-felon doctrine had at last been put to rest in the United States.

The impact of *Garner* will be greatest for smaller police agencies. Fyfe and Blumberg (1985) report that in a 1982 survey of 75 police departments that served populations of 100,000 or more, only one agency allowed the use of deadly force to apprehend all fleeing-felons. On the other hand, a survey which included county sheriffs' departments and police agencies serving a population of 20,000 or more indicated that slightly more than a third of the departments had no written policy whatsoever (Nielson, 1983). These departments will need to develop policies to insure compliance with the requirements of *Garner*.

The *Garner* decision does not completely resolve the debate regarding policy. In its ruling, the Court held that a police officer may use deadly force to prevent the escape of a suspect when there is probable cause to believe that the individual would present a threat of serious physical harm, either to the officer or to the public. As the majority opinion in this case noted, such probable cause would exist if the suspect had threatened the officer with a weapon or committed a crime which involved the infliction or threatened infliction of serious physical injury. Others would impose more restrictive policies, however. The National Organization of Black Law Enforcement Executives (NOBLE) and the American Civil Liberties Union (ACLU) have advocated the adoption of policies which permit the use of deadly force only in defense of life (Matulia, 1985:61). For a critique of this position, see Fyfe and Blumberg (1985).

# THE IMPACT OF A RESTRICTIVE FIREARMS POLICY

Police administrators have the option of adopting departmental firearms policies which are more restrictive than state law. Therefore, beginning in the early 1970s, some large urban police agencies located in common law states began to implement policy guidelines which were more restrictive than state statute. Because officers who violated these guidelines could not be prosecuted, only terminated, some questioned the efficacy of these policies for reducing the level of violence directed at citizens. Fortunately, a number of research studies have addressed this issue.

Fyfe (1979) examined shootings by New York City police officers and concluded that a more restrictive policy did reduce the number of shootings, even in the absence of a change in state law. Meyer (1980) reached the same conclusion in Los Angeles. Binder et al. (1982) report a decline in the monthly shooting frequencies for three cities (Birmingham, Newark, and Oakland) following the introduction of a more restrictive policy. Finally, Sherman (1983) reports a similar conclusion regarding the effect of more restrictive firearms policies in Atlanta and Kansas City.

The effect that restrictive firearms policies have on officer safety is another issue that has been addressed by researchers. Fyfe (1979) reports that line-of-duty deaths actually declined in New York after the implementation of the more restrictive firearms policy. Although he does not necessarily attribute the decline to the adoption of the policy, it is clear that a more restrictive policy does not make the police officer's job more dangerous. Not only was this relationship between policy change and officer safety replicated in Atlanta (Sherman, 1983), but it has also been observed by Sherman et al. (1986) that despite increasingly restrictive departmental firearms policies and despite the fact that the number of citizens killed by police officers has been cut in half for the 50 largest cities over the last 15 years (1970-84), the number of "citizen killings of police in those cities fell by two-thirds in the same fifteen year period" (p. 1). Clearly, restrictive firearms policies do not make a police officer's job more risky. They may even contribute to a safer working environment.[7]

## THE ARMING OF OFF-DUTY OFFICERS

Approximately one-quarter of the police departments in the United States require their off-duty officers to carry weapons at all times if they are within the jurisdiction. Most other police agencies leave this decision to the discretion of the officer (Police Executive Research Forum and the Police Foundation, 1981). The question of whether off-duty officers should be armed depends very much on the role that society expects them to play. Fyfe (1980) has examined the various arguments pro and con with respect to this issue and concludes that the time may have arrived when police should "leave their guns in their lockers with the rest of their uniform" (p. 81). In this section, we will explore what factors led him to this conclusion.

Several reasons are cited as justification for arming off-duty police officers. For one thing, it is asked: How can an off-duty officer intervene to stop a crime that is in progress without a firearm? Secondly, it can be argued that the presence of a substantial number of armed off-duty officers walking around the community in street clothes serves as a deterrent to potential criminals. Third, it is suggested that off-duty officers must carry weapons for their own protection.

The first argument is the most complex for its goes to the heart of the controversy surrounding the proper role to be played by off-duty police officers. Generally, police officers are expected "to respond in an appropriate manner to situations threatening to life, property, or order" (Fyfe, 1980:73) regardless of whether they are on or off duty. What is an appropriate manner, however? A hypothetical situation should suffice to make this question clearer.

Let us suppose that an off-duty officer is eating dinner at a restaurant and that two hold-up men enter and demand money from the owner. What options does the officer have? On the one hand, he can identify himself, jump up from his seat, draw his weapon, and confront the suspects. On the other hand, he can sit calmly in his chair and make careful mental notes of the suspects so that the information can be turned over to on-duty investigators in the hope of later apprehending the suspects. Another possibility, of course, is to follow the suspects after they leave the premises. What are the advantages and the disadvantages of the officer taking aggressive police action under these circumstances?

Confronting the robbers may terminate the robbery and prevent the loss of the owner's property (which is likely to be covered by insurance anyway). However, it may also lead to a violent exchange of gunfire in which the robbers, innocent bystanders, or the officer himself are killed or seriously wounded. As Fyfe (1980) has noted, off-duty officers are at a disadvantage in such situations for a number of reasons.

For one thing, they are not in radio communication with the department. Thus, there is no opportunity to call for assistance. Secondly, they have been thrust into the encounter without prior warning. Consequently, there is no opportunity, as with a radio-dispatched assignment, to plan strategy. Third, the off-duty officer may not be physically or psychologically ready for the confrontation. He may be tired, his reflexes and judgment may have been dulled by alcohol, and he may be concerned about the safety of his family or other companions. Finally, the officer in street clothes, armed with a weapon, runs the risk of being mistaken for the criminal and being shot by uniformed on-duty officers who arrive on the scene.

The other options have some drawbacks as well. If the officer refrains from taking direct action, the robbers will escape with their loot, perhaps forever. However the risk of death or serious injury occurring to either the officer or to any of the bystanders is dramatically reduced. Although many police officers believe that to be discovered as "cops" in such situations means certain death, Fyfe (1980:79-80) notes that the data from New York City suggests that this is not the case. He reports not a single incident in which an off-duty officer was shot merely "because he was a cop" (p. 80), while many were shot while attempting to forcibly intervene in such situations. Clearly, whether or not a police officer should take aggressive action in these and similar situations depends on how one evaluates the relative costs and benefits incurred.

The second reason cited for arming off-duty police officers is to deter potential criminals. The question of deterrence as Fyfe notes, is a difficult, although not impossible, issue to research. Studies could be undertaken to examine the effect on potential criminals of the presence in the community of armed individuals in street clothes who happen to be off-duty police officers. At present, no such studies exist. However, we do know that a substantial proportion of police shootings (15-20%) involve off-duty officers (Milton et al., 1977) and that many of these are not justifiable in that they violate either departmental policy or the law (Fyfe, 1980).

Off-duty police officers do use their weapons to apprehend criminals. However, they also use them on occasion to settle personal disputes with neighbors, friends, and spouses or to end their own lives. Thus, we are forced to ask the following question: Does the deterrent effect of arming off-duty officers outweigh the costs associated with this policy? Because data are not available with respect to the question of deterrence, we are unable to resolve this issue at the present time.

The third rationale for arming off-duty police officers is that they require protection from criminals seeking revenge. Intuitively, this may make sense but it also may be the weakest argument. Police are not alone in helping to send criminals to the penitentiary. Prosecutors and judges also perform this task, albeit unarmed. Nonetheless, we rarely read reports of attacks by criminals against their officials. Given the fact that criminals who tried to take revenge would incur a high risk of being recognized or otherwise identified, it is unlikely that police officers would have to worry about this danger either.

Despite the arguments pro and con, few police departments are likely to take steps to disarm their off-duty officers. As Fyfe notes, the claim that an officer has the responsibility to enforce the law twenty-four hours per day can be a powerful argument for higher police salaries at contract negotiation time. In addition, the public is likely to perceive the disarming of off-duty officers as yet another restriction on the power of the police to fight crime. Instead, the recent trend has been for departments to give officers the option of whether or not to carry a weapon off-duty and to discourage this practice while participating in sports or social events where it is likely that alcoholic beverages will be consumed. A survey taken in 1978 indicated that approximately one-half of the departments required their off-duty officers to carry weapons at all times if they were within the jurisdiction (Heaphy, 1978). Three years later, only one-quarter of the agencies still had this requirement (Police Executive Research Forum and The Police Foundation, 1981).

## MEASURING THE FREQUENCY OF POLICE KILLINGS

Statistical data encompassing a wide range of topics are routinely collected and published by all levels of government in the United States. For this reason, it is quite surprising to learn "that this country simply does not know how many of its own citizens it kills each year under the authority of the state" (Sherman and Langworthy, 1979:553). There is no reporting system with respect to police-caused homicides and no accurate count of the number of citizens shot/killed by the police each year in the United States. Although the FBI collects information on killings by police officers in the supplementary homicide reports filed by law enforcement agencies with the Uniform Crime Reporting Section, it does not publish these data due to reservations with respect to their quality (Sherman and Langworthy, 1979:547).

In the absence of any centralized reporting system, researchers have often relied on the *Vital Statistics of the United States* to measure the number of police-caused homicides (Kuykendall, 1981; Kobler, 1975; and Takagi, 1974). These data are based on death certificates which have been completed by coroners (or medical examiners) and submitted to the state health department. In turn, the various state health agencies transmit these reports to the National Center for Health Statistics (U.S. Public Health Service) which publishes the information in the *Vital Statistics*. Because there is a category on the death certificate entitled, "death by legal intervention—police," these reports should provide an accurate account of the number of police homicides in the U.S. Unfortunately, this is not the case.

According to the *Vital Statistics,* the number of police-caused homicides in the U.S. between 1965 and 1979 ranged from a low of 265 to a high of 412 per year (Binder and Fridell, 1984:255). However, Sherman and Langworthy (1979) observed, based on an examination of data supplied by police agencies in 13 jurisdictions, that *Vital Statistics* may underreport the number of police killings by as much as 51 percent (p. 553). This system of reporting has so many flaws that the information generated is unreliable with respect to both the total number of police killings and the relative incidence of police-caused homicide from one city to another. It is ironic, as the authors note (Sherman and Langworthy, 1979:560), that "while the police may have the most to gain by undercounting the number of citizens they kill...it is the police that have provided the largest figures on the numbers of citizens killed."

More recently, researchers have relied on data voluntarily supplied by police departments in urban areas (Sherman et al., 1986; Matulia, 1985; and Milton et al., 1977). These studies have provided reliable information for large cities. However, the number of citizens killed for the nation as a whole remains unknown. Sherman et al. (1986:21) has recommended that a national reporting system be established within the U.S. Department of Justice to correct this problem. These authors note that such a system is already in place to collect information regarding capital punishment statistics. Because the police are responsible for many more deaths, why not do the same with respect to these killings?

The most important finding to emerge from this body of research is that the number of police-caused homicides has declined substantially in recent years.

Sherman et al. (1986) reports that the total number of annual killings by officers in 50 of the nation's largest cities (>250,000 pop.) declined by one-half between 1970 (353) and 1984 (172). This decrease was not accompanied by either a drop in the over-all homicide rate or in the general level of violence within these communities. The authors attribute this decline in police killings to several factors: increasingly restrictive shooting policies, more intensive training and discipline by police departments, a rise in civil litigation, and greater participation by the black community in the political process.[8]

Another important finding that emerges from the studies which have relied on data supplied by law-enforcement agencies is that the rate of killings/shootings varies dramatically across departments. Sherman et al. (1986:3) reports that officers in Atlanta killed citizens (between 1970-74) at a rate 44 times higher than was the case in Oklahoma City. These differences between cities are not explained by population size, the number of police officers or the overall general homicide rate. In an earlier report, Milton et al. (1977) had observed that the variation in police shooting rates could not be explained by population size (p. 29), or police department size (p. 31). The finding that consistently emerges is not that cities with high levels of crime will necessarily have a large number of citizens shot/killed by law enforcement officers, but that the level of police violence within a jurisdiction is more a function of policy considerations than the general crime rate.

Finally, it should be noted that the use of deadly force is a rare event in the career of a police officer, even in cities with very high rates of police-caused homicide. Sherman et al. (1986:5) observe that in Jacksonville, Florida (a city which was ranked at the top according to one measure for the period 1980-1984), a police officer, on the average, could be expected to work 139 years before killing a citizen. On the other hand, a Milwaukee officer in the same period would have waited 1,299 years and a Honolulu officer could be expected to work 7,692 years before fatally wounding a citizen.

## THE RELATIONSHIP BETWEEN OFFICER CHARACTERISTICS AND THE USE OF DEADLY FORCE

If it could be demonstrated that certain officer characteristics are related to a decreased risk of involvement in shooting incidents, police departments could recruit officers with these traits and reduce the level of police-citizen violence in their community. Unfortunately, there has not been a great deal of empirical research on the relationship between individual officer characteristics and firearms usage. Nonetheless, a few studies have examined this question.

One of the few data sets that allowed analysis of this issue was made available to this author by the Kansas City (MO) Police Department. Demographic data were collected for all officers who fired their weapons at citizens between

1972 and 1978. Identical information was also gathered for a randomly selected control group representing all nonshooters who had served with the department during this period of time (Blumberg, 1983a: Chapter IV). Because the research design incorporated data with respect to the unit and beat of assignment for each of the officers, it was possible to compare shooters and nonshooters in terms of a number of social characteristics while controlling for exposure to risk due to work assignment.

The findings indicated that most officer characteristics were not related to shooting behavior. Race, height, prior military service, marital status at appointment, preservice officer experience with firearms, and whether or not the officer himself had been arrested prior to joining the department all failed to distinguish between shooters and nonshooters. Only age and length of police service were strongly related to shooting behavior. Younger officers and those with fewer years of police experience were significantly more likely to become involved in a shooting (controlling for assignment). In addition, there was some evidence indicating that females and middle-class officers were less likely to shoot at citizens. However, the relatively small number of female officers[9] in the sample and the larger number of missing cases with respect to officer-social class precluded a precise analysis of these relationships.

The other studies that have attempted to find relationships between officer characteristics and shooting behavior have had even less success. Sherman and Blumberg (1981) examined the relationship between officer education level and deadly force. The authors find little relationship between these variables. Geller and Karales (1981) and Fyfe (1981a) examined the relationship between officer race and shootings. Both researchers observed that black officers have a higher shooting rate than white officers. Geller and Karales attribute this disparity primarily to a black overrepresentation in off-duty shootings (stemming in large part from officer residence patterns). Because black officers more often reside in high-crime areas of the city, they have a greater risk than white officers of becoming involved in shootings when off-duty. There is no significant overrepresentation in on-duty shootings by these officers. Fyfe (1981a) did find racial disparities among both on- and off-duty shooting rates, but reports that when officer assignment and residence are controlled, most of the differences disappear. Thus, it does not appear that police departments can reduce the number of shootings by hiring additional black officers.

Finally, it must be noted that Alpert (1984) failed to find a relationship in Miami between officer age or length of police service and shooting behavior. This finding was unexpected, given the strong relationships observed between these variables by Blumberg (1983a: Chapter IV) in Kansas City, Missouri. Alpert does report, however, that younger, inexperienced officers are more frequently involved in unintentional shootings. It has been suggested that at the time of this research, many of the Miami officers were so young that they were not at risk of intentional shooting because they were still in training and not on the street.[10]

The limited body of research suggests that attempts to reduce the number of police shootings by hiring certain types of officers may not be very effective in the short-term. There is little relationship between most officer characteristics and shooting behavior. However, as Walker (1985) notes, the long-term impact on the police culture resulting from an infusion of a substantial number of minority and female officers remains unknown. Although there is little relationship between officer race and the use of deadly force, it is conceivable that a predominantly white department in a community with a large black population would have a less harmonious relationship with its citizens, and thus more shootings, than a department with a substantial number of black officers. What is clearly needed, as the Dade County Grand Jury (1983:4-5) has noted, is more research which examines the relationship between officer characteristics and police use of deadly force. In the interim, police administrators may wish to explore policies which are designed to reduce the number of shootings by younger officers, a group which has been shown to have a high rate of involvement. Increased supervision, better training, lateral entry, and raising the minimum age for policework to 25 years should be considered as possible options in this regard.

# RACE DISCRIMINATION AND
# POLICE USE OF DEADLY FORCE

There is probably no other issue with respect to police use of deadly force that evokes as much controversy and generates as much attention as police shootings of blacks. Such incidents were often the catalysts that sparked many of the riots that occurred in our urban areas during the 1960s. Throughout the 1970s and into the 1980s, controversial shootings involving blacks have continued on occasion to create mistrust between police agencies and the citizens they serve. Los Angeles, Houston, Birmingham, Miami, New York, and other cities have all experienced incidents that created a storm of controversy, led to polarization between the police and the black community and to protests directed against the unnecessary use of deadly force. On occasion, such shootings have even led to violence. Consequently, it is not surprising that a great deal of research has been conducted on the issue of police shootings that involve blacks.

All studies are in agreement that blacks are the victims of police deadly force in numbers disproportionate to their representation in the general population (Matulia, 1985; Geller and Karales, 1981; Blumberg, 1981, Fyfe, 1981B, Meyer, 1980; Fyfe, 1978; Milton et al., 1977; Jenkins and Faison, 1974; Dallas Police Department, 1974; Takagi, 1974; Burnham, 1973; Knoohuizen, Fahey and Palmer, 1972; and Robin, 1963). What the studies disagree about is the reason for this finding. In fact, the range of opinion with respect to this question is quite broad.

Goldkamp (1976), after surveying the literature on race and police shootings, concludes that researchers generally subscribe to one of two belief perspectives. Belief Perspective I links the disproportionately high minority shooting rates to the impact of differential policing (i.e., race discrimination by the police). The best known proponent of this point of view is Takagi (1974) who has argued that "the police have one trigger-finger for whites and another for blacks." Belief Perspective II links the number of minority shootings to disproportionate minority arrest rates for crimes of violence. Arrest rates are seen as reflecting a disproportionate participation by minorities in violent criminal activity and therefore, to account for the relatively great number of minorities shot by the police. A number of researchers subscribe to this point of view (Matulia, 1985; Geller and Karales, 1981; Blumberg, 1981; Fyfe, 1981B; Milton et al., 1977; and the Dallas Police Department, 1974).

Studies seeking to explore the question of why blacks are overrepresented among victims of police deadly force have utilized a variety of techniques. Matualia (1985), Blumberg (1983a), Geller and Karales (1981), Meyer (1980), Fyfe (1978), Milton et al. (1977), Takagi (1974), Dallas Police Department (1974), Burnham (1973), and Robin (1963) compared arrest statistics and shooting data to determine if blacks are more likely to be the victims of police shootings than would be expected by their representation among those arrested for various types of criminal activity. We will call this technique Methodology I.

Fyfe (1982), Blumberg (1981), Geller and Karales (1981), Meyer (1980), and the Dallas Police Department (1974) examined the situational characteristics of shooting incidents to determine whether blacks are shot/killed under circumstances that present less danger to the officer, and thus less justification, than those incidents which involve white victims. We will call this technique Methodology II. The assumption underlying this approach is that if race discrimination is present, we should find that blacks are shot and/or killed under circumstances that present less justification. For example, a finding that an equivalent proportion of white and black victims are unarmed would be taken to indicate that race discrimination on the part of the police was not responsible for the disproportionate involvement of blacks as shooting victims in that particular community.

Finally, Blumberg (1983b) has utilized a new approach to examine this question (Methodology III). Analysis of the situation characteristics of police shootings that occurred in the white and minority neighborhoods of New York City was conducted to determine whether citizens were shot and/or killed under circumstances that present less justification in minority communities. No evidence was uncovered to indicate that this is the case. However, the importance of this study lies not so much in its findings with respect to New York, but in the fact that it lays out a new methodology for the examination of this question.

Each of these approaches has shortcomings. Examination of arrest statistics is problematic for a couple of reasons. For one thing, there is the question of which set of arrest statistics is the appropriate comparative measure with which to examine the issue of race discrimination in police shootings (Blumberg, 1981). Should the proportion of black shooting victims in a particular jurisdiction be compared to the proportion of black arrestees in that community who are charged with violent index crimes, with any index crime, or with any crime? Secondly, there is concern whether arrest statistics really are a valid indicator of the extent to which minority citizens commit crimes (Peirson, 1978). If arrest statistics themselves reflect discriminatory law enforcement by the police, they obviously have little value for addressing the question of whether shootings are the result of race discrimination by police.

There is a problem with the other techniques as well. Because baseline data are not usually available with respect to all police-citizen encounters, Methodology II is not able to determine whether the police are more likely to shoot blacks than whites under the circumstances. Thus, even if the data indicate that an equal proportion of blacks and whites who were shot were unarmed, it still does not tell us if unarmed blacks were more likely to be shot since one does not know the relative number of unarmed whites and blacks who come into contact with the police.[11] One can only determine whether the situational characteristics of shooting incidents are similar for both races. Fyfe (1982) was able to overcome this limitation by using property crime arrests as baseline data for his analysis in Memphis and New York.

Methodology III has the same shortcomings. Because baseline data are not available regarding all police-citizen contacts in white and minority communities, it is only possible to determine if the situational characteristics of shooting incidents are similar. Although we can compare, for example, the proportion of shooting victims in white and minority communities who are unarmed, it is not possible to discern whether the police are more likely to shoot at an unarmed person in the minority community.[12]

Obviously, resolving the question of why blacks are disproportionately the victims of police deadly force is not an easy matter. As we have observed, any attempt to do so is plagued by a number of methodological difficulties. For this reason, future researchers should utilize all three methodologies in conjunction with each other to examine the question of whether the disproportionate number of blacks shot in a particular community is the result of race discrimination on the part of the police. If none of these various approaches produces evidence of discrimination, administrators and citizens alike could be reasonably confident that a problem does not exist in their community.

Having examined the methodological difficulties which surround this issue, we turn our attention to the findings of these studies. For the most part, the research suggests that race discrimination on the part of the police does not explain the disproportionate representation of blacks as shooting victims.

Generally, studies which utilize Methodology I find that the proportion of black shooting victims is comparable to their representation among those arrested for violent crimes (Matulia, 1985; Blumberg, 1983a; Geller and Karales, 1981; Fyfe, 1978; Milton et al., 1977; Dallas Police Department, 1974; and Burnham, 1973). Studies which utilize Methodology II have reached different conclusions, depending on the city which was examined.

Blumberg (1981) has observed that the situational characteristics of police shootings are similar in Kansas City (MO) and Atlanta regardless of opponent race. On the other hand, Meyer (1980) was able to conclude that shooting incidents involving black suspects in Los Angeles differ in circumstances from those involving others (1980:107). Geller and Karales (1981) found that a greater proportion of the black opponents (than whites) in Chicago were shot under circumstances that either presented serious danger or no danger to the police. Because many of the remaining incidents were classified in an ambiguous manner,[13] it is not possible to clearly determine whether white or black citizens were shot under circumstances that presented less justification in Chicago. Finally, Fyfe (1982) has utilized this approach to examine shootings in Memphis and New York. He finds evidence of racial discrimination in Memphis, but not in New York.

A number of observations are in order with respect to these findings. For one thing, it is clear that the question of why blacks are disproportionately the victims of police shootings must be examined on a city-by-city basis. What is true in one department may not be the case in another. As the Fyfe (1982) study illustrates, because there is evidence of race discrimination in Memphis does not mean that this is also true in New York. Indeed, previous research (Blumberg, 1983a: Chapter VII, Milton et al., 1977) has demonstrated that there is variation between communities not only in the rate of police shootings, but in their nature as well. Secondly, we must entertain the possibility that those departments which have allowed analysis of their shooting data by outside researchers may not be representative of other police agencies. It is conceivable that these departments are more progressive and have less to fear than other agencies. If that is the case, we must be very cautious about over-generalizing from those studies which suggest that race discrimination on the part of the police does not explain the disproportionate representation of blacks as victims of police shootings. Indeed, our suspicions are buttressed somewhat by the fact that the one study which discerned clear evidence of discrimination (Fyfe, 1982) was based not on information willingly supplied by the department, but obtained as a result of a subpoena served in a civil suit.[14]

Finally, we must recognize that race discrimination at the societal level is clearly responsible for much of the disproportionate representation of blacks as shooting victims. It should be remembered that blacks are also overrepresented as victims of justifiable homicides committed by private citizens (Matulia, 1985:34). As long as institutional discrimination continues to exist, the social conditions that are responsible for the disproportionate black involvement in violent crime will go unabated. Until this situation is remedied, blacks will continue to be overrepresented not only as the victims of police shootings, but in the jail, prison, and death-row populations as well.

## SUMMARY

This chapter has examined a number of key issues with respect to police use of deadly force. The first section examined the history of the "fleeing-felon" doctrine and the successful battle to abolish it. Next, various research studies which have examined the impact of more restrictive firearms policies were explored. This was followed by a discussion of the relative advantages and disadvantages of arming off-duty police officers. Fourth, we examined the question of how many police killings actually occur in the United States each year. It was clear from the discussion that this is not an easy question to answer. Fifth, the relationship between officer social characteristics and shootings was explored. We noted that younger, less-experienced officers are more likely to become involved in shooting incidents. There is also some preliminary evidence that females and officers drawn from middle-class backgrounds are less likely to use their weapons. Finally, the controversy surrounding the disproportionate number of black shooting victims was examined. The growing body of research in this area, the methodological problems inherent in resolving this question, and the findings of the various studies were discussed.

# Notes

1    Between 1977 and 1987, approximately 100 persons were executed by judicial order upon conviction for murder in the United States.

2    *Coker v. Georgia,* 422 U.S. 584 (1977).

3    Because clearance rates are quite low for many crimes, some have argued that fleeing felons are not likely to be apprehended at a later date. However, as Silberman (1978) notes, these clearance rates are misleading. Because offenders generally commit many offenses, not just one, the likelihood of eventually being arrested is much greater than clearance rates would suggest.

4    The Model Penal Code was drafted by the American Law Institute (ALI) in 1962 as a guide which states may wish to follow when revising their criminal statutes and procedures.

5    *Tennessee v. Garner* 105 S. Ct. 1694 (1985).

6    The Police Foundation is a private research institute that came into existence in 1970 with an endowment from the Ford Foundation. It is dedicated to improving the quality of law enforcement in the United States.

7    Because these restrictive policies in no way inhibit the officer from using deadly force in self-defense, it is not surprising that officer safety is not jeopardized.

8    The decline in the number of police-caused homicides did not result from *Tennessee v. Garner.* This decision was handed down by the U.S. Supreme Court in 1985 and the Sherman et al. (1986) report examined the period 1970-84. As previously noted, by the mid-1980s, most large urban police departments already had firearms policies more restrictive than state statute.

9    There were 44 female officers serving with the Kansas City (MO) Police Department on 12/31/78, comprising only four percent of the agency's personnel.

10   Personal communication from Dr. James J. Fyfe, May 20, 1985.

11   E.g., let us say that 50 percent of both white and black opponents were armed. It could still be argued by some that this does not eliminate the possibility that blacks are more likely to be shot than whites under similar circumstances. Because baseline data with regard to the number of armed citizens of each race who came in contact with the police are not available, a definite answer to this question is not possible.

12   E.g., three of these methodologies have been utilized to examine shootings by New York City officers and the findings consistently suggest that the disproportionate number of black victims in that community does not result from racial discrimination by the police.

13   Geller and Karales classified many of the other incidents as involving the use of or a threat with either another deadly weapon (not a gun) or physical force. Clearly, these

responses do not represent equivalent levels of risk for a police officer. Consequently, how does one interpret the finding that black shooting victims are less likely to respond in this manner (pp. 123-124)?

[14]    *Wiley v. Memphis Police Department,* 548 F. 2d 1247 (6th Cir. 1977).

# REFERENCES

Alpert, G.P. (1984). *Police Use of Deadly Force: The Miami Experience.* Center for the Study of Law and Society, University of Miami.

Binder, A. and L. Fridell (1984). "Lethal Force as a Police Response." *Criminal Justice Abstracts,* Vol. 16:2, pp. 250-280.

Binder, A., P. Scharf and R. Galvin (1982). "Use of Deadly Force by Police Officers." *Final Report.* Washington, DC: National Institute of Justice.

Blumberg, M. (1983A). "The Use of Firearms by Police Officers: The Impact of Individuals, Communities and Race." Ph.D. dissertation, School of Criminal Justice, State University of New York at Albany.

Blumberg, M. (1983B). "Police Shootings in Minority Communities." A paper presented at the *Annual Meeting of the Criminal Justice Sciences,* San Antonio.

Blumberg, M. (1981). "Race and Police Shootings: An Analysis in Two Cities." In J.J. Fyfe (ed.) *Contemporary Issues in Law Enforcement.* Sage Publications, Inc.

Burnham, D. (1973). "3 of 5 Slain by Police Here are Black, Same as the Arrest Rate." *The New York Times.* August 26.

Dade County Grand Jury (1983). *Final Report.* Eleventh Judicial Circuit of Florida.

Dallas Police Department (1974). *Report on Police Shootings.* Dallas, TX: Center for Police Development, South Methodist University.

Fyfe, J.J. and M. Blumberg (1985). "Response to Griswold: A More Valid Test of the Justifiability of Police Actions." *American Journal of Police,* Vol. 4:2, pp. 110-132.

Fyfe, J.J. (1982). "Blind Justice: Police Shootings in Memphis." *The Journal of Criminal Law and Criminology* (2) (Summer).

Fyfe, J.J. (1981A). "Who Shoots? A Look at Officer Race and Police Shooting." *The Journal of Police Science and Administration* 9 (4).

Fyfe, J.J. (1981B). "Race and Extreme Police-Citizen Violence." In R.L. McNeely and C.E. Pope (eds.) *Race, Crime and Criminal Justice.* Sage Publications, Inc.

Fyfe, J.J. (1980). "Always Prepared: Police Off-Duty Guns." *The Annuals of The American Academy of Political and Social Science* (42).

Fyfe, J.J. (1979). "Administrative Interventions on Police Shooting Discretion: An Empirical Examination." *Journal of Criminal Justice* (7).

Fyfe, J.J. (1978). "Shots Fired: A Typological Examination of New York City Police Firearms Discharges 1971-1975." Ph.D. dissertation, School of Criminal Justice, State University of New York in Albany.

Geller, W.A. and K.J. Karales (1981). *Shootings of and by the Chicago Police.* The Law Enforcement Study Group.

Goldkamp, J.S. (1976). "Minorities as Victims of Police Shootings: Interpretations of Racial Disproportionality and Police Use of Deadly Force." *Justice System Journal* 2 (Winter):169-183.

Heaphy, J.F. (1978). *Police Practices: The General Administrative Survey.* Washington, DC: The Police Foundation.

Jenkins, B. and A. Faison (197). *An Analysis of 248 Persons Killed by New York City Policemen.* New York, NY: Metropolitan Applied Research Center, Inc.

Knoohuizen, R., R. Faley and D.J. Palmer (1972). *The Police and Their Use of Fatal Force in Chicago.* The Chicago Law Enforcement Study Group.

Kobler, A.L. (1975). "Police Homicide in a Democracy." *Journal of Social Issues* 31 (November): 163-184.

Kuykendall, J. (1981). "Trends in the Use of Deadly Force by Police." *Journal of Criminal Justice,* Vol. 9:5, pp. 359-366.

Matulia, K.J. (1985). *A Balance of Forces: Model Deadly Force Policy and Procedures* (2nd edition). Gaithersburg, MD: International Association of Chiefs of Police.

Meyer, M.W. (1980). "Police Shootings at Minorities: The Case of Los Angeles." *Annals of the American Academy of Political and Social Science* 452 (November) :89-110.

Milton, C.H., J.S. Halleck, J. Lardner and G.L. Albrecht (1977). *Police Use of Deadly Force.* Washington, DC: The Police Foundation.

Nielson, E. (1983). "Policy on the Police Use of Deadly Force: A Cross-sectional Analysis." *Journal of Police Science and Administration.* Vol. 11:1, pp. 104-108.

Peirson, G.W. (1978). *Police Use of Deadly Force: Preliminary Report.* National Minority Advisory Council on Criminal Justice.

Robin, G.D. (1963). "Justifiable Homicide by Police Officers." *Journal of Criminal Law, Criminology and Police Science* 54:225-231.

Sherman, L.W. and E.G. Cohn (with P.R. Gartin, E.E. Hamilton, and D.P. Rogan). (1986). *Citizens Killed by Big City Police,* 1970-1984. Washington, DC: Crime Control Institute.

Sherman, L.W. (1983). "Reducing Police Gun Use: Critical Events, Administrative Policy and Organizational Change." In M. Punch (ed.) *The Control of Police Organization.* Cambridge, MA: M.I.T. Press.

Sherman, L.W. and M. Blumberg (1981). "Higher Education and Police Use of Deadly Force." *Journal of Criminal Justice* 9 (4).

Sherman, L.W. and R.H. Langworthy (1979). "Measuring Homicide by Police Officers." *Journal of Criminal Law and Criminology* 70.

Silberman, C.E. (1978). *Criminal Violence, Criminal Justice.* Random House, New York.

Takagi, P. (1974). "A Garrison State in a 'Democratic' Society." *Crime and Social Justice: A Journal of Radical Criminology* (Spring-Summer).

Walker, S. (1985). "Racial Minority and Female Employment in Policing: The Implications of 'Glacial' Change." *Crime and Delinquency,* Vol. 31:4, pp. 555-572.

Wukitsch, D.J. (1983). "Survey of the Law Governing Police Use of Deadly Force." *New York State Bar Journal* (January).

# Study Questions

1. What criticisms have been leveled at the common law "fleeing felon" doctrine?

2. What is the impact of *Garner v. Tennessee* on police use of deadly force?

3. Discuss the arguments which have been cited on behalf of arming off-duty police officers as well as the criticisms that are directed at this practice.

4. Discuss the various data sources that researchers have employed to study the question of police deadly force and the strengths and weaknesses of those sources.

5. Discuss some of the difficulties that researchers have encountered in trying to determine why blacks are disproportionately the victims of police use of deadly force.

# 13

# EXECUTION WITHOUT TRIAL: POLICE HOMICIDE AND THE CONSTITUTION* **

## Lawrence W. Sherman

The national debate over the state's right to take life has been focused on the issue of "capital punishment," or more precisely, execution after trial. Far more deadly in impact is the body of law permitting execution without trial through justified homicide by police officers. In 1976, for example, no one was executed and 233 persons were sentenced to death after trial, yet an estimated 590 persons were killed by police officers justifiably without trial.[1] Even in the 1950s, when an average of 72 persons were executed after trial each year,[2] the average number of police homicides was 240 a year, according to official statistics,[3] and 480 a year according to one unofficial estimate.[4] Since record-keeping began in 1949, police actions have been by far the most frequent method with which our government has intentionally taken the lives of its own citizens.

The significance of police homicide is not, however, derived solely from its frequency. Equally important is the nature of the crimes that justify police use of deadly force. Unlike executions after trial, executions before trial are not limited to extremely serious crimes such as murder, rape, and treason. Twenty-four states follow what is thought to be the traditional common-law doctrine, which permits the use of deadly force whenever necessary to prevent a felony or to arrest someone whom an officer has reasonable grounds to believe has committed a felony[5]—any felony, including, in at least one state, spitting on a policeman.[6] Eight states have adopted the more restricted version of this common-law doctrine proposed by the Model Penal Code;[7] ten other states have adopted statutes allowing police to use deadly force to arrest suspects of "violent"[8] or "forcible" felonies, which in some states may include burglary.[9] Even under these relatively recent restrictions, most police officers are still legally empowered to shoot unarmed fleeing burglary suspects in the back.

The available evidence suggests that when the police do use deadly force, their targets are often suspects of less serious crimes.[10] Approximately half of the

*Reprinted from *Vanderbilt Law Review* (January), 33:71:71-100. Copyright 1980 by *Vanderbilt Law Review*.

**This writing was supported in part by the National Institute of Mental Health, Center for Studies in Crime and Delinquency. Fred Cohen, David Wukitsch, Michael Gottfredson, Eva Sherman, Mark Blumberg, and Robert Langworthy contributed ideas and assistance.

people at whom police shots were fired in the several cities studied have not carried guns, and the proportion of those shot while fleeing is substantial.[11] To be sure, many police homicides occur in defense of life, although the data are not precise enough to determine exactly how many. There is no doubt, however, that many executions without trial occur in response to crimes against property without any defense justification.

A review of the legal history of police homicide shows that the rule that any felony warrants the use of deadly force is a common law anachronism to which our courts and legislatures continue to cling long after the Crown Courts have treated the doctrine as dead and Parliament has laid it to rest through criminal law reform. More important, an analysis of the constitutional status of the any-felony rule shows that it should be held to violate the due process clause of the Fifth Amendment, the ban on cruel and unusual punishment of the Eighth Amendment, and the equal protection clause of the Fourteenth Amendment. Both the historical and constitutional lines of inquiry suggest that only the defense-of-life doctrine is appropriate to govern police use of deadly force.

## THE ANY-FELONY RULE:
## AN HISTORICAL ANACHRONISM

The original meaning of the common-law justification for homicide to effect a felony arrest was very different from its current meaning. A barbaric legal doctrine[12] transplanted to England before the common law began,[13] the justification arose at a time when (1) there were no accurate and reliable weapons available that could kill at any distance, (2) the label "felony" was reserved for only the most serious crimes, all of which were punishable by death, and (3) there was virtually no communication among law enforcement officers in different communities. Each of these three elements of the historical context has changed drastically over the centuries, and with it the practical meaning of the doctrine.

The medieval weaponry used in "hue and cry"[14] during the early years of the any-felony rule was apparently limited to knives, swords, farm tools, and halberds. The longbow was not introduced until 1415,[15] and in 1504 the Tudors restricted the crossbow to lords and large landowners.[16] Henry VIII allowed noblemen and wealthy commoners to own guns,[17] but "[t]he musket of Shakespeare's time could not reach an enemy thoughtless enough to stand farther than eighty or ninety yards away."[18] A "typical" London street brawl in the reign of Henry VIII was put down by a band of constables, none of whom were armed with any weapons other than those used in hand-to-hand combat.[19] In this technological context, then, the practical meaning of the deadly force doctrine was that suspects could be killed if they resisted in a hand-to-hand struggle, but it did not mean that they could be killed from a distance behind while they were in flight.

That meaning changed in the nineteenth century with the invention of the revolver. Police officers in large American cities, who had been disarmed since the decline of Indian attacks before the Revolutionary War, began to carry revolvers in the 1850s after criminals used revolvers to shoot and kill their colleagues.[20] The dumping of thousands of army revolvers on the surplus market after the Civil War speeded the general rearmament of an increasingly violent urban society[21] and led to official acceptance of police use of revolvers.[22] The immediate effect of this change was that the police could, and did, shoot fleeing suspects who were posing no immediate threat to anyone.

The effect of the revolution in weaponry on police homicide was compounded by the expansion in the scope of felonies. Originally reserved under the common law for felonious homicide, mayhem, arson, rape, robbery, burglary, larceny, prison breach, and rescue of a felon, all punishable by death,[23] the felony label was attached to many more crimes after the advent of the revolver.[24] Moreover, while the scope of felonies was expanding, the scope of capital felonies contracted, leaving the death penalty in most states only applicable to treason and crimes endangering life or bodily security.[25] These changes in the legal context of police homicide significantly altered the meaning of the common-law any-felony doctrine. The changes greatly expanded the number of situations in which the police could kill without trial, and they created a gross difference in proportion between the severity of the post-trial penalty and the severity of the penalty for attempting to escape arrest.

While advances in weapon technology and changes in the criminal law were expanding the scope and potency of the any-felony rule, one of the primary reasons for its existence was fading. By the late nineteenth century, the rise of bureaucratic police agencies with the capacity to communicate information about suspects at large was undermining the necessity for the use of deadly force in the apprehension of felons. The escaping suspect of eleventh-century England might establish a new life in another community with little fear of eventual capture, and the social goal of retribution was thus easily frustrated by a fleeing felon. By the eighteenth century, however, Justice Fielding was circulating descriptions of wanted criminals outside of London,[26] and by the early twentieth century American detectives consulted their colleagues in other cities about various thieves and their whereabouts.[27] The effect of the increasingly sophisticated apprehension techniques meant that it was no longer absolutely necessary to kill a suspect, if his identity were known, in order to insure his eventual capture.

These changes in the scope and impact of the any-felony doctrine did not escape public notice and criticism. An 1858 *New York Times* editorial questioned one of the first police shootings there, making a value judgment supported by the constitutional analysis below. The *Times* suggested, "if a policeman needed to defend his life, the use of force was permissible, but if he was chasing a suspect, he had no right to shoot the man. A policeman either had to be swift enough to catch the suspect or justice must be lost."[28] Another *Times* editorial the same year expressed grave concern about the possible future in which "[e]very policeman is to be an absolute monarch, within his beat, with complete power of life and death over all within his range, and armed with revolvers to execute his decrees on the instant, without even the forms of trial or legal inquiry of any kind,"[29] a future that, to a large extent, has been realized.

These changes did not escape the notice of the courts. As early as 1888 the Supreme Court of Alabama, observing the legislative inflation of crimes to felony status, pronounced that "the preservation of human life is of more importance than the protection of property." The court restricted the common-law rule by disallowing deadly force in the prevention of secret felonies not accompanied by force.[30] Several other decisions grappled with the obsolete common-law standard,[31] but generally the courts were, as one commentator noted, "reluctant to abandon a convenient pigeon-hole disposal of cases on the basis of whether the crime was a felony or a misdemeanor."[32]

Meanwhile, the English common law had already effectively abandoned the absolute right to kill to prevent felonies or apprehend felons. It replaced the any-felony doctrine with a balancing test emphasizing necessity and proportion:

> The circumstances in which it can be considered reasonable to kill another in the prevention of crime must be of an extreme kind; they could probably arise only in the case of an attack against a person which is likely to cause death or serious bodily injury and where killing the attacker is the only practicable means of preventing the harm. It cannot be reasonable to kill another merely to prevent a crime, which is directed only against property.[33]

This principle was so well established in case law that by 1879 the Criminal Code Bill Commission took it as a "great principle of the common law" that the "mischief done by [the use of force to prevent crimes should not be] disproportioned to the injury or mischief which it is intended to prevent."[34] Moreover, a close reading of the original common-law codifiers Fosters, Blackstone, Hawkins, and East reveals so many internal contradictions and exceptions to the right to kill all felons[35] that one may question whether there was ever such a rule. Thus, in 1965 the Criminal Law Revision Committee reported to Parliament that despite "old authority" for the right to kill all felons, "the matter is very obscure; ...owing no doubt to the restraint of the police there is a dearth of modern authority on it;" and concluded that their central proposal to reclassify crimes would have no effect on police powers since "the likelihood that anything would turn nowadays on the distinction between felony and misdemeanor is very slight."[36]

In this country, however, the use of the distinction remained anything but slight. As recently as 1977 the Sixth Circuit upheld a Tennessee statute under which the Memphis police shot and killed a 16-year-old burglary suspect fleeing from a hardware store.[37] Noting that "the legislative bodies have a clear state interest in enacting laws to protect their own citizens against felons," and that the statute "merely embodied the common law which has been in force for centuries and has been universally recognized"[38] (something that we have seen is clearly *not* the case in English common law), the court rejected a broad constitutional challenge to the statute. An argument that the statute violated the Eighth Amendment's ban on cruel and unusual punishment was rejected on the grounds that police homicide is not "punishment."[39] The assertion that the statute violated due process protections was rejected on the grounds that state interests served by police homicide were more important than an individual's right to trial before being killed by police.[40] While recognizing that the Eighth Circuit had recently held that a similar Missouri statute did violate Fifth and Fourteenth Amendment due process guarantees,[41] the Sixth Circuit criticized that decision for intruding into legislative matters.[42] Finally, the Sixth Circuit case dismissed a claim of racial discrimination in violation of the Fourteenth Amendment because "both white and black fleeing felons...have been fired upon or shot by Memphis police."[43] The Supreme Court denied certiorari.[44]

The Sixth Circuit's cursory treatment of the threshold issue of whether police homicide constitutes punishment, however, is hardly definitive. Measured against well-established Supreme Court standards, police homicide clearly constitutes punishment. When police homicide is viewed as punishment, the Fifth, Fourteenth, and Eighth Amendment arguments that all present police homicide statutes and case law as constitutionally unsound are much more compelling.

# CONSTITUTIONAL ANALYSIS

## The Characterization of Police Homicide as Punishment

The often elusive definition of punishment in philosophy and jurisprudence has been a "major obsession with the English linguistic philosophers of this century."[45] The definitions vary sharply, with distinctions focusing upon the intent of the putative punisher, or the purpose of inflicting pain or suffering.[46] As the recent ruling in *Bell v. Wolfish*[47] reveals, the issue of intent has likewise proved to be divisive in the Supreme Court's efforts to define deprivations that constitute punishment. Justice Rehnquist, delivering the opinion of the Court, held that in determining whether particular conditions accompanying pretrial detention amount to punishment in the constitutional sense a "court must decide whether the disability is imposed for the purpose of punishment or whether it is but an incident of some other legitimate governmental purpose."[48] "Absent a showing of an expressed intent to punish," Justice Rehnquist continued, "that determination will turn on 'whether an alternative purpose to which [the restriction] may rationally be connected is assignable for it, and whether it appears excessive in relation to the alternative purpose assigned [to it],'"[49] (quoting *Kennedy v. Mendoza-Martinez*,[50] apparently as the controlling case on the subject). Justice Stevens, however, pointed out in his dissent that the *Mendoza* Court also recognized that evidence of intent would sometimes by "unavailable or untrustworthy."[51] "In such cases," Justice Stevens said "the [*Mendoza*] Court stated that certain other 'criteria' must be applied 'to the face' of the official action to determine if it is punitive."[52] Even Justice Rehnquist, whose opinion in *Bell v. Wolfish* reveals a very restrictive conception of what constitutes punishment, cited the seven *Mendoza* criteria approvingly. Although he did not, as Justice Marshall pointed out,[53] make full use of them, he nonetheless refers to them as "useful guideposts in determining" what is punishment, calling them "the tests traditionally applied to determine whether a governmental act is punitive in nature."[54]

With the original intent of the Gothic chieftains in establishing the kill-to-arrest rule lost in history, and determination of the subjective intent of police officers acting within the rule vulnerable to "hypocrisy and unconscious self-deception,"[55] it is necessary to turn to the criteria used in *Mendoza* and apply them "to the face" of police homicide to determine whether that action constitutes punishment. The decision offered seven criteria:

1. Whether the sanction involves an affirmative disability or restraint,
2. whether it has historically been regarded as a punishment,
3. whether it comes into play only on a finding of *scienter,*
4. whether its operation will promote the traditional aims of punishment—retribution and deterrence,
5. whether the behavior to which it applies is already a crime,
6. whether an alternative purpose to which it may rationally be connected is assigned for it, and
7. whether it appears excessive in relation to the alternative purpose assigned...[56]

The *Mendoza* Court noted that all of these criteria are relevant to the inquiry, although they "may often point in differing directions."[57] All seven criteria, however suggest that police homicide constitutes punishment, as is clear when each criterion is examined.

1. *Whether the Sanction Involves an Affirmative Disability or Restraint.*
Recent pronouncements by the Court leave no doubt that the sanction of police homicide constitutes "an affirmative disability or

restraint." It is not only a deprivation of rights, but a deprivation of "the right to have rights,"[58] not only a sanction, but a "unique sanction." As Justice Brennan stated, "[in] a society that so strongly affirms the sanctity of life,...the common view is that death is the ultimate sanction."[59] Five members of the present Court have "expressly recognized that death is a different kind of punishment from any other which may be imposed in this country" and stated that "[f]rom the point of view of the defendant, it is different in both its severity and finality. From the point of view of society, the action of the sovereign in taking the life of one of its citizens also differs dramatically from any other legitimate state action."[60] The right to life has consistently been held fundamental and preeminent.[61] Its deprivation has the same effect no matter what the expressed purpose may be.

2. *Whether It Has Historically Been Regarded as Punishment.* The historical record clearly demonstrates that executions without trial, including the kill-to-arrest doctrine, were generally viewed as punishment. Thieves were often killed outright during the hue and cry, even after they had been captured. "Let all go forth where God may direct them to go," urged the tenth-century laws of Edgar; "Let them do justice on the thief."[62] Suspicion sufficed to convict thieves without any trial at all, and "execution in such cases often followed immediately on arrest."[63] According to the preamble to Act 24 of Henry VIII, it appears the common law authorized the victims of crimes and attempted crimes to kill the criminal, regardless of whether it was necessary to prevent the felony.[64] In the twelfth and thirteenth centuries "outlaws could be beheaded by anyone, and a reward was paid for their heads under Richard I."[65] Abjurors of the real (felons who had escaped into religious sanctuary and agreed to leave the country forever) who strayed from the highway on their journey to the sea could also be beheaded by anyone.[66] In the context of the times in which the kill-to-arrest doctrine evolved, it was clearly linked to a philosophy of summary justice that can only be viewed as punishment.

Modern commentators have taken the same view of the historical status of the doctrine. Professor Perkins notes that "as the felon had forfeited his life by the perpetration of his crime, it was quite logical to authorize the use of deadly force."[67] Another commentator on killing fleeing felons described "the extirpation [as] but a premature execution of the inevitable judgment" in the era of capital punishment for all felonies.[68] With the passing of that era, premature execution is of course more severe than the "inevitable judgment." The historical character of police homicide as punishment, however, is not altered by the modern disproportion between pre-trial and post-trial sanctions.

3. *Whether It Comes into Play Only on a Finding of Scienter.* The basis and parameters of the *Mendoza* Court's *"scienter"* criterion are unclear. Of the two cases cited to support the relevance of *scienter* to a punishment characterization,[69] one in fact holds that penalties may constitute punishment regardless of *scienter,* apparently contradicting the point for which it was cited. The holding stated that, regardless of *scienter,* any fine imposed on an import merchant for underestimating the value of certain goods was "still punishment and nothing else."[70] The other case cited in *Mendoza* only mentions in passing that the exemption from a federal child labor "tax" of employers who do not know that their workers are underage suggests that the tax is really a penalty. The Court in that case opined that, "[S]cienter is associated with penalties, not with taxes."[71] Neither case actually holds that punishment is only imposed after finding a *scienter.*

The apparent contradictions notwithstanding, the Supreme Court has held that "the general rule at common law was that *scienter* was a necessary element...of every crime."[72] Regardless of criticisms of this usage,[73] one may proceed from it to infer that when an officer finds sufficient cause to believe someone is a felon and thus has met a requisite justification for killing him, the officer finds *scienter* at the same time. If the officer does not have probable cause to believe that *scienter* is present, then he does not have probable cause to believe the person is a felon, and killing is not justified. Justified police homicide therefore historically presumes *scienter,* and satisfies the apparent meaning of this *Mendoza* criterion of punishment.

4. *Whether Its Operation Will Promote Traditional Aims of Punishment—Retribution and Deterrence.* Police homicide clearly promotes retribution, the first of the two "traditional aims of punishment" named by the *Mendoza* Court. As the dissent in *Mattis v. Schnarp,*[74] a recent Eighth Circuit decision argued in support of the any-felony rule, which the court had found unconstitutional; "[t]here is no constitutional right to commit felonious offenses and to escape the consequences of those offenses." In that context, "consequences" strongly implies "just desserts," or retribution.

Whether police homicide, or indeed any punishment, actually promotes deterrence, the second of the two traditional aims named, may be an impossible question to answer.[75] If undisputed empirical evidence of a deterrent effect is required to evaluate whether a sanction is a punishment, then many social scientists would argue that few sanctions qualify. If, on the other hand, a deterrent effect need only be hypothesized for the sanction to be a punishment, then police homicide passes the test. The assumption by legal scholars that police homicide has a deterrent effect is reflected in the American Law Institute's debates over the issue. The deterrence of flight from arrest[76] and the deterrence of robbery[77] were both specifically mentioned, albeit with differences of opinion. The deterrence hypothesis is also implied in recent federal cases, such as *Jones v. Marshall*,[78] a Second Circuit opinion in which a three-judge panel upheld Connecticut's common law permitting police to kill fleeing felons, observing that the states had the right to place a higher value on order than on the rights of suspects. The only way such a homicide could achieve order is through deterrence.

5. *Whether the Behavior to Which It Applies Is Already a Crime.* All of the behavior to which police homicide applies is already a crime, or the officer must reasonably believe it to be a crime. There is however, some question about *which* crime police homicide is punishing. As Professor Mikell asked in his often-quoted statement to the American Law Institute:

> May I ask what we are killing [the suspect] for when he steals an automobile and runs off with it? Are we killing him for stealing the automobile?...It cannot be...that we allow the officer to kill him because he stole the automobile, because the statute provides only three years in a penitentiary for that. Is it then...for fleeing that we kill him? Fleeing from arrest...is punishable by a light penalty, a penalty much less than that for stealing the automobile. If we are not killing him for stealing the automobile and not killing him for fleeing, what are we killing him for?[79]

No matter how little sense it makes in relation to the post-trial penalty, we are in fact killing the auto thief for the volatile combination of felony and flight, both of which are crimes.

6. *Whether an Alternative Purpose to Which It May Rationally be Connected is Assignable For It.* The purposes of capture and crime prevention, rather than punishment, may no doubt be rationally connected to police homicide as alternatives to the purpose of punishment. Just as the *Wolfish* Court held that overcrowding and other disabilities imposed on pretrial detainees in a federal jail did not constitute punishment because they were merely an "inherent incident" of the objective of insuring detainee's presence at trial. It could be argued that death is merely an inherent incident to insuring that felony suspects are captured and that felonies are prevented. By this logic, death from police homicide is not a punishment if the expressed intent of the officers using deadly force is to apprehend felony suspects.

An equally strong case, however, could be made that the presence of multiple purposes in a governmental action does not automatically grant preeminence to the non-punitive purpose. One purpose of prison systems in some states is the manufacture of license plates, but a penitentiary sentence could hardly be described as merely an inherent incident of a legitimate state interest in manufacturing license plates. Implicit in the *Wolfish* Court's reasoning is a judgment about the primary purpose of any governmental action that has more than one purpose. Punishment rather than apprehension can be judged the primary purpose of police homicide. As one court once noted, "[t]he reason for...killing felons...in attempts to arrest them...is obvious...[T]he safety and security of society require the speedy arrest and punishment of a felon."[81]

Unlike the other *Mendoza* criteria, this one is explicitly qualified by the succeeding criterion, which questions whether the possible alternative purpose to punishment appears excessive. No matter what the primary purpose of police homicide is judged to be, then, if it appears excessive in relation to a nonpunitive purpose, it must be defined as punishment. As Justice Stevens interprets *Mendoza* in his *Wolfish* dissent, "when there is a significant and unnecessary disparity between the severity of the harm to the individual and the demonstrated importance of the regulatory objective,...courts must be justified in drawing an inference of punishment."[82]

7. *Whether It Appears Excessive in Relation to the Alternative Purpose Assigned to It.* The disparity between the death of a suspect and the purposes of prevention (of nonviolent crimes) and capture is both significant and unnecessary, and therefore excessive in relation to those purposes. It is significant in the case of capture because, once

again, the means used to prevent the suspect's escape is far more severe than the maximum penalty that would be imposed upon sentencing for all crimes (depending on the jurisdiction) except murder, treason, and rape. It is significant in the case or prevention of nonviolent crimes because the evil imposed is greater than the evil presented. It is unnecessary in the case of capture because most suspects can eventually be recaptured, and in the case of prevention because nonlethal intervention is usually possible. A sanction that takes a life to prevent the theft of an ear of corn[83] or a chicken[84] cannot, in a society that values life, be other than excessive.

Each of the *Mendoza* criteria point to the conclusion that the use of deadly force to capture felons and prevent felonies constitutes punishment, and is therefore subject to the constitutional restraints on the use of punishment. Even if it were ruled not to be punishment, however, it is still a deprivation of rights subject to due process of requirements of the Fifth and Fourteenth Amendments. Although a ruling that police homicide constitutes punishment has the added advantage of subjecting it to Eighth Amendment review, that review is generally reached only after due process guarantees have been satisfied.[85] In the case of police homicide, the due process guarantees are anything but satisfied.

## Due Process Requirements

Although police homicide raises serious due process questions if viewed merely as a deprivation of rights, when recognized as punishment its apparent violation of due process guaranties is striking. The framers "intended to safeguard the people of this country from punishment without trial by duly constituted courts"[86] and "under the due process clause, a detainee may not be punished prior to an adjudication of guilt in accordance with due process of law."[87] The limitation on imposing death, under the Fifth Amendment, is particularly strict. It requires that "[n]o person shall be held to answer for a capital, or otherwise infamous crime unless on a presentment or indictment of a grand jury." Indeed, the Eighth Circuit observed that a literal reading of the due process clause would mean that "life could never be taken without a trial."[88] And that is precisely what it should mean, with respect to life taken under the authority exercised on behalf of the state. A less rigid standard, however, must be applied when deadly force is used by an individual in accordance with the self-defense doctrine.[89] In addition to personal defense, this doctrine includes the defense of "another person against what is reasonably perceived as an immediate danger of death or grievous bodily harm to that person from his assailant."[90]

The Eighth Circuit, the only circuit to hold that the any-felony rule violates the Fourteenth Amendment, finds this interpretation too extreme. "Such a literal reading," it stated, "would fail to recognize the interests of the state in protecting the lives and safety of its citizens." Therefore, the court held that the situations in which the state can take a life, without according a trial to the person whose life is taken, are to be determined by balancing society's interest in public safety against the right to life of an individual.[91] Irrespective of their conclusion, the use of the balancing test is a fundamentally flawed procedure for determining whether the right to a form of due process specified in the Constitution is applicable. The Fifth Amendment does not depend upon a showing that it is in the community's best interests that the procedures be accorded.[92] As Professor Dworkin has observed, "a right against the Government must be a right to do something even when the majority would be worse off for having it done."[93] The majority is no doubt worse off when a fleeing felon escapes, but that should not alter the felon's Fifth Amendment right to grand jury review and trial before he is executed.

The balancing test is, however, the prevailing method of determining how much process is due once it is determined that due process applies.[94] Although the severity of individual deprivation and the relative importance of governmental interest in summary action is arguably incommensurable,[95] even a balancing procedure should lead reasonable men and women to a more restrictive scope of executions without trial. Both the Fifth and Fourteenth Amendments specifically forbid deprivation of life without due process of law, so there is no question that some process is due. The issue of when to allow executions without the due process of trial must then balance the individual's fundamental right to life[96] and the right not to be deprived of life without the due process of trial[97] against the state's interest; not just the interest in general public safety, but its narrow interest in protecting the property and lives of other specific individuals. We have long since decided that life is more important than property, and that no property offender, no matter how serious or recidivistic, may be executed after trial for his offenses. It should follow that the state's interest in protecting the property of others is not compelling enough to allow execution without the due process of trial.

The state's interest in protecting the lives and bodies of other individuals is, however, far more compelling, and much more appropriate for a balancing test.[98] When someone poses an immediate threat of grievous injury to another, the use of a balancing test would lead to the conclusion that the state's interest in protecting the other person allows it to commit an execution without the due process of trial. It is not necessary, however, to adopt the balancing test procedure in order to conclude that police officers may kill in defense of life. The self-defense doctrine gives them that power as individuals irrespective of their association with the state. The police can kill those posing an immediate threat of violence without violating the Fifth Amendment rights of those killed, just as any citizen can. The legitimate concern some courts have shown with police officer's safety[99] can, accordingly, be satisfied without violating the Fifth Amendment rights of those killed. If a fleeing felon whom the officer reasonably believes to be armed turns toward the pursuing officer with reasonably apparent intent to shoot the officer, the officer may kill him under the self-defense doctrine. The fleeing-felon rule in no way increases the officer's safety beyond the safeguard of the self-defense rule.

If a balancing test is used, however, the final and most difficult problem is to assess the state's interest in insuring public safety. An escaped felony suspect is certainly free to commit other crimes, but that should not be a compelling justification for the use of deadly force. A released convict who has served a full penitentiary sentence may be equally likely to commit more crimes, but that justifies neither his execution nor the incarceration beyond the end of his sentence. Far more compelling is the deterrence argument that the failure to kill fleeing felons will encourage more felonies. No empirical attempt to evaluate this argument has been made to date, but let us assume, *arguendo,* that each police homicide prevents eight or even eighty, robberies. Are we to measure the value of life in such utilitarian terms? Is it a lesser evil that a life be lost than several hundreds or thousands of dollars be stolen? In a society that punishes million-dollar white-collar frauds with a four-month prison term, it seems difficult to answer that question affirmatively.

Our primary concern, however, is with the Constitution, and not with the greatest good for the greatest number. Even if a balancing test determined that the state's interest in maintaining public safety allowed it to execute fleeing and in-progress felons without trial under the due process requirements of the Fifth and Fourteenth Amendments, those executions could still be ruled unconstitutional as either cruel and unusual punishment under the Eighth Amendment, or a denial of equal protection under the Fourteenth Amendment.

## Police Homicide As Cruel and Unusual Punishment

The lack of guidance on the framers' intent in banning cruel and unusual punishment makes that phrase difficult to define precisely.[101] Nonetheless, four criteria for judging whether a given punishment is cruel and unusual can be clearly discerned in *Furman v. Georgia*[102] and its predecessor cases. The criteria are whether the penalty is (1) inherently cruel,[103] (2) disproportionately severe to the offense it punishes,[104] (3) unacceptable to contemporary society,[105] or (4) inflicted arbitrarily.[106] None of the four seems to have been overruled in the death penalty cases since *Furman,* and all but the third are specifically addressed in the opinion of the Court—a consensus the *Furman* Court lacked—in *Gregg v. Georgia.*[107] Any of the four criteria can make a punishment cruel and unusual. Police homicide satisfies at least three, and on occasion all four-criteria.

1. *Inherent Cruelty.* The present Court has consistently held that death is not, per se, an unconstitutional punishment.[108] Previous courts have, however, considered whether particular modes of inflicting death are unconstitutionally cruel.[109] Shooting and electrocution have both withstood challenges, but it is doubtful that any court would uphold death inflicted by a sustained beating after a suspect had been subdued,[110] or by a drowning or a choke-hold.[111] Nonetheless, police have used all three methods to kill suspects in cases that have received widespread attention, and have sometimes received light penalties for doing so. Yet most police homicides do not receive much attention or review.[112] Under the present any-felony rule, prosecutors are on firm ground for declining to prosecute police officers who beat felony suspects to death when the beating is necessary to effect an arrest. Unless such action can be justified by the self-defense doctrine, it would seem to be an inherently cruel and unusual form of punishment.

2. *Disproportionate Severity.* The determination whether a punishment is proportionately severe to the crime it punishes is essentially a moral judgment, not based on objective assessments of the necessity or efficacy of the penalty imposed.[113] When judged in accord with contemporary standards, police homicide is "grossly out of proportion to the severity"[114] of most of the crimes it punishes.[115] As a former Oakland, California police chief graphically explained with restricting his officers' right to shoot fleeing burglars beyond the state law's limitations:

> Considering that only 7.65 percent of all adult burglars arrested and only .28 percent of all juvenile burglars arrested are eventually incarcerated, it is difficult to resist the conclusion that the use of deadly force to apprehend burglars cannot conceivably be justified. For adults, the police would have to shoot 100 burglars in order to have captured the eight who would have gone to prison. For juveniles, the police would have to shoot 1,000 burglars in order to have captured the three who would have gone to the Youth Authority.[116]

Comparisons to actual punishments typically imposed after trial would probably show that killing a fleeing suspect of any crime, even murder, would impose a more severe punishment without trial than could be expected after conviction. In the case of murder, treason and rape, a state's decision to make available the death penalty for post-trial punishment might mean that pretrial execution would not be disproportionately severe. But murder and rape do not even appear as categories in most studies of police use of deadly force, since they comprise such a small percentage of all crimes punished by police homicide. Under the proportional severity test used for the past century in English law, which embodies social values quite similar to our own, even fleeing murderers could probably not be killed justifiably in order to arrest them once they no longer posed an immediate threat of violence.[117]

When analyzed from a utilitarian perspective, police homicide is as disproportionately severe as it is when evaluated by moral standards as a punishment.[118] Assuming that prevention of escape is the utilitarian goal served by police homicide, the fact that modern apprehension techniques have diminished considerably the importance of immediate capture leaves police homicide disproportionately severe in relation to the utilitarian purposes it might serve. Whether viewed as a punishment or a method of capture, the severity of police homicide is disproportionate to its objective.

3. *Lack of Acceptability in Contemporary Society.* Although police homicide in arresting serious felons did not shock the conscience[119] of medieval England, the Eighth Amendment must be interpreted in light of the evolving standards of a maturing society.[120] Three of four available objective indicators,[121]—police department administrative policies, scholarly opinion, and mass public protests—show a considerable evolution in the attitudes toward police homicide in recent years. A fourth indicator—legislative authorization—lags behind the others, but that alone does not demonstrate the acceptability of police homicide to society. Moreover, even the legislative arena has markedly changed its approach toward police homicide over the past decade.

Until quite recently, police department policies were either vague or silent on the use of deadly force,[122] but that is rapidly changing. Since 1977, police policies in Los Angeles, Birmingham, and Houston, among others, have restricted the use of deadly force far beyond the limits of state law. Los Angeles adopted a modified defense-of-life policy after officers shot and killed a naked chemist.[123] Houston reportedly adopted a defense-of-life policy in the wake of the beating and drowning of a young Chicago male.[124] Birmingham adopted a more restrictive policy after a Police Foundation study of seven cities showed Birmingham to have the highest police shooting rate[125]—the public outcry over which lends some support to Justice Marshall's hypothesis that the public is more likely to find a punishment unacceptable when it knows the full facts.[126]

Police policies more restrictive than state law are far from new, however. A 1974 study of the Boston Police Department found that the majority of the large cities surveyed permitted their officers to use deadly force only to apprehend suspects who present a threat of serious injury or death to someone.[127] In 1975 the California Peace Officers' Association and the California Police Chiefs' Association jointly adopted a similar policy.[128] The policy of the Federal Bureau of Investigation since at least 1972 has been "that an agent is not to shoot any person except, when necessary, in self-defense, that is, when he reasonably believes that he or another is in danger of death or grievous bodily harm."[129] The Federal Bureau of Narcotics and Dangerous Drugs, which operates one of the most hazardous types of law enforcement programs,[130] adopted a similar policy in 1971.[131]

These policies were preceded by some 50 years of nearly unanimous scholarly criticism of the any-felony rule. Law reviews,[132] professional police publications,[133] and a Presidential commission[134] all lobbied for a change in the rule. A more powerful force for change, however, has been the long series of public protests—often violent—over police use of deadly force in minority communities. In the 1960s, several race riots were precipitated by police shootings.[135] In the 1970s, police homicides have produced more limited protests with less violence, but with a clear focus on the problem of police homicide. New York, Houston, Los Angeles, Dallas, and other cities repeatedly felt such protests throughout the late 1970s.[136] In the Southwest, minority groups even managed to enlist President Carter's concern for the problem,[137] leading to an intensified effort at federal prosecution of police for civil rights violations.[138] Yet as long as the any-felony rule survives, many of the incidents that stir public outrage will remain legal and beyond prosecution.

Although state legislatures appear less vulnerable to such protests than police chiefs and mayors, a steadily growing number of legislatures have nonetheless reflected the apparent change in public sentiment toward police homicide. Since 1973, at least eight states[139] have adopted the Model Penal Code limitations on the use of deadly force to arrest. Minnesota has even required that all police shootings be reported to the state government, in part for monitoring purposes.[140] Taken in conjunction with the developments in police policy, scholarly opinion, and public protests, the state legislative actions are consistent with the general trend toward restricting executions without trial.

4. *Arbitrary Infliction.* Relative to the total number of arrests and police-citizen encounters, police homicide is inflicted so rarely and with such arbitrariness as to be wanton and freakish.[141] It can be likened to a virtual lottery system in which there are no safeguards for the capricious selection of criminals for the punishment of death.[142] Even in police departments with comparatively restrictive deadly force policies, the discretion that even those policies allow officers in the use of deadly force is so uncontrolled that people literally "live or die, dependent on the whim of one man."[143] The available evidence strongly suggests that police homicide is inflicted in a trivial number of the cases in which it is legally available, through procedures that give room for the play of racial and other prejudices. Unlike convictions for capital offenses, there are no records kept of the number of felony suspects whose actions make them legally vulnerable to execution without trial. The fact that the rate of police homicide was only one per 6,822 Part I Index[144] arrests in 1975, however, provides a reasonable inference that the sanction is rarely used even when it is available, since the rate of flight per attempted arrest seems likely to be much larger. Moreover, the extreme rarity of occurrence alone raises a strong inference of arbitrariness.[145]

Despite the progressive policies of many police departments, many other departments still allow their officers total discretion to use their legal power to kill.[146] Even the departments with restrictive policies typically say when officers *may* use their weapons, and not when they *must*. Noninvocation of available legal penalties is the common practice in American policing, as extensive research has shown, and police homicide is no exception.[147] As a Kansas City, Missouri, police officer recently said about the control of firearms discretion in that department (one of the best managed police agencies in the country), "they pretty much leave it up to your own conscience to decide" whether or not to shoot someone when their restrictive policy allows it.[148] Many police officers are punished for using their guns when they should not have, but recent research[149] has found no case in which an officer was punished for not using force when he or she could have.

The inconsistency among police officers in deciding when to use force is further demonstrated by a recent experimental study of twenty-five randomly selected Connecticut police officers who were given identical information about three arrest situations. When asked if they would be likely to use deadly force, their responses were almost evenly split, even though they were all making decisions under Connecticut common law.[150]

In comparison to the vigorous controls on the post-trial death penalty which were approved in *Gregg v. Georgia*,[151] the use of deadly force by police is virtually uncontrolled. The trier of fact, without any information from a recordkeeper about what the typical police action has been in previous situations similar to an instant case must also determine the sentence. If decision-making without access to the information is an unconstitutionally arbitrary way to impose the death penalty after the careful finding of facts at trial, then surely it must be so without a trial.

## Police Homicide and Equal Protection

A final argument against the use of deadly force to arrest is that present practices deny equal protection to blacks. The argument is not without its weaker points, for discrimination in the use of deadly force is methodologically difficult to prove. Nonetheless, the extremely disproportionate impact of executions without trial on blacks compels consideration of the argument.

According to official statistics, blacks constituted forty-six percent of the people killed by official police action in 1975,[152] while they only constituted 11.5 percent of the population.[153] The national death rate from police homicide of black males over age ten in a recent ten-year period was nine to ten times higher than the rate for white males.[154] Studies in specific cities have found even greater racial disparities in the rate of police homicides.[155] There have been some attempts to explain the disparity using arrest rates for FBI Part I Index crimes,[156] but the approach has several limitations. First, the power to use deadly force under the common law rule is not limited to arrests for "index" crimes. Indeed, as the empirical studies[157] show, most police shooting incidents arise out of situations in which the initial criminal offense is clearly not an Index crime. Second, in many police shooting situations there is no offense recorded unless the police intervention precipitates more violence. Many violent family fights, for example, are not reported as crimes,[158] although they are reported if a police officer is assaulted. Third, the evidence of racial discrimination in arrests undermines any use of arrest rates to show an absence of discrimination in police homicide.[159]

Even if arrest rates by race were an appropriate means of showing that the disparity in police homicide rates is not discriminatory, they do not always match the police homicide rates. In Philadelphia from 1950 to 1960, for example, where 87 percent of the police homicide victims but only 22 percent of the city's population were black, only 31 percent of the arrest population was black.[160] More recently, a study of the Chicago police found the police homicide rate per 10,000 arrests (for all charges) in 1969-70 to be 1.00 for whites and 2.01 for blacks.[161] Nationally, in 1975 blacks accounted for 46 percent of the police homicide victims and only 33 percent of the FBI Part I Index offense arrests.[162]

The existence of racial discrimination in police homicides can be neither proved nor disproved with the available evidence. Resolution of the issue would require data on the number of blacks and whites who committed acts that made them legally vulnerable to police homicide: assaulting or threatening to assault police or others, fleeing from arrest for felonies, participating in a riot, or engaging in other specifically covered behavior.[163] Short of a mammoth systematic observation study[164] costing millions of dollars, there is no reliable way to obtain such data. A sample of the narrative accounts found in arrest reports, somewhat less expensive, would be the next best measure of legal vulnerability of whites and blacks, but no such study has yet been done.

In the absence of more conclusive evidence, the demonstrably higher rates of police homicide for blacks strongly suggests[165] racial discrimination on a national basis. Although such patterns are quite likely to vary from one city to the next, such a variation would support the argument that present procedures allow police homicide to be administered in a discriminatory fashion.

## SUMMARY AND CONCLUSION

This analysis of police homicide and the Constitution leads to the conclusion that the present state laws are unconstitutional, not just in the common-law states, but in the Model Penal Code and "forcible felony" states as well.[166] The present laws of every state in the union deny police homicide victims Fifth and Fourteenth Amendment rights to due process, allow the punishment of death to be imposed in a cruel and unusual fashion, and appear to deny equal protection to blacks. The only constitutional alternative apparent is to remove police homicide from the realm of punishment and confine justification for it to the self-defense doctrine. In short, the conclusion is that the police throughout the country should adopt the first section of the firearms policy of the Federal Bureau of Investigation.[167]

The defense-of-life policy has the virtue of being both constitutional and highly practical. It is constitutional, first, because it demonstrably does not constitute punishment. Since self-defense is an individual action rather than a state action, it is not subject to evaluation by the *Mendoza* criteria. The right to life is fundamental, and so the right to defend life need not be granted by the state; it is, rather, something the state may not restrict. Police and other citizens may kill under self-defense on the same evidentiary basis—eyewitnessing an immediate threat to life. If police were not granted special powers, police killings in self-defense could be distinguished from punishment administered by the state. The adoption of such an approach would signal a return to the English tradition of citizen-police officers, whose only special power is to arrest on probable cause (as citizens could only do during the hue and cry), and a rejection of the Continental tradition of soldier-police that we have unconsciously adopted by giving the police special powers to kill.[168] Police homicide in defense of life is nonpunitive by its very nature. It is inherently preventive. It uses an overt act—such as refusing to drop a gun on demand—as the evidentiary basis for taking preventive action. By preventing the consummation of a violent crime threatened by an overt act, the defense-of-life killing looks toward the offender's behavior in the future. Present police homicide rules all look primarily toward the offender's past behavior, and therefore constitute punishment.

Moreover, the defense-of-life policy is constitutional because it does not violate due process. As a solely individual action, police killings in defense of life do not deprive citizens of rights on behalf of the state, but merely on behalf of protecting their own rights. Finally, the defense-of-life policy does not constitute cruel and unusual punishment. It is neither inherently cruel, nor disproportionate to the conduct to which it responds, nor unacceptable to society, nor imposed in an arbitrary and capricious manner. The defense-of-life policy would still leave room, hypothetically, for racial discrimination, but it seems most unlikely that police would grant preferential treatment to whites who pose immediate threats to life and limb.

The defense-of-life policy would also be more practical to implement than any of the other attempts to create a policy more restrictive than the common-law doctrine. The Model Penal Code exemplifies the practical problems. As the dissent observed in *Mattis v. Schnarr,*[169] a policy that allows police to kill someone who the officer reasonably believed "would use deadly force against the officers or others if not immediately apprehended" required too much guessing and analysis for an emergency situation. This language differs sufficiently from the "immediate danger" language of the FBI's policy to include the killing of a fleeing felon merely because he is labeled "armed and dangerous," (as opposed to someone who is actually committing an overt act such as pointing a gun at someone else). The police are not armed with a crystal ball. Predicting that a fleeing felon is likely to kill someone is no more possible than predicting that a paroled felon is likely to kill someone. Such a policy places an undue burden on the police officer. When people commit overt threatening acts, however, there is much less ambiguity.

A self-defense policy avoids the Model Penal Code's problems in allowing police officers to shoot fleeing felons only when they have used or threatened to use deadly force. Professor Perkins argues that this provision of the Code "goes too far" because officers making split-second decisions will find it difficult to evaluate all the details of the suspect's conduct.[170] On the contrary, for precisely that reason, the Model Penal Code does not go far enough.

The self-defense policy also avoids the practical problems of allowing officers to shoot fleeing suspects of specified "forcible" felonies, the approach used in ten states. As a former Los Angeles Police Department policy observed, "[it] is not practical to enumerate specific felonies."[171] An informal survey of police officers from three New York state police departments found that none of them could remember the types of felonies which warranted the use of deadly force under New York state law.[172] With a self-defense policy, there is nothing complex to remember, and no need to consider prior events; the officer need only evaluate the information he observes to assess whether someone is committing an overt act signaling an immediate threat to the officer or someone else.

It is not the practicality of the defense-of-life rule that makes it constitutional, however; that is merely a fortunate by-product. Rights cannot depend on administrative convenience, especially not the right to life. The defense-of-life is necessary for the simple reason that anything else constitutes execution without trial, in violation of the Constitution.

# Notes

1   The official death records of the National Center for Health Statistics, preserved on tape, show a total of 295 deaths by legal intervention of police for 1976. Independent tests of the death record data, however, reveal that they are rather consistently under-reporting police homicides by about 50 percent. Sherman & Langworthy, "Measuring Homicide by Police Officers" 70 *Journal of Criminal Law and Criminology* 546 (1979). On the number of post-trial death sentences, *see* U.S. Department of Justice, Law Enforcement Assistance Administration, National Criminal Justice Information and Statistics Service, Capital Punishment, 1976; National Prisoner Statistics Bulletin SD-NPS-CP5 at 3 (1977) [hereinafter cited as Capital Punishment Statistics].

2   Capital Punishment Statistics, *supra* note 1, at 13.

3   Vital Statistics of the United States, 1950-1959 (Annual).

4   *See* note 1 supra.

5   Comment, "Deadly Force to Arrest: Triggering Constitutional Review," 11 *Harv. C.R.-C.L. Rev.* 361, 368 (1976); Note, "Justifiable Use of Deadly Force by the Police: A Statutory Survey," 12 *William & Mary Law Review* 67 (1970). On the common law, *see* e.g., 2 Hale's P.C., 76-77.

6   Comment, "Policeman's Use of Deadly Force in Illinois," 48 Chi.-*Kent. L. Rev.* 252, 252 (1971).

7   The Code provides, in part: The use of deadly force is not justifiable under this Section unless:
     (i) the arrest is for a felony; and
     (ii) the person effecting the arrest is authorized to act as a peace officer or is assisting a person whom he believes to be authorized to act as a peace officer; and
     (iii) the actor believes that the force employed creates no substantial risk of injury to innocent persons; and
     (iv) the actor believes that:
          (1) The crime for which the arrest is made involved conduct including use of threatened use of deadly force; or
          (2) there is a substantial risk that the person to be arrested will cause death or serious bodily harm if his apprehension is delayed. Model Penal Code, 3.07(2)(b) (1962).

8   Sherman, "Restricting the License to Kill—Recent Developments in Police Use of Deadly Force," 14 *Criminal Law Bulletin* 577, 581 (1978).

9   Comment, *supra* note 5, at 365 n. 34.

10   Table 13.1 is constructed from four empirical studies of police use of deadly force: (1) a study of the 32 persons killed by Philadelphia police officers in 1950-1960. *See* Robin, "Justifiable Homicides by Police," 54 *J. Crim. L.C. & P.S.* 225 (1963), (2) A study

of 911 police killings reported in newspapers around the country in 1965-1969. *See* Kobler, "Figures (and Perhaps Some Facts) on Police Killings of Civilians in the United States, 1965-69," 31 *J. Soc. Issues* 185 (1975). (3) A study of police department records, producing pooled data for 1973 and 1974 in Birmingham, Alabama; Oakland, California; Portland, Oregon; Kansas City, Missouri; Indianapolis, Indiana; and Washington, DC, and in Detroit for all of 1973 and part of 1974, on 320 police firearms discharges in which a bullet wounded or killed someone. *See* C. Milton, J. Halleck, J. Lardener, G. Abrecht, Police Use of Deadly Force (1977) [hereinafter cited as C. Milton]. (4) A study of 2,926 incident in which New York City Police Department officers discharged their weapons, regardless of impact, during 1971-1975. See J. Fyfe, "Shots Fired: A Typological Examination of New York City Police Firearms Discharges" (1978) (unpublished Ph.D. dissertation, School of Criminal Justice, State University of New York at Albany.

TABLE 13.1

**EVENTS PRECEDING POLICE USE OF DEADLY FORCE**

| | Robin, 1963 (N = 32) | | Kobler, 1975B (N = 911) | | Milton, et al., 1977 (N = 320) | | Fyfe, 1978 (N = 2,926) | |
|---|---|---|---|---|---|---|---|---|
| | % | Rank | % | Rank | % | Rank | % | Rank |
| Distrubance Calls: Family Quarrels Disturbed Persons Fights Assaults "Man with a Gun" | 31 | (2) | 17 | (4) | 32 | (1) | 12 | (2) |
| Robbery: In Progress Pursuit of Suspect Burglary: In Progress Larceny Tampering with Auto | 28 | (3) | 20 | (3) | 21 | (2) | 31 | (1) |
| Traffic Offenses Pursuits Vehicle Stops | 3 | (4) | 30** | (1) | 9 | (5) | 11 | (4) |
| Officer Personal Business: Dispute Horseplay Accident | ? | — | ? | — | 4 | (6.5) | ? | — |
| Stakeout/Decoy | ? | — | ? | — | 4 | (6.5) | ? | — |
| Other | 0 | (5) | 6 | (5) | 11 | (4) | 14 | (3) |

STUDY FINDINGS*

*Percentages may not total 100 due to rounding.
**Includes other misdemeanors not listed above.

[11]    Of the studies cited in note 10, *supra,* Kobler, at 188, found 50 percent of those shot by the police to have carried guns at the time and 25 percent to have been completely unarmed. Milton, at 22, found 45 percent to have been unarmed. Fyfe, at IV-30, found 54 percent to have had guns and 30 percent to have lacked a gun or a knife. Another study found 53 percent of the 1969-70 police homicide victims in Chicago to have carried a gun, and 23 percent to have lacked any weapon. Harding & Fahey, "Killings by Chicago Police, 1969-70: An Empirical Study," 46 S. *California Law Review* 284, 292-93 (1973).

Kobler, at 165, also found that measured by a defense-of-life standard, only 50 percent of the killings would have been justified; the rest were either killings of suspects in flight or to prevent a nonviolent crime. In contrast, Fyfe, at 279, found that 71.5 percent of the police firearms incidents in his New York sample were reportedly in defense of life, a finding consistent with the tradition of relative restraint in that department. Other cities are quite different. A study of Philadelphia police use of deadly force in 1970-74 found that approximately 45 percent of those people shot had been fleeing at the time, and in approximately 25 percent of the incidents the shooting victim was both fleeing and unarmed. A study by the Boston Police Department found that 102 of the 210 targets of Boston police firearms discharges in 1970-73 were fleeing at the time, and 80 of the 102 were unarmed. *See* Mattis v. Schnarr, 547 F. 2d 1007, 1019-20 n. 30 (8th Cir. 1976).

[12]    *See* 4 W. Blackstone, Commentaries 180 (1800) (citing Von Stiernhook, Treatise on Gothic Law).

[13]    W. Melville-Lee, *A History of Police in England* 35 (1901).

[14]    "Hue and cry," under old English Law, refers to the loud outcry with which robbers, burglars, and murders were pursued. All who heard the outcry were obliged to join in pursuit of the felon. *See* 4 W. Blackstone, *supra* note 12, at 293.

[15]    L. Smith, *This Realm of England 1399-1688,* at 15 (1966).

[16]    L. Kennett and J. Anderson, *The Gun in America* 22 (1975).

[17]    *Id.* at 23.

[18]    R. Sherrill, *The Saturday Night Special* 4 (1973).

[19]    G. Elton, *Policy and Police* 4, 5 (1972).

[20]    L. Kennett and J. Anderson, *supra* note 16, at 151; R. Lane, *Policing The City* 103-04 (1967); J. Richardson, *The New York Police* 113 (1970).

[21]    L. Kennett and J. Anderson, *supra* note 16, at 91.

[22]    This did not occur without the strenuous objections of some commanders who thought the use of revolvers was cowardly. *See* W. Miller, *Cops and Bobbies,* 51-53 (1977).

23    R. Perkins, *Criminal Law* 10-11 (2d ed. 1969). As Blackstone noted, "The idea of felony is indeed so generally connected with that of capital punishment, that we find it hard to separate them..." 4 W. Blackstone, *supra* note 12, at 98.

24    Comment, "Use of Deadly Force in the Arrest Process," 31 *La. L. Rev.* 131, 132-33 (1970); *see* 4 W. Blackstone, *supra* note 23.

25    Furman v. Georgia, 408 U.S. 238, 333-41 (1972) (Marshall, J., concurring).

26    P. Pringle, *Hue and Cry* 133 (1955).

27    *The Professional Thief, by a Professional Thief* (E.H. Sutherland, ed.) 112 (1937).

28    *Quoted in* L. Kennett and J. Anderson *supra* note 15, at 150.

29    *Quoted in* Miller, *supra* note 21, at 146.

30    Storey v. State, 71 Ala. 329, 340 (1882 involving the theft of a horse).

31    *E.g.,* United States v. Clark, 31 F. 710, 713 (8th Cir. 1887); Reneau v. State, 70 Tenn. 720 (1879).

32    Pearson, "The Right to Kill in Making Arrests," 28 *Mich. L. Rev.* 957, 976 (1930).

33    Regina v. McKay [1957] V.R. 560, 572-73 (Smith, J., dissenting); 11 *Halsbury's Laws of England* 1179 (4th ed. 1976) (emphasis added). The question of deadly force to prevent flight is either implied in this formulation, or so far beyond the pale that the current formulations make no mention of it. *See also* Lanham, "Killing the Fleeing Offender," 1 *Crim. L.J.* (Australia) 16, 17-18 (1977).

34    *Quoted in* Regina v. McKay, [1957] V.R. 560, 572-73 (Smith J., dissenting).

35    *Id.* at 572.

36    Criminal Law Revision Committee, Seventh Report: *Felonies and Misdemeanours* 7 (1965); 18 *Parliamentary Papers* (House of Commons and Command (1964-65).

37    Wiley v. Memphis Police Department, 548 F.2d 1247 (6th Cir.), *cert. denied,* 434 U.S. 822 (1977).

38    *Id.* at 1252.

39    *Id.* at 1251.

40    *Id.* at 1252.

41    Mattis v. Schnarr, 547 F.2d 1007 (8th Cir. 1976).

42    Wiley v. Memphis Police Department, 548 F.2d 1247, 1252-53 (6th Cir.), *cert. denied,* 434 U.S. 822 (1977).

43    *Id.* at 1254.

44    Wiley v. Memphis Police Department, 434 U.S. 822 (1977).

45   G. Newman, *The Punishment Response* 7 (1978).

46   Professor Hart, for example, suggests five defining characteristics of punishment:
>    (1) It must involve pain or other consequences normally considered unpleasant.
>    (2) It must be for an offense against legal rules.
>    (3) It must be imposed on an actual or supposed offender for his offense.
>    (4) It must be intentionally administered by human beings other than the offender.
>    (5) It must be imposed and administered by an authority constituted by a legal system against which the offense is committed.

H. Hart, Punishment and Responsibility 4, 5 (1968).

Professor Packer, in contrast, finds that definition insufficiently clear as to the distinction between the purposes and effects of punishment, and purposes a sixth defining characteristic of punishment: "It must be imposed for the dominant purpose of preventing offense against legal rules or of exacting retribution from offenders, or both." H. Packer, *The Limits of the Criminal Sanction* 21-23, 31 (1969).

47   99 S. Ct. 1861 (1979)

48   *Id.* at 1873.

49   *Id.* at 1873-74.

50   372 U.S. 144 (1963).

51   99 S. Ct. at 1899.

52   *Id.*

53   *Id.* at 1887 (Marshall, J., dissenting).

54   *Id.* at 1873.

55   *Id.* at 1898 (Stevens, J., dissenting; H. Packer *supra* note at 33.

56   372 U.S. at 168-69.

57   *Id.* at 169.

58   Furman v. Georgia, 408 U.S. 238, 290 (1972) (Brennan, J., concurring).

59   *Id.* at 286.

60   Roe v. Wade, 410 U.S. 113, 157 (1973); Screws v. United States, 325 U.S. 91, 123 (1945); Johnson v. Zerbst, 304 U.S. 458, 463 (1938); Yick Wo v. Hopkins, 118 U.S. 356, 370 (1886); Mattis v. Schnarr, 547 F.2d 1007, 1018 (1976).

62   *Quoted in* T. Critchley, *A History of Police in England and Wales* (2d ed. 1972).

63   J. Bellamy, *Crime and Public Order in England in the Later Middle Ages* 134 (1973).

64   *Cited* in Regina v. McKay, [1957] V.R. 560, 571-72 (Smith, J., dissenting).

65    R. Hunisett, *The Medieval Coroner* 67 (1961).

66    *Id.* at 49

67    R. Perkins, *supra* note 23, at 985.

68    Note, "Legalized Murder of a Fleeing Felon," 15 *Va. L. Rev.* 582, 583 (1929).

69    Helwig v. United States, 188 U.S. 605 (1902).

70    *Id.* at 612.

71    Child Labor Tax Case, 259 U.S. 20 (1921).

72    United States v. Valint, 258 U.S. 250, 251 (1922).

73    *See e.g.,* R. Perkins, *supra* note 23, at 771.

74    547 F.2d 1007, 1023 (8th Cir. 1976).

75    J. Gibbs, *Crime, Punishment and Deterrence* (1975).

76    Professor Waite argued for extending the right to kill to arrest all offenses in order to deter flight, for otherwise "we say to criminal, 'You are foolish...if you submit to arrest. The officer dare not take the risk of shooting at you. If you can outrun him, outrun him and you are safe...If you are faster than he is you are free and God bless you.' I feel entirely unwilling to give that benediction to the modern criminal." 9 ALI Proceedings 195 (1931), *quoted in* J. Michael & H. Wechsler, *Criminal Law and its Administration* 81-82 n. 3 (1940).

77    Judge Learned Hand once commented that "It has been constantly supposed here that if you are able to shoot a robber you are less likely to have a robber. I question that. I challenge it altogether. I don't believe that possibility figures at all in the commission of crime." 35 ALI Proceedings 258-334 (1958), *quoted in* Mattis v. Schnarr, 547 F.2d 1007, 1015 (8th Cir. 1976). While Judge Hand's remarks were directed specifically towards private citizens' rights to defend property, the *Mattis* court observed that he was speaking to the larger problem of justification to use deadly force in general. *Id.* at 1015 n. 17.

78    528 F.2d 132, 142 (2d Cir. 1975).

79    ALI Proceedings, 186-87, *quoted in* J. Michael and H. Wechsler, *supra* note 76.

80    99 S. Ct. at 1873.

81    Holloway v. Moser, 193 N.C. 185, 136 S.E. 375, (1927), *quoted in* Pearson, *supra* note 32, at 964.

82    99 S. Ct. at 1899 (Stevens, J., dissenting).

83    Storey v. State, 71 Ala. 329, 341 (1882).

84    Regina v. McKay, (1957) V.R. 560.

85   Ingraham v. Wright, 430 U.S. 651, 671-72, n. 40 (1977).

86   United States v. Lovett, 328 U.S. 303, 317 (1946).

87   99 S. Ct. at 1872.

88   Mattis v. Schnarr, 547 F.2d 1007, 1018-19 (8th Cir. 1976).

89   Brown v. United States, 256 U.S. 335 (1921).

90   40 Am. Jur. 2d *Homicide* 170-71, *quoted in* Mattis v. Schnarr, 547 F.2d 1007, 1015 (1976).

91   Mattis v. Schnarr, 547 F.2d 1007, 1019 (1976).

92   Note, "Specifying the Procedures Required by Due Process: Towards Limits on the Use of Interest Balancing," 88 *Harv. L. Rev.* 1510, 1524 (1975).

93   Dworkin, "Taking Rights Seriously," in *Oxford Essays in Jurisprudence* 202, 214 (2d Series 1973), *quoted in* Note, *supra* note 92, at 1527 n. 76.

94   Morrissey v. Brewer, 408 U.S. 471, 481 (1972); Cafeteria & Restaurant Workers Union v. McElroy, 367 U.S. 886, 895 (1961).

95   Note, *supra*, note 92, at 1519.

96   *See* note 61 *supra* and accompanying text.

97   *See* Palko v. Connecticut, 302 U.S. 319, 327 (1937); Comment, *supra* note 5, at 378.

98   Note, *supra* note 92, at 1528-29.

99   Wiley v. Memphis Police Department 548 F. 2d 1247, 1251-52 (8th Cir. 1976). *See also* Terry v. Ohio, 392 U.S. 1, 23 (1968).

100  For an example of such a sentence, see the case of nursing home operator Bernard Bergman, reported in *New York Times,* June 18, 1976, A, at 1, col. 7.

101  Furman v. Georgia, 408 U.S. 238, 258 (1972) (Brennan J., concurring).

102  408 U.S. 238 (1972).

103  Robinson v. California, 370 U.S. 660 (1962); Louisiana v. Resweber, 329 U.S. 459 (1947); In re Kemmler, 136 U.S. 436 (1890); Wilkerson v. Utah, 99 U.S. 130 (1878).

104  Robinson v. California, 370 U.S. 660, 676 (1962) (Douglas J., concurring); O'Neil v. Vermont, 144 U.S. 323, 339 (1892) (Field, J., dissenting).

105  Trop v. Dulles, 356 U.S. 86 (1958).

106  408 U.S. at 256 (Douglas, J., dissenting).

107  428 U.S. 153 (1976).

108  *Id.* at 169, *see* Coker v. Georgia, 433 U.S. 584 (1977); Roberts v. Louisiana, 428 U.S. 325 (1976); Woodson v. North Carolina, 428 U.S. 280 (1976); Jurek v. Texas, 428 U.S. 262 (1976); Proffitt v. Florida, 428 U.S. 242 (1976).

[109]   *See* Louisiana v. Resweber, 329 U.S. 459 (1947); Wilkerson v. Utah, 99 U.S. 130 (1878).

[110]   *See* Screws v. United States, 325 U.S. 91 (1945).

[111]   *See* Sherman, "The Breakdown of the Police Code of Silence," 14 *Crim. L. Bull.* 149, 150-51 (1978) discussing the Joe Campos Torres beating and drowning case. At least four southern California men died from police choke-holds in one recent year. *See* Cory, "Deadly Force," *Police Magazine,* Nov. 1978, at 5, 6.

[112]   One study found that police homicide cases are typically not referred to a grand jury, and that only three cases in some 1,500 led to police officers being criminally punished. Kobler, "Police Homicide in a Democracy," 31 *J. Soc. Issues* 163 (1975). A study of police use of deadly force in 49 Los Angeles county police agencies found that of 18 incidents officially designated as having been in violation of the department's firearms policies, only one was referred for criminal prosecution; only two led to dismissals, two led to suspensions, and 13 (72 percent) led to either a reprimand or no punishment at all. Uelman, "Varieties of Police Policy: A Study of Police Policy Regarding the Use of Deadly Force in Los Angeles County," 6 *L.A.L. Rev.* 1, 40 (1973). A study of police records in six cities found that of the eight percent of shooting incidents judged improper by administrative reviews punishment "generally consisted of a reprimand rather than suspension or termination." Milton, *supra* note 10, at 28.

[113]   408 U.S. at 394 (Burger, C.J., dissenting).

[114]   *Id.,* at 393 (Burger, C.J., dissenting).

[115]   See note 10 *supra.*

[116]   Milton, *supra* note 10, at 46.

[117]   The justification, however, is up to the jury to determine in light of all the circumstances of a particular case. *See* 11 Halsbury's Laws, *supra* note 33, 1180.

[118]   *See* 408 U.S. at 279-80 (Brennan, J., concurring).

[119]   "[The Court], before it reduces a sentence as 'cruel and unusual,' must have reasonably good assurances that the sentence offends the 'common conscience'," which not even opinion polls can measure. United States v. Rosenberg, 195 F.2d 583, 608 (2d Cir. 1952), *quoted in* Furman v. Georgia, 408 U.S. 238, 360 (1972) (Marshall, J., concurring).

[120]   Trop v. Dulles, 356 U.S. 86, 100-01 (1958).

[121]   408 U.S. at 278 (Brennan, J., concurring).

[122]   Milton, *supra* note 10, at 45-49.

[123]   "Gun Rules Rightened," *Los Angeles Times,* Sept. 9, 1977, at 1.

[124]    Cory, "Police on Trial in Houston," *Police Magazine*, July 1978, at 33, 40.

[125]    "Findings of Police Deadly Force Study Spark Three-Way Controversy in Birmingham," *Law Enforcement News*, June 21, 1977, at 1, col. 1; Personal Communication with B.R. Myers, Police Chief, Birmingham, Alabama. (November 1978).

[126]    *See also* Sarat and Vidmar, "Public Opinion, the Death Penalty, and the Eighth Amendment: Testing the Marshall Hypothesis," 1976 *Wisconsin Law Review* 171, 179.

[127]    Planning and Research Division, Boston Police Department, the use of Deadly Force by Boston Police Personnel, (May 3, 1974), *cited in* Mattis v. Schnarr, 547 F.2d 1007, 1016 n. 19 *See also* Clance, "Police Tell Firearm Policies," *San Diego Union*, Oct. 16, 1975, (nine of ten cities in San Diego County employ a defense-of-life police firearms policy). Contra, Leeds & Lowe, "Survey Finds Few Rules on Police Use of Guns," *Chicago Tribune*, Dec. 6, 1977.

[128]    Baker, "Model Firearms Policy for California Law Enforcement," 10 *Journal of California Law Enforcement* 5 (1975).

[129]    FBI, Memorandum 31-72 (Nov. 21, 1972), *quoted in* Mattis v. Schnarr, 547 F.2d 1007, 1015 (8th Cir. 1976) Policies more restrictive than state law are also reported in Comment, "The Use of Deadly Force in Arizona by Police Officers," 1973 *Law and Social Order* 481.

[130]    In the 40-year history of federal narcotics enforcement, 17 agents have been killed by assault in the line of duty, almost as many as in the FBI which has had at least four times as many agents and a longer history. J. Wilson, *The Investigators* 48 (1978).

[131]    Mattis v. Schnarr, 547 F.2d 1007, 1015 (8th Cir. 1976). Even these policies, however, may be ambiguous. The FBI policy reportedly goes on to allow the use of any force necessary to effect an arrest. Personal communication with Dr. Charles Wellford, Office of the United States Attorney General (Dec. 7, 1979).

[132]    *See, e.g.,* Pearson, *supra* note 32; Safer, "Deadly Weapons in the Hands of Police Officers, On Duty and Off Duty," 49 *Journal of Urban Law* 565 (1972); Note, *supra* note 68; Note, *supra* note 5; Comment, *supra* note 24; Comment, *supra* note 6; Comment, *supra* note 23. *But see* Miller, "The Law Enforcement Officer's Use of Deadly Force: Two Approaches," 8 Am. *Criminal Law Quarterly* 27 (1969).

[133]    *See, e.g.,* "Police Policy on the Use of Firearms," *The Police Chief*, July 1967, at 16.

[134]    President's Commission on Law Enforcement and Administration of Justice, Task Force Report: The Police 189-190 (1967).

[135]    For example, such riots occurred in San Francisco, St. Louis and Los Angeles in 1966. *See id.* at 189.

136    "Killings of Chicanos by Police Protested," *New York Times,* Oct. 12, 1977, A, at 17 col. 1; "Houston Quiet After Violence Hospitalizes Over 12," *New York Times,* May 9, 1978, at 22 col. 1; "2,000 Assail Police at Black Rally As Off-Duty Officers Meet Nearby," *New York Times,* July 17, 1978, B, at 3, col. 1; "Los Angeles Police Scored on Shooting," *New York Times,* Aug. 15, 1977, at 13 col. 1.

137    Gilman, "In Washington, A New Zeal for Prosecuting Police," *Police Magazine,* Nov. 1978, at 15, 18.

138    *Id.* Measured by the number of cases in which the victim died, however, Justice Department prosecutions of police officers have actually declined under the Carter administration. From 1970 through 1976, the average number of federal civil rights prosecutions for police homicide was four per year; in 1977, and 1978 it was only two per year. Personal communication from Daniel F. Rinzel, Civil Rights Division, U.S. Department of Justice (November 30, 1978).

139    *See* Minn. Stat. 609.066 (1976); Comment *supra* note 5, at 368-69.

140    Minn. Stat. 626.553 (1976).

142    *Id.* at 293 (Brennan, J., concurring).

143    *Id.* at 253 (Douglas, J., concurring).

144    Computed from National Center for Health Statistics, Public Health Service, Department of Health, Education and Welfare, Vital Statistics of the United States 1975 II *Mortality* part A 1-168; FBI, Crime in the United States 1975-1979. Using the unofficial estimated number of police homicides, the rate was one per 3,411 Part I Index arrests.

145    Goldberg and Dershowitz, "Declaring the Death Penalty Unconstitutional," 83 *Harvard Law Review* 1773, 1790 (1970), *quoted in* Furman v. Georgia, 408 U.S. 238, 249 (1972) (Douglas, J., concurring).

146    Until 1968, one large southwestern department employed the following policy on the use of a firearm, quoted in its entirety: "Never take me out in anger; never put me back in disgrace." Milton, *supra* note 10, at 47. Other "policies" have included "Leave the gun in the holster until you intend to use it," and "It is left to the discretion of each individual officer when and how to shoot." *Id.* at 47-48.

147    K. Davis, *Police Discretion* (1975); National Institute of Law Enforcement and Criminal Justice, *Police Discretion: A Selected Bibliography* (1978); Black, "The Social Organization of Arrest," 23 *Stan. L. Rev.* 1087 (1971); Goldstein, "Police Discretion Not to Invoke the Criminal Process: Law Visibility Decisions in the Administration of Justice," 69 *Yale Law Journal* 543 (1960).

149    The Project on Homicide by Police Officers, Criminal Justice Research Center, State University of New York at Albany, has studied this area.

150   G. Hayden, "Police Discretion in the Use of Deadly Force: An Empirical Study of Information Usage in Deadly Force Decision Making" (1979) (unpublished paper, University of New Haven).

151   428 U.S. 153 (1976).

152   National Center for Health Statistics, *supra* note 144. The total figure for all minority group members is probably somewhat higher, but no official statistics for other nonwhites are reported.

153   Bureau of the Census, Department of Commerce, Statistical Abstract of the United States 25 (1976).

154   P. Takagi, "A Garrison State in a "Democratic" Society," in *Police Community Relations* 358 (A. Cohn & E. Viano eds.).

155   *See* note 10 *supra*.

156   *E.g.*, Milton, *supra* note 10, at 19; Burnham, "3 of 5 Slain by Police Here are Black, Same as the Arrest Rate," *New York Times*, Aug. 26, 1973, at 50, col. 3. *See also* "The Management of Police Killings," *Crime and Social Justice*, Fall-Winter 1977, at 34; Goldkamp, "Minorities as Victims of Police Shootings: Interpretations of Racial Disproportionality and Police Use of Deadly Force," 1 Just, Sys. J. 169 (1977).

157   *See* note 5 *supra* and accompanying text.

158   Parnas, "The Police Response to the Domestic Disturbance," 1967 *Wisconsin Law Review* 914.

159   *See* Black, *supra* note 147. The fact that the greater likelihood of police to arrest black suspects can be largely attributed to (a) the greater tendency of blacks to be antagonistic to the police and (b) the greater tendency during street encounters with the police—to demand an arrest does not remove discrimination in a legal sense. Neither a suspect's attitudes nor a complainant's preference constitute proper grounds for enforcement decisions. *Id.* at 1097-1107.

160   Robin, *supra* note 10.

161   R. Knoohuizen, R. Fahey, & D. Palmer, "The Police and Their Use of Fatal Force in Chicago" 21 (1972) (unpublished study).

162   National Center for Health Statistics, *supra* note 144; FBI, *supra* note 144.

163   Comment, *supra* note 5.

164   *See, e.g.*, A.J. Reiss, "The Police and the Public" (1971); Reiss, "Systematic Observation of Natural Social Phenomena," in *Sociological Methodology* 3-33 (H. Costner, ed. 1971). Since police only draw their weapons once in every hundred citizen encounters (and patrol cars in many large cities average no more than ten encounters in eight hours), it could typically require two weeks of observation in order to capture one

drawing of a weapon. *See* Cruse and Rubin, "Determinants of Police Behavior," in Project Report to National Institute of Law Enforcement 194 (1972).

[165]  Other equal protection arguments can be made in addition to those concerning race. *See* Comment, *supra* note 5, at 375-80.

[166]  For a survey of the differing state approaches, *see* materials cited in note 5 *supra*.

[167]  *See* notes 129 & 131 *supra* and accompanying text.

[168]  *See generally* B. Chapman, Police State (1970); R. Fosdick, European Police Systems 17-20 (1915); Bayley, "The Police and Political Development in Europe in the Formation of National States in Western Europe" 328-79 (C. Tilly, ed. 1975).

[169]  *See* Mattis v. Schnarr, 547 F. 2d 1007, 1023 (8th Cir. 1976) (Gibson, C.J., dissenting).

[170]  Perkins, *supra* note 23, at 986.

[171]  Milton, *supra* note 10, at 48.

[172]  This survey was conducted by the Project on Homicide by Police Officers, Criminal Justice Research Center, State University of New York at Albany.

## Study Questions

1.    Sherman refers to homicides by the police as "executions before trial." Explain his concept in this phrase in light of (a) the "fleeing-felon" rule in deadly force and (b) constitutional issues associated with the use of deadly force by police.

2.    What is meant by the "any-felony rule" with respect to the police use of deadly force?

3.    Discuss the issue of police deadly force as being "punishment" meted out by officers as opposed to an action to apprehend felons.

4.    What issues of due process arise when considering the use of deadly force by the police? At what point does the state's interest take priority over individual rights regarding deadly force?

5.    What are the constitutional and practical benefits of having only a "defense-of-life" policy for the use of deadly force by the police? What are the problems with such a policy?

# 14

# THEORETICAL CONSIDERATIONS OF OFFICER PROFANITY AND OBSCENITY IN FORMAL CONTACTS WITH CITIZENS*

Mervin F. White, Terry C. Cox, and Jack Basehart

Interacting with citizens constitutes an important part of a police officer's daily activities. Many aspects of these interactions have the potential for influencing how the police and citizens perceive and evaluate each other and, more importantly, for influencing the effectiveness with which officers are able to do their job. Research over the years has established the fact that contacts between officers and citizens influence police-community relations in major ways, often for the worse. This is especially true of those contacts that citizens evaluate negatively. Recent research is beginning to indicate that the verbal communication between officer and citizen is an important, if not the most important, dimension of these exchanges.

The research literature has long since established the fact that contacts between citizens and the police reflect more than a simple exchange of information, or an officer's effort to enforce the law. Undercurrents of pre-established perceptions, prejudices, knowledge, and presumptions color both sides of these exchanges. Citizens often bring to the interaction an array of attitudes and preconceived notions about the police and their conduct that sometimes are inaccurate. These include preheld perceptions of officer insensitivity, prejudice, incompetence, and abusiveness that color the citizen's receptiveness to the officer's efforts at interaction and communication.

Likewise, the officer brings to the interaction a similar attitude of presumptions, prejudices, and perceptions of the citizen. Prior research has established that the officer is sometimes racially prejudiced, calloused by contacts with undesirable and unrepresentative population elements, and is trained to assert authoritative control in these contacts. In addition, the police culture abounds with perceptions of the public as uncooperative, unsupportive, and antagonistic toward the police.

This chapter addresses the issues of the influence of police-citizen verbal exchanges on citizen's *attitudes toward the police* (hereafter referred to as ATP). More specifically, it attempts to address the use of offensive language by police

---

*This chapter was written expressly for inclusion in this book.

officers in addressing citizens. The offensive language of concern will focus upon the use of profanity and obscenity, although other forms of offensive language (e.g., racial, ethnic, and sexual slurs, or language that is perceived as degrading, sarcastic, angry, or threatening) are included by inference. This chapter is theoretical and attempts to integrate the small body of research currently emerging on this issue. It is argued that much of the negative attitudes held by the public toward the police are the outcome of officer behavior and, thus, the power to reshape these public attitudes and perceptions lies within the hands of the police themselves.

## EMPIRICAL BACKGROUND OF THE PROBLEM

To suggest that verbal communications exert an important influence in police-citizen interactions is to understate the obvious. Sykes and Brent's (1983) proposition that the police officer's primary task is talking reflects the potency of this function. Recognition that verbal communication directly influences police-community relations permeates the literature. Yet, there is a paucity of information regarding specific dimensions of police-citizen communication that enhances or impedes police efficiency or adversely affects the way citizens feel about the police. Research has shown that citizens who have negative contacts with the police, compared to those who do not, have more negative attitudes toward the police (Scaglion and Condon, 1980; Stark, 1972; Chevigny, 1969; National Advisory Commission on Civil Disorders, 1968; Reiss, 1970; 1971; Black and Reiss, 1967; Bayley and Mendelsohn, 1969; Skolnick, 1975; Wesley, 1970; Thornton, 1975; Griffiths and Winfree, 1982; Smith and Hawkins, 1973; Rusinko, Johnson, and Hornung, 1978; Campbell and Schuman, 1972; Walker, 1977; Cox and Falkenberg, 1987; Cox, White, and Lewis, 1987; Cox and White, 1988). Scaglion and Condon (1980), consistent with many other researchers, report that citizens' attitudes toward the police appears most affected by actual contact with a uniformed officer in an official or semi-official capacity.

There is growing evidence that one of the important dimensions of police-citizen interaction is verbal communication, especially officer's use of offensive language. For example, research has established that verbal behavior is an important factor in citizens' complaints against the police (Culver, 1975; Wagner, 1980; Russell, 1978; Hudson, 1973; Stark, 1972). Numerous studies document the existence of police verbal harassment of citizens (National Advisory Commission on Civil Disorders, 1968; Reiss, 1970; Black and Reiss, 1967; Van Maanen, 1978; Bayley and Mendelsohn, 1969; Wesley, 1970; Stark, 1972). Further, Black and Reiss (1967), Reiss (1970), and the National Commission on Civil Disorders (1968) provided unequivocal evidence that police officers use racial slurs in interactions with black citizens. Reiss (1970:60) found that more than one in ten blacks said that a police officer had called them an offensive name.

Language typically labeled as profanity or obscenity has been identified as frequently used by officers to refer to certain citizens both in officer-to-officer and officer-to-citizen communications. For example, Van Maanen (1978) identified the label "asshole" as a favorite term of abuse by the police. Skolnick and Bayley (1986:91) identify "turd" as a term commonly used by members of the Houston Police Department. Furthermore, single episodes or individual examples of police use of profanity in interactions with citizens can be found in numerous training films and case-oriented books such as Baker (1985).

In more recent studies, a relationship has been established between citizen perception of officer use of profane and obscene language directed to the citizen and the citizens' negative attitudes and evaluations of the police. For example, Cox and Falkenberg (1986) in a study of adolescent involvement in alcohol and marijuana use, found that respondents who perceived being verbally harassed by the police held significantly more negative attitudes toward the police than those who report not experiencing this abuse. Another recent study of negative contacts between the police and college students reported that verbal abuse and profanity perceived by respondents as directed to themselves by the officer were highly significant factors in their negative assessment of the police (Cox and White, 1988). Some 15 percent of the respondents (n = 832) in this study reported that police officers had directed profanity toward them. In a third recent study with a large sample of college students, Cox, White, and Baseheart (1988) reported that 12.2 percent of their respondents indicated that a police officer had directed profanity toward them. In these latter two studies, student respondents reported more negative attitudes toward the police as a result of the profanity directed to them.

Finally, there is some research to indicate that officers misperceive hostility to be greater than it necessarily is from the communities they serve (Groves and Rossi, 1970); Crawford, 1973; and Cox and White, 1988 who provide the most recent research on this issue). This research suggests that officer's misperception rests on a complex dynamic of interaction of officers' perceptions, attitudes, and verbal behavior that likely provoke negative responses by various groupings of community citizens who are the object of these discriminatory responses. This research, like the others referred to above, strongly suggests that officers' verbal behavior, especially the use of language judged by citizens to be obscene, is a key factor in promoting negative perceptions and evaluations of the police by the public.

# PROFANITY AND OBSCENITY IN LANGUAGE USAGE

This discussion of officer use of profanity and obscene language in interaction with the public immediately encounters the problem of defining what language fits into these categories. The meaning of terms such as profanity, indecent language, and obscenity will vary according to vernacular, cultural, and individual interpretations, as well as contexts of everyday uses. Even so, the U.S. Supreme Court, in *Federal Communications Commission v. Pacifica Foundation* (438 U.S. 726), in 1978 confirmed the Federal Communications Commission's Declaratory Order (FCC 75-200) that specifically concludes that words such as "fuck," "shit," "piss," "motherfucker," "cocksucker," "cunt," and "tit" depict sexual and excretory activities and organs in a manner patently offensive by contemporary standards. Halonen (1987) indicates that the Federal Communication Commission currently applies the Pacifica Standards to the broadcast media. While these standards may be helpful in defining guidelines for the broadcast media, they do not include definitions for interpersonal interactions.

However, to the extent that the U.S. Supreme Court is correct in holding that words such as those identified are offensive by contemporary standards, it can be assumed that their use in interpersonal communication will be offensive, especially when one party perceives itself as the object of address (See Glassman, 1978; and Bordner and Herman, 1979 for some research on these community standards). Thus, there is reason to believe that the Pacifica Foundation standards are applicable to some conditions of interpersonal communications. In the present case, those conditions involve formal and semi-formal contact between the police and citizens in which the citizen perceives this language to be directed specifically to him/her. One of the most important elements in these specific situations is the officer's authority to significantly affect the life and liberty of the citizen.

Of course, one must consider the current vernacular as a context of use for certain terminology. In the current vernacular, words such as "bitchin" and "funky" are used as adjectives conveying a positive connotation. Thus, "John is a bitchin' guy!" and "That is a funky shirt!" are taken as compliments. However, it is difficult to imagine contexts in which statements such as "Shut-up and listen, you fucking asshole!" are likely to be taken as complimentary or to be perceived by the person addressed as appropriate language by police officers.

Actually, the use of language perceived to be profane and obscene has a long history in Western civilization and apparently is widely used in other cultures as well (Sherman, 1968; Vincze, 1985; Fine, 1976). There are reasons to believe that the use of profanity in other cultures is not unlike that in our culture (see Fine, 1976; Vincze, 1986). The research literature on various types of language uses in our society confirms the expectation that substantial differences exist between recognizable groupings in the rates, types, and functions of language that may be "off-color," profane, or obscene. Most of this research addresses differences between males and females in their use patterns and the functions these differences in patterns reflect in the relationships between the sexes (see Barron, 1971; Bauduin, 1973; Brend, 1975; Cameron, 1969; Cohen and Saine, 1977;

Foldy, 1981; Gleser, Gottschalk and Watkins, 1959; Hass, 1981; Kramer, 1975; Lakoff, 1973; 1975; Mulac, 1976; Reiber, Weidmann and D'Amato, 1979; Thorne and Henly, 1975; Warshay, 1972; Warshay and Warshay, 1978; West, 1979; Wood, 1966; and Zimmerman and Wes, 1975). It will be of some interest to the present effort to review some of these findings because they have relevance to understanding the purposes for which police officers employ profanity and obscenity in their interactions with citizens in law enforcement situations.

There is substantial evidence that men and women differ significantly in their language uses. For example, women, compared to men, reflect more emotion and feeling in their language (Gleser, et al., 1959; Wood, 1966; Barron, 1971; Bernard, 1972); they typically avoid a forceful style and use more polite words (Lakoff, 1973; Brend, 1975); they use more person-oriented language (Barron, 1971; Warshay, 1972); and their speech is more timid and uncertain (Lakoff, 1973). In contrast, men's language is more thing- or event-oriented (Barron, 1971; Warshay, 1972) and more sports- or location-oriented (Hass, 1981). In addition, males' language is more direct (Zimmerman and West, 1975; West, 1979) and they are more likely to interrupt female speakers than vice-versa (Zimmerman and West, 1975; Lakoff, 1973). Finally, men use stronger language (shit, damn) than do women (oh, fudge; oh, dear) (Kramer, 1975).

These findings establish the fact that men and women use language differently. Indeed, they show that the language used by men reflects greater concern with dominance and assertiveness and reflects long-standing, gender-role prescriptions (men—strong, dominant, rational, less emotional; women—more submissive, emotional, wishing and/or needing) (Hass, 1981).

Turning specifically to the research on differences in the uses of profanity, the research establishes that differences between males and females exist (Selnow, 1985). More specifically, males report using profanity more frequently than females and they are more likely to see profanity as appropriate when a male uses it. The one exception is when its use is in mixed company settings, where both sexes are likely to see this type of language as inappropriate (see Selnow, 1985; Kramer, 1975; Cohen and Saine, 1977; and Mulac, 1976).

Cameron (1969) offers a useful scheme for classifying profanity according to type. His scheme uses three categories for classifying offensive language. His three categories include words having religious notations (e.g., hell, Goddamn); words indicating excretory functions and organs (e.g., shit, piss, asshole, turd, fart); and words concerned with sexual organs and functions (e.g., cunt, fuck, prick). Research has demonstrated that these three categories can be ranked according to their perceived offensiveness. In general, profanity with a religious connotation is perceived to be less offensive while profanity with a sexual connotation is most offensive (Bauduin, 1973).

Operational definitions of words and phrases that are likely to be considered profane and obscene in interpersonal discourse are difficult to establish. Indeed, a precise listing of such does not exist. Even so, we have argued that such a list should not be impossible to establish. One place to begin would be the Pacifica Foundations standards. The list would need to take into account current vernacular, the contexts of usage and the special nature of the relationship that comes into being in formal and semi-formal police-citizen interactions. It is beyond the scope of the present paper to establish a list of words and phrases considered profane or obscene and therefore offensive to citizens in their interaction with the police. Instead, we turn to a discussion of the purposes for which officers may use offensive language in their interaction with the public and some of the possible consequences of that usage.

## INTENT AND CONTEXT OF OFFENSIVE LANGUAGE USE BY POLICE OFFICERS

It must be assumed that police officers who use offensive language during their formal interactions with citizens do so with control and intent. The alternative assumption, that officers' use of such language is without personal responsibility, is simply not tenable. The research consistently reflects such language usage as systematic and deliberate, whether immediate or long-term. Officers do not enter interaction with citizens with empty heads. On the contrary, they are likely to be guided by a host of previously acquired behaviors perceived as affective means of dealing with citizens in these contexts.

There is every reason to believe that the use of profanity and obscenity by officers occurs almost exclusively in interaction with selected segments of the population (e.g., racial and ethnic minorities, lower- and working-class citizens, and other powerless and disvalued persons). Likewise, it can be observed that the use of such language is far more likely to be restrained and controlled in the presence of persons of power and influence. Further, it is inconceivable that a police officer would use profanity or obscenity during a trial where tensions, stress, frustration, and anger-provoking conditions are often high. The variable that distinguishes these latter two situations from the first one is the presence of a capacity to exert controls and sanctions on officer conduct in them that is not present in the first. Thus, it is logical to reject simplistic explanations such as "lack of verbal skills" or the "loss of personal control" by officers in their interaction with certain segments of the population. These explanations are simply unsatisfactory. We argue, instead, that officers' use of such language is purposive and includes a previously acquired repertoire of behavior (e.g., tactics and strategies for performance of duties).

The issues of officer intent and control of language usage have at least three interactive contextual dimensions. The first of these is the personal dimension. Officers may engage in the use of profanity or obscenity as a means of satisfying their own psychological or personal agenda. The personal agenda includes both the satisfaction of needs brought to the role and the expression of emotional responses to the demands of the role itself. In the first instance, it can be noted that charges of bigotry, abuse of power (and other forms of corruption), and being violence-prone have a long history in police work. In the latter case, the build-up of tensions, frustrations, and angers to the role may find catharsis in verbally aggressive ways.

The second dimension is a situational one. Officers may use profane or obscene language as a means of dealing with a variety of situational contingencies in role enactment. These may include factors such as perceived dangerousness, difficulties of unpleasantries inherent in police work, emotional provocations deriving from citizens' behavior, or even simplifying the otherwise unmanageable complexities of situations. The use of profane or obscene language to attribute blame, achieve emotional release, or explain complex phenomena by focusing upon culpable individuals or groups is one way of dealing with these situational contingencies.

The third dimension, already suggested, is the police role itself. Officers' socialization experiences (including training), role expectations, and definitions (both formal and informal) may foster confrontation stances with selected population elements perceived as problematic, dangerous, or even undeserving in some manner. Preparation for the police role (both formal training and informal work-related on-the-job training) includes presenting oneself as authoritative and in control. These influences structure officers' perceptions of persons, behaviors, and situations with ready-made explanations, language forms (including profanity and obscenity), and behavioral forms designed to standardize confrontations with citizens.

## OFFICER PURPOSES FOR USING PROFANITY AND OBSCENITY

The research demonstrates that profanity and obscenity are used for several purposes. Specifically, the research indicates that profanity and obscenity are used as sources of communication power and control and to establish and/or maintain dominant-submissive relationships (Selnow, 1985; Lakoff, 1973; 1975; Cohen and Saine, 1977; West, 1979); to promote group or community solidarity (Vincze, 1985; Zimmerman and West, 1975); as weapons to degrade or insult others (Paletz and Harris, 1975); as a way of alienating others from membership in special groupings (Selnow, 1985; Thorne and Henly, 1975); as a way of labeling others (Warshay and Warshay, 1978); as a means of demarking territoriality (Vincze, 1985; Paletz, and Harris, 1975; Warshay and Warshay, 1978); as a way to defy authority (Paletz and Harris, 1975); and to make one more socially acceptable to one's own group(s) (Selnow, 1985).

Rothwell (1971) has offered an interesting listing of motives for using profanity. His typology seems primarily designed to apply to the uses of profanity by dissident and militant groups, especially in the 1960s and early 1970s. He identifies five reasons: (1) to create attention; (2) to discredit; (3) to provoke confrontation; (4) for interpersonal identification; and (5) to provide the individual with some amount of catharsis. The similarity of his listing with those identified above is noted.

In the following we present a typology of motives or purposes for which profanity and obscenity are used by police officers in their formal and semi-formal interaction with the citizenry. The typology integrates the contextual dimensions noted above with the list of motives identified in the research literature on the use of profanity and obscenity. It is assumed here that officer use of this language is role-related and expresses either personal agenda or situational contingencies or both. We recognize that these factors may not operate independently in any given instance, but rather overlap and interact to produce officer obscenity.

## PERSONAL AGENDA PROVOKED USES OF PROFANITY AND OBSCENITY

Some use of offensive language in formal and semiformal interaction between police officers and the public will reflect motives or purposes that are provoked by personal agenda concerns. While these will reflect role-related concerns, they are not intrinsic to the law enforcement role. They include the following.

### Aggression

Profanity and obscenity may be used by officers in formal and semi-formal police-citizen contacts as a form of aggression. The history of organized policing in the United States is replete with charges of bigotry, abuse of power (and other forms of corruption), being violence-prone and so on. Further, research in the last couple of decades confirms that in some situations, and with some segments of the population, officers are likely to be violently aggressive (see Black, 1968; National Advisory Commission on Civil Disorders, 1968). Buss (1971) asserts that verbal behavior is an active and direct form of aggression. Bartol and Bartol (1968:163) define aggression as "behavior perpetrated or attempted with the intention of harming another individual physically or psychologically or to destroy an object."

Conceptually, verbal behavior involving profanity or obscenity directed toward citizens in formal and semi-formal interactions is likely intended to attack one's identity in a condescending fashion. When this is done, then aggression is a primary factor associated with this type of behavior. In fact, when using Bartol and Bartol's (1986) definition of aggression, two reasons (to discredit and to provoke confrontation) presented by Rothwell (1971) are readily encapsulated. In the instances of police aggression, officers will likely be attempting to accomplish defined goals (effecting an arrest) that are confounded by frustration, anger, or even confusion on behalf of the officer.

Aggression can be classified as either instrumental or expressive. Rothwell's (1971) classification scheme suggests that some individuals enter situations in which they intend to use profanity and obscenity in a rational and controlled way with forethought. That is, their use of such language is designed to achieve some preselected end. He suggests that this was true of the dissidents and militants of the 1960s and early 1970s. In contrast, aggression that is a behavioral outgrowth of situationally provoked anger, hostility, fear, or frustration is expressive. That is, this aggression is not premeditated, but is an outgrowth of situational contingencies not rationally and intentionally anticipated.

It is expected that much of police (verbal) aggression is of the expressive variety, reflecting officer response to emotional provocations in particular policing situations. However, instrumental aggression should not be discounted. Van Maanen (1978:235) suggests that the arrest of citizens labeled as "assholes" may serve an important occupational purpose since "real" police work is seldom available and the arrests of such persons provide the opportunity to apply valued skills. In this context, confrontational provocation may include obscenity and profanity as means of instigating citizen behavior that legitimizes the arrest. Even so, it bears repeating that much of the aggression expressed in officer profanity and obscenity likely reflects situational emotional provocations deriving from actual or misinterpreted citizen behavior.

Why some police officers resort to aggressive language patterns when frustrated by the actions and behaviors of citizens is, in part, consistent with certain considerations of the frustration-aggression hypothesis (Dollard, et al., 1939; Berkowitz, 1962, 1969, 1973, 1983). This hypothesis argues that people who are frustrated, annoyed, or threatened will behave aggressively since aggression is a natural, almost automatic response to frustrating circumstances. In short, frustration facilitates and increases the probability of aggressive responses in some people. For some persons, frustration results in the generation of anger that predisposes them to act aggressively. Whether actual engagement in verbal aggressive responses that are the focus of this paper will occur or not will depend upon either personality factors of the individual officer, the situational factors in the specific circumstances in which the police-citizen interaction occurs, or some combination of the two.

Personality factors will vary considerably among officers to include a variety of coping skills, emotional dispositions, inner conflicts, experience, prejudices, and other similar factors. Regardless, aggression (including verbal) is learned behavior that involves a pattern perceived as effective for that individual in past interactions. When confronted with interactions that are emotionally provocative, some officers may revert to previously learned patterns of verbal aggression that likely include profanity and obscenity.

Situational dimensions will also vary considerably for police officers working in widely heterogenous populations. Reactions to frustrations by use of profanity and obscenity are likely to be controlled. As suggested previously, officers do not enter situations empty-headed. The use of such language patterns will be directed most likely toward groups defined as disvalued, powerless, or who are in conflict with the police. In contrast, police officers exposed to potentially frustrating experiences in situations involving powerful persons, including situations not directly controlled by the police (e.g., court), are unlikely to target profanity or obscenity directly toward others.

## Identification With the In-Group

Rothwell suggests that the use of profanity and obscenity may be directed toward gaining acceptance by or identification with significant others, that is, to be "one of the gang." Use of such language for this purpose would, of course, reflect the fact that this language is characteristic of the identified group. This use of the language would imply, as Rothwell (1971:237) suggests, "...a planned rhetorical strategy to create identification...(between user)...and potential allies."

It can be anticipated that this motive would most likely be active in circumstances where the offending officer is in the presence of another officer (or officers) where such observed behavior could confirm the officer's "likeness" with these others. That such language is part of the vernacular of policing is beyond question. Further, the prohibition against use of such language in formal and semi-formal police-citizen contacts by most or all police departments, notwithstanding, research has documented that officers do use such obscenity and profanity in their interactions with selected segments of the population. It can be concluded, then, that such language as a "rhetorical strategy" to create identification between officers and their colleagues is likely.

## Catharsis

Rothwell (1971) suggests that one might use profanity for the purpose of catharsis. This purpose or motive is consistent with the psychodynamic or hydraulic model involving the release of built-up aggressive energies or pent-up hostilities in persons who have not released these in more appropriate or acceptable ways. To the extent that verbal behavior of the officer is defined as aggressive, the process of catharsis involved in police-citizen interactions is likely discharged in the form of displaced aggression. Van Maanen (1978:235) suggests that encounters and subsequent actions in encounters with persons defined as "assholes" provides an expressive outlet for the frustrations that policing engenders. Moreover, responses by officers (these are certain to include both verbal and physical behaviors) release pent-up energies, hostilities, and frustrations suffered by the police at the hands of the community elite, courts, and numerous others. This type of release of pent-up hostilities displaces them to less directly responsible individuals who are simply scapegoats in a larger social process. To the extent that what is being described is accurate, it is little wonder that individuals who are members of disvalued and powerless groups report such high frequencies of experiencing profanity and obscenity directed toward them by police officers.

## SITUATIONALLY PROVOKED USE OF PROFANITY AND OBSCENITY

Profanity and obscenity are sometimes used by police officers for purposes that reflect situational contingencies affecting role performance demands. Like the personal agenda motives, these are not intrinsic to the law enforcement task. That is, other more professionally acceptable tactics and strategies could be used to achieve the same ends. These include the following.

### Gaining the Attention of the Target

It is banal to point out that profane and obscene language is generally frowned upon in "polite" society. Yet, it is precisely for this reason that use of such language is likely to gain the attention of others, particularly when these others are the target of such language use. More directly, it is asserted that in some circumstances officers may resort to the use of such language specifically for the purpose of gaining the attention of citizens who may be less than cooperative. Some citizens stopped by the police for some suspected law violation or investigative purpose are not likely to be cooperative, to acknowledge their culpability, or in other ways facilitate the officers task. Instead, they may become argumentative, confrontational, and resistant to the officer's intervention. Getting the attention of such citizens and effectively communicating with them will be a high priority for the officer. Offensive language, as noted, is a well-established way of doing this.

## Establishing Social Distance From Target

The use of profane and obscene language is an effective means of establishing social distance between the speaker and the target of address. In police work this may work well with certain segments of the public with whom they must have rule-enforcing contact. Van Maanen (1978) suggests that maintaining this social distance helps guarantee that the target citizen(s) will not come uncomfortably close to the officer(s). However, to the extent that this language is associated with condescension and derogation, the primary purpose may be to gain social distance by reducing human characteristics through the process of dehumanization.

The application of names connoting excretory or sexual organs and functions is likely an attempt to reduce human characteristics to objects or functions seen as socially undesirable or offensive. Dehumanization can permit an officer to take more harmful or negative actions in situations where physical or psychological discomfort is inflicted on the citizen. This is especially important in situations where the officer experiences dissonance between the actions of the citizens and legal mandates imposed upon him. Findings by Bandura, Underwood, and Fromson (1975) demonstrated that it becomes more difficult to treat people hurtfully or cruelly as they become more personalized and humanized. Black's (1971) findings that the probability of the occurrence of an arrest increases as the relational distance between complainants and suspects decreased lends some support to this idea, also. One can reasonably speculate that as the relational distance increases between the officer and the offender, the probability of an arrest will be increased. Most likely, this will be effected as the offensive language of the officer achieves social distance and dehumanizes the target citizen(s).

## Labeling and Degrading the Target

Negative labeling and stereotyping are associated with prejudiced attitudes toward some target groups(s). Labels containing profanity and obscenity serve to identify out-groups who are the targets of prejudice and discrimination. Verbal rejection serves as a fundamental state in the degradational processes of out-group rejection. Allport (1958) suggests that intense hostility is reflected in the name-calling processes of verbal rejection. Further these epithets generally result from deep and long-standing hostility (Allport, 1958:49). Van Maanen (1978:224) notes that the term "asshole" arises from a person's failure to meet police expectations in the interaction situation itself. That is, "asshole" is applied to those persons who do not accept the police definition of the situation (Van Maanen, 1978:223). Consistent with Van Maanen (1978), these labeling and classification schemes identify those who are "like" and those who are "unlike" police officers.

Emphasizing profane and obscene labels associated with disvalued out-groups to actual interactions with certain citizens or citizen groups is consistent with Van Maanen's (1978) description of the purpose for which labels are used. They help make meaningful the actions of these citizens, thus justifying the actions of the police officer(s). In attaching simple profane and obscene terms to complex behavior, the underlying complexity is stripped away. Applying these labels serves as confirmation in the attempt to interpret complex events with simplistic measures.

## Dominance and Control of Target

Finally, it is noted that officers may use profane and obscene language in formal and semi-formal police-citizen interaction for the purpose of dominance and control of both the situation and the citizen(s) involved in the interaction. Specifically, research indicates that profanity and obscenity are frequently used as sources of communication, power and control, and as means of establishing and/ or maintaining dominant-submissive relationships (Selnow, 1985, 1985; Lakoff, 1973; 1975; Cohen and Saine, 1977; and West, 1979). This use of profanity and obscenity in interaction with citizens likely includes many of the other uses indicated above.

With regard to personal agenda concerns, use of this type of language reflects a pattern of learned behavior perceived by the officer as effective for dealing with particular situations. For example, officers lacking confidence in their ability to handle a particular situation may rely on aggressive verbal responses as compensatory means of gaining control of, or of dominating, the situation.

Situational contexts may include elements perceived by the officer as anger-evoking, dangerous, or frustrating. Role demands and constraints to deal with these situational factors, likely perceived as originating with the citizen(s) involved in the interaction, may well lead to the officer seeking to control and dominate the situation through the use of profanity and obscenity.

While most or all police agencies formally prohibit the use of profanity and obscenity in formal and semiformal interactions with the public, officers are trained to use verbal and nonverbal approaches designed to control and dominate citizens in law enforcement-related interactions. Concepts such as "command presence" and "command voice" are taught as part of the skills officers need to gain and maintain such control and dominance. Complications of interaction control are likely to stem from informal normative arrangements that define the extent to which offensive language, including profanity and obscenity, will be tolerated both by other officers and by certain groups of citizens. Common attitudes among officers, reflecting the strength of this informal norm, are that officers should not take any "shit" from citizens or go on duty to see what the "assholes" are up to tonight. This factor accounts for, or at least influences, some of the variances that are likely to exist not only among various police agencies, but among individual officers as well.

## EFFECTS OF USING PROFANITY AND OBSCENITY

One can hardly discuss the reasons why police officers might choose to use profanity and obscenity in interaction with the public without raising the related question of the effects the use of this language might have on the outcome of such an interaction. Before discussing the effects of the use of profanity, however, it would seem appropriate to mention three additional factors that may significantly influence the effects of profanity and obscenity on target individuals and groups. These include *who* uses the profanity, *where* the profanity is employed, and *how* the profanity is used. Each of these deserve some brief comment.

It is commonplace to observe that women have been expected, traditionally, to refrain from the use of verbal obscenities (at least in public discourse). The same expectations have applied to certain categories of men (e.g., clergy, public officials, and perhaps most professionals) as well. The social "revolutions" of the 1960s and 1970s changed some of these expectations for most people in American society. Certainly, it became more acceptable for most men and women to use profanity in public discourse. While this acceptability seems to be waning somewhat, it still remains more acceptable today than before the 1960s. In this context, it is commonplace for police departments to prohibit their officers from using profanity and obscenity in their interaction with the public. Thus, while it is usually recognized that profane and obscene language is commonplace among police officers while interacting among themselves (even when both sexes are present), it is expected that they will refrain from such language in the performance of their duties.

*Where* profanity is employed is a second factor that significantly influences the outcome of an encounter. One would not expect to encounter the use of profanity in public discourse, in church, or in "polite society." Such usages are quite likely to draw attention to the user and the message. However, the effect might well be alienation of the audience from the user and his/her message. It would not be outside the realm of possibility that the user and the message would be rejected by the audience, thus achieving the opposite of what the user intended. In like fashion, it can be recognized that the use of such offensive language by a police officer may well gain the attention of the target citizen(s). However, that officer may well find that the effect of this use may alienate the target citizen(s) from him/her, the department, and, research has shown, from the occupational group as a whole. The continued frequency of citizen complaints about racism, abuse, and violence undoubtedly reflect some of these concerns.

To say that someone is a "mean bastard" can have at least two interpretations: one, that it is an insult that may invite reprisals, and two, as a phrase expressing admiration and/or affection. This example suggests a third factor that likely mediates the effect of the use of profanity, that being *how* the profanity is used. An instance of profanity, for example, may be used in a very laudatory sense, or as an insult (perhaps designed to precipitate confrontation). One needs, therefore, to be aware of the context in which the profanity is used to determine the possible meanings intended in its use and to better predict the possible consequence(s) of its usage. In the present context, our reference has been to uses by police officers in which the object of address *understands* that the language was used in the negative and derogatory sense. It should be recognized that sometimes the citizen may interpret the uses negatively, even when the officer intends otherwise.

These three factors, then, undoubtedly tend to mediate the effect that the use of profanity will have on the outcome of an interaction. Exactly what effect the use of profanity might have on the receivers is a difficult question to answer, and one for which there is no clear answer. Rothwell (1971), however, has suggested that polarization is the most likely outcome of obscenity reflecting the strong social disapproval of this type of language. This suggests that very few individuals are able to remain totally neutral in their attitudes toward issues/persons in the face of verbal obscenities. Instead, people tend to polarize themselves into one camp or another. Difficulty for the officer will arise because of his/her inability to accurately predict who will disapprove of the use of profanity, for what reasons, and in what situations. Thus, seemingly mild and inoffensive forms of profanity and obscenity may be highly disapproved of by those who have attached a negative semantic significance to the particular term chosen.

Given this effect of using profanity, police officers who choose to use it in their interactions with the public might well expect the outcome to be further alienation toward the police, especially when these individuals are already negatively disposed toward them. This would seem to have particular relevance in situations where an officer uses profanity in a directed or aggressive fashion.

Rothwell further states that polarization created by the use of profanity may have additional consequences. Using profanity may cloud the issues involved in the intervention focusing the emphasis on the obscenities themselves. The clouding of issues in a law enforcement encounter may have important, even devastating, consequences for the police and/or the citizen(s) involved. Police officers must continuously be concerned with misconduct allegations; a procedure that has more potentially serious consequences in some organizations than in others. Further, arrests include important decision-making properties including use of sound judgment. Verbal abuse of this sort may become the basis for a challenge to the officer's judgments, clouding such issues as probable cause, evidence interpretation, and may even provide a basis for impeaching his/her immediate and long-term credibility. This would seemingly become a serious issue in confrontational events between citizens and police officers where key decisions surround judgment and discretionary factors.

A potentially momentous effect having significant relevance to the police-public interactions is that profanity and obscenity serve as stimuli capable of producing aggressive responses because of their semantic significance. Berkowitz and Knurek (1969; see Berkowitz, 1973; 1983) suggest that verbal and/or symbolic stimuli can elicit impulsive aggressive responses from those persons who are set to act aggressively. Prior learning plays a prominent role in predisposing persons to respond aggressively to verbal symbols with semantic significance attached to something one considers to be negative.

There is every reason to believe verbal behavior in the forms of profanity and obscenity by police officers sets the occasion for an aggressive response. Theoretically, these behaviors substantially increase the risk of a consequential physical altercation where the use of force becomes necessary. Consequently, risk of physical injury for the combatants is increased. Buss (1961) has pointed out that an anger stimulus will likely elicit an anger reaction or even a counterattack. The counterattack may take the form of either a counter-obscenity or perhaps even physical aggression. Support for this position is found in research focusing on the "situated transactional" properties of assaults and murders. Luckinbill's (1977) findings reveal that murder is frequently the outcome of a "character contest" that begins with an attack on one of the contestant's identity. Retaliatory attacks often escalate to the ultimate form of physical violence.

Obviously, numerous cases involving the use of profanity or obscenity by police officers result in passive submission. Reinforcement resulting from such submission will likely strengthen this approach for the officer into a routine pattern for some categories of behavior and of people. This vision is fatally flawed because of variances in the semantic significant, aggressive predisposition, and situational factors among individuals being affected. Anger stimuli presented to some people may result in total disengagement from cognitive regulatory measures under conditions of high emotional arousal associated with anger. Disengagement processes are further enhanced with alcohol or drug intoxication. Given these factors, it is small wonder that assaults on police officers occur with such high frequencies during disturbance-related calls.

While profanity and obscenity used in a condescending and derogatory fashion may not result in immediate aggressive retaliatory responses, this language will likely result in suppressing the anger or "biting one's tongue" with deference extended to police authority. A potentially harmful effect is the formulation of negative attitudes toward the police. Concrete experiences associated with negative contacts with police have consistently been identified as a factor associated with the development of negative attitudes toward the police. Recent research findings (Cox and Falkenberg, 1987; Cox and White, 1988; and While, Cox, and

Basehart, 1988) confirm the expectation that a police officer's verbal abuse will subsequently diminish citizens' positive attitudes toward the police.

Research by White, Cox, and Baseheart (1988), unfortunately, demonstrates how negative experiences involving the use of profanity, obscenity, and other verbal abuse are generalized to other agencies and members of the occupation. Their findings are consistent with those of Berkowitz and Knurek's (1969) who conclude that persons having certain stimulus properties are particularly likely to be victims of displaced hostility following anger arousal. Consistent with classical learning concepts, then, persons possessing aversive stimulus properties (e.g., uniform, authority) evoke aggressive responses learned in association with previous negative experiences, even when they have not behaved in a provocative manner.

In conclusion, police officers must interact with the public to achieve the public mandates that are their *raison d'être*. As Sykes and Brent (1983) suggest, the police officer's primary task is talking to the public. Verbal communication skills, then, are critically important to the achievement of the officer's mission. Yet, the available research strongly suggests that officers sometimes behave in a fashion that complicates their work in highly undesirable ways.

In this chapter, we presented a typology of motives that helps to explain why officers sometimes use profane and obscene language in the course of their law enforcement duties. We have assumed that their use of such offensive language is rational and purposive. The motives for using this language may be provoked either by personal agenda concerns or by situational contingencies, including the conduct of the citizen(s) with whom they are interacting. Finally, we have suggested that the consequences for engaging in this type of language usage poses both immediate and long-term consequences for the officer, the department, and the occupation as a whole. Furthermore, these consequences may, on some occasions, be devastating for the officer, the citizen, or both.

# REFERENCES

Allport, G. (1958). *The Nature of Prejudice*. Revised Edition. Reading, MA: Addison and Wesley.

Baker, M. (1985). *Cops: Their Lives in their Own Words*. New York: Simon and Schuster.

Bandura, A., B. Underwood, and M.E. Fromson (1975). "The Disinhibition of Aggression Through Diffusion of Responsibility and Dehumanization of Victims." *Journal of Research and Personality*. 9:253-269.

Barron, W. (1971). "Sex-Typed Language: The Production of Grammatical Cases." *Acta Sociologica*. 14:24-72.

Bartol, C.R. and Bartol, A.M. (1986). *Criminal Behavior: A Psychosocial Approach*. Englewood Cliffs, NJ: Prentice-Hall.

Banduin, F. (1973). "Obscene Language and Evaluative Responses: An Empirical Study." *Psychological Reports*. 32:399-402.

Bayley, D.H. and H. Mendelsohn (1969). *Minorities and the Police*. New York: The Free Press.

Berkowitz, L. (1962). *Aggression: A Social-Psychological Analysis*. New York: McGraw-Hill.

Berkowitz, L. (1969). "Frustration-Aggression Hypothesis Revisited." In Leonard Berkowitz (ed.) *Roots of Aggression*. New York: Atherton Press.

Berkowitz, L. (1973). "Words and Symbols as Stimuli to Aggressive Responses." In J.F. Knutson (ed.) *The Control of Aggression*. Chicago: Aldine.

Berkowitz, Leonard (1983). "The Expression of Anger as a Parallel Process in the Display of Impulsive, 'Angry' Aggression." In R.G. Geen and E.I. Donnerstein (eds.) *Aggression: Theoretical and Empirical Reviews*. Vol. 1. New York: Academic Press.

Berkowitz, L. and D.A. Knurek (1969). "Label-Mediated Hostility Generalization." *Personality and Social Psychology*. 13:200-206.

Bernard, J. (1972). *The Sex Game*. New York: Atherton.

Black, D.J. (1971). "The Social Organization of Arrest," *Stanford Law Review*. 23:1087-1111.

Black, D. and A.J. Reiss, Jr. (1967). *Studies in Crime and Law Enforcement in Major Metropolitan Areas*. Washington, DC: U.S. Government Printing Office.

Bordner, D.C. and M.S. Herman (1979). Perceived obscenity in a Southern Community. Paper presented at the Southern Sociological Society Meetings.

Brend, R. (1975). "Male-Female Intonation Patterns in American English." In B. Thorne and N. Henly (eds.), pp. 84-87. *Language and Sex: Differences and Dominance*. Rowley, MA: Newberry House.

Buss, A.H. (1971). "Aggression Pays." In J.L. Singer (ed.) *The Control of Aggression and Violence*. New York: Academic Press.

Cameron, P. (1969). "Frequency and Kinds of Words in Various Social Settings, or What The Hell's Going On." *Pacific Sociological Review*. 12:101-104.

Campbell, A. and H. Schuman (1972). "A Comparison of Black and White Attitudes and Experiences in the City," In C.M. Haar (ed.) *The End of Innocence: A Suburban Reader*, pp. 97-110. Glenview, IL: Scott Foresman.

Chevigny, P. (1969). *Police Power: Police Abuses in New York City*. New York: Pantheon Books.

Cohen, M. and T. Saine (1977). "The Role of Profanity and Sex Variables in Interpersonal Impression Formation." *Journal of Applied Communication Research*. 2:45-52.

Cox, T.C., and S.D. Falkenberg (1987). "Adolescents' Attitudes Toward the Police: an Emphasis on Interaction Between the Delinquency Measures of Alcohol and Marijuana, Police Contacts and Attitudes." *American Journal of the Police*. 6:45-62.

Cox, T.C. and M.F. White (1987). "Traffic Citations and Student Attitudes Toward the Police: An Examination of the Interaction Dynamics." *Journal of Criminal Justice*. Forthcoming.

Cox, T.C., M.F. White and W.D. Lewis (1987). "Police Perceptions of Hostility from College Students." Paper presented at the Annual Meeting of the Academy of Criminal Justice Sciences. St. Louis.

Crawford, T.J. (1973). "Police Overperception of Ghetto Hostility." *Journal of Police Science and Administration*. 3:168-174.

Culver, J.H. (1975). "Policing the Police: Problems and Perspectives." *Journal of Police Science and Administration*. 3:125-135.

Dollard, J., et al. (1939). *Frustration and Aggression*. New Haven: Yale University Press.

Fine, G.A. (1976). "Obscene Joking Across Cultures.: *Journal of Communication*. 26:134-140.

Foldy, W.A. (1981). "Obscenity Reactions: Toward a Symbolic Interactionist Explanation," *Journal for the Theory of Social Behavior*. 11:125-146.

Federal Communications Commission (1975). *Declaratory Order (FCC 75-200) in Commission Report*. Washington, DC: U.S. Government Printing Office.

Glassman, M.B. (1978). "Community Standards of Patent Offensiveness: Public Opinion Data and Obscenity Law." *The Public Opinion Quarterly*. 42:162-170.

Gleser, G., L. Gottschalk, and J. Watkins (1959). "The Relationship Between Sex and Intelligence to Choice of Words: A Normative Study of Verbal Behavior." *Journal of Clinical Psychology*. 15:182-191.

Griffiths, C.T. and L.T. Winfree (1982). "Attitudes Toward the Police: A Comparison of Canadian and American Adolescents." *Journal of Police Science and Administration.* 11:127-141.

Groves, W.E. and P.H. Rossi (1970). "Police Perceptions of a Ghetto." *American Behavioral Scientist.* 13:727-743.

Halonen, D. (1981). "FCC Launches Attack on Indecency." *Broadcasting.* 112(110) (April 20): 3-37.

Hass, A. (1981). "Partner Influences on Sex Associated Spoken Language of Children." *Sex Roles.* 7:925-935.

Hudson, J.R. (1973). "Police-Citizen Encounters That Lead to Citizen Complaints." *Social Problems.* 18:179-193.

Kramer, C. (1975). "Women's Speech: Separate But Equal?" In B. Thorne and N. Henly (eds.) *Language and Sex: Differences and Dominance,* pp. 45-49. Rowley, MA: Newberry House.

Lakoff, R. (1973). "Language and Women's Place." *Language and Society.* 2:45-49.

Lakoff, R. (1975). *Language and Women's Place.* New York: Harper and Row.

Luckinbill, D.F. (1977). "Criminal Homicide as a Situated Transaction." *Social Problems.* 25:176-186.

Mulac, A. (1976). "Effects of Obscene Language Upon Three Dimensions of Listener Attitude." *Communication Monographs.* 43:300-307.

National Advisory Commission on Civil Disorders (1968). Report of the National Advisory Commission on Civil Disorders. Washington, DC: U.S. Government Printing Office.

Paletz, D. and W.F. Haris (1975). "Four-Letter Threats to Authority." *Journal of Politics.* 37:955-979.

Piliavin, I.M. and S. Briar (1964). "Police Encounters With Juveniles." *American Journal of Sociology.* 70:206-214.

Reiber, R.W., C. Weidmann, and J. D'Amato (1979). "Obscenity: Its Frequency and Context of Usage as Compared in Males, Nonfeminist Females and Feminist Females." *Journal of Psycholinguistic Research.* 8:201-223.

Reiss, A.J., Jr. (1970). "Police Brutality: Answers to Key Questions." In M. Lipsky (ed.) *Law and Order: Police Encounters.* New York: Aldine.

Reiss, A.J., Jr. (1971). *Police and the Public.* New Haven: Yale University Press.

Rothwell, J.D. (1971). "Verbal Obscenity: Time for Second Thoughts." *Journal of Western Speech.* 35:231-242.

Rusinko, W.T., K.W. Johnson, and C.A. Hornung (1978). "The Importance of Police Contact in the Formulation of Youths' Attitudes Toward the Police." *Journal of Criminal Justice.* 6:53-67.

Russell, K.V. (1978). *Complaints Against the Police: A Sociological View.* Leiester: Oldham and Manton, Ltd.

Scaglion, R. and R.G. Condon (1980). "Determinants of Attitudes Toward City Police." *Criminology.* 17:485-494.

Selnow, G.W. "Sex Differences in Uses and Perceptions of Profanity." *Sex Roles.* 12:303-312.

Sherman, J. (1968). *A Cursory History of Swearing.* New York: B. Franklin.

Skolnick, J.V. (1975). *Justice Without Trial.* New York: Wiley.

Skolnick, J.H., and D.H. Bayley (1986). *The New Blue Line: Police Innovation in Six American Cities.* New York: The Free Press.

Smith, P.E., and R.O. Hawkins (1973). "Victimization, Types of Citizen-Police Contacts, and Attitudes Toward the Police." *Law and Society Review.* 8:135-12.

Stark, R. (1972). *Police Riots: Collective Violence.* Belmont, CA: Wadsworth Publishing Company.

Sykes, R.E., and E.E. Brent (1983). *Policing: A Social Behaviorist Perspective.* New Brunswick, NJ: Rutgers University Press.

Thorne, B. and N. Henly (1975). "People and The Police: An Analysis of Factors Associated With Police Evaluation and Support." *Canadian Journal of Sociology.* 1:1975.

Thornton, L.M. (1975). "People and The Police: An Analysis of Factors Associated With Police Evaluation and Support." *Canadian Journal of Sociology.* 1:1975.

*Federal Communications Commission v. Pacifica Foundation* 438 U.S. 726.

Van Maanen, J. (1978). "The Asshole." P.K. Manning and J. Van Maanen (eds.) *Policing: A View From the Street.* Santa Monica, CA: Goodyear Publishing Co.

Vincze, L. (1978). "Hungarian Peasant Obscenity: Sociolinguistic Implications." *Ethnology.* 24:33-42.

Wagner, A.E. (1980). "Citizen Complaints Against The Police: The Accused Officer." *Journal of Police Science and Administration.* 8:373-377.

Walker, D. (1977). "Citizen Contact and Legal System Support." *Social Science Quarterly.* 58:3-14.

Warshay, D.W. (1972). "Sex Differences in Language Style." In C. Safilios-Rothschild (ed.) *Toward a Sociology of Women,* pp. 3-9. Lexington, MA: Xerox.

Warshay, D.W. and L.H. Warshay (1978). "Obscenity and Male Hegemony." Paper presented at the ISA Meetings.

West, C. (1979). "Against Our Will: Male Interruption of Females in Cross-Sex Conversations." *Annals of the New York Academy of Sciences.* 327-81-97.

Wesley, W.A. (1970). *Violence and the Police: A Sociological Study of Law, Custom, and Morality.* Cambridge, MA: Harvard University Press.

White, M.F., T.C. Cox, and J. Basehart (1988). "Perceptions of Police Verbal Abuse as an Influence on Respondent Attitudes Toward the Police." Paper presented at the Annual Meetings of the Academy of Criminal Justice Sciences, April 4-8, San Francisco, CA.

Wood, M. (1966). "The Influence of Sex and Knowledge of Communication Effectiveness on Spontaneous Speech." *Word.* 22:112-137.

Zimmerman, D. and C. West (1975). "Sex Roles, Interruptions and Silences in Conversation." In B. Thorne and N. Henly (eds.) *Language and Sex Difference and Dominance,* pp. 105-129. Rowley, MA: Newberry House.

# Study Questions

1.  What is meant by obscene and profane language?

2.  What effect can profane language by police officers have on the public's perception of law enforcement?

3.  How might a police department control the language of officers to ensure that police personnel do not use profane or obscene language when speaking to members of the public?

4.  In your opinion, are there situations wherein an officer's use of profane language would be permissible? If so, under what circumstances would the use of profanity be acceptable and why?

5.  Are there factors within the occupational environment of the police which induce an officer to use profanity? If so, what are those factors? If not, what do you feel leads to a police officer's use of profanity toward a citizen?

# 15

# A TAXONOMY OF PREJUDICE AND DISCRIMINATION BY POLICE OFFICERS*

## David L. Carter

## INTRODUCTION

This chapter explores the issues associated with prejudice and discrimination in policing. Its intent is to identify the nature of prejudice and discrimination, consider their implications on the practice of policing, propose alternate perspectives of the problems, and empirically illustrate their existence within a police department. Since there has been relatively little research done on prejudice and discrimination in policing per se, this particular article has been developed to provide "food for thought" on the issue.

It is commonly asserted that the police are a generally prejudicial occupational group whose treatment of racial and ethnic minorities (as well as that of women) is different from that afforded to the dominant white male society. The assertion continues that the police believe minorities are inferior (particularly intellectually inferior) and thus are enigmatic for the maintenance of the social order.

There is evidence that the police have, in fact, treated minorities in a discriminatory manner.[1] Some of this behavior is based on deep-rooted racial or ethnic prejudice developed through one's life socialization process. However, this writer maintains that other dysfunctional behaviors are a product of occupational socialization. For example, officers may be socialized by occupational variables to note that a significant number of persons with whom they come in contact for official police action (other than traffic) are minority group members.[2] This is largely because a disproportionate number of minority group members are of a lower socioeconomic status, reside in high-crime areas, and thus are incidental to more police contacts (Coffey, et al., 1982).

During his/her working hours, the white officer, particularly one assigned to a predominantly minority area, has a significantly increased degree of contact with minority group members. Unfortunately, most of this contact is with persons who have "police problems" thereby causing the officer to lose the perspective that many of the people are victims or in need of general police service; they are not all criminals. Thus, the officer's decision-making process to deal with minority

*This chapter was written expressly for inclusion in this book.

group members is based on a fallacious, intuitive correlation between race, ethnicity, and criminality.

Police administrators have recognized these problems and set out to correct them in different ways. Paramount among the remedies is a battery of "human relations" training programs. One presumption underlying this type of training is that one may change the prejudicial attitudes of police officers—and subsequently their behavior—by educating the officers about the dynamics and effects of interpersonal and intergroup relations.

There are a number of problems with this remedy for police prejudice. First, many "human relations" training programs have been poorly designed with the subject matter only intuitively selected.[3] Second, the quality of instruction in such programs is frequently suspect, it is not uncommon for the instructor to be an individual who is experienced in policing, but unfamiliar with the complex social-psychological constructs involved in prejudice and discrimination. Third, human relations training is frequently treated as "tokenism." That is, the training is dealt with cavalierly and presented with less sincerity and importance than other more traditional policing subjects.

The final problem is perhaps the most significant of all; the assumption that ingrained attitudes of prejudice can be changed with a few hours of police training in human relations is fallacious. While the intent of such training programs is desirable, one must recognize that these programs are not based on any theoretical foundation. They are too commonly developed on a priori premise that has not been scientifically tested. The compounding effects of these problems are (1) better human relations are not typically achieved; (2) officer attitudes are not changed; and (3) cost-effectiveness of the organization is reduced in that resources are wasted on non-effectual training.

These problems were clearly exemplified by Reese (1973) who studied the effect of human relations training on Los Angeles police cadets. Reese found, in part, that,

> little or no change takes place in an attitude, as a result of the basic training in a police academy...[Furthermore] there is significant wors-
> ening of attitude in the behavioral level...after the recruit has had
> exposure to field conditions in a one-month field training session.
> [1973:265]

This finding has significant implications not only for the impact (or lack thereof) on human relations training, but also the strong effects of occupational socialization.

# THE PROBLEM

In addressing this multidimensional problem, the author challenges the fundamental premise of human relations training. The premise is that such training can change officer attitudes toward certain classifications of people. As a function of this approach, this chapter addresses issues of prejudice and discrimination and how they relate to the training process.

At the outset, one must recognize that prejudice is a normal phenomenon manifest in all humankind. While there are significant conflicts among the psychological theories of prejudice and discrimination (c.f., Record, 1983; Blalock, 1982), there remains a sufficient body of knowledge available from which one may gain an understanding of the problem.

Simply increasing one's awareness and understanding of racial and ethnic discrimination is insufficient to generate or sustain social programs designed to protect minorities, or to ensure the equal opportunity and treatment of minority group members by the mainstream social order (Record, 1983). This chapter attempts to translate the theory of prejudice and discrimination into practice. This is accomplished by presenting a pragmatic taxonomy of these phenomena, to propose realistic systemic dynamics of prejudice and discrimination, and to present a functional understanding of the phenomena by police officers that can lead to a behavioral control mechanism.

At this point the author should reinforce the fact that race and ethnicity are different human attributes. While the former is based on physiological factors, the latter is characterized by cultural variables including norms, values, and customs. Regardless of this distinction, persons who are members of a minority group whether it is racial (e.g., black) or ethnic (e.g., Hispanic), experience similar discriminatory treatment as an artifact of their membership with a group that is distinct from the dominant social group. Thus, the concepts discussed in this chapter apply to both racial and ethnic minorities in their relationship with the police.

# LITERATURE REVIEW

Prejudice, as described by Coffey et al, (1982), includes "... an avertive or hostile attitude toward a person simply because he or she belongs to a certain group and is, therefore, presumed to have the objectionable qualities ascribed to the group" [p. 8]. While this definition may not be completely comprehensive, it clearly illustrates a pervasive characteristic of prejudice—it is a generalized attitude.

As implied by the genesis of the term, prejudice is "prejudgment." More specifically, as observed by Newman, [prejudice] involves judgment at two levels. The prejudiced person makes certain judgments about people and he makes certain judgments about their characteristics. Prejudgements about their characteristics are empirical errors. Prejudgments about people are logical errors; errors in inference. The empirical errors are normally not difficult to detect or refute; the logical errors are more problematic, for often we mistake them for ordinary empirical errors, and often we are confused about how value conclusions follow from factual premises [1971:56-57].

In a conceptually similar approach, Takagi (1978) links the development of prejudice to cultural determinism. To follow Takagi's logic, observed variance in appearance, language, and/or customs would be empirical errors under the assumption that those differences are "wrong" or "inferior" when compared to one's own social characteristics. Similarly, variance in behaviors among individuals or groups of people which are generalized to the larger cultural group are logical errors.

To expand on this concept, the author maintains that a great deal of prejudice is based simply on a lack of knowledge or understanding without malice, per se, toward other persons or groups. That is, we have learned, via socialization, alternate norms and values which are peculiar to our individual, social experience. Thus, variance from these standards leads to the assumption that anything that is different is "incorrect." We therefore treat those who are different in a manner inconsistent to our own values; i.e., in a discriminatory manner. This is similar to cultural conflict but it exists at the interpersonal rather than intergroup level (Carter, 1983).

While most literature focuses on the "recipient group" with respect to prejudicial attitudes, it is interesting to note the findings of Ward (1981) with respect to prejudice against women. Ward's research indicated that prejudice against women (regardless of race or ethnicity) was not based on sex role stereotypes but was primarily dependent upon the personal characteristics of the assessor. This is somewhat supported by previous research of this author wherein the Hispanic male trait of machoism dictated a prejudicial attitude toward females (Carter, 1983). Thus, in these cases it was the characteristic of the assessor (i.e., Hispanic male) which precipitated the prejudice.

These findings infer that the understanding of prejudice must focus on an individual's "internal" characteristics as they interact with perceived characteristics of the recipient group. Moreover, it appears that observations of minority separatism (e.g., Afro hairstyles of blacks or the Spanish language of Hispanics) may be viewed as a threat to the dominant society as perceived from the individual's socially defined position. If this is the case, then prejudice and discrimination may be reactive mechanisms to offset that threat (Lazin, 1975). Moreover, the interaction of personal and group (or empirical and logical) characteristics further fuels the prejudicial relationship.

## THE DEVELOPMENT OF PREJUDICE

An attitude is the cumulative product of the perception process. When we perceive phenomena, we align that perception within our self-definition of rationality which is produced through socialization. This rationality takes on the characteristics of universality wherein we assume that our values and beliefs are "right" and deviation from those attitudes is abnormal. Thus, humankind views phenomena selectively based on one's socialized perception. The process permits us to prejudge phenomena and attach our values in order to determine the level of acceptability of those phenomena. The outcome of this process is the manifestation of prejudice.

Based on this developmental procedure, we may expand on the earlier definition of prejudice and describe it as an emotionally based attitude about persons, objects, or locales founded on values which are universally applied to phenomena as determined by one's own life experiences. It is important to understand that prejudice is an attitude in that one's attitude is a predisposition to behavior.

Prejudice—like attitudes in general—has three characteristics which dictate one's behavior. The first characteristic is *direction*. That is, one is either for or against something. Thus, prejudice can be a favorable attitude as well as an unfavorable one. Second, prejudice varies in *intensity*. This refers to the degree to which one's attitude varies. One may be "for or against" something; however, the range of this direction will vary with different subjects. The final characteristic is *importance*. This is the hierarchical position of our attitudes. Whereas each attitude has horizontal variability (i.e., direction and intensity) each also has vertical variability wherein we conceptually rank, by order, the attitudes (Gunderson and Hopper, 1984).

The variability of one's prejudicial attitudes is directly related to the manner in which the prejudice was acquired. This writer maintains that the acquisition of prejudice can be explained as a product of either normative or cognitive development. Normative development means that prejudice is the result of perceiving values which are inconsistent with our own, that is, value conflict. As the diversity of the values increase so does the intensity of the prejudice. This is a dynamic developmental process in that one's prejudice changes with one's norms.

Cognitive development means that prejudice is learned through the direct teaching or observation of others, notably significant others. For example, if a child's parents are avid apostles of the Ku Klux Klan, the child will directly learn his/her prejudice against blacks. Similarly, occupational socialization will shape one's attitudes in a like manner. For example, police training and both the formal and informal instruction of a field training officer will have a significant influence on a police officer's attitudes and prejudices. While cognitive development is also value-laden, it is less subtle than normative development and more difficult to change.

One can be more precise in describing prejudice by examining how the phenomenon manifests itself in one's attitudinal system. In analyzing the types of prejudices present in our society, the author proposes a four-point descriptive typology.

The first type is *sycophantic prejudice,* wherein the prejudice toward a person, object, locale, or value is favorable and usually in exchange for friendship, acceptance, favors, or self-gratification. Second is *homeostatic prejudice.* This is the desire to maintain behavior and attitudes in a manner consistent with one's social group standards (i.e., maintenance of the social "steady state"). Those who do not conform with the defined *status quo* will experience discrimination which will increase with the variance from the *status quo.*

*Normalized or institutional prejudice,* the third type, is where custom, law, or policy discriminates against individuals or groups. The prejudicial attitude becomes a convention of institutional behavior without the sanction of moral legitimacy. The prejudices of the dominant social group become ingrained as a defined facet of acceptable behavior within organizations. Finally, one can identify *phrenetic prejudice.* This is overt bigotry or frenzied and fanatical prejudice typically directed toward racial, ethnic, religious, and/or ideological minorities. Whereas in the former types of prejudice the motivations are largely value-laden, in phrenetic prejudice the motivation appears to be pathological hatred.

## THE TRANSITION BETWEEN PREJUDICE AND DISCRIMINATION

Regardless of the development or classification methods, one must recognize that an underlying element of prejudice is one's values. Values are an expression of one's personality characteristics which, as argued by Rosenburg (1957), may be distinguished as being either "occupational" or "non-occupational" in nature. This infers that one's prejudices may vary, both horizontally and vertically, based on their source(s).

In that prejudice evokes both attitudinal reactions (i.e., emotions and feelings) and behavioral reactions (i.e., discrimination) perhaps one may rely on Rosenburg's typology to understand discrimination among police officers. Since, as noted previously, prejudice is a behavioral predisposition, one may assume that a person's prejudices are consistent over reasonably long periods of time. However, this is not necessarily the case in the instance of behavior. In behavior one is extending the attitude into an overt decision-making arena of whether or not to actually behave in a manner consistent with the attitudinally determined beliefs.

If one does decide to behave as per the dictates of prejudice, then there is discrimination. Conversely, if this predisposition to behave does not come to fruition, then there is no discrimination.

With respect to policing, the writer maintains that the decision to behave is significantly affected by the Rosenburg model. Specifically, discrimination may be either *occupational* or *personal*. Occupational discrimination is an officer's behavior as exhibited as part of his/her job. It is confined because of organizational and/or legal sanctions and may include so-called "reverse discrimination" to avoid the appearance of officer impropriety. In occupational discrimination the officer's behavior may not be consistent with his/her true attitudes. This is not the case with personal discrimination wherein one's prejudicial attitudes are more likely to be acted on because of no obligation imposed by one's official status. If this is true, then this thesis may have significant implications for understanding and controlling police discrimination.

In general, Rafky (1975) observed that discrimination implies conscious, intentional, and systematic inequitable treatment of others. It is, therefore, the behavioral product of prejudice. In understanding why one discriminates, Rafky sets forth the idea of "role divestment." This concept refers to the reluctance of members of the dominant society to relinquish various behaviors, status, and authority. The concept assumes that such characteristics are viewed as exclusive privileges of the dominant society and discrimination is a preventive mechanism to avoid divestiture. Role divestment does not, however, adequately explain discrimination by minority groups against the dominant society nor does it explain "within group" discrimination.

Rafky (1975) explores a more pliable understanding of discrimination by examining the locus of behavior. This essentially refers to the location (or origin) of discriminatory dynamics. Within this framework, Rafky proposes that one's discriminatory actions can be correlated to precipitative variables in the *individual,* the *organization,* and *society.* It is important to recall that the prejudicial attitude sets the stage for discriminatory behavior. Thus, characteristics of interpersonal relations, the organizational environment, or social circumstances can induce one to behave (i.e., discriminate) as defined by his prejudice.

Based on this author's previous research, it is postulated that the characteristics of discrimination can surface at either the intragroup or intergroup level. With respect to policing, intragroup discrimination would occur within the "police subculture." For example, a white supervisor discriminating against a black subordinate (individual level), detectives discriminating against patrol officers (organizational level) or federal officers discriminating against municipal officers (social level). The permutations for such behaviors are infinite; however, a fundamental element remains consistent—there is the everpresent link of occupational culture which binds the officers together as cohesive groups when confronted by or dealing with "non-police" groups. Discrimination in the latter case would therefore occur as an intergroup phenomenon.

This writer proposes that intergroup discrimination by the police can take two forms. The first is *external discrimination* which is the police (Group A) versus defined community collectives (Group B). The discrimination is based on an observed or perceived status as defined by either the normative or cognitive development of prejudice. This behavior focuses on defined demographics such as race, ethnicity, religion, age, sex, socio-economic status, etc.

The second form is *circumstantial discrimination*. Based on an officer's perception of another person's values, attitudes, and beliefs the officer may discriminate. The perception is developed by the circumstances surrounding the encounter with the citizen and does not typically rely exclusively on demographic traits. Moreover, this form of behavior is the type to most likely be a form of harassment. Conceptually, circumstantial discrimination is closely akin to Van Maanen's (1978) descriptive typology of "the know-nothing, suspicious person, and asshole" wherein a police officer classifies an individual on perceived characteristics within the likely outcome of the encounter to be defined by that perception.

When examining police discrimination, Griswold (1978) stressed the need to assess the role of the victims and complaints. He maintains that if victims are identifying minority group members as criminal offenders with greater frequency than those of the dominant society, then the police are going to be concentrating their enforcement efforts toward those minorities in response to the victim identifications. Similarly, one must look at the racial/ethnic consistency of a geographic area as related to allegations of police discrimination. If most officers are white, while the preponderance of citizens in a given geographic area are of a racial or ethnic minority, then interaction between the police and the community may have the *appearance* of discrimination. In both cases, police discrimination may largely be perceived rather than a real phenomenon.

In earlier works (c.f., Carter, 1983; 1985c) this author closely examined a number of elements related to prejudice and discrimination by the police. In sum, the writer disagrees with that portion of the literature which suggests that the bulk of police prejudice is an overt, malicious attitude toward racial and ethnic minorities. Rather, the propositions of the current work are:

1. Prejudice is based on our perception of others which consequently permits the classification of a person into a category (e.g., "troublemaker;" "suspect;" "asshole;" "transient;" etc.).
2. While racial and ethnic prejudices exist, they are not any more pervasive among police officers than other social or occupational groups.
3. Police discrimination is largely an unconscious phenomenon precipitated by homeostatic prejudice; it is predominantly a habitual behavior rather than an intentionally malicious act.

4. When police officers discriminate, it is most likely a product of a "good faith" belief that the officer is performing a legitimate police function (such as the "stop and frisk" of a person the officer defines as suspicious) rather than intentional harassment of a minority group member. That is, a person draws police attention because of his/her behavior or "classification variables" thereby the officer responds to what he/she perceives to be a potential police situation.

5. Police officers attempt to avoid occupational discrimination because of organizational, legal, and social sanctions. This avoidance is most likely not altruistic, but motivated by the threat of punishment.

6. Efforts by police administrators to control police prejudice are largely ineffectual. The initial locus of change should be toward behavioral alteration of discrimination with only long-term change agents directed toward prejudice.

The last proposition can have significant implications in the effort to minimize discrimination by officers. If an administrator seeks to control dysfunctional behavior, he/she must introduce realistic remedies that have a reasonable chance of success. As noted previously, most police efforts to minimize discrimination have followed the path of human relations training in the hope that such academy instruction will change attitudes. As illustrated in this article, such a goal is unrealistic in light of the evolutionary process by which attitudes are developed. As observed by Fisher (1982), social habits and prejudices are so deeply rooted that they are extremely difficult to change. Moreover, such beliefs are not willingly surrendered even after it is obvious that they no longer sustain their initial functions. These observations lend support for this writer's position that it is organizationally nonfunctional and inefficient to attempt to change officer attitudes (e.g., prejudices) during a training academy program. Gunderson and Hopper (1984) reinforce this position by stating it is easier to change behaviors than attitudes. In this author's opinion, while behavioral change may be accomplished, it will probably not be lasting without a motivational influence that is either in the form of reward or punishment.

In a universal sense, changing prejudice and discrimination may occur only through education, legislation, and/or revolution. While these may be philosophically acceptable egalitarian remedies, they lack the pragmatic framework required in the organizational environment. At a more operational level, Ward and McCormack (1979) suggest strategies that police organizations may employ to minimize corruption. With only minor modification these approaches may be useful for effecting change, first in discriminatory practices and, second, in prejudicial attitudes.

The first strategy which must be implemented is the *power-coercive* model. This employs the use of formal authority to force the acceptance of change. Under this approach there will be no change in attitude but the behavioral change occurs. Essentially, the organization relies on its resources to ensure acceptable behavior. If behavior deviates from the window of acceptability, then "swift and sure" punitive action is imposed. Tactics in this approach would include stringent supervision, discipline (the more autocratic the better), and the threat of lawsuits against individual officers. The theory, therefore, is that officers will avoid discrimination simply to avoid punitive sanctions. The major advantage of this strategy is its immediacy, although it is only a short term "stop-gap" that may have an undesirable influence on morale or job satisfaction. The next stage would involve the *normative-re-educative* strategy. This approach relies on behavioral research findings to strategically plan changes in one's belief and value systems. In essence, it employs intrusive activities/variables to re-socialize the individual away from long-held prejudices. This is obviously a long-term change process and must be imposed with patience. Once institutionalized with constant reinforcement, the strategy will have a more meaningful effect than the power-coercive model. The reason is that with the normative-re-educative approach individual prejudices are actually being changed, therefore, the predispositions toward behavior have been desirably altered.

The final strategy is the *rational-empirical* model. Underlying this method is the philosophy that employees will rationally do what is in their best interest. Thus, to effect change one merely justifies the change by convincing the organizational members that the change is in their best interest. While the dynamics of this approach are different for corruption control, as discussed by Ward and McCormack (1979) when compared to discrimination, the approach does have a significant role. Notably, the rational-empirical model can serve as a means of reinforcement through in-service training and via supervision of line personnel. It must, however, follow a successful resocialization.

The reader should note that these strategies are suggested for the *control* of discrimination—not to remedy the problem. It is a virtual impossibility to totally eliminate discrimination and one is utopian to believe that this could occur. Elimination of prejudice and discrimination would be an abnormal human condition within the framework of Durkheim's conceptualization of normality relating to crime (Durkheim, 1938). Instead, the materials proposed in this article are devised to provide a better understanding of the phenomenon with the goal of containing the "worst-case" incidents of discrimination.

# AN EMPIRICAL ASSESSMENT OF PREJUDICE AND DISCRIMINATION IN THE PRACTICE OF POLICING

The propositions set forth in this chapter were developed *a posteriori* to data collection on a research project dealing with the relationship between police training and the police personality. Because of this, the propositions cannot be directly tested, thereby limiting the construct validity of the results. Despite this limitation some interesting findings on prejudice and discrimination emerged.

The instrument used in this study was a derivation of that used by the Police Foundation (Kelling and Wycoff, 1978) in their study of the Dallas Police Department. Changes in the instrument were made to alleviate non-applicable issues, to adjust organizational nomenclature, and to add questions on specific issues of force and civil rights litigation unique to the study's population: The McAllen, Texas Police Department. The amended instrument was pretested on a purposive sample of demographically similar officers in a police department at a city contiguous to McAllen. After the instrument was amended based on the pretest results, it was administered to 96 of the 104 sworn McAllen police officers. Those excluded from the study were the chief, two captains, and five officers who were logistically unable to complete the instrument. The survey was administered in a controlled confidential environment during time allotted for a new in-service training program. The respondents represented all shifts and assignments within the department as well as ranks ranging from patrol officer through lieutenant. Only three instruments were excluded from the analysis due to inaccurate completion.

A particularly interesting aspect of this population is that 73 percent of the respondents were Hispanic. The remaining 27 percent were all Anglo-American (no blacks or other racial/ethnic minority groups are represented on the department). At the time of the study the department had only six female officers, all of whom were surveyed.

## Sexual Discrimination Issues

Since Ward (1981) found that prejudice against women is not based in sex role stereotypes but in the personal characteristics of the assessor, the writer expected to find reasonably strong evidence of sexual discrimination. This expectation was further fueled by the impression of policing as being a male-dominated occupation (52.1% agreed that "policing is a man's work") and the large proportion of Hispanic males (characterized by the cultural trait of *machismo*) in the population. However, the overall findings infer reasonably strong support for females.

Nonetheless, the results did produce some conflict. For example, 50.5 percent agreed that female officers are equally effective as males, yet 44.2 percent agreed that they did *not* feel comfortable on a call with a female. Perhaps this latter finding is explained by the result that 56.4 percent did not feel females were capable of using force in the same manner as a male. This is reinforced by the respondents who reported that of all non-officer males they knew, a mean of 39.7 percent would make good police officers. This appears significant in comparison to the belief that of all non-officer females only 17.2 percent were perceived as being "good officer material."

A number of variables were tested on possible sexual discrimination issues of which only two non-spurious significant findings were identified. The data indicated that spousal disapproval of working with females increased significantly as length of employment increased ($X^2 = 135.815$, df = 90, p < .001, V = .488). Perhaps this is a product of general spousal distrust engendered by the policing occupation interacting with a fear that as time increases "on the street" so does the probability of injury. In the case of the latter variable there is an assumption that police spouses do not believe that female officers are as capable as their male counterparts.

The second significant finding regarding female officers was that as length of employment increased, so did the belief that female officers have an equal opportunity for promotion. ($X^2 = 113.682$, df = 90, p < .05, V = .447). This finding was most likely influenced by the fact that two female officers had successfully completed an assessment center for promotion about two months prior to the survey. Furthermore, the females had been harassed by their male subordinates but were able to "hold their own" and had "earned" the reluctant support (although not true respect) of the male officers.

## Ethnic Discrimination Issues

A number of variables were tested which fall within the genre of ethnic discrimination issues. Essentially, the officers were surveyed based upon their observations and perceptions of officer behavior. One interesting finding indicated that as job satisfaction decreased there was a significant increase in the belief that officers discriminate because of race or ethnicity ($X^2 = 56.864$, df = 24, p < .001, V = .387). The question that this brings to mind is whether low job satisfaction entices officers to discriminate as a means of retaliation. Unfortunately, the data to answer this question was not available.

In this particular study, length of employment was tested against a number of cynicism variables. Somewhat atypically, length of employment was consistently a significant indicator of cynicism in this study (Carter, 1985b). This is noteworthy given the findings of employment as related to various discrimination variables. Length of employment was significantly associated with the belief that promotions are based on ethnicity ($X^2 = 150.961$, df = 90, p < .001, V = .515); the belief that officers discriminate based on race/ethnicity (x2116.115, df = 90, p < .05, V = .451); and that minority group members are the recipients of intentional discrimination ($X^2 = 142.716$, df = 90, p.001, V = .500). These findings are particularly important in that it appears that prejudice and discrimination are directly correlated with increased cynicism.

Given the large proportion of Hispanic officers in the study, ethnic background was a prime variable to be tested on prejudice/discrimination issues. The results showed that Hispanic officers not only believed that ethnicity effects promotion ($X^2$ = 43.993, df = 18, p < .001, V = .438) but also that promotion is based on ethnicity ($X^2$ = 54.572, df = 18, p < .001, V = .436). Thus, the evidence of intragroup discrimination appears to be substantial.

On other issues Hispanic officers significantly indicated the belief that discrimination exists within the department ($X^2$ = 54.101, df = 18, p < .001, V = .438), and they do not feel that the department should actively recruit Anglo officers ($X^2$ = 36.532, df = 18, p < .005, V = .363). Based on interviews with the officers, these findings indicate that there is external and circumstantial intergroup discrimination by Anglo officers and circumstantial discrimination by Hispanic officers. However, the Hispanic officers felt the recruitment of Anglo officers would disrupt a growing internal power base currently being realized by Hispanics.[5]

Hispanic officers further indicated the belief that departmental recruitment procedures are discriminatory ($X^2$ = 54.091, df = 18, p.001, V = .436) and agreed that minority officers are better with minority citizens in the resolution of police-associated problems ($X^2$ = 41.794, df = 18, p < .001, V = .383).

## SUMMARY

This chapter has examined prejudice and discrimination as operational variables in interpersonal, intergroup, and intragroup relations. Functional descriptions of the phenomena have been proposed as they relate to both the practice of policing and police organizational membership. A fundamental proposition of the author was that police human relations training cannot change prejudice because prejudice is the culmination of one's life-long socialization experience. Rather, police training, departmental policies and procedures, and supervision should focus on containing discriminatory behavior.

The intent of this chapter was to provide an exploratory examination of issues associated with discrimination. While not all issues were thoroughly examined—such as discrimination by minority group members and interorganizational discrimination—the dominant themes of prejudice by officers from the dominant society have been addressed. It is hoped that this discussion lays a foundation for future study of the problem.

Finally, a comment on the empirical data. The reader is reminded that the study was not designed to test the propositions of prejudice and discrimination set forth earlier in this chapter. Conversely, the propositions and typologies suggested were a product of the research endeavor. Nonetheless, the data analysis does provide some support for certain elements of the author's thesis. At the minimum, the findings suggest that alternate approaches for controlling discrimination should be examined.

# Notes

1   As evidence of discrimination by the police, *see* United States Commission on Civil Rights (1961); (1965); (1970); (1981).

2   *See* Carter (1985a) for a detailed discussion of occupational socialization in policing.

3   Excellent reviews of police human relations training can be found in Dearth (1984) and Das (1983).

4   Newman (1979) provides a comprehensive discussion of the variable meanings of prejudice and the evolution of the term.

5   This is a somewhat justified concern given the sociopolitical history of the city. Although a lengthy discussion is not appropriate at this point, suffice it to note that the city government has traditionally been in the hands of the Anglo community despite the fact that the city is over 80 percent Hispanic.

# REFERENCES

Blalock, H.M. (1982). "Race and Ethnic Relations." In A. Inkeles (ed.) *Foundations of Modern Sociology*. Englewood Cliffs, NJ: Prentice Hall.

Carter, D.L. (1983). "Hispanic Interaction with the Criminal Justice System in Texas: Experiences, Attitudes, and Perceptions." *Journal of Criminal Justice* 11(3):213-227.

Carter, D.L. (1985a). "A Systems Approach in the Explanation of Dysfunctional Police Behavior." Paper presented at the Academy of Criminal Justice Sciences annual meeting, Las Vegas.

Carter, D.L. (1985b). "Police Brutality: A Model for Definition, Persceptive, and Control." In A. Blumberg and E. Niederhoffer (eds.) *The Ambivalent Force*. 3d ed. New York: Holt, Rinehart and Winston.

Carter, D.L. (1985c). "Hispanic Perceptions of Police Performance." *Journal of Criminal Justice* 13(6).

Coffey, A., et al. (1982). *Human Relations*. 3d ed. Englewood Cliffs, NJ: Prentice Hall.

Das, D. (1983). *Analysis of Police Human Relations Training: An Evaluation of State Mandated Curricula*. Unpublished doctoral dissertation, Huntsville, TX: College of Criminal Justice, Sam Houston State University.

Dearth, D.K. (1984). *An Analysis of the McAllen, Texas Police Department's Human Relations Program*. Unpublished doctoral dissertation, Huntsville, TX: College of Criminal Justice, Sam Houston State University.

Durkheim, E. (1938). "Les Regeles de la Methods." In G.E.G. Catlin (ed.) *The Rules of Sociological Method*. New York: The Free Press.

Fisher, S. (1982). *From Margin to Mainstream: The Social Progress of Black Americans*. New York: Praeger Publishers.

Griswold, D.B. (1978). "Police Discrimination: An Elusive Question." *Journal of Police Science and Administration* 6(1):61-67.

Gunderson, D.F. and R. Hopper (1984). *Communication and Law Enforcement*. New York: Harper and Row Publishers.

Kelling, G.L. and M.A. Wycoff (1978). *The Dallas Experience: Human Resource Development*. Washington, DC: The Police Foundation.

Lazin, F.A. (1975). "The Police and Black Separatism: A Problem for Public Policy." *Journal of Police Science and Administration* 3(1):1-8.

Newman, J. (1979). "Prejudice as Prejudgment." *Ethics*. 90(October):47-57.

Rafky, D.M. (1975). "Racial Discrimination in Urban Police Departments." *Crime and Delinquency* (July) 233-242.

Record, W. (1983). "Race and Ethnic Relations: The Conflict Continues—A Review Essay." *The Sociological Quarterly* 24(Winter):137-149.

Reese, C.D. (1973). "Police Academy Training and its Effect on Racial Prejudice." *Journal of Police Science and Administration* 1(3):257-268.

Rosenburg, M. (1957). *Occupation and Values*. Glencoe, IL: The Free Press.

Takagi, P. (1981). "Race, Crime, and Social Policy: A Minority Perspective" *Crime and Delinquency* (January):48-63.

United States Commission on Civil Rights (1975). *A Report on Equal Protection in the South*. Washington DC: U.S. Government Printing Office.

United States Commission on Civil Rights (1967). *A Time to Listen...A Time to Act*. Washington DC: U.S. Government Printing Office.

United States Commission on Civil Rights (1961). *Justice: Book 5*. Washington DC: U.S. Government Printing Office.

United States Commission on Civil Rights (1970). *Mexican-Americans and the Administration of Justice in the Southwest*. Washington DC: U.S. Government Printing Office.

United States Commission on Civil Rights (1981). *Who is Guarding the Guardians?* Washington DC: U.S. Government Printing Office.

Van Maanen, J. (1978). "The Asshole." In P.K. Manning and J. Van Maanen (eds.) *Policing: A View from the Street*. Santa Monica, CA: Goodyear Publishing Co.

Ward, C. (1981). "Prejudice Against Women: Who, When, Why?" *Sex Roles* 7(2):163-171.

Ward, R. and R. McCormack (1979). *An Anti-Corruption Manual for Administrators in Law Enforcement*. New York: John Jay Press.

# Study Questions

1.   Distinguish between "prejudice" and "discrimination." Can one occur without the other? Discuss your responses.

2.   The author maintains that human relations training has been a misguided and ineffective remedy for police prejudice. Discuss the reasons for this argument.

3.   Describe the four types (or degrees) of prejudice discussed in this chapter. Illustrate your responses with an example of each type.

4.   Can the police behave in a proper manner yet have their actions appear to be discriminatory? Explain your response.

5.   Discuss various methods which may be used to control or minimize discrimination by police officers.

# PART IV: MANAGING POLICE DEVIANCE

# 16

# CONTROLLING AND REVIEWING POLICE-CITIZEN CONTACTS*

## Herman Goldstein

## CONTROL AND REVIEW IN CONTEXT

Complaints arising from police-citizen contacts account for much of the attention police receive. Many proposals have been made in the last 20 years for improving the methods by which allegations of police misconduct are investigated. These proposals have evoked such strong reaction from the police, however, most discussions and writings on the subject now reflect only the polarization that has occurred. Before one can begin to deal with the issue of how to control and review police actions, one must put these passionate and extremely divergent positions into proper perspective.

Interest in the control of police conduct first began to accelerate in the 1950s. The U.S. Supreme Court and other courts throughout the country, as part of the "due process revolution," became highly critical of police practices revealed in the cases that came before them. It was largely in response to this concern that the Supreme Court in 1961 imposed on the state courts the requirement that evidence obtained through an illegal search or seizure be excluded from a criminal prosecution—a decision generally accepted as an effort to provide judges with more effective control over police conduct.[1] Also starting in the 1950s, various citizen groups—contending that existing means for seeking redress were ineffective—began to demand some form of civilian review of complaints filed against police officers. A widespread movement developed to establish civilian review boards that would be empowered to receive, investigate, and hold hearings on complaints filed with them.[2] Interest in control over the police peaked in the late 1960s when the police dealt first with urban rioting and then with massive political protest.

---

*Reprinted with permission from Goldstein's *Policing a Free Society,* Copyright 1977, Ballinger Publishing Company.

Participants in these confrontations who were aggrieved by police actions added their voices to those who had previously been calling for new, more effective mechanisms for airing their complaints.

Because minority groups and political dissidents were among those complaining most vigorously about police conduct, the debate over control and review mechanisms became entangled with strong and often bitter feelings on political and racial matters. The referendum on a civilian review board in New York City in 1966 was converted into a rather crude tabulation of public attitudes on the racial conflict in that city.[3] But even where such tensions were absent, the debate over control of the police generated strong antagonisms.

The police saw much of the criticism directed at them coming from groups and individuals against whom they were required to take action—alleged criminal offenders and disruptive protesters. They feared that the proposed review mechanisms would be used by these groups to retaliate against them. Officers in agencies which did not engage in the practices most commonly criticized resented the wholesale distrust implied both in the criticism directed at them and in the proposals that were made. They were offended by the notion that their actions would be judged by individuals removed from the situations they confronted. And they claimed such review would eliminate much of the initiative and aggressiveness on which—they believed—police work heavily depends. Less commonly articulated, but of no small concern, was police recognition that the patchwork nature of policing did indeed make the police terribly vulnerable to an outside review if such review were to be based upon formal concepts and criteria rather than the realities of police work. It is understandable, too, that the police should tire of the continued emphasis on abuses, feeling that quality police performance deserved a proportionate share of public attention. Together, all of these concerns produced a solid wall of resistance to the whole notion of civilian review. In fairness it must be recognized that many of the objections of the police were not unlike those expressed by other occupations and professional groups when faced with proposals for review of their activities by individuals outside their field.

The proponents of more effective civilian review, however, had ample basis for concern. Case after case and study after study have documented situations in which police authority has been abused and in which citizens were left without an effective avenue for redress. Many of these accounts were compiled by groups such as the American Civil Liberties Union and other champions of civil liberties and minority rights whose business it is to draw attention to such concerns.[4]

The fact that the studies were conducted and published by groups viewed as inherently antagonistic to the police was often used by the police to discredit the claims that were made. But criticism came from more neutral sources as well.[5] As recently as 1973, for example, the *Chicago Tribune*, which in the past had taken strong editorial positions defending the police from censure by civil libertarians, published the results of an investigation which was highly critical of Chicago

Police practices.[6] A team of reporters persuasively documented incidents of wrongdoing by officers and the failure of the department to investigate effectively the complaints that had been filed about them.

If one looks objectively at the anguish, humiliation, loss of income, and physical suffering experienced by those who have been wronged by the police (through false imprisonment, false prosecution, or beating) and who have unsuccessfully sought redress through established channels, one can appreciate the intensity of the feelings that underlie demands for more effective control of police conduct. And one can understand, too, how these feelings get translated into sweeping proposals that do not always communicate clearly the primary source of concern.

In order to bring the problem back into perspective, both the police and citizen critics of the police must be jarred from their extreme positions. The police cannot afford to bury their heads in the sand and maintain that there are simply no problems. Nor can they, under a system of government that attaches so high a value to protection from improper action by its agents, continue to resist in blanket fashion all efforts to provide aggrieved citizens adequate opportunities to air their grievances. Critics of the police, on the other hand, have an obligation to recognize the realities and complexities of police work, the handicaps under which the police function, and the difficulty in achieving effective control in a police operation. They must recognize, too, that many of the specific wrongs upon which they focus, though inexcusable, nevertheless are symptomatic of more basic problems that will be solved only if citizen interest extends to matters beyond control and review.

This brings us, then, to two factors that must be recognized in restoring a more balanced perspective in the quest to control police conduct. First, we have seriously erred in placing so heavy a burden on control mechanisms as a way of solving long-standing problems in the police field. Second, we have erred, too, in viewing control almost exclusively in terms of identifying and taking action against wrongdoing. It is inevitable that people who take an interest in police matters because they have suffered some abuse will concentrate on creating methods for controlling police behavior. Yet, there are serious limits to what one can do, through this essentially negative procedure, to change police performance. However well-designed a system of control and redress might be, it is not likely to have a significant impact on police conduct in an agency that is in a state of disarray—that suffers from lack of clarity as to its function, from lack of clear direction, from internal conflicts, and, in addition, is often poorly organized, poorly administered, poorly staffed, and poorly trained.

The police field would have profited greatly if the energies devoted to both advocating and resisting new forms of control in recent years had instead been applied, for example, to better defining the police task; to providing police with needed alternatives for carrying out their duties; or to improving the recruitment and screening of police personnel, their training, and especially their leadership. Leadership is of special importance, for a competent police administrator has much greater potential for achieving a higher quality of police service than can ever be realized by others attempting to control a poorly administered organization from the outside.

The second failing of proposals for control—the narrow concentration of wrongdoing—commits the police to waiting for complaints to be filed. It commits them to focusing their attention on investigations, disciplinary procedures, and sanctions. Both the police and the public become so preoccupied with identifying wrongdoing and taking disciplinary action against errant officers that they lose sight of the primary objective of control, which is to achieve maximum conformity with legal requirements, established policies, and prevailing standards of propriety. This objective is far more likely to be attained by fostering an atmosphere in which the police conform because they want to conform, rather than out of fear of the consequences if they do not.

# FACTORS COMPLICATING CONTROL AND REVIEW

Although new positive approaches to achieving control would reduce the need to concentrate on wrongdoing, it would nevertheless be necessary, under the best of circumstances, for police administrators to maintain and perfect procedures for identifying improper conduct, reviewing police actions, and imposing sanctions. Many factors inherent in the police function make this task extremely complex and at times almost impossible.

## The Adversary Nature of the Police Function

Tensions and hostility are parts of policing. Police officers must, as part of their job, issue orders to people, catch them in violation of laws, deprive them of their freedom, and bring charges that may lead to the imposition of severe punishment. Contacts between officers and citizens are often initiated under conditions that are emotionally charged, such as immediately after a fight or other disturbance, or following the commission of a crime. Even the person getting a traffic ticket frequently becomes indignant. However scrupulous the police may be in carrying out their responsibilities, they are bound to incur the wrath of some of those against whom they must proceed. This hostility manifests itself in various forms—sometimes immediately, by verbal abuse or physical resistance to the police; sometimes later, by alleging that the officer's actions were improper or illegal. Under such circumstances an officer must be able to count on support for actions taken in the line of duty. The police officer expects and indeed needs some insulation from the community being served. But insulation can serve as a shield for the officer who is not so scrupulous—who in fact acts improperly.

The most difficult cases to review are those alleging improper use of force or verbal abuse, for it is often impossible to establish, in the rapid escalation that characterizes such encounters, who provoked whom, recognizing of course that the officer is under an obligation to exercise restraint and not respond in kind. To this must be added the fact that most police encounters occur under isolated conditions. Police usually apprehend criminals in such places as closed commercial establishments, residential areas in the early hours of the morning, and areas closed to the public after dark, where the absence of witnesses makes it likely that a crime will be committed. Even the giving of a traffic citation on a crowded street is often unobserved.

That otherwise honorable citizens resort to lying as a defense against police is well established. It is also clear that some police officers lie to justify action they have taken. The task of getting at the truth is further complicated because many of the people with whom the police have contact are unscrupulous individuals. Hard-core criminal offenders do not hesitate to make a false allegation if they think it might help to cloud the issue of their own guilt. People in organized crime also use this technique to discourage the police from taking action against them.

The frequency with which such allegations are made and the degree to which investigation shows them to be unfounded leads some police supervisors to discredit all complaints from known criminals. At the same time, these people are especially vulnerable to police abuse. A violence-prone officer, for example, may conclude that an offender's reputation is such that his word would not be trusted in any subsequent review. Thus complaints filed by the most discredited people require the most careful investigation.

## The Insensitivity that Stems from Dealing Routinely with Crises

For the individuals involved, the events that lead to contact with a police officer (and the contact itself, as previously noted), may be quite traumatic. This is especially true of complainants and victims who have never previously had occasion to call the police. They often have high expectations as to what they will receive in the way of a response.

By contrast, what citizens view as crises may seem trivial to the police, who are in the business of handling such matters routinely. At the start of his career, an officer may respond with some urgency to such incidents as a family squabble, a traffic accident, a typical home burglary, or a drunk causing a disturbance. But after handling a hundred domestic disturbances, a hundred accidents, a hundred burglaries, or a hundred drunks, the officer understandably may not display the same degree of concern and inquisitiveness. Moreover, there are often department pressures on the officer to take shortcuts in disposing of such cases. And the full resources of the department, such as technicians equipped to search for physical evidence, are generally not available for assignment in minor cases. In large-city departments, where high volume results in some forms of crimes being handled by special units, the members of these units, may develop an insensitivity over such serious matters as rapes, robberies, and aggravated assaults.

The sharp contrast between the state of mind of the officer in these cases and that of the complainant victim, or arrestee is a common source of conflict and dissatisfaction.

## The Absence of Adequate Guidelines

Outrageous as an incident may seem to a citizen, the action about which he or she complains is quite often within the limits of the officer's legal authority. Relatively few departmental regulations or policies establish narrow standards of conduct for those sensitive actions about which complaints are most commonly received. The question, then, becomes not whether the officer acted illegally or in violation of departmental rules, but whether the officer acted improperly. Furthermore, in making that judgment everything depends upon whose standard of propriety is employed. Many police agencies follow a practice of vindicating officers unless their actions can be classified as illegal. This is a convenient way of disposing of cases for a police administrator who is—from the outset—inclined to react adversely to citizen complaints. For the police administrator who concludes the behavior was improper and who wants to take corrective action, the absence of a specifically applicable standard or rule makes it difficult or even impossible for him to do so. (Civilian review boards, during their brief life in some cities, found themselves in the same predicament.)

Occasionally a police chief may attempt to deal with such a situation by taking action based on some peripheral element in the case, such as the fact that the officer may have been off his beat when the alleged misconduct occurred. This explains why so many disciplinary actions taken against police officers appear to be for violation of trivial or obscure administrative regulations. There was a time, too, when an administrator could simply bring a charge of conduct unbecoming a police officer, but recent litigation in some jurisdictions has established that an officer is entitled to know in specific terms what he is charged with, and beyond this, is entitled to know in advance the specific definition of the conduct that will subject him to discipline.[7]

This situation adds support to the proposals made in the preceding chapters for structuring police discretion. The most elaborate apparatus for reviewing police conduct will not succeed unless explicit rules and policies are established to which police officers can then be held.

# Department-Wide Practices That Are Themselves Questionable

A citizen's complaint alleging wrongdoing by an officer may in effect challenge a practice that is common throughout the agency. Police officers are frequently accused of having acted improperly despite the fact that their actions were in accord with their instructions from their supervisors, in harmony with the actions of fellow officers, and in conformity with long-standing practice.

Thus, for example, a citizen may complain that an officer stopped his car, ordered him out of it, and frisked him without adequate grounds for doing so, but, in many departments, officers are encouraged to do precisely this without being held to strict legal guidelines on when such action can be taken. When this is the case an agency can hardly penalize the accused officer, nor can it offer effective redress to the citizen. Likewise, an agency is not likely to discipline an officer against whom a complaint is filed because the officer ordered street-walking prostitutes to move on, or seized a weapon in an illegal search, or arrested a petty gambler without adequate evidence, if personnel are instructed and sometimes even rewarded for doing these very things.

For the progressive administrator, citizen complaints are often the best indicators of long-standing practices in need of correction. They bring to light police procedures that are often more traditional than necessary. A woman taken into custody for a traffic violation, for example, may accuse a policewoman of a gross indignity for subjecting her to a complete body search. But inquiry may reveal that all women who are detained, whatever the charge, are searched in this manner. Given the offensive nature of the procedure, the number of occasions on which it must be followed could be greatly reduced by such steps as eliminating the need for jailing minor offenders; refining the standard operating procedure regarding the search of prisoners to specify when body searches are necessary; and housing unsearched prisoners separate from those who have been searched.

However, where the administrator supports continuation of a procedure considered offensive by some, a form of control and review is needed that gets at the practice rather than just the action of one officer. This has implications for the design of systems for citizens redress that will be examined later.

# Atmosphere of Duplicity and Hypocrisy

Effective control requires honesty in dealing with subordinates. Ideally a police administrator should be in a position to mean what he says. But the great inconsistencies between articulated policies and actual practices often require a police administrator to play a hypocritical role. The police are told they enforce all laws equally, but are expected to be highly selective in their enforcement practices. They are told they have no discretion, but are constantly expected to use discretion. If a discretionary action results in a complaint being filed, however, they know their performance will be judged by the formal requirements of the law. They are told they are responsible for all crime, but know their potential for preventing crime is limited. The net result of this hypocrisy is that, understandably, officers often do not take seriously what they are told. This has a devastating effect on the capacity of the administration to control their conduct. The situation is so serious in some agencies that the administrator who desires total compliance with a specific order has to send a special message through informal channels making it clear that he really means, in this particular case, what the formal promulgation says.

The problem surfaces time and again in reviewing police conduct. The police often act in violation of the law on the grounds they are acting in the public interest—as, for example, in arresting inebriates for their own safekeeping. They do so with the support of the community, the police administrator, and the vast majority of police officers. Along comes an officer who, without adequate legal grounds, breaks into several private homes in search of a person responsible for a brutal attack on a small child. He argues that his violation of the law also was in the public interest. Can the administrator contend that one violation is to be condemned, while the other is justified? How does one weigh the relative seriousness of one illegality compared with another?

This dilemma of being expected to operate illegally in some situations is almost certainly what police officers have in mind when they contend that laymen do not have the kind of understanding required to review police conduct; that police behavior should be judged by those who have themselves been police officers. Interpreted, this plea means that police want their conduct measured by the informal code by which they operate rather than the formal criteria that define their function and authority.

## Fear of Incurring Tort Liability

Still another bind in which the police administrator is caught stems from the liability of the subordinates or of the municipality to civil suit. The success of the city attorney or corporation counsel in defending officers and the department against civil actions is measured in some degrees by an ability to avoid judgments against the city and its employees.[8] This official is, as a result, constantly enlisting the aid of the police in the defense of actions brought against them as well as in the defense of actions brought against other city agencies. This makes the police sensitive to the possibility of civil action and especially to the adversary nature of such a proceeding.

It follows that, whenever it appears that there is the slightest possibility that the agency or officers may be sued in connection with a complaint filed with the department, the police begin to think in terms of defending the action. As soon as a civil action is filed or the city attorney learns of the possibility of a suit from some other source, interest in defending the case usually takes precedence over the agency's interest in establishing the facts and especially in assessing blame.

The classic example of this dilemma is found in police efforts to promote safe driving on the part of their officers. Elaborate programs are frequently set up to review accidents involving departmental vehicles in order to establish the cause. If it is concluded that the accident was avoidable, the officer may be required to take a driver-improvement course. If the officer is adjudged guilty of careless or reckless driving, he may be punished. When, however, the accident causes serious injury or death, the process is likely to be stopped short on orders of the city attorney because of the high probability that a suit will be filed. So in the most serious accidents the officer is, for all purposes, exempt from immediate disciplinary action and, especially in large jurisdictions where the litigation may extend over several years, may never be called to account, even if eventually found to have been responsible for the accident.

Ideally the interests of a city attorney would transcend the possible liability incurred in single cases and extend to correcting the practices that give rise to suits by full and immediate implementation of existing administrative controls and by development of new guidelines as suggested in Chapter 5. As noted there, this should produce a gradual decrease in the number of suits filed and, in addition, a gradual improvement in the quality of police service. But as a practical matter, short-termed city attorneys are generally unwilling to incur the immediate costs inherent in so long-range a proposal, and as a result the dilemma continues.[9]

## The Blue Curtain

Those most likely to witness police actions are other police officers. It follows that review of a specific incident often is heavily dependent upon the testimony of other officers. But police will rarely incriminate a fellow officer.[10] They will either support the officer's actions or deny knowledge of the incident. This attitude has come to be referred to in police circles as "the blue curtain."

Of course unwillingness to testify against a co-worker is not a characteristic unique to the police. Many other occupations and some of the most highly regarded professions, such as the legal and medical professions, protect themselves in the same manner. While there is no basis for making precise comparisons on this score between professional and occupational groups, those who work in the police field say that the code of secrecy among police officers is tighter and more absolute than in any other field. A number of factors, which also contribute to the police subculture, may account for this situation:

(1) The police see themselves as members of a group aligned against common enemies. An attack upon any one of their members is consid-

ered an attack on the group. (2) Officers are greatly dependent upon one another for help in difficult situations. If an officer wants to count on fellow officers when his own life is endangered, he cannot afford to develop a reputation for "ratting." (3) The police are vulnerable to false allegations. An officer can easily imagine himself accused of wrong-doing in a difficult-to-review incident. He hopes that his defense of fellow officers when so accused will result in their willingness to assist him should their situations be reversed. (4) Police officers are as aware as their administrators of the disparity between formal policy and actual practice. The feeling emerges that it is necessary to cover up wrong-doing because practices that have developed which the police have rationalized as serving the public interest will not stand up to scrutiny. (5) An officer has no occupational mobility. He must anticipate con-tinuing to work in the same place with the same people. He cannot ordinarily avoid an uncomfortable situation by transferring to another agency. He may even have to work, at some time in the future, under the supervision of an officer whose wrongdoing he observed.

Under these conditions it is not surprising that an officer at the bottom rung in an organization, concerned about such pragmatic things as supporting a family, will maintain the blue curtain. It is the easier alternative; he avoids subjecting himself to the harassment and anguish he may suffer on being ostracized by his fellow workers. For the police administrator, the challenge is in attempting to create the kind of administrative atmosphere and arrangements that will enable the most principled among his subordinates to put integrity above loyalty to their peers. But his potential for achieving such an atmosphere is seriously limited unless steps are taken to reduce drastically or eliminate altogether the underlying problems of policing in this country, which buffet officers between conflicting pressures and make their actions so vulnerable to criticism, if not prosecution, that they must depend on one another for protection.

## Dealing With Abuse While Building Morale

Police at the operating level would like their leaders to subscribe to the same informal code that dictates relationships among themselves. Specifically they want supervisors and a police chief who will defend their agency from outside criticism. This is why police personnel usually prefer a chief selected from their own ranks. It is why they support a candidate who has a reputation for having been "one of the guys."

How subordinates view their leader is important in a police agency, for it has a major influence upon morale. It is usually argued that morale is of central concern in an agency where much of the work is frustrating, routine, and seemingly endless; where its quality depends on the initiative of the individual; and where the authority and capacity of operating personnel are so often challenged. Moreover, if police leaders are to carry out new programs, they can do so only with the respect and support of their subordinates.

Can a police chief support his subordinates without committing himself to defend everything they do? For some chiefs this presents no problem, for they place a much higher value on maintaining a good relationship with their subordinates than upon being responsive to public criticism. Many are prepared to defend the actions of their officers, however illegal or improper they may have been; or, as a minimum, resolve all questionable cases in favor of their personnel. The chief who attempts to balance, in a judicious manner, the interests of men with the public's interest undertakes the more difficult chore, for he must be prepared to incur the wrath of his subordinates or the public or, in borderline cases, both. His conclusions may lead to his punishing an officer who has a reputation for many accomplishments and acts of bravery. To cite a specific case, an officer had become a local hero of sorts for his daring exploits in apprehending street robbers. But behind the cover of his reputation, he had engaged in some brutal attacks on disrespectful teenagers. Despite overwhelming evidence supporting the charges of wrongdoing, the disciplinary action brought against him by the administration was unsuccessful, primarily because of the tremendous amount of support for the officer expressed by the police themselves and by the mass media, whose hero the officer had become. The reverse is also true. A chief finds it extremely difficult, on weighing the evidence, to dismiss charges against an officer who was at the center of an incident about which there was an outpouring of public criticism.

Ideally a chief with a reputation for fairness in the investigation and review of alleged wrongdoing will gradually alter the prevailing code somewhat, making it clear that he can indeed be counted on to support those whose behavior is proper. But it takes time to establish such a reputation, and the tensions in most large police agencies today simply do not afford such an opportunity. The rank and file typically are quick to criticize disciplinary actions resulting from citizen complaints. Well-intentioned administrators committed to open and fair investigation of citizen complaints are especially vulnerable to allegations that morale, under their leadership, has declined. Important as morale may be, it is not an objective to be pursued independently at any cost.[11] Yet large segments of the public—uninformed on the dynamics of police operations—tend to view an allegation of poor morale as an especially serious indictment of a police chief's ability to run an agency. So a police administrator who wants to take appropriate action against wrongdoing must be concerned not only with the impact that those actions will have on the attitudes of subordinates toward their work; the administrator must also be prepared to do battle in public forum in response to the charge that personnel are unhappy and morale is low.

## OPPORTUNITIES FOR IMPROVEMENT THROUGH CHANGES IN ADMINISTRATIVE PRACTICES

### Making Maximum Use of Positive Approaches

Police administrators can do much of a positive nature to achieve conformity with desired standards of conduct. Some of these opportunities were described in earlier chapters. Structuring discretion is perhaps the most obvious, for there is no more logical way to avoid wrongdoing than by giving police officers clearer and more positive directions on what is expected of them. One can shake one's head in dismay over the bizarre and perhaps offensive manner in which an officer handles a given incident, only to be pulled up short by the realization that no one ever told the officer to handle it differently.

A new system of incentives and rewards should be designed to elicit desired conduct. The present system, described and denounced with increasing frequency, is absurd. Police officers are rewarded in various ways for the number of arrests they make, for the tidiness of their uniforms, for their promptness in reporting for work, and for the neatness with which they maintain their notes in training programs. Police units are rewarded for the number of traffic citations issued, for the cleanliness of their facilities, and for their performance in target practice. Some or all of these measures may be important, but few directly affect the nature of the service rendered the public. An officer can register exceptionally well on all of them and still, in the eyes of the public, perform shabbily. New factors must be found that directly measure the quality of police services actually delivered.[12]

Perhaps more important than these administrative devices, however, is the need for aggressive advocacy by police leaders of a quality of police service that is more responsive to the diverse needs of the community, that is more sensitive to humanitarian concerns, and that reflects a full awareness of the delicate nature of the police function in a democracy. A skillful administrator who sincerely stands for these things and who manifests his values in everything he does—especially in the numerous opportunities he has for communicating both with his community and with his personnel—has tremendous potential for eliciting support for his values from his subordinates. Some of the most significant and often-cited differences between the police in the United States and in England are attributable to the fact that the police leadership in that country has, through hard work and long tradition, succeeded in instilling in police officers a commitment to a high set of values that guide them in their conduct even when specific direction is lacking. The prevailing character of police operations in England makes wrongdoing of the kind and magnitude that occurs in this country unthinkable.

It will take at least as much hard work and long tradition for police leadership in this country to change the values and priorities of individual officers, who are pressured by their peers into a police subculture that is greatly resistant to change. In pursuing this objective, an administrator must make use of a variety of measures—some of a very positive nature and some which, of necessity, involve the use of traditional discipline and sanctions—in seeking to accelerate the process whereby the behavior of the police is brought into line with the law and with the standards of the community.

## Viewing Individual Wrongdoing as an Agency Problem

If alleged wrongdoing is verified, police tend to defend the reputation of their agency by characterizing the wrongdoing as an isolated phenomenon not representative of their operations. This traditional response has contributed, perhaps unwittingly, to a prevalent attitude within police departments that wrongdoing is exclusively the responsibility of the wrongdoers; that the agency itself is exempt from any responsibility for the misconduct. It follows that, while sergeants, lieutenants, captains, and higher-ranking officers are held to strict account for investigating wrongdoing, they are rarely held to account for having failed to prevent the alleged misconduct in the first place or for having failed to uncover it on their own. Thus, preoccupied with defending themselves in the community, police administrators in many jurisdictions have forfeited one of the oldest and potentially most effective means for achieving conformity with legislative and administrative promulgations—the simple process of creating through traditional administrative devices an agency-wide sense of responsibility for the prevention of misconduct.

A factor that may contribute to this lack of responsibility for the wrongdoing of others is that—aside from the negative publicity—the agency incurs no direct liability or other costs when wrongdoing is proved. This is in sharp contrast to the effects on an agency when its officers have automobile accidents. Damage to the vehicles and personnel means direct costs in the form of budget expenditures for repairs and replacements; injuries may result in loss of manpower; and sizable claims may be filed against the city which are made known to the department because the funds for them are generally quite limited and closely watched. Confronted with these problems, most large police agencies and many smaller ones develop, as was previously noted, elaborate programs aimed at preventing accidents. Accidents are carefully reviewed. Drivers with a propensity for having accidents are identified, counseled, schooled, and, in the most serious cases, grounded. Safe-driving campaigns are launched within the agency. Refresher courses in defensive driving are offered to all personnel. The most common causes of accidents are described and analyzed in training programs and in safety campaigns. And awards are given to the department unit having the best safety record.[13] Departments with such programs have accepted the responsibility for preventing automobile accidents. If administrators applied these same techniques to police wrongdoing, they could eliminate many current abuses.

Accepting the responsibility for achieving conformity requires, specifically, that an administrator inculcate an administrative philosophy that holds supervisory officers responsible for the actions of their subordinates. Enough pressure should be exerted on a precinct commander, for example, to result in his viewing an overly aggressive police officer who is constantly offending citizens as a major administrative problem, rather than—as is often the case—an extremely valuable employee who frequently gets in trouble. Each captain, each lieutenant, and each sergeant should be made to feel as responsible for an officer's conduct in relating to citizens as they do for assuring that an officer appears for work on time. This would make the task of controlling police conduct far more manageable than it is today.[14]

## Measuring Performance and Identifying Patterns of Wrongdoing

If police agencies were profit-making institutions whose success depended on the marketability of their end product, they would take the initiative in conducting research to determine how their product was received. They would not simply wait for complaints. Those that were filed, however, would be carefully analyzed, not just to establish their veracity but to learn what it was about police operations that antagonized people.

Most police agencies have some form of internal administrative audit. In some an inspections unit conducts exhaustive checks of the various sections of the agency to assure compliance with standard operating procedures. But these inspections—like the systems of incentives and rewards for individual officers—dwell on matters unrelated to the quality of services rendered the public. They deal with the completeness of records, the cleanliness of facilities, the presence of required equipment in vehicles, and the appearance of personnel at roll call.[15] Occasionally an effort is made to time the response of vehicles to calls for assistance and to interview citizens who frequently need police service. But this is the closest the traditional inspection comes to evaluating the quality of police service, and the measurements employed do not assure accurate and objective results.

Techniques are available to provide police with more accurate feedback on the effects of their programs and policies. Carefully developed surveys have been used to great advantage in recent years to establish the actual incidence of crime (by identifying the victims of crime), to measure citizen attitudes toward the police, and to measure citizen satisfaction with police service.[16] Practically all of these efforts, however, have been initiated by individuals outside police agencies. Two notable exceptions were studies conducted by the police departments in

Kansas City, Missouri, and San Diego. These efforts demonstrated that the police can, by contract with established survey research organizations, employ recently developed survey techniques to get more reliable feedback on their efforts and especially on the effects of new programs. An agency that is truly committed to improving the quality of its performance could, on its own and through proper design of the survey instrument, pinpoint the areas of functioning in need of improvement. Such information would go a long way toward filling in the police administrator on what is happening "out there" and would be an extremely valuable tool for achieving greater conformity with administrative policies. It might even be used as a basis for rewarding officers for appropriate conduct.

Inspection techniques that test performance, especially if they are surreptitious, understandably rankle employees, who consider them demeaning and offensive. The techniques are particularly offensive if disciplinary action for failure to conform with established policies is automatically taken. An experiment in New York City, for example, in which the police department itself arranged for a number of wallets to be turned in to police officers with the request that they be properly processed, caused a furor among the rank and file and unfavorable comment from the public as well.[17] However, it does not follow that a police administrator who takes on the rather elementary, but often needed, chore of assuring that a call to the police department is answered quickly should be denied the opportunity to place test calls in order to measure how quickly they are answered. In many areas auditing of performance affords the clearest and most precise measurement of conformity with department policies and aspirations. If the testing offends operating personnel, it may be worthwhile to forgo disciplinary action in order to obtain a more accurate measure of actual operating conditions in the agency. Employed in this fashion, testing can be used in a positive way to support departmental conformance rather than as a means for getting at individual wrongdoing.

## Identifying Officers With a Propensity for Wrongdoing

In city after city situations arise in which a few officers acquire a reputation for being physically abusive and riding roughshod over the rights and dignity of citizens. Such officers are well known to their supervisors, to the top administrators, to their peers, and to the residents of the areas in which they work, and yet little is done to alter their conduct.

In Pittsburgh recently, residents who had been the victims of one such officer contacted each other, compared experiences, gathered witnesses, and filed a lawsuit with the United States District Court for Western Pennsylvania seeking relief for the entire class of law-abiding citizens desiring to use the city's sidewalks and streets. The court, finding against the defendant, issued a preliminary injunction enjoining the officer from continuing his abusive practices.[18]

Why should it take a court action to put an end to a pattern of conduct that was so obviously wrong and so well known? Many factors account for—but do not justify—the situation, including the fact that such officers often build up a large following of people who feel better protected because of the officer's aggressiveness.

In a positive program aimed at controlling police conduct, abusive behavior would be identified and corrected long before it reached these proportions. And the purpose in early identification would not be to discipline or dismiss the officer (although this may be necessary in some especially difficult cases), but to assist him in overcoming what, from the standpoint of both administrators and fellow officers, should be considered a serious handicap.

Several of the more advanced police departments in the country have recently been experimenting with programs to deal with the problem. In Oakland, under the direction of Professor Hans Toch, officers with a record of violent involvements were enlisted in a program of research and training aimed at preventing violence—their own as well as that of fellow officers.[19] The Kansas City, Missouri, Police Department, building on the Oakland program, experimented with a peer review program in which panels of experienced and specially trained officers counseled those officers whose records or requests for help indicated they were having trouble. But a review of the Kansas City experiment concluded that the manner in which it was conducted made an assessment of its value extremely difficult; that there were, in fact, no discernible results.[20] The review called for more rigorous tests of the concept, which is still viewed as having considerable potential as a way of reducing violence and altering conduct that offends the public.

## Training Specifically Aimed at Preventing Improper Conduct

In addition to working with officers whose conduct needs correcting, police training programs must do a more effective job in anticipating the situations that create the greatest stress and challenge for a police officer, and they must devise ways in which an officer can meet them. It is, for example, in the nature of police work that some people will resist arrest. Likewise, it is to be anticipated that officers will often be in situations in which they are taunted, provoked, and defied in various ways. How an officer handles such a situation will depend in large measure upon how he perceives it. If he sees the opposition and hostility, however expressed, as an attack upon him as an individual, he will probably react in kind. If instead he develops some understanding of the factors that produce such attacks on the police, he will be more capable of responding in a cool and dispassionate manner. Of course when the police must deal with persons who have no respect for the law or the police—and this is frequently the case—the most strenuous efforts to be tactful and persuasive will not work. In these situations the training an officer receives in using minimal force becomes extremely important.

Meeting stress with calm is counter to natural inclinations; it is certainly in conflict with the stereotype of how the police are expected to function. The young person going into police work most likely believes that one should stand up to a challenge, and this attitude is often reinforced by seasoned police officers.[21] As an officer, he must be convinced that the height of maturity and prowess is to deal with challenges to his authority in a calm, unemotional, and somewhat detached manner. He must rise above the emotions of those with whom he is dealing, even at the risk of appearing cowardly. Restrained, dispassionate conduct on the part of police in hostile confrontations has won a great deal of respect for them and has, at the same time, provided some clear and dramatic lessons for the community on the true nature of the police role in our society. It is the author's impression that officers who develop a reputation for being unflappable receive less resistance to their actions and to their authority.

Some training programs have experimented with ways to teach police to function under stress. But, on the whole, in the keen competition for available training time, this problem has not received the priority it deserves.[22]

If improvement in the quality of police service is the primary objective of a training program, those engaged in training police should take a special interest in citizen complaints. The situations that prompt a citizen to complain—no matter who is subsequently determined to be at fault—provide an excellent indication of areas to which training time might profitably be devoted, for even if a complaint stems from a misunderstanding, it is important that police learn to avoid such misunderstandings. Appropriate and often-repeated training could, for example, reduce substantially the frequency with which police are accused of verbal abuse. It could also remind officers, in an effort to keep them from appearing callous, that the situations that are routine for them are emotionally charged for others.

All of these comments about training, of course, are made with full awareness that a high percentage of current training is negated by the working environment in which the officer is subsequently placed. The most sophisticated training techniques will obviously be of little value if they are not reinforced by a form of administration that succeeds in eliciting conformity at the street level.

## Investigating Complaints

In order to adequately investigate citizen complaints, agencies must employ procedures that meet some basic criteria. Although these have been set forth and elaborated upon in many studies, some police agencies have been slow to recognize just how essential they are.[23]

The first thing the police must do is to create an atmosphere that affords people who feel they have been wronged easy access to the complaint process.

Since the police are so often the target of criticism, it is sometimes difficult for them to realize that many citizens are afraid to lodge complaints about them. The problem has recently been aggravated by the practice, initiated by some police associations, of threatening to file a defamation suit against a complainant if his allegation is proved to be without foundation.[24] The concern of police personnel over frivolous complaints is understandable. The better solution, however, is a system of investigations that is scrupulously objective. Police administrators must, therefore, despite this most recent development, work to create a situation in which complainants are not, from the outset, confronted by a challenge to their veracity. Furthermore, it is essential that all complaints be investigated; that the complainant be kept informed on the progress of the investigation; that it be conducted speedily; and that the complainant be informed of the outcome. It is, of course, equally important that officers against whom allegations are made be provided with a full opportunity to defend themselves; that all of their rights be adequately protected; and that they be kept informed about the processing of the complaint.

Adoption of elaborate procedures to receive and investigate allegations of police wrongdoing does not, however, in itself assure that the task will be carried out effectively. All administrative devices inevitably depend for their effectiveness on the commitment of those making use of them.

Internal investigations tend to take on the character of an adversary proceeding that pits a complainant against an officer. This leaves little room for flexibility and possible negotiation. Investigators feel pressed to find for or against the officer, even though the circumstances may indicate that both parties erred. As a consequence, in the difficult-to-settle case the officer feels put upon if labeled the guilty party; and the citizen feels offended if told his or her allegation was unfounded. For a large number of complaints alleging relatively minor misconduct, police might profitably consider mediation as an alternative form of disposition. This would, however, require a greater willingness than police have demonstrated in the past to acknowledge, on occasion, that a mistake was made. Many minor disputes could be settled satisfactorily with a letter of apology.

## PROVIDING CITIZEN REDRESS

Whether there ought to be some form of civilian review of police conduct is not really an issue. The need to provide means for aggrieved citizens to obtain redress—which must entail some form of review from outside the agency—is an essential element in the policing of a free society. The issue, rather, is the form such review and opportunity for redress should take.

Any arrangement for review and redress must first provide relief for the aggravated citizen. Beyond this, however, it is of the utmost importance that the arrangement work in such a way that it strengthens and supports the traditional system for controlling police conduct—the process whereby the chief supervises his personnel and is held accountable for their performance.

Why is this point so important? Given the decentralized and dispersed nature of police organizations, it is utterly hopeless to attempt to control police conduct other than by making the administrative system work. No court or specially constituted civilian body, based outside the police agency, can possibly provide the kind of day-to-day direction that is essential if the behavior of police officers at the operating level is to be effectively controlled. This means that even in the most acute situations, when administrators and supervisors are either unwilling or incapable of asserting themselves, there is simply no way to work around them. They must be replaced or forced to function properly. To attempt to compensate by giving agencies outside the police department the responsibility to carry out some control functions that are usually a part of management invites still further abdication by administrators and supervisors—the very people who have the greatest potential for achieving maximum control. Also, it seriously weakens the ability of a well-intentioned administrator who already has enough difficulties in achieving conformity to his standards.

If the administration is to be held responsible for the conduct of its personnel, it follows that it must be given an opportunity to look into allegations of wrongdoing—to conduct the initial investigation and, if it concludes that its personnel erred, to take appropriate corrective or disciplinary action. In some cases the agency may conclude that it incurred some liability and may even wish to take the initiative in recommending that damages be paid to the complainant. The more effective and open a job the police do in managing their internal investigations, the less likely it is that there will be need for external review.

When police conduct is reviewed from outside the police agency, the focus should be on the agency rather than the individual officer. Admittedly the question involved in a given case may revolve around a specific officer's use of authority. But if the agency has had the opportunity to review the case and chooses to support (and perhaps even defend) the officer's actions, then, quite appropriately, the agency's policies and judgments are at issue rather than just those of the officer. Today, civil actions can be brought against police officers without any implication that the police administrator was responsible for the behavior. As mentioned earlier, the city attorney routinely defends such cases vigorously in order to minimize judgments against the municipality. This process, like the proposed civilian review boards, is dysfunctional; it may provide some form of citizen redress, but at the cost of seriously weakening the administrative apparatus upon which effective control of the police depends in the long run.

If primary dependence is placed upon the administrator and the agency for achieving conformity, it follows that any system for citizen review and redress must cope with two distinct situations: (1) the public must have the opportunity to appeal from a decision reached by the internal investigative processes of a police agency on conclusion of its investigation of a complaint filed against a specific officer or group of officers; and (2) the public must have the opportunity to deal with the more difficult situation when an agency tolerates widespread abuse, fails to establish effective internal investigation procedures, and fails to establish sufficiently specific rules governing police conduct.

This distinction is important in examining and designing redress procedures, for a process that may be effective in achieving one objective may be of little use in achieving the other. Indeed, failure of efforts in recent years to control police conduct is a result, to a great extent, of not distinguishing between these two quite different needs.

## Appeals from Administrative Decisions on Specific Complaints of Officer Wrongdoing

Even under the best circumstances, when a police agency demonstrates a strong commitment to conformity with the law and established policies and to self-policing, there are bound to be situations in which a citizen is convinced that the agency reached the wrong conclusion in its investigation of a complaint. Whether the disagreement reflects an understandable difference of opinion in evaluating a difficult-to-judge incident or—at the other end of the spectrum— citizen outrage that the agency could dismiss a complaint in light of the evidence presented, how can one best provide for an appeal from the agency's decision?

A citizen who is displeased with the results of a police inquiry into a complaint filed with the agency currently has a few avenues to pursue, though none is wholly satisfactory. If the complaint alleged that an officer violated a law, whether it be the prohibition against false imprisonment or some more common offense, the complainant can turn to the local prosecutor in an effort to have the officer prosecuted. But prosecutors tend to be as reluctant to bring charges against police officers, on whom they so heavily depend as a group, as are police administrators. They are generally under less pressure to take action and traditionally have enjoyed great latitude in deciding whether or not to initiate a prosecution. If the aggrieved citizen had alleged a violation of constitutional rights, such as being deprived of liberty without due process of law, he can seek to institute a prosecution in the federal courts under the criminal section of the federal Civil Rights Act.[25] But the statute has been narrowly construed to require proof that the officer was motivated by a specific intent to deprive the complainant of rights.[26] Initiating a prosecution requires the cooperation of federal prosecutors, who are often as reluctant to place themselves in an adversary position with local police as are the local prosecutors. While the federal prosecutors receive numerous complaints of police misconduct, few cases are tried and in only a third of these are convictions obtained.[27]

Also at the federal level, if the complaint alleged a violation of constitutional rights, the citizen can resort to a civil action under the federal Civil Rights Act,[28] which avoids any dependence upon the federal prosecutor and which can be instituted without first exhausting state remedies.[29] But the availability of a defense based on "probable cause and good faith" and limitations on the law of damages in the federal act result in such proceedings holding the potential for redress only in the case of individuals severely injured by outrageous instances of police illegality.[30] Bringing such action, needless to say, can be an expensive and difficult undertaking.

By far the most common alternative is for the complainant to seek damages by instituting a civil action under state law. There would usually be a basis for doing so if the original complaint alleged false arrest, false imprisonment, malicious prosecution, or assault and battery.[31] The number of such suits has skyrocketed in some jurisdictions, but—except when the violation is unusually flagrant—there continues to be only a slight chance for adequate recovery.[32] The problems in pursuing this avenue have frequently been catalogued: the cost of hiring a lawyer; the delays before the case is tried; the fact that the plaintiff often was engaged in criminal activity, was an alcoholic or mentally ill or possessed other characteristics that make the case less than convincing to a jury; the difficulty in establishing damages; and the full or partial immunity of the jurisdiction from damages. Even if the plaintiff should obtain a substantial verdict, the officer's financial condition or the manner in which his assets are held usually makes collection unlikely.

Considerable emphasis has recently been placed upon the possibility of making greater use of the tort remedy. The standards set forth in *The Urban Police Function*, for example, approved by the American Bar Association and the Board of Officers of the International Association of Chiefs of Police, urged: "In order to strengthen the effectiveness of the tort remedy for improper police activities, governmental immunity, where it still exists, should be eliminated, and legislation should be enacted providing that governmental subdivisions shall be fully liable for the actions of police officers who are acting within the scope of their employment."[33] Specific proposals have been advanced by, among others, Chief Justice Warren Burger[34] and the District of Columbia government, the latter with the support of the Metropolitan Police Department.[35] If the city and, through budget arrangements, the police agency become responsible for damages incurred, the tort remedy may create the leverage that will force the police to take the necessary administrative steps to eliminate misconduct that results in suits being filed.

Important as these efforts are, it must be borne in mind that the tort remedy, in its potentially most effective form, nevertheless would be available for but a very limited range of wrongdoing. Many actions, though less damaging, are serious intrusions on the dignity and privacy of citizens and therefore warrant some form of appeal from an administrative investigation of them. Currently no effective method exists to provide for such a review.

The creation of a specially constituted appeals panel has not been seriously advocated in recent years in this country because it sounds too much like another civilian review board.[36] But in England, Sir Robert Mark, Commissioner of the Metropolitan Police, urged establishment of an independent board to review cases where complainants were dissatisfied with the results of a police force's own inquiry. He stressed that he wanted to continue the present system whereby Scotland Yard conducts its own investigations of alleged wrongdoing, but he felt public anxiety would be lessened if it were known that the Yard's findings would always be available for examination by persons other than policemen. He suggested that the review body consist of a prominent public figure and a number of assistants, including one with professional knowledge of police procedure and another entirely divorced from police administration and law.[37]

This proposal is significant for the elements it contains: it recognizes the distinct need for an appeal process, it is intended to augment rather than supplant the internal investigation procedure, and it is expected to serve a positive function by building public confidence in internal investigations. Implied is the assumption that the mere existence of such a form of review will aid the administrator in maintaining the objectivity and integrity of the internal investigation apparatus.

In many respects the concept of an ombudsman—so often advocated in recent years—is essentially a system for affording citizens the opportunity to appeal from administrative decisions. It contains many of the same elements embodied in the English proposal, except that it is typically not limited to the police. Where it is established, in the Scandinavian countries and in New Zealand, agency heads are expected to investigate allegations of wrongdoing and to take appropriate action. The ombudsman becomes involved only when there is reason to believe that a complaint alleging wrongdoing has been inadequately dealt with by administrative officials or when it appears that the policies and practices to which a complaint relates ought to be reviewed and possibly modified.[38]

The mere presence of a detached independent critic supports a police administrator desirous of making the right choice when confronted with strong pressures that move him in the other direction. Because the ombudsman concept applies to all agencies of the government employing the ombudsman, the police are not being singled out for special treatment. Furthermore, the attention typically given by the ombudsman to making constructive suggestions for change and improvement gives the appeal process positive value as a vehicle for strengthening administrative procedures and—in the end—the quality of services rendered the public.

## Dealing with Pervasive Agency-Tolerated Wrongdoing

What happens, however, if a citizen or group of citizens concludes that certain practices or policies of a police agency are illegal or improper? Or that the agency has failed to establish a fair and effective system for investigating complaints filed against the agency or its personnel?

Citizens can, of course, pursue a specific case to obtain redress and thereby also illustrate their concern, but even if they succeed there is no assurance the practice or policy will be altered. They can, for example, challenge the legality of a search in the course of a criminal prosecution, with the result that the evidence, if judged to have been illegally obtained, is declared inadmissible. But the manner in which such rulings are made usually serves neither to influence the future behavior of the officer nor to influence the policies and practices of the police agency.[39] Or in some instances, they can sue and—in the rare case—possibly even win a judgment against a police officer, but, as has been noted, a successful suit does not generally result in a reevaluation of department practices.

As another alternative, aggrieved citizens can turn to the political processes by which a police agency is—at least theoretically—directed. They can take their concerns to a mayor, city manager, city council, or special board having supervisory responsibilities over the police agency; and they may well receive a satisfactory response from these officials. But, as discussed in Chapter 6, the responsibility of these officials to supervise and, more specifically, to correct police policies and practices, is often unclear and, even where clear, commonly shirked. On the other hand the political processes and channels may be wide open, and the responsible officials may accept their responsibility for directing police operations, but they may nonetheless support the policies and practices being protested. They can do so with relative immunity if the group filing the complaint is but a small minority.

Ideally, clarification of the channels through which citizens are supposed to influence their police agency and adoption of additional systems for structuring police discretion, including administrative rule-making, will together provide the means for more effectively exposing and challenging questionable policies. Without such mechanisms a group that is aggrieved by police policies or by the lack of appropriate internal investigation procedures currently has no effective remedy available unless the alleged wrongdoing is a violation of some constitutional right. Where it is, there may be a basis for the use of the injunction authorized by the general remedy section of the federal Civil Rights Act.[40]

Federal courts have issued injunctions in widely varying circumstances.[41] In *Lankford v. Gelston* a group of neighbors in Baltimore obtained an injunction in 1966 to stop the police from indiscriminately searching private dwellings after police had searched over 300 residences in an effort to locate the person responsible for killing one police officer and wounding another. The searches were made by heavily armed officers on the basis of anonymous tips, without search warrants and without the consent of the occupants.[42] Although the searches relating to this incident had obviously ceased, the court of appeals, finding that such searches were, on a small scale, routinely carried out by the police to apprehend persons accused of serious crimes, remanded the case for entry of a decree enjoining the department from searching any private house based only on an anonymous tip.

A number of individuals who have studied the control of police conduct have urged greater use of the injunction provisions of the Civil Rights Act as a way of forcing police agencies to articulate their policies (thereby exposing those which infringe constitutional rights) and as a way of requiring an agency to take steps— such as improved training—that might prevent patterns of behavior considered unconstitutional.[43] When used in this manner the process contains a number of the elements so seriously lacking in some of the most commonly proposed systems for controlling police conduct. It operates on the top police administrator, thereby applying pressure to the entire agency rather than to individual police officers. It focuses upon administratively tolerated and continuing patterns of police violations, rather than isolated incidents of wrongdoing. It is more concerned with preventing such violations in the future than in providing redress for the past. And it has the potential for contributing, in a very significant way, to stimulating police agencies to better control their personnel through the structuring of discretion by requiring that the agency itself produce explicit guidelines for police functioning in important areas. By depending on the agency to formulate the policy, the court may produce a much more workable operating code tailored to local needs than the court could ever prepare on its own.

The United States Supreme Court, however, in *Rizzo v. Goode,* has narrowed the availability of injunctive relief as applied to the police.[44] In 1973 the United States District Court for the Eastern District of Pennsylvania, on finding that violations of constitutional rights by Philadelphia police occurred in what the court described as an unacceptably high number of instances and that, in the absence of changes in procedures, such violations were likely to continue to occur, concluded that revision of the procedures for handling civilian complaints was a necessary step in attempting to prevent abuses.[45] The court required the Philadelphia Police Department to formulate and submit to the court for approval a comprehensive program for dealing adequately with civilian complaints alleging police misconduct, and offered some specific guidelines for doing so. The decision was affirmed by the Court of Appeals for the Third Circuit.[46] On appeal, however, the Supreme Court reversed the decision, holding that the facts failed to establish a sufficient showing of controversy between the plaintiffs and the defendants to warrant the bringing of an action under the Civil Rights Act; that, in effect, there had been a failure to prove that the police chief and other city officials against whom the action was brought were responsible for the alleged violations and a failure to prove that the specific individuals seeking relief were likely to continue to be the target of such violations. The Court also concluded that the number of incidents cited did not constitute the pervasive pattern of violations that had been established in prior cases in which the use of the injunction had been upheld.

The Supreme Court distinguished the *Rizzo* case from the *Lankford* decision by pointing out that in the *Lankford* case the pattern of abuse was clear and flagrant; had extended over a long period of time; was acknowledged as the routine practice of the department in serious cases; received the tacit approval of high-ranking officials of the department; and most likely would have continued in the future without judicial intervention. The majority concluded that these conditions had not been established as present in the *Rizzo* case.

The Supreme Court's holding in *Rizzo* gives new emphasis to the reluctance of the federal courts to intrude in local police matters absent extraordinary circumstances. Except in very clear-cut situations, such as existed in the *Lankford* case, a prolonged and difficult process of proof will be required to establish a record adequate to warrant injunctive relief. The difficulty arises, in particular, from the need to prove a sufficient number of violations to document that they are in fact pervasive; to prove the authorization and approval of top officials, which requires penetrating the bureaucratic shields with which some administrators protect themselves from being held accountable for operating practices of a questionable nature; and to prove the likelihood that the pattern of deprivations will affect the same individuals in a similar fashion in the future.

Although the Court concluded that the plaintiffs failed to meet the required standards of proof in the facts presented by the record in the *Rizzo* case, those familiar with police operations in large cities recognize that the situation the plaintiffs attempted to substantiate in *Rizzo* is a fairly common one: patterns of violations engaged in by numerous officers that continue over a period of time with either the support, awareness, or indifference of top administrators. Indeed, the district court, which had concluded that the facts warranted injunctive relief, found that the problems disclosed by the record were fairly typical of the problems afflicting police departments in major cities.[47]

One method of preserving the use of an action under the federal Civil Rights Act to provide injunctive relief—while avoiding the problems which concerned the Court in *Rizzo*—would be for the federal courts to make use of a device similar to that now being recommended for the handling of prisoner civil-rights cases, whereby the judge requests that the defendant prepare a special report giving the court "the benefit of detailed factual information that may be necessary to decide a case involving a constitutional challenge to an important, complicated correctional practice."[48] This procedure has the advantage of placing the responsibility for describing the existing practice upon the government (in this case, the police department whenever high-ranking administrators are the defendants). Certainly the department itself is best equipped to supply information regarding current practice, as well as factual data on department policy, training, and supervision, as these bear on conduct alleged to violate a plaintiff's civil rights. The mere act of responding to the judge's inquiry would itself constitute a departmental review of existing policies and practices. Assuming the department would produce an accurate and adequate report of the facts, the court could use it to determine whether there was a basis for ordering injunctive or other relief. The department could even be encouraged to take administrative action to change the alleged practice without a judicially imposed requirement to do so.

In setting forth the reasons for limiting access to the federal courts for injunctive relief, the Supreme Court in the *Rizzo* case reflected the belief that the control of the police is better left to state and local governments. This suggests still another alternative, that it may be desirable to cope with pervasive agency-tolerated wrongdoing through civil actions for injunctive and other forms of relief brought in the state rather than the federal courts.[49] Plaintiffs have usually shown a preference for federal courts, presumably on the grounds that federal judges are more sensitive to and supportive of the rights of citizens to be free of improper police practices than are state judges.[50] It is assumed that state judges, because they must be concerned about reelection, hesitate to condemn police practices that have been sustained over a prolonged period of time and that—whether lawful of unlawful—generally have the approval of a majority of the community. But this situation may be changing, particularly in those states where state courts are imposing stricter controls on police than are now supported by the United States Supreme Court.[51]

# Notes

1   *Mapp v. Ohio,* 367 U.S. 643 (1961). For a comprehensive study of the development, use, and effectiveness of the exclusionary rule, see D.H. Oaks, "Studying the Exclusionary Rule in Search and Seizure," *University of Chicago Law Review* 37 (1970):665-757.

2   For a review of these developments, see J.R. Hudson, "Police Review Boards and Police Accountability," *Law and Contemporary Problems* 36 (1971):515-538; H. Beral and M. Sisk, "The Administration of Complaints by Civilians Against the Police," *Harvard Law Review* 77 (1964):499-519; W. Gellhorn, *When Americans Complain* (Cambridge, MA: Harvard University Press, 1966).

3   For an analysis of the referendum and the events leading up to it see D.W. Abbott, L.H. Gold, and E.T. Rogowsky, *Police, Politics and Race* (New York: American Jewish Committee, 1969).

4   See, e.g., American Civil Liberties Union of Southern California, *Law Enforcement* (Los Angeles: Institute of Modern Legal Thought, 1969); and P. Chevigny, *Police Power* (New York: Vintage Books, 1969).

5   See, e.g., National Advisory Commission on Civil Disorders, *Report of the National Advisory Commission on Civil Disorders* (Washington, DC: U.S. Government Printing Office, 1968). pp. 162-163; National Commission on the Causes and Prevention of Violence, *To Establish Justice, To Insure Domestic Tranquility,* Final Report (Washington DC: U.S. Government Printing Office, 1969), pp. 145-149; D.J. Black and A.J. Reiss, Jr., "Patterns of Behavior in Police and Citizen Transactions," in studies in *Crime and Law Enforcement in Major Metropolitan Areas,* Field Surveys III, vol. 2, Report of a Research Study Submitted to the President's Commission on Law Enforcement and Administration of Justice (Washington, DC: U.S. Government Printing Office, 1967).

6   G. Bliss et al., *Police Brutality,* pamphlet (Chicago: *Chicago Tribune,* 1973).

7   See, e.g., *Bence v. Breier,* 501 F.2d 1185 (7th Cir. 1974); *Perea v. Fales,* 114 Cal. Rptr. 808 (1974). For a general analysis of due process requirements vis-à-vis government agency regulations, see *Parker v. Levy,* 417 U.S. 733 (1974).

8   According to a survey by the IACP covering 1967-1971, it was estimated that 75 percent of all suits filed against the police were defended by the city attorney or other public legal officer. Counsel for insurance agencies defended 23 percent of the cases, and 2 percent were represented by attorneys for police associations. W.W. Schmidt, *Survey of Police Misconduct Litigation 1967-1971* (Evanston, IL: Americans for Effective Law Enforcement, Inc., 1974), p. 8.

9   One method of dealing with the problem has been proposed in the form of legislation in both Michigan and California that would amend the rules of evidence in those states so that written policies, procedures, rules, guidelines, orders, or directives of a law enforcement agency concerning the discharge of duties by its officers would not be

admissible as evidence of a standard of care or negligence in any civil action other than the disciplinary proceedings between the agency and its officers. See, e.g., Senate Bill No. 899 proposed in Michigan, October 17, 1973.

10 An exception to this pattern is so unusual that it receives widespread publicity when it occurs. See, e.g., "A Station House Divided: Police Debate Officers' Indictment," *New York Times,* 31 October 1975, in which it is reported that the testimony of fellow police officers resulted in the indictment of one officer on a charge of murdering a prisoner who was in custody at a station house; three others on assault; and a police sergeant on a charge of perjury.

11 Actually the relationship between morale and productivity is not clear by any means. See, e.g., C. Perrow, *Complex Organizations: A Critical Essay* (Glenview, IL: Scott, Foresman & Co., 1972), pp. 104-105, in which he concludes that a happy worker is not necessarily a good worker.

12 This need is discussed in American Bar Association, *The Urban Police Function,* Approved Draft (Chicago: American Bar Association, 1973), pp. 277-292. Some efforts to develop new measures are under way. See, especially, G.T. Marx, "Alternative Measures of Police Performance," Innovative Resource Planning Project, Working Paper WP-12-74, MIT Operations Research Center, Some Alternative Measures: Validation of the 1972 Massachusetts Police Selection Exam," Innovative Resource Planning Project, Working Paper WP-13-74, MIT Operations Research Center, mimeographed (Cambridge, MA, 1974).

13 See, e.g., National Safety Council, *Guidelines for Developing an Injury and Damage Reduction Program in Municipal Police Departments* (Washington, DC: U.S. Government Printing Office, 1973).

14 This point has frequently been made by those who have delved into the problems of handling citizen grievances and controlling police conduct. See, e.g., Gellhorn, *When Americans Complain,* p. 182; and F.M. Broadway, "Police Misconduct: Positive Alternatives," *Journal of Police Science and Administration* 2 (1974):215.

15 For an example of an inspection report in a large police agency, see O.W. Wilson, *Police Administration,* 2d ed. (New York: McGraw-Hill, 1963), pp. 494-508.

16 On victimization studies, see A. Biderman, "Surveys of Population Samples for Estimating Crime Incidence," *The Anals* 374 (Nov. 1967):16-33; P.H. Ennis, *Criminal Victimization: A Report of a National Survey,* National Opinion Research Center for the President's Commission on Law Enforcement and Administration of Justice (Washington, DC: U.S. Government Printing Office, 1975); and United States Department of Justice, *Criminal Victimization Surveys in the Nation's Five Largest Cities: National Crime Panel Surveys of Chicago, Detroit, Los Angeles, New York, and Philadelphia* (Washington, DC: U.S. Government Printing Office, 1975); and United States Department of Justice, *Crime in Eight American Cities: National Crime Panel Surveys of Atlanta, Baltimore, Cleveland, Dallas, Denver, Newark, Portland, and St. Louis,* advance report (Washington, DC: U.S. Government Printing Office,

1974). On measuring citizen attitudes and satisfaction with police services, see, e.g. G.E. Carte, "Changes in Public Attitudes Toward the Police: A Comparison of 1938 and 1971 Surveys," *Journal of Police Science and Administration* 1 (1973):182; F.F. Furstenberg and C.F. Wellford, "Calling the Police," *Law and Society Review* 7 (1973):393-406; and V. Cizanckas and F. Feist, "A Community's Response to Police Change," *Journal of Police Science and Administration* 3 (1975):284-291. For one of the latest examples of the use made of such survey techniques in getting feedback on police performance, see G.L. Kelling et al., *The Kansas City Preventive Patrol Experiment: A Technical Report* (Washington, DC: Police Foundation, 1974).

17   "15 Policemen Keep Money 'Lost' in Test," *New York Times,* 17 November 1973.

18   *Wecht v. Marsteller,* 363 F. Supp. 1183 (W.D.Pa. 1973).

19   H. Toch, "Change Through Participation (And Vice Versa)," *Journal of Research in Crime and Delinquency* 7 (1970):198-206. For the final report on this project, see H. Toch, J.D. Grant, and R.T. Galvin, *Agents of Change* (New York: John Wiley and Sons, 1975).

20   The project, as initially conceived, is described in Broadaway, "Police Misconduct: Positive Alternatives," pp. 210-218. For its evaluation, see T. Pate et al., *Kansas City Peer Review Panel* (Washington, DC: Police Foundation, 1975).

21   See, e.g., J. Van Maanen, "Working the Street: A Developmental View of Police Behavior," in *The Potential for Reform of Criminal Justice,* ed. H. Jacob (Beverly Hills, Calif.: Sage Publications, 1974), pp. 116-120.

22   Under a grant from the Police Foundation the International Conference of Police Associations has launched a major study of the causes of stress in the police occupation. One of the objectives of this study is to find effective ways in which police training programs can aid officers to deal with stress.

23   For the most recent set of detailed recommendations for police agency processing of citizen complaints, see the National Advisory Commission on Criminal Justice Standards and Goals, *Police* (Washington, DC: U.S. Government Printing Office, 1973), pp. 469-491.

24   See, e.g., "Police Protective League is Filing Defamation Suits," *Los Angeles Daily Journal,* 30 January 1975.

25   18 U.S.C. §242 (1970).

26   *Screws v. United States,* 325 U.S. 91, 107 (1945).

27   The Criminal Section, Civil Rights Division of the Attorney General's Office, reports 7,000 complaints of alleged criminal interference with the civil rights of citizens during 1973 (most of which were police misconduct). Only 61 defendants were tried during 1973, of which only 19 were convicted. *Annual Report of the Attorney General of the United States: 1973* (Washington, DC: U.S. Government Printing Office, 1974), p. 73.

28   42 U.S.C. §1983 (1970).

29   See Monroe v. Pape, 365 U.S. 167, 183 (1961); McNeese v. Board of Education for Community School District No. 187, 373 U.S. 668, 671 (1963); Preiser v. Rodriguez, 411 U.S. 475 (1973).

30   For a discussion of these limitations, see National Commission on the Causes and Prevention of Violence, Task Force on Law and Law Enforcement, *Law and Order Reconsidered* (Washington, DC: U.S. Government Printing Office, 1969), pp. 376-378.

31   Although now somewhat dated, C. Foote, "Tort Remedies for Police Violations of Individual Rights," *Minnesota Law Review* 39 (1955):493-516, continues to be one of the most helpful treatments of this subject. See also National Commission on the Causes and Prevention of Violence, Task Force on Law and Law Enforcement, *Law and Order Reconsidered,* pp. 370-375; and Joyce Blalock, Civil Liability of Law Enforcement Officers (Springfield, IL: Charles C Thomas, 1974).

32   Based upon a survey of litigation in the period from 1967-1971, the IACP estimates that, whereas there were 1,741 suits filed in police jurisdictions having ten or more officers in 1967, 3,894 such suits were filed in 1971. In the period 1967-71 the plaintiffs were successful in only 18.5 percent of the cases that went to trial. Schmidt, *Survey of Police Misconduct Litigation 1967-1971,* pp. 5-6.

33   American Bar Association, *The Urban Police Function,* supplement p. 11.

34   *Bivens v. Six Unknown Named Agents of Federal Bureau of Narcotics,* 403 U.S. 388, 422-424 (1971).

35   District of Columbia Law Enforcement Liability and Legal Assistance Act of 1971 (proposed legislation).

36   Actually there are now a number of jurisdictions where a civilian body with some general superintending responsibility over the police force is authorized to hear citizen complaints—both initially and on appeal. See, e.g., M. Berger, "Law Enforcement Control: Checks and Balances for the Police System," *Connecticut Law Review* 4 (1971/72):492; and M. Flynn, "Police Accountability in Wisconsin," *Wisconsin Law Review* 1974:1166.

37   For a summary of proposals made for the review of citizen complaints in England, and for reactions to these proposals, see *The Handling of Complaints Against the Police: Report of the Working Group for England and Wales* (London: Her Majesty's Stationery Office, 1974). Sir Robert Mark's comments appear on pp. 49-52.

38   For an exploration of the ombudsman concept, see W. Gelhorn, *Ombudsmen and Others* (Cambridge, MA: Harvard University Press, 1966); S. Hurwitz, "Denmark's Ombudsman," *Wisconsin Law Review* 1961:169-199; D.C. Rowat, ed., The Ombudsman, 2d ed. (Toronto: University of Toronto Press, 1968); Stanley v. Anderson and J.C. Moore, *Establishing Ombudsman Offices* (Berkeley, CA.: Institute of Governmental Studies, 1972).

39  See, e.g., W.R. LaFave and F.J. Remington, "Controlling the Police: The Judge's Role in Making and Reviewing Law Enforcement Decision," *Michigan Law Review* 63 (1965):987-1012; and H. Goldstein, "Trial Judges and the Police," *Crime and Delinquency* 14 (1968):18-19.

40  See "The Federal Injunction as a Remedy for Unconstitutional Police Conduct," *Yale Law Journal* 78 (1968):143-155; G.J. Siedel III, "Injunctive Relief for Police Misconduct in the United States," *Journal of Urban Law* 50 (1973):681-699; and "Injunctive Relief for Violations of Constitutional Rights by the Police," *University of Colorado Law Review* 45 (1973):91-129.

41  See Siedel, "Injunctive Relief for Police Misconduct," Wecht v. Marsteller, is another example.

42  *Lankford v. Gelston,* 364 F.2d 197 (4th Cir. 1966).

43  See, e.g., A. Amsterdam, "The Supreme Court and the Rights of Suspects in Criminal Cases," *New York University Law Review* 45 (1970):814; and "The Federal Injunction as a Remedy for Unconstitutional Police Conduct," p. 149.

44  *Rizzo v. Goode,* 18 CrL 3041 (1976), *rev'g.* 506 F.2d 542 (3d Cir. 1974).

45  *Council of Organizations v. Rizzo,* 357 F. Supp. 1289, 1318 (E.D. Pa. 1973).

46  *Goode v. Rizzo,* 506 F.2d 542 (3d Cir. 1974).

47  *Council of Organizations v. Rizzo,* 357 F. Supp. 1289, 1318 (E.D. Pa. 1973).

48  Federal Judicial Center, *Recommended Procedures for Handling Prisoner Civil Rights Cases in the Federal Courts,* Tentative Report (Washington, DC: U.S. Government Printing Office, 1976).

49  Most state courts have been reluctant to enforce 42 U.S.C. § 1983, although they clearly have authority to do so. If they do not use the federal Civil Rights Act, it is uncertain whether an alternative is available to them.

50  Also, because courts have held that a state decision precludes a subsequent litigation of the issues in federal court (res judicata), plaintiffs have been reluctant to have the door to the federal court closed. See, e.g., Spence v. Latting, 512 F.2d 93 (10th Cir. 1975); Constitutional Law—Civil Rights—Section 1983—Res Judicata/Collateral Estoppel," *Wisconsin Law Review* 1974:1180.

51  See D.E. Wilkes, Jr., "The New Federalism in Criminal Procedure: State Court Evasion of the Burger Court," *Kentucky Law Journal* 62 (1974):421-451; and "State Constitutional Requirements—Divergence from U.S. Supreme Court Opinions," 18 *Criminal Law Reporter* 2507-2508 (1976).

# Study Questions

1.  The author states that interest in the control of police conduct began to accelerate in the 1950s. What factor or factors were responsible for this acceleration?

2.  Why have proposals for control of police conduct failed in the past?

3.  The author suggests that many factors inherent in the police function make the control of police conduct complex and almost impossible. What are the factors?

4.  What are the problems with the current police incentives-and-reward system, especially as it relates to eliciting desired conduct?

5.  What forms of redress are available to citizens when there is pervasive agency-tolerated wrongdoing?

# 17

# POLICE DISCIPLINARY PROCEDURES: A REVIEW OF SELECTED POLICE DEPARTMENTS***

## David L. Carter

The disciplinary process of a police department represents a serious administrative action having a significant effect on an officer's security and career potential. Because of the wide-ranging effects of disciplinary actions, the processes and outcomes are subject to careful scrutiny and challenge. Should the department wrongfully discipline an employee, the costs to resolve conflicts through court challenges and labor arbitrations can rise quickly. Civil suits may even award punitive damages to a wrongfully terminated or wrongfully disciplined employee. Therefore, it is important that a department have a well-planned, objective, structured, and equitable disciplinary system which is clearly articulated by formal policy and procedures.

This chapter presents a descriptive model for the police disciplinary process based on a qualitative analysis of the procedures used by 20 major United States police departments. While variability is difficult to measure and validate in qualitative research, the explicit nature in which police policies and procedures are written enhanced the author's abilities to conduct a robust content analysis of the disciplinary systems.

## PROBLEM STATEMENT

The purpose of this study was to examine the different police disciplinary processes along with supporting policies and procedures[1] used in the nation's largest police agencies. Disciplinary practices in police departments vary greatly on a continuum of being informal processes reliant on custom to adversarial proceedings supported by voluminous prescriptive documentation. The intent of this study was to define the critical stages of the disciplinary process and describe both commonalities and variances to the process as actually practiced by agencies.

---

*This chapter was written expressly for inclusion in this book.

**The author expresses his appreciation to the personnel in the 20 sampled police departments for the time and assistance given in support of this research effort.

351

# PHILOSOPHY OF DISCIPLINE

The disciplinary process is critical for organizational control—it is the mechanism through which personnel who have violated department procedures and rules[2] are sanctioned. The sanctions may be viewed as positive/remedial or negative/punitive. Positive/remedial sanctions are intended to be primarily corrective in nature. That is, the errant behavior is pointed out to the officer emphasizing the negative effect it has on the practice of policing. The sanction imposed will be specifically directed to correct the problem so the behavior will not recur. Although the officer may suffer inconvenience, embarrassment, or loss of income, the *intent* is remedial. Negative/punitive sanctions are intended to be retributive in nature. The intent is to punish the offending officer for violating department rules and/or procedures. While there is a desire for a remedial effect (as a means to avoid future negative sanctions) the primary emphasis is punishment for the errant behavior.

Whether a sanction is positive or negative is largely dependent on two factors. The first, and arguably the most important, is the ideology of the police executive. If the administrator's ideology toward employee motivation and control is consistent with the assumptions of McGregor's Theory X, then the sanctions are most likely to be negative/punitive. (e.g., Most people must be coerced, controlled, directed, and threatened with punishment in order to get them to do their job and address organizational objectives.) Conversely, if the administrator subscribes to Theory Y assumptions, there would be a greater tendency toward positive/remedial sanctions. (e.g., External control and the threat of punishment are not the only means for motivating employees to achieve organizational objectives and adhering to organizational principles.) (See McGregor, 1960).

The second factor is the nature of the infraction. As the seriousness of the infraction increases, the more likely the sanction is to be punitive (if not in spirit, certainly in practice). This points to an important element in disciplinary philosophy: Neither positive nor negative discipline represent a pure model. The sanctions will exist on a continuum, however, the general practices employed in most disciplinary cases will weight the continuum to either the positive or negative approach. It should be further noted that in reality, the alternatives for the actual sanctions will be virtually the same for positive and negative discipline. However, the framework or spirit in which the disciplinary system is institutionalized is the factor that distinguishes between the two forms.

The purpose of both forms of discipline is to encourage proper behavior. Positive discipline attempts a cooperative approach to this end while negative discipline uses a coercive approach. (See also, IACP, 1976).

# RESEARCH PROCEDURES

This project was based on a contract to assist a major metropolitan police department[3] during a period of procedural review and contract negotiations with the police collective bargaining units. A brief look at the background will help place the methodology into perspective.

## Background

The genesis for this study was to assist a police department in restructuring its disciplinary system. The department had lost a number of civil rights suits wherein inadequate discipline had become a key issue. Furthermore, the department was having significant problems with officer misconduct and the entire disciplinary system—from complaint reception through appeal—did not seem to work. Officers had challenged the system in court and frequently won. The burgeoning procedures and lengthy appeals resulted in officers who had complaints against them sustained, never "serving" their disciplinary sanction. In two cases, officers had been terminated by a department trial board, yet the officers had not lost even one day's work because of the appeals procedure. As a capstone to these problems, the police officers' union was challenging the disciplinary system and attempting to get even less restrictive procedures implemented as provisions of the collective bargaining agreement. As one Deputy Chief stated:

> [This department] is out of control. The only thing[s] we can discipline people for are minor technical [rule] violations because the penalties are so limited, nobody cares. [Confidential statement of a Deputy Chief of Police.]

The information for this study was collected for a twofold purpose: (1) to identify trends and models on which to redesign the department's disciplinary system and (2) to help justify the department's policy decisions on disciplinary matters during the course of binding arbitration for the contract with the Police Officer's Association (POA).

## Methodology

Relying on applied qualitative research methods, a purposive sample of 20 police departments was selected to study the policies, procedures, rules, and other supporting documentation concerning the disciplinary system. The selection of the departments was based on several criteria. First, a department must either serve a population in excess of 500,000 inhabitants or employ more than 1,000 sworn personnel. This criterion was used under the assumption that the largest agencies would tend to have the most formalized disciplinary systems and articulated policies. Moreover, departments were needed that would most accurately reflect the magnitude of the Central Department where the disciplinary system was being restructured.

A second criterion was geographical distribution. Such distribution would expose alternate approaches to the disciplinary process based upon variation in culture, law, public sentiment, and demographic factors. This variation was desired in order to assess alternate models and develop a profile of disciplinary proceedings. Moreover, based on the authors' experience it is known that overall there is a greater propensity for structured unionization in northern and northeastern police departments than other parts of the country. The geographic dispersion would permit comparison between departments which are highly unionized, moderately unionized, and non-unionized.

The third criterion was "comparability" (from a collective bargaining perspective) with the Central Department. This was an attempt to select departments which were fairly homogeneous with respect to salary, benefits, organizational structure, and policing demands. This is admittedly a very subjective factor, yet it was necessary for purposes of the contract arbitration hearing of the Central Department.

Following selection of the 20 agencies, all were contacted via letter and asked to submit copies of policies, procedures, rules, collective bargaining agreements, civil service regulations, and any other written materials related to internal affairs investigations, the disciplinary system, and other matters not addressed in this chapter. After telephone follow-ups with some departments, all agencies responded to the requests with varying degrees of comprehensiveness.

In several cases departments asked that portions of the information contained in the policies and procedures remain confidential. These requests typically referred to the internal investigation. While such information would most likely be available under each state's Freedom of Information Act, the researchers nonetheless honored the requests in the spirit of cooperation. In those cases, information is reported based on aggregate trends or the consensus of the agencies.

Issues addressed in this study were addressed via a content analysis of the documents received. (While all departments responded, the amount and types of materials varied.) In some cases, follow-up telephone calls were made to clarify information that was vague or not contained in the materials received. Interestingly, the appeals alternatives and point of imposition of sanctions tended to be the most vague portions of the directives. Conversely, information on the internal investigation and adjudicatory hearings were very explicit—almost pathological in some instances.

The factored variables for this qualitative analysis were (a) grounds for discipline, (b) the internal investigation, (c) the adjudication process,

(d) disciplinary sanctions/alternatives, and (e) disciplinary appeals. In presenting the findings the author first describes the general literature and recommends practices associated with each variable. This is followed by an aggregate presentation of the findings from the content analysis.

## GROUNDS FOR DISCIPLINE

How can an employee be disciplined? With complex civil service regulations, complicated collective bargaining agreements, evolving case law, appellate processes, and political factors—such as public opinion and scrutiny of the police or political negotiation in a city council—it is difficult to stay abreast of the status of disciplinary proceedings.

To begin, the most basic needs which must be met are having the *grounds and notice for discipline*. The grounds for discipline are written as organizational rules (or regulations) which either proscribe or prohibit forms of behavior. The rules are supported by organizational policy which states the police department's philosophy on various responsibilities and tasks. Rules and regulations do not have to be as precise as the criminal law but need to be sufficiently clear so that employees can reasonably distinguish between which behavior is acceptable and which is not.

All organizational rules, policies, and procedures should be part of the department's manual and each employee should have a copy. Providing employees a copy of the manual, including the disciplinary process and potential sanctions, establishes notice of the types of behavior which are prohibited as well as those which are required. With this type of notice the employee has greater difficulty contending that he/she was unaware certain actions were prohibited or that the proscription of behavior applied. (Such as in the case of rule violations occurring off-duty or when the officer is out of the jurisdictional boundaries.)

If action is contemplated against an officer for misconduct, the grounds for the action must be carefully evaluated. Is it because the officer violated the criminal law? Is it because the officer's behavior posed a threat to the police responsibility of community protection? Is it because the officer violated the oath of office? The rationales for the discipline can make a significant difference in the sanction applied.

If a department relies on unarticulated custom or broad categorizations—such as "conduct unbecoming"—rather than on rules which specifically prohibit defined forms of behavior, then potential problems arise. For example, a chief may want to terminate an officer because he/she used marijuana off duty. If the officer is charged with "conduct unbecoming" or charged because he/she violated a law (e.g., misdemeanor possession of a controlled substance) it is unlikely, notably in a department with a collective bargaining contract, a penalty of termination can be sustained (c.f., Carter and Stephens, 1988). However, a more definitive rule which is supported by policy stipulating the unique problems associated with officer drug use would result in a stronger case for termination. Such a directive would give clear notice and grounds for disciplinary action.

In establishing administrative rules and procedures as grounds for discipline, it is imperative that the department ensure that the regulations adhere to substantive due process standards. That is, any rules must be clear, specific, and reasonably related to a valid public need. (See Swanson, Territo, and Taylor, 1988.) The rule must be fundamentally fair in and of itself by not imposing any unrealistic burden on the officer as a result of his/her police employment nor may the rules, per se, violate any of the officer's rights.

Having the administrative framework in place is only one element of establishing the grounds for misconduct. Before any other element of the disciplinary system can be initiated there must be an allegation that the officer violated an organizational rule or procedure. The allegation may be in the form of a complaint from a citizen concerning treatment by an officer; observations of a supervisor of either one incident or a cumulative problem involving a series of incidents; or an allegation of wrongdoing by either another officer or a citizen. Importantly, the department must have some form of reliable information indicating that an officer may have been involved in misconduct before any administrative action should take place.

## Police Department Practices

All police departments studied had a "Code of Conduct" or similar document which stipulated proscribed conduct in the form of rules. These types of malfeasance and misconduct typically represent the most serious violations of accepted organizational behavior. Most proscribed behavior was presented in departmental procedures wherein disciplinary action may be forthcoming if an officer was misfeasant or nonfeasant. As one may expect, these behaviors were typically of a less serious nature. All agencies had some form of rule requiring officers to adhere to administrative procedures, general orders, and memoranda, thus establishing a clear mechanism for invoking the disciplinary process in these instances.

All agencies had some form of a general collective rule dealing with "conduct unbecoming a police officer." Various wording was used such as prohibiting behavior which would."bring discredit on [the] police department" or behavior that "violates the tenets of [the] department's code of ethics." While the spirit of these provisions is intuitively clear—particularly when read in the context of the total Code of Conduct—the meaning of "conduct unbecoming" was never articulated (although it was illustrated by some departments to include public intoxication, disorderly conduct, sexual indiscretions, etc.). An important point to note is "context." That is, when reading the documents one can sense a clear ideology and, to a lesser extent, an impression of accepted latitudes of behavior. Interestingly, about half the departments included the Law Enforcement Code of Ethics in the "code of conduct" with the notation that ethical behavior was part of all expected behaviors. In other departments, the Code of Ethics was included in other policy materials, sometimes appearing as an appended afterthought.[4]

All of the departments in the sample made some reference to off-duty behavior. The clear trend was not to explicitly stipulate rules governing an officer's off-duty behavior; rather, several statements were promulgated clearly inferring the parameters of accepted off-duty behavior. Notable exceptions concerned the use of police authority while off duty—both when employed in an off duty capacity and when observing a criminal incident when off duty. The second area, as one might expect, was a prohibition against committing any crimes.

In sum, the departments in the sample tended to have very similar rules on officer behavior. The greatest variability concerned requirements and rules concerning off-duty employment.

The method by which the departments received complaints varied widely, ranging from an independent ombudsman to the desk officer in any precinct station. Nearly all departments had some form of statement that the complaint system should be open and accessible to citizens and that officers should courteously refer complainants to the appropriate office in the department when asked. Internal allegations by an officer concerning the actions of another were typically referred through the chain of command.

## THE INTERNAL INVESTIGATION

After a complaint has been filed, the department has the responsibility to investigate the allegation. Under the "pure model" a department will have an independent Internal Affairs (IA) section to investigate the facts and allegations of the complaint. The presence and structure of an IA section will depend on a number of organizational variables such as agency size, overall public service demands of the department, available resources, number of complaints received, and structure of the department's disciplinary process. The IA function may be performed by an individual assigned as an IA investigator on a case-by-case basis, a supervisor, a command officer, or, in sensitive cases, an outside agency.

Regardless of the structure, the factor of paramount importance is that the investigation be thorough and impartial. Importantly, this function is merely *fact-finding*—the IA investigator should not be given authority to draw a formal conclusion on whether or not the allegation is true.

The IA investigation is procedurally very similar to a criminal investigation.

Physical evidence, if any, is collected and analyzed, witnesses are interviewed, applicable records are obtained for evidentiary use, and the accused officer is interviewed. The investigator then collates the information into a logical case report with supporting evidence and statements/depositions.

The significant distinction between an IA investigation and a criminal investigation is the rules of evidence. While there is clear recognition that an officer who may face an administrative disciplinary hearing has procedural due process rights, the extent and precise nature of those rights remain in debate. Procedural due process particularly comes to issue during the course of the complaint investigation and transgresses throughout the adjudication of the complaint. Of particular concern during the investigation is the Fourth Amendment prohibition against unreasonable searches and seizures and the Fifth Amendment privilege against self-incrimination.

Generally speaking, during the course of a disciplinary investigation the Fourth Amendment guarantees apply to an officer at home and off-duty just as they would to any other citizen. However, lockers at the police station, a police car, and other elements related to on-duty performance may not be protected. Moreover, it appears that even though an unlawful search may occur, any fruits of that search may be used in a disciplinary hearing but not in a criminal trial. Some departments have established detailed procedures on conducting searches as part of internal investigations which include a provision that searches must be consistent with current criminal procedure. In those cases, the fruits of an unreasonable search may not be used in the disciplinary proceeding.

With respect to the Fifth Amendment, the Supreme Court held in *Garrity v. New Jersey*, 385 U.S. 483 (1967) that statements compelled during the course of an internal investigation cannot be used as evidence in a criminal trial. A practice which has evolved as a product of this ruling is that agencies, during the course of IA investigations, will conduct "Garrity Interviews." These are sworn statements or depositions of the accused officer taken by an IA investigator who is of a higher rank than the officer under investigation. The officer is "ordered" (on the record) to answer all questions truthfully during the interview. The officer is also told (on the record) that his/her statements will be used during the internal disciplinary process but cannot be used in a criminal proceeding. As a result, compelled testimony for administrative purposes is currently an accepted practice.

## Police Department Practices

All agencies studied had a specially designated Internal Affairs Section (alternately also called Division, Bureau, or Unit) which was functionally organized to report directly to the Police Chief/Commissioner or a Deputy Chief for Operations (or equivalent rank). The ranks of the IA investigators varied widely, although a common theme was to give IA personnel either a special "rank" (or designation such as Inspector) or have investigators possess special organizational authority as a matter of policy. All departments had written policies and procedures concerning internal investigations and the authority of IA during the course of the investigations. It appears that departments with active unions/collective bargaining associations tended to have more detailed procedures than the non-union agencies. All departments reported that searches by IA investigators followed current Fourth Amendment criminal procedure. However, searches of lockers in police facilities and police were typically performed upon approval of a unit or case supervisor. All agencies employed "Garrity Interviews" in a manner generally similar to that described above. Interestingly, on this issue it appeared that agencies which had a collective bargaining agreement tended to have more formalized depositions taken during the Garrity Interview, while the non-union departments generally relied on a witnessed sworn statement by the officer.

## THE ADJUDICATION OF THE COMPLAINT

The adjudication process is the point where a determination of the facts is made. All evidence developed during the course of the investigation is submitted to the adjudication mechanism for purposes of determining if the allegation can be sustained. This process may be a review by a command officer, a supervisor, a panel of officers, a citizen review board, or a hybrid of these standard options. The actual review may be a formal adversarial proceeding, a non-adversarial hearing, or a confidential review by command personnel.

For purposes of this study, the alternate adjudication systems used in police disciplinary cases are defined as follows:

**Command discipline/review.** That disciplinary process wherein officer culpability is reviewed and sanctions are imposed by the department's command structure rather than through a hearing or board of inquiry. Typically, the results of a complaint investigation are formulated in a written report documenting the incident. This is forwarded through the organizational chain of command to a designated command level where a determination is made and, if the complaint is sustained, a sanction is imposed. The command level varies and appears to be correlated with the size of the department.

**Hearings/proceedings.** The types of initial proceedings wherein the veracity of allegations against an officer are evaluated have been divided into three categories as noted below. These categories have been developed after assessing the narrative descriptions of hearing processes used by the departments sampled as well as consideration of practices described in the literature.

*Adversarial.* This proceeding is closely akin to a court trial. Formal rules of evidence are followed, testimony is presented, evidence is introduced, cross-examination is permitted, and transcripts are recorded. In adversarial proceedings both the police department and the accused officer are typically represented by counsel.

*Quasi-adversarial.* This trial board or hearing body has only limited presentation of evidence, usually statements only by those parties directly involved in the case. The proceeding also has very limited cross-examination and "loose" evidentiary rules or procedures. Direct testimony is frequently used only to clarify questions in reports and to permit the accused officer to make a statement on his/her behalf. The hearing body relies significantly on supervisory and internal investigations reports. Generally, the accused officer is afforded the right to counsel.

*Non-adversarial.* No testimony is presented in this type of hearing. The board typically functions in a close proceeding somewhat similar to a committee meeting. Only reports of the incident in question are reviewed, generally including the initial complaint and, importantly, the internal investigation report. The accused officer may submit a written statement on his/her behalf to be reviewed by the board. "Selectively important" written statements and/or reports may also be reviewed at the board's discretion; these are decided on a case-by-case basis. Generally the accused officer is not present during the board's deliberations nor is the officer's counsel (if afforded) permitted access to the deliberations.

Regardless of the review mechanism used, it is important that minimum standards of due process are attached to the proceedings. Standards typically include...

1. timely and adequate notice,
2. a chance to make an oral statement or argument,
3. a chance to present witnesses and evidence,
4. confrontation of adverse witnesses,
5. cross-examination of adverse witnesses,
6. disclosure of all evidence relied on,
7. a decision based on the record of evidence,

8. a right to retain an attorney,
9. a publicly compensated attorney for the indigent,
10. a statement of findings of fact,
11. a statement of reasons or a reasoned opinion, [and]
12. an impartial deciding officer [Davis, 1976:242].

These due process rights are not ironclad nor must they meet the stringent formality found in a criminal case. Moreover, other procedures may apply to an agency in light of applicable laws, contracts, and custom.

The adjudication procedure in most agencies does not issue a finding of the officer's "guilt" or "innocence." Instead, it simply attempts to determine, based on the evidence presented, whether or not the complaint or allegation against the officer can be sustained. The reason for this is twofold: First, administrative disciplinary hearings are conducted under relaxed rules of procedure, evidence, burden of proof, and disposition. As such, a finding of "guilt" may go beyond the permissible scope of constitutional limits. Second, the approach of "sustaining" or "not sustaining" complaints may afford the department some insulation from liability. Ideally, this factor should not be an element of administrative discipline, however, as a reality it is a concern.

## Police Department Practices

Departments which utilize a trial board or comparable body—regardless of the adversarial status of the hearing body—select the board members in a wide variety of ways. No definitive process exists that emerges as a clear or preferred trend. Regardless of the selection process used, it is clear that the departments strived to obtain a balanced and objective board.

The data reported from the surveys describes the formal disciplinary system that is *available* to officers accused of misconduct (See Table 17.1). In all agencies, based on the authors' experiences, informal systems of discipline also exist. For example, it is common practice that in serious cases an officer is given an option to resign rather than go through the formal disciplinary system. In such instances the option is usually to the benefit of both the officer and the department. In less serious and minor cases the officer and the department—sometimes in conjunction with the POA—will agree to a disciplinary penalty via an informal process somewhat akin to a "plea bargain" in criminal cases. When these informal processes are used it is frequently a result of clear recognition by all parties that the officer was culpable.

With respect to the type of disciplinary system used by the departments, the data show no clear preferential trend except to have different mechanisms for minor and serious infractions. To distinguish between these different infractions, the following definitions were used:

**Misconduct.** For interpretation of Table 17.1, "misconduct" is a general term referring to police officer behavior which violates police department procedures, rules/regulations, and/or the criminal law. The misconduct can be divided into two broad subcategories, serious and minor misconduct.

> *Minor misconduct/infraction.* This is a technical infraction of departmental rules or procedures wherein the penalty is a written reprimand, supervisory counseling, or mandatory training.

> *Serious misconduct/infraction.* This is defined as employee misconduct, including criminal acts, wherein the administrative penalty involves at least unpaid suspension from duty.

These definitions were developed after the policies were reviewed with the diverse provisions synthesized into manageable categories. Certain behaviors obviously transgress these categories. The departments sampled had a wide variety of options available to channel cases to the most appropriate adjudicatory forum.

Based on both the survey results and the authors' experiences, it is clear that the burden of proof in disciplinary cases fall on the department and is proof within a preponderance of the evidence. Minimal due process rights are afforded to officers in all cases, however, the degree to which those rights are extended varies depending on the nature of the disciplinary system. In general, the rights afforded to the accused officer in the sampled departments were: written notification of the specific alleged infraction or complaint; notification of the accuser(s); an opportunity to submit a written notice of the disciplinary decision. In addition, all departments utilizing an adversarial trial board afforded the accused officer the right to representation by counsel during the hearing. It appears that police departments with collective bargaining agreements extended more due process rights to officers than those departments without contracts.

# DISCIPLINARY SANCTIONS/ALTERNATIVES

If a complaint is sustained after the review, then the reviewing body or other designated person or group (typically, but not always, represented by the department's chain of command) will assess the sanction for the rule violation. Disciplinary alternatives usually depend on the seriousness and circumstances surrounding the rule violation, aggravating and mitigating factors, and the officer's personnel history. Potential sanctions include termination, loss of rank, punitive suspension from duty, placement on punitive probation, punitive reassignment, mandatory training, a reprimand for the record, or supervisory counseling.

*Termination of Employment.* Termination is complete severance from the police department including salary, benefits, and reciprocal responsibilities between the officer and the department. It is the decision that faces the greatest challenge in the administrative review process and in subsequent court proceedings. Even though termination is a difficult and costly decision for a police department, it is the only real alternative in certain serious cases.

*Demotion/Loss of Rank.* Loss of rank refers to demotion from a formally recognized organizational position which has defined authority over other organizational members. Rank does not include "grades" which are typically salary increments within a rank or "position classifications" which describe a particular functional responsibility but no specific hierarchical authority. As a penalty, loss of rank is a significant sanction because it represents a loss of earnings, a loss of status (in both the formal and informal organization), and a liability in career growth. Most frequently, an employee will be demoted because he/she abused the authority of the rank or the misconduct was of a nature to question the individual's effectiveness as a leader.

In somewhat serious cases, demotion may be a reasonable alternative to termination, particularly in cases where the officer's integrity is not of issue and where there is no violation of criminal law. Like termination, demotion carries with it some organizational side effects. One of the most obvious is the continuing reminder that a supervisor or management person committed a serious violation of policy. It can have both positive and negative effects depending on how the individual handles the action and how other employees view and understand the circumstances of the decision. Positive effects would include evidence of policy enforcement and the exhibition of organizational concern for employees in that the individual was not terminated. Negative effects might include lowered officer morale that a serious rule violation was not terminated (e.g., the belief that "a patrol officer would be fired") and the feeling of the individual that he/she "beat the system" because they were not terminated. Certainly, the way the department handles a demotion will have a significant effect on how the action is perceived.

*Punitive Suspension.* A punitive suspension is where an officer is barred from work without salary for a designated period usually not exceeding four weeks. During the suspended period the officer carries no authority as a police officer and in many jurisdictions cannot even work an "off-duty" job that may require police authority. While the officer has no authority or salary, typically personnel benefits are still accrued.

A punitive suspension has an effect similar to a monetary fine. An officer loses the salary expected when on suspension which, theoretically, will cause modification in the negative form of behavior.

*Punitive Probation.* Punitive probation is when the officer remains on duty receiving salary and benefits, however, his/her status is significantly altered because a subsequent sustained misconduct allegation of the same nature may result in suspension or termination. Punitive probation has generally been applied on a limited basis. It has been used most frequently for officers who have gone through alcohol rehabilitation programs, officers who have chronically missed work, officers who have received an unusually high number of "minor" complaints (e.g., discourteous or unprofessional, etc.) and similar circumstances.

*Reassignment.* The sanction of reassignment is most appropriately used in cases where an officer has been involved in misconduct associated with his/her current assignment. Reassignment is also frequently used in conjunction with some other form of disciplinary action. The reassignment may involve taking an officer out of a specialized position or, in the case of patrol, moving the officer to another shift and/or location. This alternative is notably appropriate in cases where the circumstances of the working environment contributed to the misconduct. In cases where potential liability may result from the officer's action, a change of assignment for a specified period of time could present some insulation from a negligent retention situation.

*Mandatory Training.* If an officer's rule or procedural violation was a product of misfeasance, a reasonable alternative may be to provide the officer with additional mandatory training on the subject(s) of issue related to the misconduct. It is conceivable that the improper behavior was a function of not being adequately prepared to perform the required functions of the job. As such, the department must recognize some of the responsibility and afford a course of remedial action.

*Reprimand.* A reprimand for the record is when the officer is officially admonished for his/her behavior. The admonishment is in written form, usually from a division commander, with a copy of the reprimand in the officer's personnel file. The purpose of the reprimand is to serve as a record (and notice) of the incident and a warning about future misconduct. The reprimand may be considered in promotional evaluations as well as in punishment decisions in any future misconduct incidents.

*Supervisory Counseling.* This is a discussion with the employee concerning a problem usually related to some performance factor or procedure. The purposes of counseling are both of a corrective and instructive nature to help remedy a minor problem before it manifests into some form of misconduct. The supervisory counseling is typically not part of the employee's official personnel record, however, the supervisor should maintain a record for reference in case it is necessary for future disciplinary problems. While this alternative is not a product of the formal disciplinary process, it points to a disciplinary alternative which is frequently used. Supervisory counseling is what one commonly hears referenced as an "oral reprimand."

## Police Department Practices

The departments studied had various disciplinary alternates largely consistent with those desribed above. The exceptions were that very few departments described punitive probation or mandatory training as possible sanctions. Despite this, the authors are familiar with departments which use such sanctions on problem employees on an "informal basis." Alternate penalties found in non-union departments were fines and requiring officers to work regularly scheduled days without pay, or working scheduled days off without pay. Questions arise about the propriety of these penalties in light of various labor laws, nonetheless these sanctions are still applied in several agencies.

# DISCIPLINARY APPEALS

Borrowing from the judicial system's procedures, most police departments in the United States offer some avenue of appeal (or review) of sustained complaints. While appeals have not been directly mandated by minimal due process rights in administrative disciplinary hearings, the implication is clear that some form of review should be available. Police agencies under civil service systems typically have the most formal appellate structure with review often occurring outside of the police administrative structure.

The primary purpose of appeal is to review the facts and evidence to determine if the complaint was properly sustained. Typically in administrative disciplinary appeals cases are not "remanded," the finding is simply reviewed. Some appeals may also review the disciplinary penalty to determine if it is "appropriate." Generally, under civil service regulations, appeals of the disciplinary sanction, (particularly when the appellate mechanism is extra-departmental) will not be reviewed except for termination.

An important personnel question associated with appeals is the point at which the penalty attaches. Should it be following the initial time a complaint is sustained or should the penalty be delayed pending the outcome of the appeal? The issue arises with notable regard to employee rights and the minimal due process afforded during disciplinary cases. Despite these issues, clear trends appear to be that discipline can be imposed immediately after a complaint is sustained. Should administrative appeals prove to be inappropriate to an officer, he/she may resort to civil court action to resolve the issues.

**Table 17.1**

**DISCIPLINARY PROCESS POLICIES**

| CITY | ADJUDICATION SYSTEM | APPEAL | PENALTY IMPOSITION |
|------|---------------------|--------|--------------------|
| Baltimore | Adversarial Trial Board w/ Automatic Review by Police Commissioner all Infractions | No Appeal after Police Commissioner Lawsuits Have Been Pursued By Some Officers | Immediate after Review by Police Commissioner |
| Boston | Minor—Command Discipline By Police Commissioner Serious—Adversarial Hearing | Minor—Hearing Available as Appeal Serious-Police Commission and Civil Service Com. | Immediately |
| Chicago | Various Internal Hearing Panels Depending on Nature of Accusation and Seriousness of Penalty | Police Board Review and Grievance Process Available | Immediately but Some Variation Possible |
| Cleveland | Adversarial System all Infractions | Civil Service Commission and Common Pleas Court | Immediately |
| Dallas | Minor—Command Discipline Serious—Quasi–Adversarial Hearing | Available—Varies Depending on Nature of Charge/Penalty | Immediately |
| Detroit | Minor—Command Discipline Serious—Adversarial Trial Board | Available—Varies Depending on Nature of Charge/Penalty | Immediately |
| Denver | Minor—Command Discipline Serious—Non–Adversarial Hearing Before Chief | Minor—No Appeals Serious—Civil Service Commission | Immediately |
| Honolulu | Minor—Command Discipline by Supervisor Serious—Command Discipline by Supervisor w/ Automatic Review by Chief | Appeal to Department of Civil Service or Discipline Amended through Arbitration With POA | Immediately |
| Houston | Adversarial Hearing for all Infractions | Civil Service Commission | Immediately |
| Kansas City (MO) | Minor—Command Discipline Serious—Board Hearing | Board of Police Commissioners | Immediately |

| Los Angeles | Command Discipline for all Infractions | Appeal to Chief of Police Followed by Arbitration | Immediately |
|---|---|---|---|
| Milwaukee | Non-adversarial Hearing w Review by Chief all Infractions | Board of Fire and Police Commissioners Some Lawsuits Filed as Appeal | Immediately |
| New York | Minor—Command Discipline Serious—Adversarial Hearing | Lawsuit against the City of New York | Immediately |
| Philadelphia | Adversarial Board of Inquiry w/Automatic Review by Police Commissioner, all Infractions | Civil Service Commission | Immediately |
| Phoenix | Minor—Command Discipline Serious—Non-Adversarial Disciplinary Review Board | Civil Service Board for Serious Infractions | Immediately |
| Pittsburgh | Quasi-adversarial Trial Board | Civil Service Commission and City Common Pleas Court | Immediately |
| St. Louis | Minor—Command Discipline Serious—A Complicated Adversarial Trial before Board of Police Commissioners | Board of Police Commissioners is Final Authority Under Missouri Law | Immediately |
| San Diego | Minor—Command Discipline w/Approval of City Manager Serious-Adversarial Internal Hearing | Adversarial Internal Hearing | After Appeal |
| San Francisco | Minor—Command Discipline Serious—Non-adversarial Chief's Hearing | Police Commission | Immediately |
| Washington (DC) | Minor—Command Discipline Serious or Complex-Quasi-adversarial Hearing | Minor—Chief Serious—Arbitration or Internal Review | After Internal Appeals Exhausted |

Generally, before a lawsuit can be filed all internal appeals and remedies must have been exhausted. Furthermore, the suit must typically be based not on an alleged misinterpretation of facts, but on a violation of the officer's rights during some course of the disciplinary proceedings.

## Police Department Practices

Table 17.1 illustrates both the appellate options offered by the different departments and the policies for imposition of the disciplinary penalty. For purposes of interpreting Table 17.1, "minor" and "serious" rule violations have the same meanings as used previously in the discussion of the disciplinary process. Additional definitions for information in the table are:

*Available appeal.* This refers to the fact that a department has an appellate mechanism from the initial disciplinary process, however, the specific nature of that appeal was not clearly articulated in the documents reviewed by the authors.

*Immediate.* Imposition of a penalty is immediately after the initial allegation review (e.g., trial board, hearing, command discipline) finds that the charges against the officer are sustained. The penalty is *not* held in abeyance until after the appeals are exhausted.

On the issue of appeals, all responding departments had some form of appellate mechanism for disciplinary cases. The nature of the appeal varied a great deal depending on civil service regulations applicable to the jurisdiction, state laws, collective bargaining agreements, and preferences of the city and police administration. The trend for appeals was clearly for review outside of the actual police department organizational structure; typically by either a civil service commission or police commission. Only Baltimore, Dallas, and Los Angeles had appeals inside the police command structure.

When asked at what point the discipline was imposed, the overwhelming response was immediately after the initial determination of culpability and before any appeals. (See Table 17.1). Fifteen departments reported immediate imposition of discipline. One department—Baltimore—indicated imposition of discipline immediately after review of the process by the Police Commissioner with Chicago reporting that imposition of sanctions was generally immediate, although some variation was possible. Only three departments—Detroit, San Diego, and Washington—indicated that sanctions would be imposed only after appeals. The irrefutable practice among the police departments studied was to immediately impose disciplinary sanctions; a practice supported by the literature.

In those departments reporting imediate imposition of discipline, information was sought on procedures followed when an officer's culpability for an incident was reversed on appeal. The departments reported that all suspended wages would be immediately paid and that all benefits would be retroactively reinstated. While not determined by the survey, experiences of the author indicate that personnel records are rarely expunged of unfounded or reversed infractions. While the *status* of the complaint will always be recorded in the files (e.g., unfounded sustained, reversed), an actual record is commonly kept in the official personnel record and/or internal affairs confidential files.

## CONCLUSION

This chapter has presented a profile of the police disciplinary process from two perspectives. First, issues and practices identified in the literature have been synthesized into a cohesive five-part model illustrating the fundamental components of a police disciplinary system. Second, the components were operationalized as variables for qualitative analysis in order to articulate the actual practices of 20 major law enforcement agencies.

While variability occurred on a number of procedural points, the departments showed a consensus of major trends in the disciplinary process. Perhaps the most significant factor which affected the structure of a police disciplinary system was the presence of a collective bargaining agreement with a POA. From a historical perspective, the most significant change in police disciplinary practices over the last 20 years is the institutionalization of more explicit due process rights of personnel.

The integration of research and practice, as illustrated in this chapter, permits a realistic view of police management issues which can serve as a guidepost for continuing development in police administrative practices.

# Notes

1    The following definitions are used for policy and procedure throughout this study:
*Policy.* The principles and values which guide the performance of a departmental activity. A policy is not a statement of what must be done in a particular situation. Rather, it is a statement of guiding principles which should be followed in activities which are directed toward the attainment of departmental objectives.
*Procedure.* A method of performing an operation or a manner of directing action in a particular situation to perform a specific task within the guidelines of policy. *Policy* establishes limits of action while *procedure* directs responses within those limits (Carter and Dearth, 1984).

2    For purposes of this study, a rule is defined as a *specific* requirement or prohibition which is stated to prevent deviations, except for stated purposes, from policy or procedure. A regulation is synonymous with rule.

3    As a condition of the contract, the identity of the police department must remain confidential. The department is referred to in this chapter as the Central Department.

4    A growing trend in police departments is the articulation of a "values statement" to guide officer behavior. The Houston Police Department, for example, has an extensive statement of values integrated with the mission statement. (See Chapter 3).

# REFERENCES

Barker, T. and D.L. Carter (eds.) (1986). *Police Deviance*. Cincinnati: Anderson Publishing Co.

Carter, D.L. and D.K. Dearth (1984). "An Assessment of the Mission. Texas Police Department." Unpublished consultants' report.

Carter, D.L. and D. Payne (1986). "An Examination of Practices in Employee Discipline and Procedures Associated With Probationary Police Officers in Detroit, Michigan." Unpublished consultants' report.

Carter, D.L. and D.W. Stephens (1988). *Drug Abuse by Police Officers: An Analysis of Critical Policy Issues*. Springfield, IL: Charles C Thomas, Publisher.

Davis, K.C. (1976). *Administrative Law of the Seventies*. Rochester, NY: Lawyers Cooperative Publishing Co.

*Garrity v. New Jersey,* 385 U.S. 483 (1967).

International Association of Chiefs of Police. (1976). *Managing for Effective Police Discipline*. Gaithersburg, MD: International Association of Chiefs of Police.

McGregor, D. (1960). *The Human Side of Enterprise*. New York: McGraw-Hill.

Swanson, C.R., L. Territo, and R. Taylor (1988). *Police Administration*. 2d ed. New York: Macmillan Publishing Co.

# Study Questions

1. What is the purpose of discipline—punishment or instruction? Support your position.

2. Why do police departments have so many different types of disciplinary systems? What are the strengths and weaknesses of these differences?

3. Design what you feel would be a "model" police disciplinary system. Explain each step in the process.

4. What is the difference between an adversarial and non-adversarial police disciplinary hearing? Which system do you feel is better? Why?

5. What rights do police officers have during the disciplinary process? Should those rights be extended or limited?

# 18

# INVESTIGATION AND REVIEW OF COMPLAINTS AGAINST POLICE OFFICERS: AN OVERVIEW OF ISSUES AND PHILOSOPHIES*

## Paul West

The power and authority which society have invested in the police ensure that officers' actions are subjected to close scrutiny by, amongst other groups, the media, lawyers, civil rights organizations, and the public in general. Procedures which ensure that citizens who are not satisfied by the standard of service provided by individual officers, or by the police as an organization, are entitled to have their complaints investigated (although details of the procedures vary from department to department).

Occasionally, well-publicized flagrant abuses of authority by officers who appear to have escaped without punishment cast doubt upon the integrity of complaints investigation procedures.

In such an environment, senior police managers are faced with the problem of developing and implementing a procedure for investigating citizen complaints against officers of their department, a process which must be thorough and impartial, and equally acceptable to the officers themselves, to members of the public, and to local political leaders and pressure groups.

## EXTERNAL VERSUS INTERNAL REVIEW— THE BACKGROUND

Ever since the first Internal Affairs Units (IAUs) were established in the USA during the 1940s, the subject of investigation of complaints against the police has been a major topic of public debate. The controversy has not, however, been concerned with any suggestions that investigating citizen complaints of police malpractice is an unnecessary and wasteful utilization of scarce public resources. On the contrary, all interest groups and writers who have addressed themselves to the issue have, without exception, agreed that citizen complaints against individual officers should be fully investigated. The factor which has created the debate

---

*This chapter was written expressly for inclusion in this book.*

is the form which this review of an officer's actions should take. In broad terms, the debate has centered around whether the investigation of alleged malpractice by officers should be investigated internally within the police department or externally by some other body independent of the police.

It has been argued that, whatever the investigative procedures are, public confidence, vital to an effective police department, can be fostered by a well-publicized and well-organized complaints investigation system (Beral and Sisk, 1964:500). The opposite situation occurs when an investigative unit, out of concern for the reputation of the police department, employs reprehensible tactics to discourage citizens from filing complaints against officers. In the early 1960s, cases were documented in which IAUs threatened complainants with criminal libel in New York City, demanded that they take a polygraph test in Cleveland, and charged them with various public order offenses in Philadelphia, Washington, D.C., and Los Angeles. In other words, the investigative units behaved as if the complainants rather than the officers were on trial, (Niederhoffer, 1967:284). Attitudes and actions such as these can only harm police-community relations. However, without any quantitative data available which relates police-community relations to methods utilized for investigating citizen complaints against the police, writers have only been able to express their opinions on the nature of the relationship between the two factors. Whilst it is logical to argue that a good investigative system will give rise to good police-community relations (Beral and Sisk, 1964:516; Radclet, 1986), the negative argument that a less-than-good investigative system will give rise to less-than-good police-community relations is more reasonable, pragmatic, and realistic.

Most police departments, aware of constant community tensions, do everything within their power to prevent worsening of police-community relations. A serious consideration of the ways in which their complaints investigation procedures are viewed by the general public is therefore a crucial step in this process.

One important point which is all too frequently overlooked is that, even allowing for the aggressive tactics described above which are sometimes utilized by recipients of complaints, the volume of reported complaints in most jurisdictions is not great considering the number of police involved (Barton, 1970:450; Cray, 1972:255-257). Therefore, it might reasonably be inferred that poor police-community relations arising from citizen complaints against the police are associated not so much with the number of complaints made as it is with the way in which they are investigated.

It is perhaps surprising to discover that, in the wake of the collapse of the New York City Civilian Complaint Review Board (CCRB) in 1966, after only four months' operation, The President's Commission on Law Enforcement and Administration of Justice took the apparently naive view that:

> The Police Review Board should never have been the central issue;
> Police Review Boards are only symptomatic of a much more serious

matter, ie: the loss of confidence by the public in some police forces. It is the loss of confidence which is the central issue in the controversy (Field Survey V 1967:296-297).

The President's Commission did not, however, totally adopt an ostrich stance on the effect of perceived shortcomings in police departments' IAUs on public confidence in the police. The Commission recommended, albeit reluctantly, that in those communities where it was obvious that even revised and improved internal review procedures would not restore public confidence, measures to establish some form of external review should be taken.

The development, during the late 1950s and the 1960s, of a number of external review mechanisms to monitor citizen complaints against the police, either in addition to or as replacements for existing internal review mechanisms, whatever else it achieved, certainly led to a polarization of opinions on the issue by the end of the 1960s. These opinions and their related arguments have, despite the passage of time, remained largely unchanged to the present day, and have been cataloged by a number of writers (Beral and Sisk, 1964; Cray, 1972; Terrill, 1982; Walker, 1983; as well as various reports of the U.S. Civil Rights Commission and hearings before the House Subcommittee on Criminal Justice). The arguments themselves are worthy of consideration and analysis, however, it is useful to first discuss the early attempts at complaints investigation, followed by the major event which gave rise to the polarization of views.

## Investigation of Complaints in the Early 1960s

The first major attempt to identify the various methods utilized to investigate citizen complaints against the police was undertaken by Beral and Sisk in a classic article published in the *Harvard Law Review* in 1964. At the time of writing, complaints against the police were only administered by civilian groups in two cities: Philadelphia, since 1958, and Rochester, N.Y., since 1963. Consequently, most of Beral and Sisk's discussion focused upon the differences in the organization of internal mechanisms for complaints investigation within some 200 of the larger police departments.

Three basic types of investigative mechanisms were found to exist— local supervisor investigation, local supervisor investigation supplemented by a specific unit within the police department (for example, Internal Affairs), and investigation exclusively by a specific unit within the police department.

The advantage of local supervisor investigation was that it was believed to heighten the awareness of supervisors of the specific actions of officers under their command which tended to generate friction and cause citizens to complain;

the disadvantage was that it was felt that many supervisors could have a great interest in covering up violations, both to shield their friends and favored officers and to conceal their own shortcomings.

In police departments with an Internal Affairs Unit (IAU), invariably it was found that all complaints made against officers of the departments were initially forwarded to the IAU for central recording. Officers of the IAU then generally had broad discretion in deciding whether to investigate the allegation themselves, which they would normally do in potentially serious or complex cases, or whether to refer the complaint to the accused officer's immediate supervisor for investigation. In the latter case, the supervisor's completed investigation report would be returned to the IAU for examination. As an added deterrent to biased investigation, in some departments IA officers would reinvestigate at random some of the cases which had initially been referred to officers' supervisors.

Two advantages of this two-tiered mechanism over the simple local investigation were the degree of independence and impartiality which the IAU provided, together with its apparatus which could handle large scale investigations beyond either the capability or the time and resources of officers' immediate supervisors.

Beral and Sisk's survey reported that, in 1964, less than 5 percent of the police departments in their sample relied exclusively upon a special unit—Internal Affairs—to investigate citizens' complaints. Arguments against IAUs were based mainly on practical problems of limited resources. Departments argued that they found it difficult to justify the creation of a separate unit which would effectively remove a number of officers from 'real policing.' Arguments in favor of IAUs stressed the potential of a separate unit to gain investigative experience, develop more objectivity, and convey to the community the impression that police departments gave serious attention to the processing of citizen complaints.

## CIVILIAN REVIEW IN ITS INFANCY

The concept of civilian review of complaints against the police dates from the 1950s and was initially prompted by a belief in certain quarters that the existing means for seeking redress against police misconduct were ineffective (Goldstein, 1977: 157). It is popularly assumed to include the participation of individuals representing a cross section of the community, and to be established and operated externally to the police department (Walker, 1983: 237). In practice, the first attempts at civilian review varied in type, ranging from civilian-dominated boards sitting externally to the police department to committees and offices established within the police department, but including citizen representation. The earliest Civilian Review Boards (CRBs) also operated with varying degrees of success.

In 1967, the President's Commission compared four CRBs which had been operating prior to that time. It concluded that they had generally been seen to be toothless bodies, having little power and only advisory capacities. The advice which they had been entitled to give, however, had varied. In Philadelphia (established in 1958) and Rochester (established in 1963), the boards' advice could include specific recommendations for disciplinary action to be taken against officers who had been found responsible for malpractice. One result of this was that both boards were regularly involved in litigation and injunctions initiated by police officers' associations. In New York City (established in 1966) and Washington, D.C. (established in 1948), however, the boards' powers were severely limited and they were not empowered to give views on the merits of cases. Effectively, their only jurisdiction was in making recommendations regarding whether a hearing should be held or not. Indeed, Washington D.C.'s early attempt at civilian review can only very loosely be described as such, since it was very heavily criticized for its inactivity. It seems clear that the vast majority of the public, and perhaps even of the members of the police department, were unaware of its existence (Task Force, 1967: 200-202; U.S. Commission on Civil Rights, 1981: 125). Other early efforts to establish CRBs in York, Pennsylvania and in Minneapolis, Minnesota, both in 1960, never left the drawing board.

Of the above early attempts at civilian review, two boards, those in Philadelphia and New York City, provoked the most interest at the time and the most literature since. It is useful to consider their respective histories in some detail.

## The Philadelphia Police Advisory Board (PAB)

The Philadelphia Police Advisory Board (PAB) was formed in 1958 directly as a result of the election of a new reforming mayor. The Board members, initially five but subsequently increased to eight, were all members of the public appointed by the mayor, usually including at least one sociologist, criminologist, or other person with a legal background. The only salaried staff member was the executive secretary who was responsible, amongst other things, for receiving complaints and interviewing complainants. The first executive secretary was an attorney, succeeded in 1963 by a black minister. The Board did not have its own investigative staff. Consequently, its only alternative courses of action during the investigation process were either for the executive secretary to attempt to resolve the matter informally, a course of action which was undertaken quite regularly (Beral and Sisk, 1964: 514), or to refer the investigation to the Philadelphia police commissioner who would then direct his community relations division to look into the matter.

Following an investigation undertaken by the community relations division of the police department, the completed police report would be studied by a legal subcommittee of the Board who would decide whether a hearing was warranted.

If it was concluded that a hearing was appropriate, then generally the complainant and the accused officer would both be represented by counsel, and the hearing would be adversarial in nature. Nevertheless, efforts were made to ensure that the hearings were as informal as possible, and to this end the rules of evidence were relaxed. The decision of the Board was based on a majority vote, but normally no formal opinion would be written regarding this decision. Following hearings in which the case was found proved against the officer, the Board would send its recommendation of disciplinary sanction to both the police commissioner and the mayor. The police commissioner would normally follow the Board's recommendations, but if there were any disagreement, the mayor would informally arbitrate the decision. Effectively, then, the mayor had the final say on the disciplinary recommendation (Hudson, 1971: 530-532; Brown, 1985: 149-150).

Writing in 1964, six years into the Board's life, Beral and Sisk (1964: 515) argued that the most serious obstacle to its attempts to win citizens' confidence in its independence and impartiality had been its necessary reliance, due mainly to budgetary restrictions, upon the police to investigate the complaints themselves. Another problem was the disappointingly low number of complaints being lodged with the Board, given that one of the major reasons for its establishment had been the belief that many potential complaints were not being made because of fear of police reprisals and distrust in the previous purely internal investigation procedure. Additionally, many people considered that the Board's recommendations for disciplinary sanctions were even more lenient than those which the police themselves would have initiated. Overall, however, perhaps the most fundamental weakness of the Philadelphia Advisory Board was that it existed entirely at the discretion of the mayor.

During the PAB's nine year existence, 20 percent of complaints were handled through the informal process by the executive secretary and approximately the same proportion resulted in a Board hearing. Of the cases heard by the Board, approximately one-third resulted in a finding of guilt and a disciplinary recommendation. The number of complaints made to the PAB averaged something in the region of 100 per year, a disproportionate number of which were filed by members of minority groups (Task Force, 1967: 200).

During its stormy lifetime, the PAB was subjected to a number of lawsuits by police officer's associations including the Fraternal Order of Police (FOP). One of these, concerned with a departmental regulation compelling personnel to submit to polygraph tests during internal investigations being carried out on behalf of the PAB, stopped the Board's activities and brought about certain procedural changes following the temporary stoppage. A second injunction effectively suspended the Board's activities indefinitely until a new mayor was elected. The new mayor's opposition to any form of civilian review of the police brought about the Board's sudden and largely unlamented demise (Hudson, 1971: 525-527; Halpern, 1974: 562-565; Brown, 1985: 150).

## The New York City Civilian Complaint Review Board (CCRB)

Allegations of officer misconduct in the New York City Police Department (NYCPD) during the 1950s reached such a peak that, at one point, the Justice Department threatened to conduct its own investigation of the department if the situation did not improve. Against this background in the early 1960s, as the civil rights movement gained momentum, the issue of police misconduct became even more explosive (Walker, 1983: 237). Sensing popular dissatisfaction with the situation, a new reforming mayor introduced civilian review as an issue in his election campaign, and subsequently founded the New York Civilian Complaint Review Board (CCRB) in the summer of 1966. The new CCRB was effectively a transformation of a previously existing internal police review board and consequently, as a concession to police opponents of the new board, the mayor decided that its membership should not be entirely civilian. In the end, the Board was made up of seven members: four civilians appointed by the mayor and three police officials appointed by the police commissioner. Civilians were thus in a majority on the new CCRB. The Board also had a strong ethnic minority representation, two blacks and one Puerto Rican being included in the original four civilian appointees. All four civilians were full-time salaried staff and, although they, like their counterparts in Philadelphia, had to rely upon police officers to carry out investigations on their behalf, the arrangement was unusual in the sense that the investigating officers had no other duties and worked exclusively for the Board. In effect then, rather than representing true civilian review of the complaints investigation procedure, establishment of the New York City CCRB simply resulted in jurisdiction over complaints being shifted within the police department, although civilians were now involved in the process (Brown, 1985: 151).

Conciliation, undertaken by the Board's assistant director, was attempted whenever possible, usually in situations where an officer was clearly guilty of either mistaken action or neglect, but where the damage to the complainant had been minimal. Where this conciliation process was inappropriate, an investigation would be commenced, following the conclusion of which the Board would meet to study the report and decide whether or not to hold a hearing. Hearings, similar to the arrangement in Philadelphia, were usually adversarial in nature, involving counsel for both parties, but again, the rules of evidence were relaxed. The hearing board always consisted of an odd number of members of the CCRB with the civilian members in the majority. Decisions were based upon a majority vote but, unlike in Philadelphia, if the case was found proved against the officer, the CCRB was not empowered to recommend a specific disciplinary action. Discipline was retained as being the sole responsibility of the police commissioner, in consultation with the mayor when appropriate. Hearings of cases had to be held within 20 days of the receipt by the CCRB of the completed investigation report (Hudson, 1971:529-530).

For reasons which will be discussed later, New York City's CCRB experienced a highly publicized and stormy short life of only four months, but in that time it received over 400 complaints, twice as many as the police department's internal complaint review board had previously been averaging in a whole year. Nearly half of the complaints involved allegations of unnecessary force (Cray, 1972: 319). Of the 146 complaints which were fully disposed of by the Board prior to its abolition, 11 were outside of the Board's jurisdiction and were referred elsewhere, 21 were conciliated, 109 were found to be unsubstantiated after investigation, and in one case the officer concerned received a reprimand. In only four instances were charges against the officer recommended by the Board (Task Force, 1967: 201).

As had already been the case with the Philadelphia PAB, the New York City CCRB faced constant opposition from the police. The unofficial, but extremely powerful Fraternal Order of Police (FOP) was enraged by the idea of a civilian majority on the Board and saw the activities of the CCRB not as a constructive attempt to improve community relations, but as unwarranted interference in police affairs. Their efforts and their anti-CCRB publicity, initially taking the form of a 500,000 signature petition and a police picket of City Hall, eventually resulted in the issue of the CCRB being put to the ballot in a referendum of the city population in November, 1966. The result of the referendum was a three to one vote against the Board, which was immediately abolished, after only four months of operation, and was replaced by a police-dominated review board which, with slight changes made since, continues to exist today (Cray, 1972:319; Hudson, 1971:524-25; Walker, 1983:239).

The success and impact of Philadelphia's PAB and New York City's CCRB are difficult to evaluate, particularly in the case of New York given the Board's limited lifetime. Nevertheless, as mentioned earlier, if they achieved nothing else, these two boards served to polarize opinions on the issue of investigation of complaints against the police towards the end of the 1960s.

## POLARIZED OPINIONS BEGIN TO EMERGE

Those who opposed the existing internal review mechanisms were drawn mainly from civil rights and civil liberties organizations. They cited evidence of a general loss of confidence among large sections of the population in the effectiveness of internal departmental procedures for reviewing police misconduct to support their arguments for a more balanced and genuinely accountable system. Those who supported the *status quo* were drawn mainly from police associations and conservative groups who occasionally hinted that their opponents were, in part, a manifestation of a "Communist Conspiracy" (Hudson, 1971:517; Cray, 1972:321). Despite having accepted the evidence of past failings of internal review mechanisms, these groups saw the way ahead towards redressing the balance in investigations to be reliant upon improved existing internal procedures together with more professional personnel systems.

(Describing internal review as the status quo in the mid-1960s is not strictly accurate since, in 1967, the President's Commission on Law Enforcement and the Administration of Justice reported that, of those departments which dealt with civilian complaints against the police, half had no special unit to carry out this function.)

Because of the polarizing effect which the emerging arguments were tending to have on opinions, a number of writers in the late 1960s and the early 1970s began searching for some middle ground in the debate. The result was that they settled upon the concept of a police ombudsman.

## Proposals for a Police Ombudsman

The police ombudsman proposal was presented by the President's Commission in 1967, but was initially ignored because the entrenched polar opinions which had developed were generally concerned with CRBs and avoided the issue of an ombudsman altogether.

The ombudsman proposals were originally based upon the Scandinavian system, in which the ombudsman is an executive officer of the highest prestige and integrity whose powers are limited to investigating and criticizing public agencies in direct response to complaints from private citizens. The ideal police ombudsman was therefore seen as being an individual who would rely upon moral authority to enforce recommendations and who would only resort to publishing such recommendations upon determining that, following an investigation, the chief executive of the police agency involved would not adopt the course of action which had been suggested. Certain writers urged that consideration be given to the creation of an ombudsman to investigate complaints against all agencies of government, and not just against police departments (Sharpley, 1969:16). Others put forward proposals for an organizational ombudsman—as far as the police were concerned, merely the CRB wolf in sheep's clothing—but these proposals were not well received. An organizational ombudsman would, it was argued, lack most of the advantages of the office of ombudsman whilst retaining most of the disadvantages of the CRB. Disunity in a board comprising members of various interest groups would be counterproductive to the requirement of impartiality in the office of ombudsman. Furthermore, a group would be unable to apply moral authority in enforcing their recommendations with an agency chief in the same way as a single executive official of high integrity potentially could (Sharpley, 1969:16).

The police ombudsman based upon the Scandinavian model would be an advocate of the people; he/she would have no authority to award damages, only authority to bring about reforms. Any financial compensation sought would have to be obtained through the courts. The ombudsman would need to be an official above politics, widely respected and impartial, and only concerned with satisfying valid complaints through the power to effect reforms. An important distinction was made between an ombudsman who would rely on legal authority and the CRBs which in the past had depended upon public pressure (Cray, 1972:327).

In the politically charged public sector, concern was given to the problem of how such an ombudsman would achieve independence from political control. Selection by the legislature, preferably not by a partisan vote but on the basis of an all-party concensus, was proposed as one possibility. At the municipal level a number of other alternatives were suggested, each having its own unique and unusual features. One such suggestion involved the appointment being made by the mayor and the council for a term overlapping that of the mayor; another involved the appointment being made from a list provided by a respected group of informed citizens, such as the heads of local universities or colleges (Barton, 1970:468).

The 1970s therefore arrived with a number of variations on the theme of external review of complaints investigation having been proposed and indeed implemented with varying degrees of success. The major problem was not to invent new ideas or proposals, but how to persuade those people whose lives would potentially be affected most by the proposals, the police themselves, that the new ideas were worthy of consideration.

## Police Unions and External Review

Traditionally, opposition to CRBs and indeed any form of external review, has been one of the major rallying points of police unions and associations in their efforts to organize their members. Their vigorous campaigns in the courts, in the political arena, and through public relations campaigns, have forewarned citizen groups, police administrators and politicians who have favored external review that, if proposed, the issue would be strongly contested (Halpern, 1974:569; Lynch and Diamond, 1983:1164).

Their major arguments have been based upon the beliefs that police officers possess unique skills, training, and experience which makes it impossible for civilians to make sound decisions regarding police behavior. Such beliefs can contribute towards maintaining high morale amongst officers, which is in itself often seen as a fundamental indicator of an effective police organization. Line officers thus assert that review boards staffed by laymen will severely threaten morale and that, in consequence, officers may feel restrained from taking necessary and justifiable actions in their duties when dealing with members of the public (Hudson, 1971:521). Civilian review would thus undermine officers' professionalism.

The unions' arguments based upon their advocacy of employee rights for line level and first line supervisory personnel have argued the need to have input on complaint review mechanism. Police senior administrators, through the vehicle of the International Association of Chiefs of Police (IACP), have long argued that one of the major features of the professional status which they desire for their organizations is the autonomy of chief officers in disciplinary matters. Consequently, they have sought the types of purely internal control mechanisms already exercised by the medical and legal professions (Halpern, 1974:570; Walker, 1983:242-243). As in any profession, they argue, discipline of deviant members comes properly and most effectively from fellow members of the profession. The argument that adequate public accountability is already provided by locally elected officials, the courts, prosecutors, the FBI, and Justice Department through Civil Rights complaints has also been popular (Leonard and More, 1971:92).

In this context of concerted police opposition throughout all ranks towards the notion of external review, looking back upon the demise of the New York City CCRB and the Philadelphia PAB, a number of comparisons can be made. Both the CCRB and the PAB were products of liberal reform politics, each being established at times of public concern over the use of excessive force and the alleged denials of civil rights by police officers. In Philadelphia, the creation of the Board was one of a number of reforms introduced to improve the efficiency and accountability of local government following more than 60 years of one-party (republican) rule. In New York City, on the other hand, civilian review was introduced as a political issue in the 1965 mayoral campaign, largely in an attempt to capture the black vote, since external review represented a promise of an opportunity to redress long-standing grievances against the police (Hudson, 1971:527-528; Bouza, 1985:253). (In a third case, in McAllen, Texas a quasi-civilian review board—called the Police Human Relations Committee—was part of a Civil Rights injunction against the police department to open avenues for complaints and reviews, notably for Hispanics who had been abused by police.)

Just as similar considerations led to the establishment of the PAB and CCRB, similar political decisions brought about their defeats. The opposition in both cities was a well-mobilized interest group orchestrated by the police officers' associations (Bouza, 1985:253-254). It is certainly true to say that, at least in the case of New York City and Philadelphia in the 1960s, supporters of civilian review were never as single-minded in their dedication to maintaining it as the police were to defeating it (Hudson, 1971:528).

The early experiences of these two cities bring into focus the major problem facing any administration making any attempt at introducing some form of external review of the police, that of establishing a review mechanism which will be acceptable both to the community and to the police officers involved. On the one hand, officers feel that they are betrayed when their actions are being scrutinized by outsiders, and on the other hand, citizens feel that police solidarity effectively prevents any satisfactory form of redress. In jurisdictions within which police-community relations have been damaged to the extent that little confidence and credibility is enjoyed by the existing complaints investigation procedure, any delays in introducing new procedures which aim to satisfy both parties can only serve to magnify the problem and lead to an increased polarization of views.

## INTERNAL AFFAIRS UNITS DURING THE 1970S

The increasing controversy surrounding investigation of citizen complaints against the police continued to grow during the 1970s, the flames periodically being fanned by examples of police excesses apparently going unpunished, spawning a number of further variations on the theme of civilian review. However, those police departments which continued to strongly resist the idea of being subjected to any form of external review, the vast majority of departments in fact, were still preoccupied with increasing their professionalism, and were looking for ways to improve their internal review mechanisms, either by modifying the roles of existing IAUs or through creating new Units in departments which did not already have them (Wilson and McLaren, 1977:212).

One such attempt at increased professionalism was made in 1974 by the new Police Chief of Tampa, Florida. Consideration of the influences involved in the establishment of a new IAU in that department helps to give an indication of the prevailing views on internal review procedures at that time.

### Establishing and Staffing an IAU in the Mid-1970s

Prior to 1974, internal investigations within the Tampa Police Department, had, at best, been disorganized and inconsistent due both to the lack of an IAU and the absence of written policies and procedures setting down investigative guidelines. Having decided that the creation of an IAU was essential, the new police chief undertook a survey of departments of similar size in an effort to acquire information which would help him to create a Unit with two clear goals. First, he required a Unit which would be well-organized and scrupulously fair and impartial in its investigations. Second, he wanted the unit to have the trust and respect both of the community and the members of the police department (Territo and Smith, 1976:66).

From the research carried out with other departments, the following factors emerged, all four of which were generally considered in police circles to be essential features in the selection process for staffing an IAU:

1. All personnel serving in an IAU must be volunteers; the nature and sensitivity of the work involved was generally considered to make it

both unwise and unfair to assign someone to Internal Affair's duties who was not happy with the idea.

2. Personnel must have demonstrated in their previous police performance that they possess a high degree of investigative skills.

3. Personnel must have excellent reputations amongst their peers and supervisors with regard to integrity and overall police performance; specifically, they must not themselves have been found guilty of serious official misconduct in the past.

4. Personnel must have a knowledge and understanding of the various ethnic minorities in the local community since, for a number of complex social, political, and economic reasons, past experience has shown that many citizen complaints will be initiated by members of these groups (Territo and Smith, 1976:68).

In the case of the new Tampa IAU, in addition to complying with the four generally agreed essential criteria listed above, three further specific decisions were made which helped to shape the Unit. These are also worthy to note:

(a) Investigators would serve in the Unit for a maximum period of two years so as to minimize the possibility of alienation of officers within the Unit from the rest of their colleagues, and also to foster acceptance and respect for the IAU through greater employee participation in it.

(b) A polygraph would be utilized in complaint cases when, following a complete investigation, a final decision was not possible because, due to the lack of independent witnesses to the event which had provoked the complaint, it could not be established which party was being untruthful. Refusal to submit to the polygraph test on the part of the officer could lead to dismissal in a serious case, although there was no such serious potential consequence for a complainant who might refuse to submit to the test.

(c) In 1973 the National Advisory Commission on Criminal Justice Standards and Goals had recommended (p. 479) that police departments should publish statistics, although not complete details, of internal discipline case disposition on a regular basis, in order to dispel allegations of disciplinary secrecy voiced in certain elements of the community. Tampa chose to act upon this recommendation by distributing a monthly summary of activities of the IAU both to the community and within the police department (Territo and Smith, 1976:68).

The mid-1970s thus saw new IAUs emerging. They were staffed by individuals who were involved in the work out of choice and who were committed to the ideal of police professionalism. Investigators would be of unchallenged integrity with unblemished past records and would undergo training in community and minority relations. Typically, they would be experienced detectives who would complete two years of service within the Units prior to being transferred back to operational duties. IAUs normally worked directly for the chiefs of the department, and consequently, being offered a transfer into Internal Affairs was seen as an indication of approval of an officer by the Chief himself. The IAU being staffed by such individuals, the Chief had nothing to fear from publicizing the disposition of cases by the Unit, since he/she was satisfied that, if challenged, the Chief could point to the undisputed abilities, qualities, and integrity of the IAU staff in order to dispel any allegations of unprofessionalism and dubious practices. It was argued that IAUs staffed and organized along these lines were effective mechanisms of accountability as long as they had the full support of their chief officers with regard to recommendations for disciplinary action and public statements of commitment to thoroughly investigate alleged deviant behavior by officers. Conversely, the effectiveness of IAUs would be undermined in those cases where, despite misconduct by the officer having been proven, the chief officers chose not to impose disciplinary sanctions (Goldstein, 1976: 40-41).

The first major attempt at an international study of police complaints procedures was undertaken in 1978, following which the writer concluded that the majority of police departments still processed complaints entirely internally (Russell, 1978). Whilst no indication was given of the proportion of American police departments which contained specialized IAUs or similar units exclusively used for complaints investigation, four principal variants of the internal system were identified:

1. investigation at local level in which the matter is disposed of entirely by the local commander.

2. investigation at local level subject to external supervision and scrutiny by a senior officer at headquarters.

3. investigation of minor complaints at local level, supplemented by specialist department investigation of serious matters.

4. investigation exclusively by a specialist department (Russell, 1978: 40).

It is interesting to note that these four subsystems are very similar, if not identical to the categories of internal review which had been identified over a decade earlier (Beral and Sisk, 1964). The indication is that, although efforts had been made over the intervening years to professionalize the staffing of IAUs, as far as the procedures themselves were concerned, very little had changed.

If the staffing, but not the procedures of internal review mechanisms, had changed during the 1970s, then what changes were apparent in the field of external review?

## EXTERNAL REVIEW DURING THE 1970s

Whilst the number of new external boards which were established during the 1970s was still minimal in comparison with the number of police departments in the USA, nevertheless some significant successes were achieved. Several of these newly created bodies have been well-documented and are to be described below. It is interesting to note at this point that their establishment was not generally greeted with the outcry and furor which had been typical in the 1960s. This is not, however, to be taken as an indication of reduced police opposition. In reality, their relatively smooth inceptions were more attributable to the fact that the various boards were not such political footballs as their predecessors had been in the 1960s. Additionally, in general they were much more carefully and considerately introduced following, in some cases, extremely lengthy negotiations with police associations and unions. In effect, the boards of the 1970s were carefully legit- imized prior to their creation rather than hastily thrust upon hostile and resistant police departments. That they have generally continued to function to the present day is in some measure due to the personalities and police chiefs involved, but, more importantly, is largely due to the preparatory groundwork which was under- taken prior to their establishment.

A brief description of the functions and roles of the most well-known exter- nal review bodies created during the 1970s (and two during the early 1980s) follows. The agencies are listed chronologically with respect to their dates of establishment.

## Kansas City's Office of Civilian Complaints (OCC)

Kansas City's Office of Civilian Complaints (OCC), established in 1970 and staffed by five civilians, operates from an office which is physically separate from the police headquarters. It acts as a central clearinghouse for all citizens' com- plaints, whether made directly to the OCC or to the police department. Following initial receipt of the complaint, the director of the OCC may either choose to attempt to conciliate the matter which, if carried out successfully, leads to the case being closed, or he/she may decide to forward the case to the police department's

IAU for investigation. Completed investigation reports are returned from the police department to the OCC for review and analysis, and at this stage the OCC director is empowered, if he/she is not satisfied with the quality of the investigation, to require that additional work be done by the police investigators. Having made a determination on the case, the OCC staff and director then forward their recommendation to the police chief. This recommendation merely constitutes a suggested disposition of the case; authority for selecting and imposing disciplinary sanctions has remained with the police chief, who normally involves the police supervisory staff in the process of identifying an appropriate sanction in cases where the complaint has been found to be sustained. In practice, the OCC director is very rarely dissatisfied with the quality of the police investigation, and similarly, the police chief rarely disagrees with the OCC recommendation (Perez, 1978: 319-314; US Commission on Civil Rights, 1981: 125; Walker, 1983: 239; Kerstetter, 1985: 165-166).

One additional point worthy of note with respect to the Kansas City OCC is that, whilst the appointment of a former police officer as OCC Director undoubtedly helped to allay police fears about the new agency, this decision may have been an obstacle in convincing the public of the Office's independence (Walker, 1983:233).

## San Jose's Ombudsman

An Ombudsman's office was created in San Jose in 1971, partly in response to community pressure for some form of external review of the police following a series of allegations of serious malpractice. In common with the Scandinavian model, the San Jose Ombudsman's responsibilities are not merely restricted to reviewing the police department, since the office reviews complaints regarding all municipal government agencies. Complaints against the police may either be filed with the police department's own IAU or with the Ombudsman. In the former case, the Ombudsman does not carry out a full investigation, but is empowered to monitor the internal police enquiry; in the latter case a copy of the complaint is forwarded to the IAU by the Ombudsman and both agencies carry out parallel investigations, the results of which in practice are invariably the same. Only limited use has been made of the traditional ombudsman capacity to mediate complaints (Kerstetter, 1985: 166-167).

Research has shown that, despite its independence from the police department, the San Jose Ombudsman has not been able to overcome community skepticism regarding the impartiality of the office. The most likely cause of this is that the office of ombudsman, having limited tradition in the USA, is generally regarded as constituting yet another branch of municipal government, and consequently is seen as an institution which should rightly be viewed with a fair degree of suspicion (Perez, 1978: 383).

## Berkeley's Police Review Commission (PRC)

During the 1960s, the campus of the University of California at Berkeley became established as a popular meeting center for demonstrations concerning a wide range of issues. Riots resulting from the disintegration of demonstrations were regular occurrences, usually accompanied by serious injuries sustained by a number of demonstrators at the hands of the police. The situation proved to be a fertile environment for proposals of civilian review of the police, which were initially voted on and defeated in 1971 by the Berkeley electorate, but, with subsequent amendments, were passed by a second vote in 1973.

Created in 1973, the Berkeley Police Review Commission (PRC) both investigates and holds hearings on citizen complaints against the police. It is a nine-member commission, each member of the Berkeley City Council appointing one commissioner. Commissioners serve for two-year terms and are part-time and unsalaried, but the PRC does employ two of its own full-time salaried investigators, and therefore does not need to rely upon the police department for the investigative process. The Berkeley Police Department has, however, retained its own Internal Affairs Bureau (IAB) so that citizens have the option to pursue redress of their grievance using either avenue (Kerstetter, 1985: 161). In practice, citizens generally seem to favor notifying the IAB rather than the PRC when making complaints. (During 1985 and 1986 a total of approximately 100 complaints were filed with the PRC whilst the number filed with Internal Affairs in the same period was nearer 250.) Both agencies notify each other regarding complaints which have been filed with them, but whilst the IAB will investigate all complaints regardless of where they were filed, the PRC only investigates those complaints initially filed with them. If, however, a complainant is not satisfied with the disposition of a complaint filed with and investigated by the IAB, they can appeal the case to the PRC for further investigation.

Generally, because of operational advantages and free accessibility to officers and personnel information, which the PRC does not enjoy, the IAB tends to complete its investigations first. Indeed, on occasions difficulties experienced by the PRC investigators resulted in Berkeley's 120-day limit on complaints investigations passing without a satisfactory resolution having been arrived at by the PRC.

Whatever the outcome of its investigation and hearing, Commission findings are only advisory for the benefit of the city manager, the Chief of Police, and the city council. If there is a discrepancy between the PRC finding and the IAB finding, then the city manager will access the two investigations and mediate with the Chief of Police with regard to recommended discipline. In practice, such discrepancies are rare events (Terrill, 1982:404).

## Detroit's Board of Police Commissioners

In 1974 the city of Detroit established a Board of Police Commissioners (BPC), the five members of which are mayoral appointees, to oversee a range of policies and procedures of the police department, including the investigation of citizen complaints. To handle complaints of police misconduct the Board created the Office of the Chief Investigator (OCI). The 12 civilians who staff the OCI perform legal, investigative, and clerical duties on behalf of the Board.

The Board of Police Commissioners handle three types of citizen complaints: original complaints, reviews, and appeals. All original complaints, wherever they are filed, are forwarded to the executive secretary of the BPC, and those which cannot be resolved informally are subsequently referred to the OCI. The OCI staff will then either refer the case for investigation to the supervisory staff of the police officer concerned, to the police department's Professional Standards Section (the equivalent of an IAU), or they will investigate it themselves. In the case of investigations which are referred to the police department, which in practice constitute the majority, the OCI has a monitoring role in the procedure. Complaint reviews are carried out by the OCI in cases where the complainant believes that either some error or omission has affected the outcome of the case. Complaint appeals are administered by the OCI in cases where it is established that there are sufficient grounds to warrant a complete reinvestigation.

Upon completion of all three investigative processes, the Director of the OCI decides upon case disposition and forwards, where appropriate, a recommendation on disciplinary action via the Board of Police Commissioners to the Chief of Police. The Board has the additional authority to review and either set aside or affirm disciplinary sanctions imposed by the Chief (U.S. Commission on Civil Rights, 1981: 125-126; Terrill, 1982: 404-405; Walker, 1983: 239-240).

While it may appear that the Detroit Board of Police Commissioners is an extremely powerful body, it has been pointed out that, in practice, the peculiarities of Detroit's present political system ensure that its power is strictly limited. On one hand, the formal disciplinary process in Detroit is governed by the collective bargaining contract established between the city and the police union. Imposition of discipline can only follow a separate fact-finding process, outlined in the collective bargaining agreement, which guarantees due process for the individual officer (Walker, 1983:240). On the other hand, the Board works well in Detroit because its recommendations are invariably in step with the views of both the present mayor and the present Police Chief. The city charter which established the Board allows the mayor to remove a commissioner at any time for any reason, and it might therefore be argued that members of the Board are consequently restricted from making decisions of any importance with which the mayor disagrees (Pomeroy, 1985:186).

## Chicago's Office of Professional Standards (OPS)

The extent of police brutality and abuse of authority in Chicago had been a major issue throughout the 1960s, but the community outcry, fueled by numerous reports in the Chicago newspapers of blatant officer misconduct, only really became audible to the politicians in the early 1970s. In response to these external pressures, the Superintendent of the Chicago Police Department created the Office of Professional Standards (OPS) in the summer of 1974. The OPS was established as a civilian body, principally intended to investigate allegations of brutality and excessive force made against officers of the police department, although it also acts as a recipient and registrar of complaints. Less serious complaints continue to be investigated by the police department's Internal Affairs Division.

The idea of introducing civilians into the complaints process, not merely to oversee the procedure but to actually carry out the investigations, was a unique feature of the OPS when it was first established, but it was not without problems. If police officers were not to be involved in investigations of serious allegations of police misconduct, the question was from where could competent and experienced investigative staff be obtained? The Superintendent chose to staff the OPS with 30 civilian investigators and 4 supervisors the majority of whom were former military personnel or investigators with other government departments. The staff was multiracial and included both male and female investigators. The three senior administrative officers, one black, one white, and one hispanic, were all experienced and established lawyers (Letman, 1980: 16).

The OPS was established not as an external body, but internally within the police department. Its staff was, and still is, answerable to the Superintendent, the idea being to avoid allegations of loss of authority by the Superintendent in disciplinary matters. This administrative arrangement, not surprisingly perhaps, brought allegations from various sources off a lack of real independence from the police department and accusations of a whitewash, criticisms which have continued to be leveled at the OPS to the present time. Although civilians are employed as investigators in the OPS, they have no input into the disciplinary process once an investigation has been completed. The responsibility for hearing complaints and recommending appropriate disciplinary actions to the Superintendent is that of an internal police Complaint Review Panel, which is generally composed of a lieutenant, a sergeant, and an officer of the same rank as the accused.

Chicago's OPS has continued to operate for over a decade, but not without a number of problems, chief among which has been the tendency of civilian investigators to side with the police to such an extent that accused officers have preferred to be interviewed by OPS investigators than by members of the department's Internal Affairs Division. Policies, including using different hiring and training procedures have been introduced in an effort to correct this bias in recent years, but nevertheless the Office has struggled to establish its identity, being generally viewed as neither a civilian nor a true police organization (Letman, 1980; Letman, 1981; Terrill, 1982; Brown, 1985; Kerstetter, 1985: 165).

## The Dade County (Florida) Independent Review Panel (IRP)

This office, fashioned after the ombudsman concept, was created in early 1980 following a serious credibility crisis during which even the usually supportive members of the Dade County community were doubting the ability of their Department of Public Safety (DPS) to police itself. Since its inception, the IRP has placed considerable emphasis upon its informal authority and has used its conciliatory and mediatory powers widely and with a good deal of success (Kerstetter, 1985: 170). It has jurisdiction to receive and investigate complaints against any county employee or agency, but it tends to act mainly as a "watchdog" body in that it defers its own investigation into complaints until after the subject agency's own internal enquiry has been completed. Where investigations are concerned, therefore, although it retains authority to conduct fact-finding investigations when appropriate, the IRP is primarily concerned with reviewing completed internal investigations and judging their propriety.

The difficulty of establishing an ombudsman-like panel that is generally perceived as being truly independent has been addressed in the way in which members of the IRP are selected and appointed. The full-time salaried Executive Director is appointed by the Chief Judge of the county, and, of the other six part-time unsalaried panel members, five are nominated by community organizations for appointment by the board of county commissioners and the sixth is appointed by the county manager. The Executive Director has no designated individual or group to whom he/she is accountable, rather this post implicity assumes the accountability to all relevant interest groups and particularly to the electorate of Dade County (Pomeroy, 1985: 185).

Criticisms of the IRP have centered around the undue delay in investigations caused by the operational arrangement described above and, as in Detroit, allegations that its successful functioning depends too heavily upon the present personalities involved as Executive Director of the IRP and Director of the DPS. The suggestions are that future personnel changes in these executive ranks could threaten the continued effective operations of the IRP (Kerstetter, 1985: 172-173).

## Portland's Police Internal Investigations
## Audit Committee (PIIAC)

The issue of civilian review of complaints against the police was raised in Portland, Oregon, in 1981 following two specific incidents of police malpractice which outraged the community and received widespread publicity. In response to public discontent, the Portland city council appointed a thirteen member civilian task force to analyze the police department's internal investigation procedures. In its subsequent report, the Task Force concluded that the existing police Internal Investigation Division (IID) was biased in favor of police officers over civilians and consequently that it was not held in very high regard by the Portland community. Task Force recommendations included the establishment of some form of citizen committee to oversee complaints investigation.

Despite opposition from the mayor, the city council provisionally created an eight-member civilian subcommittee of the city council, the Police Internal Investigations Audit Committee (PIIAC), pending the outcome of police union efforts to put the issue to a referendum of the Portland community.

Between May and November of 1982, events in Portland were very similar to those during the build up to the 1966 New York City CCRB referendum, but with two significant differences. First, contrary to the New York experience, the mayor of Portland was opposed to civilian review, and second, the police union, despite massive and costly local publicity, lost the vote and the referendum result narrowly approved the creation of the PIIAC, which subsequently commenced its operation in December, 1982.

The PIIAC has three specific functions: monitoring police internal investigations of complaints to ensure that they are conducted in a correct manner, making public the results of their findings in the form of reports, and providing an avenue of appeal for citizens who are dissatisfied with the outcome of their complaints which have been investigated by the police. The PIIAC is therefore not a complaint review mechanism intended to replace the police department's own internal procedures, rather the emphasis of its responsibilities is upon the review of procedures as distinct from the resolution of individual complaints.

This monitoring of procedures rather than individual cases makes the PIIAC unique. It works on two levels, on the individual level in the form of appeals made to it by citizens and on the aggregate level in the form of routine auditing of complaint files. Members of the committee see their contribution towards improving police-community relations as being the process of identifying to the police those areas of their internal review procedures which obstruct the detection of misconduct and therefore implicitly reward officer deviance (Jolin and Gibbons, 1984).

## McAllen, Texas Police Human Relations Committee (PHRC)

The American Civil Liberties Union (ACLU) filed a series of Federal Civil Rights Suits (so-called "1983 cases") against the McAllen, Texas Police Department for the use of excessive force by officers. In nearly all the cases the plaintiffs were Hispanic. The ACLU maintained that the police department lacked empathy for and understanding of the Hispanic culture which contributed to ethnic discrimination and a failure of the department to take affirmative action in investigating complaints and disciplining officers. Moreover, the ACLU charged that the department had taken no action to effectively prevent such abuses of authority nor was there an effective method of dealing with complaints against officers.

In one particular case in 1981 the evidence was punctuated by a series of police department videotapes vividly showing officers brutalizing arrestees. As a result of this evidence and the pattern of Civil Rights cases the department had lost, the Federal District Court for the Southern District of Texas issued an injunction to remedy the problems. Among the mandates of the injunction was the requirement to establish a police review board called the Police Human Relations Committee (PHRC).

The PHRC was composed of five members. Three members were un-paid citizens reflecting the demographic make-up of the city and appointed by the city council. The two other PHRC members were police officers appointed by the Chief of Police.

In an attempt to solidify its authority and autonomy, the PHRC was charged with developing its own procedures for review of cases. Investigations were the responsibility of the police department's designated IA officer who would turn investigation reports over to the PHRC to review on matters where a citizen complaint had been filed. The Committee would make recommendations for discipline if it found the complaint to be sustained, however, actual discipline was the prerogative of the chief.

There are two distinguishing points worthy to note about this board. First, the PHRC was established by a federal court order, not by a departmental decision or a citizen mandate. Second, the PHRC was given the autonomy to develop *all* of its operating procedures—a process which has caused notable indecision and delays.

While the intent of the court order is apparent, operationally the PHRC has been problematic. Interestingly, the problems have not been a product of officer, departmental, or citizen rejection. Rather, the independence of the PHRC to establish its own rules and agenda as mandated by the federal court has significantly contributed to its awkward and slow nature.

## Varieties of External and Internal Review Procedures

The development of agencies and systems such as those described above during the past decade-and-a-half has recently led Kerstetter (1985: 160-161) to reiterate the three models of external review of complaints investigation which he first proposed in 1970: civilian review, civilian input, and civilian monitor. According to Kerstetter, civilian review, the strongest mechanism, places the authority to investigate, adjudicate, and recommend punishment to the police chief, within the external agency. Civilian input, not such a strong mechanism, places authority only for complaints reception and investigation in the external agency, whilst adjudication and discipline functions are discharged internally within the police department. Finally, in the weakest system, civilian monitor, the investigation, adjudication and discipline functions are all discharged internally within the police department, but the procedures are subject to some form of external review regarding their adequacy and impartiality. Within this three-model structure, civilian review would describe the existing arrangements in Berkeley, and McAllen, civilian monitor would describe the systems in Kansas City and Chicago, and civilian input those in San Jose, Dade County, and Portland.

In many ways this three-tiered structure is comparable with the three broad types of police department internal investigation systems identified by Beral and Sisk in 1964 and discussed earlier. Under this scheme, within police departments the review mechanism can first be considered to describe those systems within which investigations are carried out exclusively by an IAU. Second, the input mechanism can be considered to describe the situation whereby the responsibility for undertaking investigations is jointly shared by an IAU and the accused officer's supervisory officers. Third, the monitor mechanism can be identified with those systems in which supervisors are given full responsibility and discretion in complaints investigation, although their completed investigation reports are subject to review afterwards by an individual or office at headquarters.

Kerstetter's model, however, only relates to jurisdictions in which external review is present in some form, whilst Beral and Sisk's work described those police departments without external review. An attempt to describe the global situation involving both external and internal review mechanisms was made by Russell (1978) who again utilized a three-tier model.

Under this model, three types of investigative mechanism were discerned: Exclusively internal, internal with external review of certain cases, and bilateral. Exclusively internal mechanisms described those jurisdictions, which were still the vast majority, in which citizen complaints were entirely administered by the police with no external scrutiny. New York and San Francisco were described as cities in which all complaints were partially administered by the police with formal external scrutiny of criminal and some non-criminal complaints. Finally, Berkeley, Chicago, and Detroit were identified as having bilateral administration of complaints by both the police and a formally constituted external organization (Russell, 1978:37).

# RECENT DEVELOPMENTS

There have been a number of significant developments in the area of complaints investigation in the United States during the 1980s which may have future wide-ranging implications for communities and police departments searching for improvements in their existing procedures. Specifically, two relatively new organizations which take a particular interest in the investigation of complaints against the police, CALEA (Commission on Accreditation for Law Enforcement Agencies) and IACOLE (International Association for Civilian Oversight of Law Enforcement) have been formed, whilst a third organization PERF (Police Executive Research Forum) has become increasingly involved in researching the area and identifying future implications for police departments.

## Commission on Accreditation for Law Enforcement Agencies (CALEA)

Following joint initiatives taken by the International Association of Chiefs of Police (IACP), the Police Executive Research Forum (PERF), the National Sheriffs Association (NSA) and the National Organization of Black Law Enforcement Executives (NOBLE), CALEA was founded in 1979. Its objective is to administer an accreditation program by which law enforcement agencies at local, county, and state levels can voluntarily demonstrate their compliance with exacting professional criteria. CALEA's overall purpose is, through the accreditation program, to improve the delivery of law enforcement services. Accreditation is carried out by measuring the performance of law enforcement agencies against a set of 944 standards of evaluation which have been drawn up. On-site assessments of agency compliance with these criteria are undertaken by assessors, generally police officers, who have been recruited, selected, and trained by the Commission.

A number of CALEA standards relate to the area of complaints against the police and disciplinary procedures, although since the accreditation process can only be undertaken by law enforcement agencies, internal rather than external review procedures tend to be emphasized. Standards are continuously being revised, updated, and amended, however, and consequently it can be anticipated that future moves towards greater external review of complaints investigation will be reflected in new standards being set by CALEA with respect to the interagency relations between police departments and external review boards.

After a lengthy period of research and planning, CALEA only commenced accepting applications for accreditation at the beginning of 1984. In the fall of 1986 it reported that 29 agencies had successfully achieved the distinction of completing the accreditation process but that, rather more significantly, a further

501 agencies from across the USA had signaled their intention of undertaking assessment within the next two years. At present, the largest accredited agency is in the Illinois State Police with 3390 full-time personnel; the smallest agency is the Indian Hill, Ohio, Police Department with 21.

Indications are that police executives, ever searching for evidence of the professional status of their agencies, see being awarded the distinction of accreditation by CALEA as becoming a benchmark of efficiency and effectiveness in the future. (Commission Update, Fall 1986:5).

## International Association for Civilian Oversight of Law Enforcement (IACOLE)

The formation of an association for individuals actively involved in civilian review of police agencies, rather than merely for people who are interested in the concept, is a relatively new venture. IACOLE was formed in 1985 and membership is open to persons who are not sworn law enforcement officers and who work for or constitute agencies established by legislative authority to investigate and/or review complaints against the police.

Membership of IACOLE includes officers from each of the external review bodies currently operating in the USA (described earlier), together with representatives of a number of other US civilian oversight agencies. In addition, it is interesting to note that the international flavor of the Association intimated by its title is a reality and not merely a hope. Registrants at IACOLE's second annual conference held in December, 1986 included members of the Association from Australia, Canada, England, Northern Ireland, and Nigeria as well as from the USA.

Although IACOLE is still in its early days of existence, it appears to have a healthy and thriving membership. The implication would appear to be that this organization appears to have the capacity to do for external review agencies in terms of increased professionalism what CALEA is presently attempting to achieve in the area of internal review procedures.

## Police Executive Research Forum (PERF)

Founded in 1975 following a series of informal discussions among ten police chiefs who were particularly interested in exchanging new ideas and encouraging innovation in the management of law enforcement agencies, the Police Executive Research Forum (PERF) has always been associated with efforts to promote research and development in policing (Duffy, 1983:14). The Forum's founders placed a great deal of emphasis upon academic learning, professionalism, and the opportunity for police chiefs to discuss mutual concerns with colleagues sharing similar crime and police problems. Consequently, general membership of PERF is limited to college-educated leaders of police departments which have at least 200 members or are the main police agencies for jurisdictions of at least 50,000 people. (Although a current proposal would significantly expand the membership pod.) The present general membership is in excess of one hundred, those members having responsibility for the delivery of police services to over 25 percent of the population of the United States.

PERF's specific interest in complaints investigation began in 1981 when it identified both real and perceived grievances about citizen complaint investigations as being an early warning signal regarding deteriorating police-community relations. A Forum policy committee was formed which initially reviewed and analyzed the prevailing complaints procedures amongst PERF's member departments (which numbered 60 at that time), and then, utilizing the information obtained from the review, produced a model policy statement on handling citizen complaints. The intention was that the model policy could be used by law enforcement agencies across the United States and, in addition, could be used to establish standards for the development of new procedures (Duffy, 1983:12).

The model policy statement covers an agency's mission, specific mechanisms to prevent misconduct, a code of conduct, penalties, and the disciplinary process. It emphasizes the prevention of misconduct as being the primary means of reducing and controlling it and describes a number of mechanisms which can be utilized to achieve the goal of prevention. These include improved selection and recruitment procedures, training in police ethics, increased training of supervisors, and creating community outreach. With regard to the complaints system itself, the policy statement stresses that it must be accessible to all persons who wish to file a complaint, must function consistently, and must collect and analyze misconduct complaints on a monthly basis. Additionally, it argues for a 120-day limit on the disposition of all complaints (PERF, 1983).

The emphasis of the model policy is thus upon creating increased police professionalism in a number of areas, and it is not simply addressed towards those areas directly concerned with the operation of IAUs. Recently, however, PERF has itself questioned whether indeed police departments, no matter how professional their policies and procedures, can effectively defend themselves against accusations of cover-ups without meaningful external reviews of police internal investigations of complaints. A Task Force established in 1987 researched the question of how police departments can better handle (solicit, investigate, and resolve) complaints against the police, and whether there is a role for external review of police conduct (see West, 1987). Its findings could potentially have widespread implications for the investigation of complaints against the police in the United States well into the 1990s, and perhaps even further.

# CONCLUSION

As evidenced throughout this chapter, a variety of investigative and complaint review schemes are being used in the United States. There is obviously not "one best model" that can be placed within a police organization. Rather, factors such as community attitude and support for the police, the presence of police malpractice problems, allegations of police department cover-ups, and the sociopolitical environment of the community must all be considered in a complaint review program. One may borrow from the structure and lessons learned from the agencies described herein, however, the specific review mechanism must nonetheless be designed to meet the specific needs and characteristics of one's own agency.

# REFERENCES

Barton, P.G. (1970). "Civilian Review Boards and the Handling of Complaints Against the Police," *University of Toronto Law Journal,* Vol. 20, pp. 448-468.

Bell, J. (1986). "PACE and Complaints Against the Police," *Policing,* Vol. 2 No. 4 (Winter), pp. 283-293.

Beral, H. and M. Sisk (1964). "The Administration of Complaints by Civilians Against the Police," *Harvard Law Review,* Vol. 77, pp. 499-519.

Bouza, A.V. (1985). "Police Unions: Paper Tigers or Roaring Lions?" in W.A. Geller, (ed.) *Police Leadership in America: Crisis and Opportunity.* (Chicago: American Bar Foundation), pp. 241-280.

Box, S. (1985). *Power, Crime and Mystification.* London and New York: Tavistock Publications, 1983.

Brown, D. (1983) "Civilian Review of Complaints Against the Police: A Survey of the United States Literature," *Home Office Research and Planning Unit Paper No. 19,* (London: Home Office).

Brown, D. (1987). "The Police Complaints Against the Police: A Survey of Complainants' Views," *Home Office Research and Planning Unit Paper No. 93.* London: HMSO.

Buckley, W. (1967). *Sociology and Modern Systems Theory.* Englewood Cliffs, NJ: Prentice-Hall.

CALEA, *Commission Update No. XXXIII.* (1986) Fairfax, VA: Commission on Accreditation for Law Enforcement Agencies, Fall.

Cray, E. (1972). *The Enemy in the Streets: Police Malpractice in America.* New York: Anchor Books.

Crook, T. (1987). "My Blokes Did Not Assault Youths'—Sergeant," *Police Review,* Vol. 95 No. 4920 (July), p. 1363.

Duffy, J.F. (1983). "PERF: Acts to Improve Citizen Complaint Procedures," *FBI Law Enforcement Bulletin,* (May), pp. 11-14.

Geller, W. A. (1984). "Police misconduct: Scope of the Problems and Remedies," *ACJS Today,* (February), pp. 6-11.

Goldstein, H. (1977). *Policing a Free Society.* Cambridge, MA: Ballinger.

Goldstein, H. (1976). *Police Corruption.* Washington, DC: Police Foundation.

Halpern, S.C. (1974). "Police Employee Organizations and Accountability Procedures in Three Cities: Some Reflections on Police Policy-Making," *Law and Society Review,* Vol. 8 No. 4 (Summer), pp. 561-82.

Hewitt, P. (1982). *The Abuse of Power: Civil Liberties in the United Kingdom.* Oxford: Martin Robertson.

Hiliard, B. (1987). "The Holloway Incident," *Police Review,* Vol. 95 No. 4921 (July 17), p. 1426.

Hudson, J.R. (1971). "Police Review Boards and Police Accountability," *Law and Contemporary Problems,* Vol. 36 No. 4 (Autumn), pp. 515-538.

IACOLE, (1985). *Proceedings of the First International Conference on Civilian Oversight of Law Enforcement,* Toronto, October 1985. Toronto: OPCC, 1986.

Jolin, A.I. and D.C. Gibbons, (1984). "Policing the Police: The Portland Experience," *Journal of Police Science and Administration,* Vol. 12 No. 3, pp. 315-322.

Kerstetter, W.A. (1985). "Who Disciplines the Police? Who Should?" In W.A. Geller (ed.) *Police Leadership in America: Crisis and Opportunity,* pp. 149-182. Chicago: American Bar Foundation.

Labour Party (1987). *Protecting our People: Labour's Policy on Crime Prevention,* London: The Labour Party.

Lambert, John L. (1986). *Police Powers and Accountability.* London: Croom Helm.

Leonard, V. and H. More (1971). *Police Organization and Management.* New York: Foundation Press.

Letman, S.T. (1980). "Chicago's Answer to Police Brutality: The Office of Professional Standards," *Police Chief,* (January), pp. 16-17.

Letman, S.T. (1981). "The Office of Professional Standards: Six Years Later," *Police Chief,* (March), pp. 44-46.

Liddy, D. (1986). *Durham Constabulary Complaints and Discipline Department.* Durham, England: Durham Constabulary Unpublished Paper.

Lynch, G.W. and E. Diamond (1983). "Police Misconduct." In S.H. Kadish (ed.) *Encyclopedia of Crime and Justice.* New York: The Free Press.

Meek, A. (1985). *A Comparison of the PACE Act 1984 with the Present System Relating to Police Complaints and Discipline.* Bramshill, Hampshire, England: Police Staff College Unpublished Paper.

*Metropolitan Toronto Office of the Public Complaints Commissioner 1985 Annual Report.* Toronto: OPCC, 1986.

Moores, G.H. (1982). "Civilianisation of the Police Complaints Procedure," *P-a-S Papers,* (April), pp. 6-7.

Niederhoffer, A. (1967). *Behind the Shield: The Police in Urban Society,* Garden City, NY: Anchor Books.

"Off with his Helmet," *Police,* Vol. 19 No. 9, pp. 9-10, (May, 1987).

Packer, H. (1966). "The Courts the Police, and the Rest of Us," *Journal of Criminal Law, Criminology and Police Science,* Vol. 57.

"PCA Calls for Dismissal of 'Unsuitable' Officers," *Police Review,* Vol. 95 No. 4908, p. 722, (April 10, 1987).

Perez, D.W., *Police Accountability: A Question of Balance,* Ann Arbor: University Microfilms, 1979.

PERF (1983). *Police Agency Handling of Citizen Complaints: A Model Policy Statement.* Washington DC: PERF.

Philips, Sir C. (1984). "Change and Reform in the System of Dealing with Complaints against the Police," *Policing,* Vol. 1 No. 1, pp. 6-19, (Autumn).

Pike, M.S. (1985). *The Principles of Policing.* London: Macmillan.

Plowden Report (1981). *Report of a Working Party on the Establishment of an Independent Element in the Investigation of Complaints against the Police,* London: HMSO.

*Police Act 1964.* London: HMSO, 1964.

*Police Act 1976.* London: HMSO, 1976.

*Police and Criminal Evidence Act 1984.* London: HMSO, 1984.

*Police Complaints Authority Annual Report 1985.* London: HMSO, 1986.

*Police Complaints Authority Annual Report 1986.* London: HMSO, 1987.

*Police Complaints Board Triennial Review Report.* London: HMSO, 1980.

*Police Complaints Board Annual Report 1981.* London: HMSO, 1982.

*Police Complaints Board Final Review Report 1977-1985.* London: HMSO, 1985.

Pomeroy, W.A.C. (1985). "The Sources of Police Legitimacy and a Model for Police Misconduct Review." In W.A. Geller (ed.) *Police Leadership in America: Crisis and Opportunity,* pp. 183-186. Chicago: American Bar Foundation.

President's Commission on Law Enforcement and the Administration of Justice, *Field Survey IV (2): The Police and The Community.* Washington, DC: USGPO, 1967.

President's Commission on Law Enforcement and the Administration of Justice, *Task Force Report: The Police.* Washington DC: USGPO, 1967.

*R v PCB ex parte Rhone and Madden,* 1983 2QB 353.

Robin, G.D. (1980). *Introduction to the Criminal Justice System.* New York: Harper and Row.

Russell, K. (1976). *Complaints Against the Police: A Sociological View.* Leicester, England: Milltak Limited.

Russell, K.V. (1978). "Complaints Against the Police: An International Perspective," *Police Journal,* Vol. 52 No. 1 (January), pp. 34-44.

San Francisco Office of Civilian Complaints, *The Professional,* Vol. 1 No. 3, (Spring 1986).

San Francisco Office of Civilian Complaints, *The Professional,* Vol. 2 No. 1, (Fall 1986).

Scarman Report, *The Brixton Disorders 10-12 April 1981.* London: HMSO, 1981.

Sharpley, G.R. (1969). "Ombudsman: A Representative Democracy's Finest Hour," *Police Chief,* (January), pp. 12-17.

Stalker, J. (1987). "This Crumbling Irrelevance," *Police,* Vol. 19 No. 9, p. 12, (May).

Stowell, G.F. (1977). "Civilian Review Boards," *Police Chief,* Vol. 44 No. 4 (April).

Terrill, R.J. (1982). "Complaint Procedures: Variations on the Theme of Civilian Participation," *Journal of Police Science and Administration,* Vol. 10 No. 4, p. 398-407.

Territo, L. and R.L. Smith (1976). "The Internal Affairs Unit: The Policeman's Friend or Foe?" *Police Chief,* (July), p. 66-69.

U.S. Commission on Civil Rights, *Who is Guarding the Guardians?* Washington, DC: U.S. Government Printing Office, 1981.

Waddington, P.A.J. (1987). "Wanted: a Permanent Police Watchdog," *The London Times,* (April 8.)

Warren, K. and D. Tredinnick (1982). *Protecting the Police,* London: Conservative Political Centre.

*Washington D.C. Civilian Complaint Review Board 1985 Annual Report,* Washington DC: Government of the District of Columbia, 1986.

Walker, S. (1983). *The Police in America.* New York: McGraw-Hill.

Wilson, O.W. and R.C. McLaren (1977). *Police Administration.* New York: McGraw-Hill.

# Study Questions

1. Distinguish between "internal" and "external" review of complaints against officers.

2. What critical factors have occurred in history which influenced changes in procedures in dealing with complaints against the police?

3. What is meant by a "civilian review board"? Explain the concept in detail. What are the arguments in favor and in opposition to civilian review boards?

4. Should a civilian review board's authority be limited to simply determining whether accusations against an officer are true or should the board also make decisions on an officer's discipline? Explain the rationale of your position.

5. What is an "ombudsman"? What role does the ombudsman fulfill as related to complaints against police officers?

# 19

# CIVIL AND CRIMINAL LIABILITIES OF POLICE OFFICERS

## Rolando V. del Carmen

During the last few years, headlines similar to these below have become familiar in the United States:

City of Houston and Two Police Officers Ordered to Pay $1.4 Million to Parents of Slain Police Victim[1]

Police Brutality Lawsuit Results in $2.1 Million Award[2]

California City Loses Police Brutality Suit: $3 Million Judgment to Victims' Families May Force Cutbacks in Services[3]

$5 Million Awarded to Innocent Bystander Who Lost Both Legs When Officer Violated Departmental Policy During Vehicle Pursuit of Bank Robbers[4]

Man Files $20 Million Suit Against City Over Shooting[5]

These headlines are no figment of any writer's imagination. These are actual cases recently decided against police officers and departments in various parts of the country. They are by no means isolated. Figures show that in 1981, over $325 million in suits or claims were filed against police officers in one state alone—Oregon.[6] Multiply that by the number of states and governmental agencies in the country and you begin to get an idea of the pervasive extent of liability lawsuits against law enforcement officers and their employees.

There are reasons to believe that suing public officials has become the second most popular indoor sport in the country. This is particularly true in law enforcement work. Figures compiled by the Americans for Effective Law Enforcement show that from 1967 to 1971 the number of civil cases against the police rose from 1,741 to 3,894. Reliable estimates indicate that by 1976 the number of suits filed alleging police misconduct exceeded 6,000 per year.[7] In 1960, there were a total of only 247 civil rights cases filed in federal district courts throughout the United States. In 1970, there were 3,985 such suits, an increase of 1,614 percent; and in 1976, the figure had grown to 12,329 an increase of 4,991 percent over 1960. In

1982, there were 16,741 cases filed by state prisoners, representing a 115.6 percent increase since 1977.[8] The number of lawsuits continues to escalate and shows no sign of abatement.

Despite these figures, only a small percentage of cases actually go to trial. For example, in 1979, 9,943 out of the 10,301 civil rights cases filed by prisoners (96.5%) in federal court were dismissed or otherwise concluded prior to trial. Only 358, or 3.5 percent, of state prisoner civil rights cases went to trial.[9] Nonetheless, a tremendous amount of effort and anxiety is spent by both parties-litigants even if the case never gets to trial. Moreover, many cases never reach the trial state because they are settled out of court—with the defendant paying expenses and damages.

It is therefore important for police officers to have ample knowledge of legal liabilities. Court intervention, leading to accountability, has become a way of life for criminal justice personnel in this country. This chapter first acquaints the officer with an overview of the array of laws to which he may be exposed in connection with his work. It then discusses the two types of cases often brought against police officers, namely: state tort and Section 1983 actions. Supervisory liability is discussed and police lawsuits against their detractors is addressed. The chapter ends with bits of advice on how legal liabilities might be minimized or avoided.

## AN OVERVIEW

The sources of legal liabilities to which police officers may be exposed are many and varied. They range from state to federal laws and from civil to criminal. For the purpose of an overview, legal liabilities may be categoried as illustrated on Table 19.1.

An officer may be held liable or punished under any and all of the above laws, based on essentially a single serious act, if all the elements are present. Moreover, administrative disciplinary measures may also be imposed by the agency, resulting in suspension, demotion, reassignment, or dismissal. The protection against double jeopardy does not apply because double jeopardy may be invoked by the defendant only if both cases are criminal in nature, hence it does not apply where one case is civil and the other criminal. It also applies only if the successive criminal prosecutions are by the same jurisdiction. A state or federal prosecutor may decide not to press charges against an officer after trial in one jurisdiction, but the danger remains that a second prosecution may be undertaken if the prosecutor so desires, particularly if justice, as perceived by the prosecutor, is not obtained in the first trial.

Although several legal remedies are available, as the above classification depicts, plaintiffs strongly prefer to use two remedies: (1) civil liability under state tort law, and (2) civil liability under federal law, particularly under 42 U.S.C., Section 1983. These two liability sources therefore merit extended discussion.

# LIABILITY UNDER STATE TORT LAW

A tort is defined as a wrong in which the action of one person causes injury to the person or property of another, in violation of a legal duty imposed by law.[10] A tortious act may be against a person or property; it may also be intentional or unintentional (as when caused by negligence). There are four requirements for liability to ensue under state tort. These are:[11]

(1) a duty on the part of the officer or department to act with care toward the plaintiff;
(2) a breach of that duty;
(3) injury to the plaintiff as a result of that breach; and
(4) the defendant's act must have been the proximate cause of the injury.

---

**TABLE 19.1**

**Legal Liabilities of Police Officers**

| | I. FEDERAL LAW | II. STATE LAW |
|---|---|---|
| A. CIVIL LIABILITIES | 1. Title 42 of U.S. Code, Section 1983— Civil Action for Deprivation Civil Rights<br>2. Title 42 of U.S. Code, Section 1985— Civil Action for Conspiracy to Deprive a Person of Civil Rights<br>3. Title 42 of the U.S. Code, Section 1981—Equal Rights Under The Law | 1. State Tort Law<br><br>2. State Civil Rights Law |
| B. CRIMINAL LIABILITIES | 1. Title 18 of U.S. Code, Section 242— Criminal Liability for Deprivation of Civil Rights<br><br>2. Title 18 of U.S. Code, Section 245— Violation of Federally-Protected Activities | 1. State Penal Code provisions specifically aimed at public officers for such crimes as<br>  a. official oppression<br>  b. official misconduct, and<br>  c. violation of the civil rights of prisoners<br>2. Regular Penal Code provisions punishing such criminal acts as assault, serious bodily injury, homicide, etc. |

There are several tortious acts for which law enforcement officers, by virtue of their responsibilities and high public exposure, are particularly susceptible. The most notable are:[12]

1. *False arrest and imprisonment:* The plaintiff alleges that the officer made the arrest and subsequently imprisoned the suspect without probable cause. Chances are that liability does not exist if the arrest or seizure was made by virtue of a warrant. This is because in these cases, probable cause has been determined to exist by the issuing magistrate and therefore the burden is on the plaintiff to show, by clear and convincing evidence, that the magistrate was wrong, a burden which is not easily met. A warrant is good protection for an officer in liability cases arising from arrest or imprisonment.

2. *Malicious prosecution:* This refers to both a criminal case which was filed maliciously and to the civil case which arises therefrom. The tort action is filed if the previous criminal trial ended in plaintiff's favor, was instituted by the officer maliciously and without probable cause, and the plaintiff was damaged by the criminal proceeding.

3. *Use of Excessive Force:* This results when plaintiff alleges and proves that the force used by the officer to effect arrest or subdue the plaintiff went beyond that which was necessary to accomplish the desired result. Use of excessive force may take the form of assault, battery, or serious bodily injury. Assault is merely menacing conduct, the result of which puts a person in fear of imminently receiving a battery, while battery is the unlawful and hostile touching of another, however slight. The general rule is that the officer is justified in using only as much force as is reasonably necessary to subdue or take the person into custody. The term "reasonably necessary" is difficult to define with precision because each case is different, depending upon circumstances present. What is important is for the officer to be able to articulate in court, should a tort case be brought, why a particular level of force was used under the circumstances. The use of force for punitive purposes is never justified, regardless of the provocation. The use of deadly weapons is usually governed by departmental rules which are usually more restrictive than state law.

4. *Wrongful Death:* This tort case is brought by the surviving family or relatives of a person whose death was caused by the officer's intentional or negligent act or omission. Any time a suspect or any person dies as a result of the officer's action or inaction, the stage is set for a wrongful death lawsuit. Examples are when an officer shoots and kills a fleeing suspect, or when shots are fired at a suspect in a shopping center, killing an innocent bystander. While the tort of use

of excessive force usually involves the use of non-deadly force, wrongful death results from the use or misuse of deadly force by the officer.

Other tort cases which may be filed against officers are libel or slander, invasion of privacy, abuse of process, cruel and unusual punishment of prisoners, negligent vehicle operation, negligent administration of first aid, failure to arrest (in some cases), and intentional infliction of emotional distress. It is said that the types of tort cases which may be brought against a police officer are limited only by the creativity and imagination of the plaintiff's lawyer. This is literally true, yet if won, the officer must pay token, compensatory, or punitive damages. Token damages are usually negligible and are given to redress a slight injury; compensatory damages are imposed to pay for the actual expenses; while punitive damages are designed to penalize and teach the officer a costly lesson. Punitive awards can run into millions of dollars.

## LIABILITY UNDER SECTION 1983 (CIVIL RIGHTS CASES)

By far, the most widely-used provision of law in the whole arsenal of legal liability statutes is 42 U.S.C. Section 1983, otherwise referred to by lawyers as Section 1983, or civil rights cases. Estimates are that around 80 percent of cases filed against public officers fall under this provision of federal law. Title 42 U.S.C. Section 1983 reads as follows:

Civil Action for Deprivation of Rights: Every person who, under color of any statute, ordinance, regulation, custom, or usage, of any State or Territory, subjects, or causes to be subjected, any citizen of the United States or other persons within the jurisdiction thereof to the deprivation of any rights, privileges, or immunities secured by the Constitution and laws, shall by liable to the party injured in an action at law, suit in equity, or other proper proceeding for redress.

Section 1983 is not new. It was passed in 1871 and was originally known as the Ku Klux Klan law because it was designed to control and punish the activities of state officers who refused to go after violations of rights of blacks by the Ku Klux Klan. For a long time, however, it was given a narrow interpretation by the U.S. Supreme Court as applying only to instances when a state officer deprived blacks of the right to vote. A much broader interpretation came about in 1961 in the case of *Monroe v. Pape*.[13] Since then, Section 1983 has been held applicable to cases where a public officer violates a person's constitutional rights. The law applies to citizens, aliens, and illegal aliens alike because the law includes "any citizen of the United States or other persons within the jurisdiction thereof." Hence, even illegal aliens have successfully brought suit under the law.

## Basic Elements of a Section 1983 Suit

There are four basic elements of a Section 1983 suit, as interpreted by the courts. These are:

1. The defendant must be a natural person or a local government;
2. The defendant must be acting under "color of state law";
3. The violation must be of a constitutional or a federally-protected right; and
4. The violation must reach constitutional level.

1. *The Defendant Must Be a Natural Person or a Local Government.* Until recently, only natural persons could be held liable in 1983 suits. State and local governments were exempt because of the doctrine of sovereign immunity. In 1978, however, the U.S. Supreme Court in *Monnell v. Department of Social Services of the City of New York,*[14] held that local units of government may now be held liable if the allegedly unconstitutional action was taken by the officer as a part of an official policy of custom. What "policy or custom" means has not been clear and is subject to varying interpretations. State immunity is still alive despite *Monnell* because that decision applies to local governments only. This is not of much consolation to state probation/parole officers, however, because the suit can be filed against the state officer himself (although not against the state) who then becomes liable.

2. *The Defendant Must Be Acting Under "Color of State Law."* This means the misuse of power was possessed by virtue of state law and made possible only because the wrongdoer is clothed with authority of state law. The problem is that while it is easy to identify acts which are wholly within the term "color of state law" (as when a police officer, while on patrol, arrests a suspect), there are gray areas which defy easy categorization (as when a law enforcement officer who moonlights as a private security guard illegally shoots a shoplifter in a department store). As a general rule, anything a police officer does in the performance of regular duties and during the usual hours is considered under color of state law. Conversely, what he does as a private citizen during his off-hours falls outside of the color of state law.

The term "color of state law" has been interpreted by the courts broadly to include local laws or regulations. Therefore, a police officer who acts in accordance with a county or city ordinance is acting under color of state law. Moreover, the phrase does not mean that the act was in fact authorized by law. It is sufficient if the act appeared to be lawful even if it was not in fact authorized; hence, if the police officer exceeded his lawful authority, he is still deemed to have acted under color of law. An example is an officer who detains somebody without legal authorization. The officer, though acting outside the scope of his authority, is nonetheless considered to have acted under color of law, hence may be sued under Section 1983.

3. *The Violation of a Constitutionally or Federally Protected Right.* Under this element, the right violated must be one guaranteed by the U.S. Constitution or that given by federal law. Rights given by state law are not protected under Section 1983. The difficulty is that while certain acts of a police officer may be grossly violative of a constitutional right (as when an officer searches a suspect's house without probable cause or any authorization whatsoever), other acts are difficult to categorize. The constitutional rights guaranteed in the Bill of Rights which police officers must be aware of and respect are summarized as follows:

FIRST AMENDMENT: includes—
   1. Freedom of religion,
   2. Freedom of speech,
   3. Freedom of press,
   4. Freedom of assembly,
   5. Freedom to petition the government for redress of grievances.

SECOND AMENDMENT: Right to bear arms.

FOURTH AMENDMENT: Prohibition against—
   1. Unreasonable arrest,
   2. Unreasonable searches and seizures.

FIFTH AMENDMENT: includes—
   1. Right of a grand jury indictment for capital or otherwise infamous crime,
   2. Right against double jeopardy,
   3. Right against self-incrimination,
   4. Prohibition against the taking of life, liberty, or property without due process of law,
   5. Right against the taking of private property for public use without just compensation.

SIXTH AMENDMENT: includes—
   1. Right to a speedy and public trial,
   2. Right to an impartial jury,
   3. Right to be informed of the nature and cause of the accusation against him,

4. Right to be confronted with the witnesses against him,
5. Right to have compulsory process for obtaining witnesses in his favor,
6. Right to have the assistance of counsel.

EIGHTH AMENDMENT: includes—
1. Prohibition against excessive bail,
2. Prohibition against cruel and unusual punishment.

FOURTEENTH AMENDMENT: includes—
1. Right to due process,
2. Right to equal protection of the laws.

Right to privacy—derived from the First, Fourth, Fifth, Sixth and Fourteenth Amendments.

A violation of any of the above rights leads, if sued and proved, to officer liability. The problem is that it is often difficult to determine the actual extent of a person's constitutional rights. For example, may an officer constitutionally disperse picketing strikers or prohibit religious demonstrations on the streets without permit? Or, when does an officer deprive a suspect of his rights to due process or equal protection? The answers to these, and a myriad of questions involving constitutional rights, are complex and require a thorough knowledge of constitutional law with which lawyers may not even be familiar. This leaves the officer vulnerable to legal liability lawsuits and argues for acquiring legal knowledge in police work.

4. *The Violation Must Reach Constitutional Level.* This means that not all violations of rights lead to liability under Section 1983. The violation must be of constitutional proportion. What this means is not exactly clear except that generally serious violations are actionable whereas non-serious ones are not. In the words of the 8th Circuit Court of Appeals:[15]

> Courts cannot prohibit a given condition or type of treatment unless it reaches a level of constitutional abuse. Courts encounter numerous cases in which the acts or conditions under attack are clearly undesirable...but the courts are powerless to act because the practices are not so abusive as to violate a constitutional right.

Mere words, threats, a push, a shove, temporary inconvenience, or even a single punch in the face do not necessarily constitute a civil rights violation.[16] Neither does Section 1983 apply to such cases as the officer giving a false testimony, simple negligence, or name-calling.[17] On the other hand, the use of excessive force to compel a suspect to confess constitutes a clear violation of constitutional rights.

A police officer is liable if all of the above four elements are present. Absence of any of these means that there is no liability under Section 1983. The officer may be liable, however, under some other provisions of law, such as under state tort or the Penal Code, but not under Section 1983.

# Why Section 1983 Lawsuits are a Popular Remedy

There are a number of reasons for the popularity of Section 1983 cases as a legal remedy. First, they almost always seek damages from the defendant, meaning that if the plaintiff wins, the officer pays. This can be very intimidating to an officer who may not have the personal resources or the insurance to cover liabilities. Second, civil rights lawsuits are usually filed in federal court where procedures for obtaining documents from the defendant (called "discovery") are often more liberal than in state courts. This facilitates access to important agency documents and records needed for trial. Third, civil rights lawsuits, when filed in federal courts, do not have to exhaust state judicial remedies, thus avoiding long delays in state courts. A fourth and perhaps more important reason is that since 1976, under federal law,[18] a prevailing plaintiff may recover attorney's fees. Consequently, lawyers have become more accommodating of civil rights cases if they see a semblance of merit in the case.

Civil rights lawsuits also continue to be used by plaintiffs extensively despite the availability of criminal sanctions against the police officer. One reason is that the two are not mutually exclusive. A case filed under Section 1983 is a civil case in which the plaintiff seeks vindication of his rights; the plaintiff is therefore in control. The vindication that an injured party may realize, if a criminal case is brought because of his injury, is less direct. Moreover, the reality is that there are definite barriers to the use of criminal sanctions against erring law enforcement officers. Among these are the unwillingness of some district attorneys to file cases against public officers with whom they work and whose help they sometimes need. Another difficulty is that serious criminal cases in most states must be referred to a grand jury for indictment. Grand juries are not enamored with having to indict police officers, unless it be shown clearly that the act was a gross and blatant abuse of authority. In many criminal cases involving alleged violation of rights, the evidence may come down to the word of the complainant against the word of the officer. The grand jury may be more inclined to believe the officer's testimony. Lastly, the degree of certainty needed to succeed in civil cases is mere preponderance of evidence (roughly more than 50% certainty), much lower than the guilt-beyond-reasonable-doubt measure that is needed to convict criminal defendants.

## Defenses in Section 1983 Lawsuits

Various legal defenses are available in civil rights cases. Some are the usual defenses available under state tort actions, while others are technical defenses (such as collateral estoppel, res judicata, laches, justiciability, and the Younger Doctrine) which only lawyers need to know. The defenses most often invoked by police defendants are (1) probable cause, and (2) good faith.

1. *The Probable Cause Defense.* This is an extremely limited defense in that it applies only to cases of false arrest or imprisonment and illegal searches and seizures. Under the Fourth Amendment, probable cause exists when the officer has sufficient knowledge of facts and circumstances that would lead a reasonable officer to conclude that the suspect probably committed the crime or that the item sought is in the place to be searched.[19] This definition, however, does not apply to Section 1983 cases brought against police officers. For the purpose of a legal defense in Section 1983 cases, probable cause simply means "a reasonable good faith belief in the legality of the action taken."[20] That expectation is lower than the Fourth Amendment definition of probable cause, as stated above. Thus, an officer who makes an arrest which is later determined to be without probable cause, may nonetheless be exempt from liability if he reasonably and in good faith believed at the time of the act that there were sufficient grounds for the arrest.

2. *The Good Faith Defense.* Good faith is by far the most-often invoked defense in civil rights cases. It has been made available since 1967 in actions seeking damages under Section 1983. Good faith basically means that the officer is acting with honest intentions, under the law, and in the absence of fraud, deceit, collusion, or gross negligence. The opposite of good faith in legal language is bad faith. For good faith to succeed as a defense, the defendant must prove two elements, namely:[21]

1. The officer must be acting sincerely and with a belief that what he is doing is lawful; and
2. The judge or jury must be convinced that such belief was reasonable.

The first element probes into the officer's state of mind at the time of the commission of the act, something which is obviously difficult to ascertain. In most cases, this is a matter of testimony by the officer as to his state of mind at the time the action was taken. The second element somehow diffuses this subjectivity by interjecting a third-party standard—that of the reasonableness of the act based on the conclusion of the judge or jury before whom the case is tried. Even if the defendant proves that he sincerely believed that his act was lawful, he is still liable if he cannot prove that his belief was reasonable.

The good faith defense is strongly enhanced by a number of acts which tend to establish that the officer did not in fact act in bad faith. Courts will most likely consider the officer's act to be in good faith under the following circumstances:

    a. if the officer followed agency manual or guidelines;
    b. if the officer acted on advice or legal counsel;
    c. if the officer followed the order of a superior; and
    d. if the officer acted in accordance with law or court decision.

## Legal Representation and Indemnification

A police officer facing a liability lawsuit, under state or federal law, has two immediate concerns. One is legal representation and the other is monetary indemnification if held liable.

Agencies use various guidelines in deciding the kinds of officer's acts the agency will defend. In general, agencies are more willing to provide legal assistance in civil cases than to those accused of criminal wrongdoing. Most states provide representation in civil actions, at least some of the time.[22] The situation is different in local law enforcement agencies. In most counties, cities, towns, or villages, there is no articulated policy (such as that set by law for state officers) for defending public officials. Legal representation by the agency is decided on a case-by-case basis. This means that the local agency is under no obligation to provide a lawyer should an officer be sued. If the agency refuses to defend, then the officer must provide his own lawyer. A suggested approach is to make legal representation an obligation of the agency. This can be provided for in the agency guidelines or manual or may be formally stated as an employment benefit.

If an officer is held liable in a lawsuit, who pays for attorney's fees and the damages assessed against him? A majority of states provide for some form of indemnification for public employees.[23] Local agencies vary in practice from full indemnification to no indemnification at all. The amount states and agencies are willing to pay varies considerably; some states set no limit, but most states do. If the court awards the plaintiff an amount larger than the maximum allowed by the agency, the employee pays the difference.

Although most agencies provide some form of indemnification, it does not follow that the agency will automatically indemnify. Most agencies will pay the judgment only if the officer acted "within the scope of employment." Moreover, most agencies also require that the employee acted in good faith. These provisions exclude agency coverage for acts which are gross, blatant, or outrageously violative of individual rights, as determined by the court.

## Professional Liability Insurance

If police officers are unable to obtain legal representation or indemnification from their agencies if sued, professional liability insurance provides a reasonable alternative. The problem is—who pays the premium? Some agencies purchase insurance for their officers, otherwise the officers pay for the premium themselves. Professional liability insurance coverage carries a number of advantages. Aside from paying for any damage award, the insurance company will most likely undertake the officer's legal defense because if he loses the insurance company pays. If provided for in the policy, the company will also pay for punitive damages, something which governmental agencies will seldom do because it may be against public policy. Professional liability insurance is sometimes discouraged on the ground that it serves to encourage the filing of lawsuits against the officer. It is also feared that the amount of damages will increase if the judge or jury is aware that the costs will be undertaken by an insurance company. There is no data to support these apprehensions. Moreover, in many jurisdictions, insurance coverage cannot be mentioned at the trial or hearing, hence negating this possible adverse effect.

## LIABILITIES OF SUPERVISORS

Although lawsuits against law enforcement officers are directed mainly at field officers, plaintiffs have recently become more inclined to include supervisory officials and agencies as parties-defendant. This strategy is based on the theory that the officer acts for the agency and therefore what he does is reflective of agency policy and practice. As a matter of legal tactic, there is wisdom in including supervisors and agencies in a liability lawsuit. Lower-level officers may not have the financial resources to satisfy a judgment, neither are they in a position to prevent similar future violations by other officers or the agency. Moreover, chances of financial recovery are enhanced if supervisory personnel are included in the lawsuit. The higher the position of the employee, the closer the plaintiff gets to the "deep pocket" of the county or state agency. Inclusion of the supervisor and agency may also create difficulty in the legal strategy for the defense, hence strengthening plaintiff's claim against one or some of the defendants.

Supervisory liability may be either direct or vicarious. Direct liability holds a supervisor responsible for what he does personally, whereas vicarious liability is indirect or substituted responsibility where the supervisor is held liable for what his subordinates do. The general rule is that a supervisor is liable only under direct liability, meaning that he is liable only if he personally authorized, participated in, directed, or ratified the act.[24] Vicarious or indirect liability for supervisors is therefore the exception rather than the rule. Court decisions of late, however, have greatly expanded the possible sources of vicarious liability under state and federal law, hence it has become a major source of concern for supervisors.

# Negligence of Supervisors

Vicarious liability stemming from the negligence of a supervisor is perhaps the most frequently litigated area of supervisory liability, and therefore deserves extended discussion. Based on case law, there are seven general areas from whence supervisory liability for negligence may arise. These are:

1. Negligent failure to train
2. Negligent hiring
3. Negligent assignment
4. Negligent failure to supervise
5. Negligent failure to direct
6. Negligent entrustment
7. Negligent retention

1. *Negligent Failure to Train.* The usual allegation in these cases is that the employee has not been instructed or trained by the supervisor or agency to a point where he possesses sufficient skills, knowledge, or activities required of him in the job. The rule is that administrative agencies and supervisors have a duty to train employees and that failure to discharge this obligation subjects the supervisor and agency to liability if it can be proved that such violation was the result of failure to train or improper training.[25]

In *McClelland v. Facteau*,[26] the Tenth Circuit held that a police chief may be held liable for civil rights violation for failure to train or supervise employees who commit an unconstitutional act. Plaintiff was booked by the New Mexico State Police at a local jail facility, and while there, was beaten by the officers, as well as denied use of the telephone and access to an attorney. In holding the officers liable, the court said in order for liability to attach, there must be a breach of an affirmative duty owed to the plaintiff and the action must be the proximate cause of the injury. In this case, it was well known that instances of constitutional violations were occurring in the department because they had been thoroughly aired by the press. Additionally, the jail itself was under lawsuit in two instances of wrongful death.

Lawsuits against supervisors and agencies for failure to train emanate from two sources, namely: a client whose rights have been violated by an officer who has not been properly trained, and from a subordinate who suffers injury in the course of duty because he has not been trained adequately. The obvious defense in these cases is proper training, but training may in fact be deficient due to circumstances beyond a supervisor's control, such as lack of funds and a dearth of expertise. Will the supervisor be liable if no resources have been allocated to provide the desired level of training? Budgetary constraints generally have not been considered a valid defense[27] by the courts and, therefore, place the supervisor in a difficult position. With proper documentation, however, the supervisor should be able to establish good faith if he repeatedly calls the attention of those who hold the purse-strings to the need for training. Even if financial resources are available, unstructured training alone may not be sufficient. The nature, scope, and quality of the training program must be properly documented and its relevance to job performance identified. There is need to document training sessions with detailed outlines to substantiate course content. Attendance sheets are necessary for defense purposes in lawsuits brought by one's own subordinates.

2. *Negligent Hiring.* Negligent hiring stresses the importance of proper background investigation before employing anyone to perform a job. Liability ensues when an employee is unfit for appointment, such unfitness was known to the employer or that the employer should have known about it through background investigation, and when the act is foreseeable.[28] In one case,[29] the department hired a police officer despite a record of preemployment assault conviction, a negative recommendation from a previous employer, and a falsified police application. The officer later assaulted a number of individuals in separate incidents. He and the supervisor were sued and held liable. In another case,[30] the court held a city liable for the actions of a police officer who was hired despite a felony record and who appeared to have been involved in many street brawls. Liability was based on the complete failure of the agency to conduct a background check prior to the hiring of the applicant.

3. *Negligent Assignment.* Negligent assignment means assigning an employee to a job without ascertaining whether or not he is adequately prepared for it, or keeping an employee on a job after he is known to be unfit. Examples would be a reckless driver assigned to drive a government motor vehicle or leaving an officer who has had a history of child molestation in a juvenile detention center. The rule is that a supervisor has an affirmative duty not to assign or leave a subordinate in a position for which he is unfit. In *Moon v. Winfield*,[31] liability was imposed on the Police Superintendent for failure to suspend or transfer an errant police officer to a non-sensitive assignment after numerous disciplinary reports had been brought to the supervisor's attention. In that case, the superintendent had five separate misconduct reports before him within a two-week period and also a warning that the officer had been involved in a series of acts indicating mental instability. The court held that supervisory liability ensued because the supervisor had authority to assign or suspend the officer, but failed to do so.

4. *Negligent Failure to Supervise.* Failure to supervise means negligent abdication of the responsibility to properly oversee employee activity. Examples are tolerating a pattern of physical abuse of inmates, racial discrimination, and pervasive deprivation of inmate rights and privileges. One court has gone so far as to say that failure on the part of the supervisor to establish adequate policy gives rise to legal action.[32] Tolerating unlawful activities in an agency might constitute

deliberate indifference to which liability attaches. The usual test is: Does the supervisor know of a pattern of behavior but fail to act on it?[33] The current law on liability for negligent failure to supervise is best summarized as follows:[34]

> To be liable for a pattern of constitutional violations, the supervisor must have known of the pattern and failed to correct or end it...Courts hold that a supervisor must be "casually linked" to the pattern showing that he had knowledge of it and that his failure to act amounted to approval and hence tacit encouragement that the pattern continue.

A writer gives this succinct advice: "The importance of this principle is that supervisors cannot shut their eyes and avoid responsibility for the acts of their associates if they are in a position to take remedial action and do nothing."[35]

5. *Negligent Failure to Direct.* Failure to direct means not sufficiently telling the employee of the specific requirements and proper limits of the job to be performed. In one case[36] the court refused to dismiss an action for illegal entry, stating that it could be the duty of a Police Chief to issue written directives specifying the conditions under which field officers can make warrantless entries into residential places. The court held that the supervisor's failure to establish policies and guidelines concerning the procurement of search warrants and the execution of various departmental operations made him vicariously liable for the accidental shooting death of a young girl by a police officer.

The best defense against negligent failure to direct is a written manual of policies and procedures for departmental operations. The manual must be accurate, legally updated, and form the basis for agency operations in theory and practice.

6. *Negligent Entrustment.* Negligent entrustment refers to the failure of a supervisor to properly supervise or control employee's custody use, or supervision of equipment or facilities entrusted to him on the job. Examples are improper use of vehicles and firearms which result in death or serious injury. In *Roberts v. Williams,*[37] an untrained trusty guard was given a shotgun and the task of guarding a work crew by a convict farm superintendent. The shotgun discharged accidentally, seriously wounding an inmate. The court held the warden liable based on negligence in permitting an untrained person to use a dangerous weapon. In *McAndrews v. Mularchuck,*[38] a periodically employed reserve patrolman was entrusted with a firearm without adequate training. He fired a warning shot which killed a boisterous youth who was not armed. The city was held liable in a wrongful death suit. Courts have also held that supervisors have a duty to supervise errant off-duty officers where an officer had property, gun, or a nightstick belonging to a governmental agency.

The test of liability is deliberate indifference. Plaintiff must be able to prove that the officer was incompetent, inexperienced, or reckless, and that the supervisor knew or had reason to know of officer's incompetence.[39] The supervisor's defense in these cases is that proper supervision concerning use and custody of equipment was exercised, but that the act occurred anyway despite adequate precautions.

7. *Negligent Retention.* Negligent retention means the failure to take action against an employee in the form of suspension, transer, or terminations, when such employee has demonstrated unsuitability for the job to a dangerous degree. The test is: Was the employee unfit to be retained and did the supervisor know or should he have known of the unfitness?[40]

The rule is that a supervisor has an affirmative duty to take all the necessary and proper steps to discipline and/or terminate a subordinate who is obviously unfit for service. This can be determined either from acts of lesser misconduct indicating a pattern of unfitness. Such knowledge may be actual or presumed. In *Brancon v. Chapman,*[41] the court held a police director liable in damages to a couple who had been assaulted by a police officer. The judge said that the officer's reputation for using excessive force and as an officer with mental problems was well-known among the police officers in his precinct, hence the director ought to have known of the officer's dangerous propensities and fired him before he assaulted the plaintiffs. This unjustified inaction was held to be the cause of the injuries to the couple for which they could be compensated.

The defense against negligent retention is for the supervisor to prove that proper action was taken against the employee and that the supervisor did all he could to prevent the damage of injury. This suggests that a supervisor must know what is going on in his department and must be careful to investigate complaints and document those investigations.

# CAN POLICE OFFICERS SUE BACK?

The huge increase in the number of cases and the resultant damage awards given in some jurisdictions have made officers feel that the balance of rights has shifted in favor of the consumers of criminal justice, at the expense of the police. Officers want to know if the police can strike back by filing lawsuits against their detractors.

The answer is yes, and the police in fact are striking back. Illustrative is a recent newspaper heading saying: "Grand Jurors Face $1.7 Million Suit for Criticism of Police."[42] The Americans for Effective Law Enforcement, Inc., an organization monitoring lawsuits filed by the police, has a quarterly publication titled "The Police Plaintiff" which reports cases filed by officers against the public. Charles E. Friend, author of a book on *Police Rights: Civil Remedies for Law Enforcement Officers,*[43] estimates that the number of actions brought by officers as plaintiffs has doubled during the last few years. Nonetheless, actual civil cases brought by the police have remained comparatively small.

While it is true that an officer may file the same type of tort lawsuits against a member of the general public as the public may bring against them, there are inherent impediments to doing that. The first is that in a tort case the officer will have to hire his own lawyer. In Section 1983 cases, as stated above, the defendant officer may be made by the federal judge to pay plaintiff's attorney's fees if the plaintiff prevails in at least one of his allegations. In contrast, if an officer sues back and wins, he cannot recover attorney's fees unless the original lawsuit against him was "utterly frivolous."[44] An officer cannot bring a Section 1983 lawsuit against the former plaintiff because one element of Section 1983 is that the defendant must have been "acting under color of law." Private persons, except in rare cases, do not come under requirement. Moreover, if the officer goes ahead and files a tort case against the plaintiff, his chances of real success are slim. Figures show that approximately 60 percent of those who run afoul of the law and have encounters with the police are indigent, hence financial recovery is remote even if the lawsuit is won.

Police officers often refrain from filing tort cases for damages because it is less expensive and more effective to punish the culprit criminally. Almost every state has provisions penalizing such offenses as: deadly assault of a peace officer, false report to a police officer, resisting arrest or search, hindering apprehension or prosecution, and aggravated assault. These can be added to the regular criminal offense against the arrested person and therefore enhance penalty of facilitates prosecution. Moreover, many officers feel that the sometimes-harsh treatment they get from the public is part of police work which is to be accepted without thought of retaliation. Whatever the attitude, it must be noted that the police have ample legal remedies available to them for aid, protection, or vindication in the course of task performance.

## MINIMIZING LEGAL LIABILITIES: GENERAL ADVICE

Liability lawsuits may be filed by anybody against an officer at any time. One of the fundamental rights in American society is the right of access to court. Whether or not the lawsuit will succeed is an entirely different matter. Figures show that most cases filed against public officers fail for various reasons. Nonetheless, it is perhaps Pollyannism in modern-day policing to expect that no lawsuit will ever be filed against an officer during his years of police work. There are bits of advice of which police officers should be aware if they are to minimize the number and potential adverse effect of liability lawsuits. In no particular order of importance, these are:

1. Act within the scope of your duties.
2. Act in a professional and responsible manner at all times. When faced with a difficult situation, use reason instead of emotion.
3. Know and follow your department's rules and regulations and your state laws. If you do, you will have a strong claim to a good faith defense.
4. Know the constitutional rights of your constituents and respect them.
5. Keep accurate written records in controversial cases.
6. Consult your legal counsel or supervisor if you have doubts about what you are doing. Be able to document the advice given.
7. Establish and maintain good relations with your community.
8. Keep yourself well-informed on current issues and trends in civil and criminal liability cases.

The above list is by no means exhaustive. There is no substitute for the specific advice of a competent lawyer when an officer is faced with a difficult situation which carries potential legal consequences. When a lawsuit is in fact filed, it is important for the officer to obtain the services of a good lawyer, either on his own or given him by the department. Liability lawsuits must be taken seriously, even if the allegations appear to be groundless or trivial, otherwise undesirable consequences may ensue.

## CONCLUSION

Gone are the days when law enforcement officers could do just about anything they pleased in the performance of responsibilities. Since the mid-1960s, the courts have abandoned their "hands-off" attitude toward cases filed against public officials, bringing on an "open door" era in litigation. Like it or not, liability lawsuits are here to stay.

Judicial intervention has brought mixed blessings for the police. Fear of liability has led to more intensive effort at police professionalization and a constant review of police practices to make certain that they comport with the law and court decisions. Thus, police departments have become proactive instead of simply being reactive in practices and policies. On the other hand, liability lawsuits have made police work less discretionary and more demanding. This can be immensely challenging. It is never easy to react rationally in crisis situations where a mistake in split-second judgment can mean the loss of life, but that is what officers must learn to do. This expectation is stiff, but by no means new. As August Vollmer, an erstwhile police chief and insightful observer once wrote:[45]

one may well wonder how a group of men could perform the task required of policemen. The citizen expects police officers to have the wisdom of Solomon, the courage of David, the strength of Samson, the patience of Job, the leadership of Moses, the kindness of the Good Samaritan, the faith of Daniel, the tolerance of the Carpenter of Nazareth and finally, an intimate knowledge of every branch of the natural, biological and social sciences. If he had all of these, he might be a good policeman.

# Notes

1   *Liability Reporter,* No. 103, July 1981, p. 1.

2   *Houston Chronicle,* June 15, 1983, p. 3.

3   *Houston Chronicle,* June 17, 1983, p. 22.

4   *Liability Reporter,* No. 125, May 1983, p. 1.

5   *Houston Chronicle,* November 14, 1984, section 2. p. 7.

6   *Liability Reporter,* No. 122, February 1983, p. 11.

7   See Schmidt, "Recent Trends in Police Tort Litigation," 8 *The Urban Lawyer* 682 (1976).

8   E. Brown, T. Flanagan and M. McLeod (eds.) *Sourcebook of Criminal Justice Statistics—1983,* 515 (1983).

9   *Recommended Procedures for Handling Prisoner Civil Rights Cases in the Federal Courts,* Federal Judicial Center, January 1980, p. 10.

10   Intergovernmental Report, *Handbook of the Law of Personal Tort Liability of Texas Public Employees and Officials,* No. VI-3, Texas Advisory Commission on Intergovernmental Relations, September 1978, at 1.

11   W. Prosser, *Handbook of the Law of Torts* 143 (1971).

12   The material in this section is generally taken from W. Schmidt, "Overview of Civil Liability," *The AELE Workshop on Police Liability and the Defense of Misconduct Complaints* 1-1 (1982).

13   365 U.S. 167 (1961).

14   98 S. Ct. 2018 (1978).

15   *Wiltsie v. California Department of Corrections,* 406 F.2d 515, 517-518 (8th Cir. 19168).

16   *See Burszka v. Johnson,* 351 F. Supp. 771 (E.D.Pa. 1972).

17   *See Smith v. Sinclair,* 424 F. Supp. 1108 (W.D. Okla. 1976).

18   *Civil Rights Attorney's Fees Awards Act of 1976,* 42 U.S.C. Sec. 1988 (1976).

19   *See Carroll v. U.S.* 267 U.S. 132 (1925).

20   *See Rodriguez v. Jones* 473 F.2d 599 (5th Cir. 1973).

21   *See Scheurer v. Rhodes,* 416 U.S. 232 (1974).

22   See R. del Carmen, *Legal Responsibilities of Probation and Parole Officers: A Manual,* at pp. 246-271 (1981), as submitted to the National Institute of Corrections, NIC Grant Award #BZ-5.

[23]   *Ibid.*

[24]   *See Hampton v. Hanragan,* 600 F.2d 600 (7th Cir. 1979).

[25]   *See Owens v. Haas,* 601 F.2d 1242 (2nd Cir. 1979), cert. denied, 100 S. Ct. 483.

[26]   610 F. 2d 693 (10th Cir. 1979).

[27]   *See Alberti v. Sheriff of Harris County,* 460 F. Supp. 649 (S.D. Tex. 1975).

[28]   *See* in general *AELE Law Enforcement Legal Defense Center: Special Report—The AELE Workshop in Police Civil Liability and the Defense of Misconduct Complaints* 12-1 (1982).

[29]   *Moon v. Winfield,* 383 F. Supp 31 (N.D. Ill. 1974).

[30]   *Peters v. Bellinger,* 159 N.E. 2d 528 (Ill. App. 1959).

[31]   383 F. Supp 31 (N.D. Ill. 1974).

[32]   *Ford v. Brier,* 383 F. Supp 505 (E.D. Wis. 1974).

[33]   *Moon v. Winfield,* 383 F. Supp. 31 (N.D. Ill., 1974).

[34]   *See* Hardy and Weeks, *Personal Liability of Public Officials Under Federal Law* 7 (1980).

[35]   *See* J. Palmer, *Civil Liability of Correctional Workers* 24 (1980).

[36]   *Ford v. Brier,* 383 F. Supp. (E.D. Wis. 1974).

[37]   302 F. Supp. 1972 (N.D. Mass. 1969).

[38]   162 A.2d 820 (N.J. 1960).

[39]   *See Moon v. Winfield,* 383 F. Supp. 31 (N.D. Ill. 1974).

[40]   *See AELE Special Report, supra* note 28, at 12-2.

[41]   LR #10509 (W.D. Tennessee 1981).

[42]   *Houston Chronicle,* January 29, 1984, p. 31.

[43]   Charlottesville, Virginia, The Michie Company, 1979.

[44]   *See Christianburg Garment Co., v. EEOC,* 98 S. Ct. 694 (1978).

[45]   As quoted in Silberman, *Criminal Violence, Criminal Justice* 199 (1978).

# Study Questions

1. In general, classify the types of cases which may be brought against police officers.

2. Give four types of cases which may be filed against police officers under state tort law.

3. What are the four essential elements of a Section 1983 case? Discuss each.

4. What is the good faith defense?

5. In what instances may a police supervisor be held liable for negligence? Discuss each.

6. Give reasons why police officers usually do not bring lawsuits against the general public.

# EPILOGUE

Policing... "What other job can you go to work horny, hungry, sober, and broke, and have all your needs satisfied by the end of your shift?"

CBS Movie, "One Police Plaza"

This conceptualization of law enforcement is one which persists, perhaps subliminally, by many people—including police officers. As evidenced by the readings in this book, there is a ring of truth to the statement, however, police administrators are attempting to understand and manage police deviance fairly and effectively.

Police misconduct is not a dichotomous problem. There are many police acts which are tangential and fall within the gray areas of propriety on the continuum of police behavior. It is safe to say that most police officers stray from the straight and narrow on some occasion for a variety of reasons. Sometimes it is a case of frustration and revenge (e.g., "street justice"), sometimes it is a product of poor judgment (e.g., isolated cases of sexual misconduct), it may be a product of not recognizing the long-range effects of the behavior (e.g., accepting gratuities), or it may be the influence of peer pressure (e.g., smoking marijuana at an off-duty party).

How do officers justify their actions in these anamolous cases? By using "doughnut shop" ethics. That is, while recognizing a specific behavior or act is improper, they justify their action in light of the unique circumstances and rationalize that the impropriety is insignificant because it is an aberration from one's normally proper behavior. Such as when the midnight officer goes into the doughnut shop for a cup of coffee and comes out with a free sack of doughnuts because the manager was glad the officer stopped by.

The authors, both former police officers, are realists: While recognizing that the anamolous circumstances occur, our focus is to control those instances through informal controls and concentrate more effort on problem prevention and remedying systemic problems. We have experienced the frustration of an unresponsive criminal justice system and the temptation of a free meal. We have been cajoled into writing creatively to put a "known criminal" in jail and to speak aggressively to maintain control of a situation or lecture a man who was robbed by a prostitute. We have felt growing prejudice creeping in as a result of repeatedly dealing with the worst side of humankind and experienced the wrath of internal investigations. We have empathy for police officers, most of whom will experience some aspect of impropriety during their professional lives. We also, from our current perch in the ivory tower, now have a better perspective on the impact of these acts on the individual, the organization, and the community.

Through discussion of these issues we hope to bring overt recognition of the forces affecting these sensitive topics. We also hope to spur individual and organizational self-recognition that the problems can occur in any police organization. Police authority is awesome, particularly for the young rookie officer who, perhaps, is holding his/her first career position. Keeping that authority in check requires firm organizational guidance during the formative occupational socialization. Police departments must recognize the influence of the environment and ensure reasonable measures of training, supervision, review, and discipline are in place to maintain control of police deviance problems. Our intent is to contribute to this end.

# AUTHOR INDEX

Abbott, D.W., 320

Abrams, R.I., 105

Abrecht, B., 241

Alpert, G.P., 228

Amsterdam, A., 342

Anderson, J., 242, 244

Anderson, S.V., 340

Baker, M., 277

Barker, T., 5, 24, 45, 52, 139
156, 160

Barrett, J.K., 45

Barron, W., 278

Barton, P.G., 374, 382

Barthel, J., 183

Bartol, C.R., 283

Bauduin, F., 278

Bayley, D.H., 260, 276

Belair, R.R., 156

Bellamy, J., 247

Beral, H., 319, 374, 375, 377,
378, 386

Berger, M., 340

Berkowitz, L. 283, 290

Biderman, A., 332

Binder, A., 223

Bittner, E., 158, 206

Black, D.J., 258, 276, 286, 320

Blackstone, W., 242, 243

Blalock, H.M., 300

Blaylock, J., 341

Bliss, G., 321

Blumberg, M., 228, 229, 232

Blumburg, A.S., 32

Bok, S., 169

Bordner, D.C., 278

Bouza, A.V., 383

Brennan, J., 247, 253, 255, 257

Brent, E.E., 276

Broadway, F.M., 332

Brown, D., 378, 379, 392

Brown, E., 406

Bryant, C.D., 47

Burger, C.J., 254

Burgin, A.L., 256

Burnam, D., 230, 258

Buss, A.H., 282

Cameron, P., 278

Campbell, A., 276

Carter, D.L., 7, 14, 16, 17, 111,
139, 197, 302, 306, 356, 371

Chapman, B., 260

Chevigny, P., 49, 276, 320

Clinard, M.B., 47

Coffey, A., 299, 301

Cohen, M., 278

Condon, R.G., 276

Connery, D.S., 183

Cooper, G.R., 156

Couper, D.C., 15

Cordner, G., 15

Cox, T.C., 276, 290

Crawford, T.J., 277

Cray, E., 374, 375, 380, 382

Critchley, T., 247

Daley, R., 173

Daly, M., 102, 103

Davis, K.C., 17, 257, 361

Dearth, D., 14, 16, 370

del Carmen, R., 415

Dershowitz, A.W., 160, 257

Diamond, E., 5

Douglas, J., 253, 256, 257

Duffy, J.F., 397

Dull, T.R., 105

Durkheim, E., 30, 308

Elliston, F.A., 33

Elton, G., 242

Ennis, P.H., 332

Fahey, R.F., 242, 259

Falkenberg, S.D., 276

Felkenes, G., 30

Fine, G.A., 278

Fisher, S., 307

Flanagan, T., 40
Foldy, W.A., 278
Foote, C., 339
Fosdick, R., 260
Friedrich, R.J., 5, 202
Fyfe, J.J., 223, 224, 225,
        228, 229, 231, 232, 241
Geller, W.A., 5, 230, 232, 241
George, J.B., 158
Gibbs, J., 249
Gibson, C.J., 260
Glassman, M.B., 278
Gleser, G.L., 278
Gold, L.H., 319
Goldberg & Dershowitz, 257
Goldkamp, J.S., 230
Goldstein, H., 15, 102, 139, 157
        208, 257, 276, 386
Grano, J., 179
Griffiths, C.T., 276
Groves, E.W., 277
Gunderson, D.F., 303, 307
Halleck, J., 241
Halpern, S.C., 378, 382
Harding, R.W., 241
Hart, H., 245
Hawkins, R.O., 276
Hayden, G., 258
Herman, M.S., 278
Hillgren, J. 206
Hopkins, E.J., 178
Hopper, R., 303, 307
Hornung, C.A., 276
Hoy, V.L., 14
Hudson, J.R., 319, 378, 379
        380, 382, 383
Hudzik, J., 15
Hurwitz, S., 340
Inbau, F.E., 158, 179
James, G.G., 155, 159
Jenkins, B., 230
Jolin, A.I., 393

Kania, R., 5, 198
Karales, K.J., 232
Keller, P.A., 207
Kelling, G.L., 309
Kennett, L., 242, 244
Kerlinger, F.N., 199
Kerstetter, W.A., 388, 389, 392,
        394
Kevlin, T.A., 139
Kittel, N.G., 160
Knapp Commission, 46-48
Kobler, A.L., 226, 241, 254
Koehler, R.R., 116
Kraska, P.B., 106
Kukendall, J., 226
LeFave, W.R., 341
Langworthy, R.H., 226, 241
Lardener, J., 241
Latting, S.V., 344
Lazin, F.A., 302
Leeds & Lowe, 256
Leonard V., More, H., 383
Levenson, H., 203
Letman, S.T., 391
Lowenthal, M.A., 39
Lundman, R.J., 139
Lykken, O.T., 183, 185
Lynch, G.W., 382
Mackey, W.C., 5
Manning, P.K., 161, 163
Marmo, M., 39
Marshall, J., 234, 237
Marx, G.T., 154, 155
Matulia, K.J., 22, 226
Matza, D., 52
McCormack, R., 307, 308
McGarrell, E.F., 40
McGregor, D., 352
McLaren, R.C., 13
Melville-Lee, W., 242
Mendelsohn, H., 276
Meyer, J.C., 139

Meyer, M.W., 223, 229
Michael, J., 249
Miller, W., 243, 244
Milton, C.H., 225, 226, 227, 241, 254, 257, 258
Moore, J.C., 340
Murphy, P., 46
Newman, J., 301
Newman, G., 245
Niederhoffer, A., 32, 374
Oaks, D.H., 319
Packer, H., 245, 246
Pear, R., 184
Perez, D.W., 388
Perkins, R., 243, 248, 260
Perrow, C., 329
Peirson, G.W., 231
Pistone, J., 154
Phillips, W., 45
Plitt, E., 4
Polsky, N., 139
Pomeroy, W.A.C., 391, 392
Possumato, T., 114
Pringle, P., 243
Prosser, W., 407
Quinney, R., 47
Radelet, L.A., 40
Rafky, D.M., 305
Record, W., 301
Reese, C.D., 300
Reiser, M., 206, 207
Reiss, A.J., 49, 198, 259 276, 320
Remington, F.J., 341
Rinzel, D., 256
Robbins, S., 18
Robin, G.D., 47, 259
Roebuck, J.B., 6, 139
Rosenberg, M., 304
Rossi, P.H., 277
Rossum, R.A., 175
Rothwell, J.D., 284, 289

Rowat, D.C., 340
Rusinko, W.T., 276
Russell, K.V., 386, 395
Sarat & Vidmar, 256
Savitz, L., 50
Scaglion, R., 276
Schecter, L., 45
Schlesinger, A.M., 176
Schmidt, W., 326, 408
Schuman, H., 276
Schur, E.M., 52
Selye, H., 207
Sharpley, G.R., 381
Shearing, C.D., 139
Sherman, L.W., 5, 50, 139, 223, 226, 227, 228, 241, 254, 278
Sherrill, R., 242
Siedel, C.J., 341
Sisk, M., 319
Skolnick, J.H., 50, 65, 154, 155 159, 162, 171, 173, 184, 276
Smith, J., 244, 247
Smith, L., 242
Smith, P.E., 295
Snizek, W.E., 47
Spielbenger, C., 206
Stark, R., 276
Stephens, D.W., 42
Stevens, J., 246, 250
Stitt, B.G., 155, 159
Stoddard, E.R., 45, 206
Strecher, W.C., 50
Sutherland, E.H., 243
Swanson, C.R., 356
Sykes, R.E., 276, 291
Symonds, M., 46
Takagi, P., 226, 258, 302
Terrill, R.J., 375, 389, 390, 392
Territo, L., 384, 385
Thornton, L.M., 276
Toch, H., 207, 334

Van Maanen, J., 50, 276, 285,
    286, 306, 319
Vincze, L., 278
Walker, D., 276
Walker, S., 15, 17, 229, 375,
    376, 379, 380, 383, 388, 389
Ward, R., 307, 308
Wells, R.O., 5, 24
Wesley, W.A., 276
Whisenand, P.M., 211
White, M.E., 276
Wilkes, D.E., 344
Willis, C.L., 199
Wilson, O.W., 13, 16, 332, 384
Wilson, J.Q., 15, 156
Winfree, L.T., 276
Wolchover, D., 160
Wukitsch, D.J., 221
Wycoff, M.A., 309
Younger, I., 49

# SUBJECT INDEX

ABSCAM, 154
Abuse of Authority, 197-218
    Legal, 201
    Physical, 201
    Verbal, 201
American Bar Association, 339
American Civil Liberties
    Union, 222, 320
Approved Deviance, 52
"AssHoles," 285, 286
Atlanta, 223, 232
*BELL v. WOLFISH,* 245
Berkeley, 389
Birmingham, 255
"Blue Code," 163
"Blue Curtain," 327
Boston, 161, 256
    Boston Licensing Board, 76
    Police Commissioner Robert
        J. di Grazia, 76
    Police Commissioner Francis
        M. Roache, 76
    Police Commissioner Joseph
        Jordan, 77
    Police Corruption, 66-79
BRILAB, 154
*CALVERT v. PONTIAC,* 33
Chicago, 391
*CICENIA v. LAGAY,* 178
Civil Rights Act, 9, 18
Civilian Review Boards, 324, 374,
    376-380
    New York City Civilian
        Complaint Review
        Board, 379
    Philadelphia Police
        Advisory Board, 377
"Clean" and "Dirty" Money, 124
Cocaine, 64, 66
Code of Conduct, 356

*COKER v. GEORGIA,* 220
Commission on Accreditation for
    Law Enforcement Agencies, 396
Community-Based Policing, 64
Citizen Complaints Against Officers,
    External Review, 387
    Investigation and Review,
        373-404
Conduct Unbecoming, 355
Contacts (Sexual)
    Citizen Initiated, 147-150
    Crime Victims, 143, 144
    Non-Sexual, 140-142
    Offenders, 144-146
    Voyeuristic, 142-143
"Cooping," 32, 128
Corruption, 5, 6
    Definition, 48
    Drugs, 102
    Patterns, 51
*CROOKER v. CALIFORNIA,* 178
Dade County, 392
Dallas, 41, 230, 256
Deception, 169-193
    Interrogatory, 177
    Investigative, 174
    Testimonial, 171
Detroit, 390
Differential Containment
    Strategies, 209-214
"Dirty Harry" Problem, 155
Disciplinary Review
    Adversarial, 360
    Non-Adversarial, 360
    Quasi-Adversarial, 360
Discrimination, 299-315
    Ethnic, 310, 311
    Sexual, 309, 310
Drinking on Duty, 129
"Dropsy" Evidence, 125
Drugs and Corruption, 102

Entrapment, 155, 156
    Objective Test, 153, 175
    Subjective Test, 155, 175
Federal Civil Rights Act, 338
*FEDERAL COMMUNICATION*
    *COMMISSION v. PACIFICA*
    *FOUNDATION*, 278
"Fix," 162
"Fleeing Felon," 220-222
Force
    Deadly, 220-239, 241, 274
*FURMAN v. GEORGIA*, 253
Garrity Interviews, 107
*GARRITY v. NEW JERSEY*, 358
Gay Rights, 65
General Orders, 14
"Good Faith" Defense, 19
*GREGG v. GEORGIA*, 253, 258
Hispanic, 309-311
"Hole," 128
Hoover, 176
Houston, 255, 256, 277
"Hue and Cry," 242
International Association of
    Chiefs of Police, 339
Informal Quota System, 125
Informants, 109
Internal Affairs Units, 373, 384-387
Internal Investigations, 357
International Association for
    Civilian Oversight of Law
    Enforcement, 397
Jacksonville, Florida, 227
*JONES v. MARSHALL*, 249
Judge Ginsberg, 104
Kansas City, 223, 232, 257,
    333, 334, 387
*KENNEDY v. MENDOZA*
    *MARTINEZ*, 246
Knapp Commission, 63, 72-75
*LANKFORD v. GELSTON*, 341
Legalization of Gambling, 62

Liability,
    Individual, 18, 19
    Department, 18, 19
Los Angeles, 255
Lying (Police)
    Accepted, 153-156
    Deviant, 160-164
    Taxonomy, 153-164
    Tolerated, 156-159
Mothers Against Drunk Driving, 157
Madison, Wisconsin, 34, 35
Mafia, 154
Malfeasance, 23
*MAPP v. OHIO*, 125, 172
*MATTIS v. SCHNARR*, 248, 260
McAllen, Texas, 40, 309, 393
*McCLUNG v. CRIMINAL JUSTICE*
    *STANDARDS AND TRAINING*
    *COMMISSION*, 115
Memphis, 231
Miami, 40
    Drug Corruption, 103
    Miami Vice, 65
    Mariel Boat Lift Effects, 67
    Police Corruption, 65-72
    River Cops, 65
Michigan State Police, 35
MILAB, 154
*MIRANDA v. ARIZONA*, 177
Misconduct, 5, 6
Misfeasance, 23
Model Penal Code, 256
*MONELL v. DEPARTMENT OF*
    *SOCIAL SERVICES*, 18
New York, 46, 230, 231, 256, 333
    Civilian Complaint Review
        Board, 72
    Commissioner Benjamin Ward, 72
    Commissioner Patrick Murphy, 73
    Police Corruption, 72-76
    77th Precinct, 75

Normalization of Deviance
    Technique, 46
Oakland, California, 254, 334
Occupational Deviance, 6-7,
    61-64, 124, 135
Occupational Socialization, 50
Off-Duty Officers
    Arming, 223-225
Opportunity Structure, 124
*OWENS v. CITY OF*
    *INDEPENDENCE,* 19
*OWENS v. HAAS,* 19
"Pad," 48
*PARKER v. LEVY,* 33, 34
Philadelphia, 129, 258
    Chief Kevin Tucker, 68
    Mayor Frank Rizzo, 69
    Mayor Wilson Goode, 70
    Police Corruption, 67-72
Police
    Brutality, 5, 126, 197-198
    Corruption
        Functional Explanation, 46
        Rotton Apple Theory, 156
    Disciplinary Proceedings,
        351-372
    Discretion, 17-18
    Drug Use, 101-113
    Ethics, 29-33
    Integrity, 33
    Liability, 405-426
    Lies, 153-167
    Misconduct, 362
    Ombudsman, 381-382
    Opportunity Structure, 48, 49
    Perjury, 49, 124-126
    Sex on Duty, 127
    Social Isolation, 50
    Stress, 107
    Subculture, 50
    Unions, 382
    Values, 34

Police Exe... JECT INDEX    435
    Forum, 3.
Police Officer As...
Policy, 14-15
Polygraph, 32, 109, 183, 113
Portland, 393
Prejudice, 299-315
Profanity and Obscenity
    Aggression, 282-283
    Catharsis, 284
    Identification With In-Group, 284
    Officer Use, 275-297
    Situationally Provoked, 285-288
"Ratting," 328
*RIZZO v. GOODE,* 342
"Rogue" Officer, 128
*ROE v. WADE,* 65
"Rotten Apple" Myth, 45, 46
*ROYAL v. ECORSE POLICE AND*
    *FIRE COMMISSION,* 33
"Rules of the Justice Games," 160
San Francisco, 78
San Jose, 388
"Scores," 49
Search Warrant, 145
Sexual Harassment, 140-150
Sexual Misconduct, 139-154
Sexual Shakedowns, 146-148
*SHERMAN v. UNITED STATES,* 174
Sleeping on Duty, 128-129
Stress and Stressors, 204-208
*TENNESSEE v. GARNER,* 221
*TERRY v. OHIO,* 24
Theory X and Theory Y, 352
*THOMPSON v. CITY OF*
    *APPLETON,* 34
Torts, 326
*TURPIN v. MAILET,* 19
*UNITED STATES v. RUSSELL,* 175
United States Commission on
    Civil Rights, 198, 208

Value Statements,,,?177
Vice Control, 62
Victimless Cr
Wickersha

# ABOUT THE AUTHOR

THOMAS BARKER is Dean of the College of Criminal Justice at Jackson State University—Jacksonville, Alabama. Dr. Barker is a former police officer in Birmingham and has held various academic appointments. He has written extensively in the areas of police misconduct and corruption as well as serving as an advisor to various law enforcement agencies on matters relating to police deviance. In addition, Dr. Barker has done extensive work related to police pursuits and police policy issues.

JACK BASEHART is on the faculty of the Department of Communications at the University of Kentucky. He received his doctorate from Michigan State University and has conducted extensive research in the areas of persuasion, credibility, and nonverbal behavior in human interaction.

MARK BLUMBERG is an Associate Professor of Criminal Justice at Central Missouri State University. A Ph.D. graduate in Criminal Justice from the State University of New York at Albany, Dr. Blumberg has conducted extensive research, consultation, and published on a wide range of policing issues. Particularly his research, consultation and special lectures have focused on the police use of deadly force as well as contributory and demographic factors associated with deadly force. Currently, Dr. Blumberg is examining the effects of AIDS on police behavior and police administrative practices.

DAVID L. CARTER is an Associate Professor of Criminal Justice at Michigan State University. He is co-author of the books *Drug Use by Police Officers* and the forthcoming *Police Systems and Practices,* as well as numerous articles in the areas of police behavior and police policy issues. Dr. Carter has served as a consultant to many law enforcement agencies on matters of police development, organizational issues, and labor issues; and provided extensive training to many law enforcement organizations including the FBI National Academy and the Police Executive Research Forum. A former Kansas City, Missouri police officer, Dr. Carter's research expertise has addressed a wide range of policing issues, including law enforcement intelligence analysis, the use of force, community policing, and Hispanic relations with the police. He holds a B.S. and an M.S. from Central Missouri State University and a Ph.D. from Sam Houston State University.

ROLANDO V. del CARMEN is a Professor of Criminal Justice at Sam Houston State University. He is the author of *Potential Liabilities of Probation and Parole Officers, 2nd Ed.* (Anderson, 1986), *Criminal Procedure for Law Enforcement*

...riminal procedure and liability of criminal
Personnel, as well as a consultant and trainer for the National
justice personnel, ...ters of correctional liability, provided training for
Institute of C... ...ional agencies, written a monograph under a Depart-
various pces on liabilities of probation and parole officers, and published
ment of degrees on matters of criminal procedure, civil rights, and liabilities.
num... degrees are an LL.M. from Southern Methodist University and the
A.. from the University of Wisconsin.

TERRY C. COX earned his doctorate from the University of Akron and currently teaches in the Department of Police Studies at Eastern Kentucky University. A specialist in police policy issues, his research interests include citizens' attitudes toward the police, violent police/citizen interactions, and police policy research.

JOHN DOMBRINK is an Assistant Professor in the program of Social Ecology at the University of California, Irvine. His research interests include study of the law and abuse of legal authority.

HERMAN GOLDSTEIN is a Professor at the University of Wisconsin-Madison Law School. A noted author in policing, Professor Goldstein's works have addressed a wide range of policing issues. His book, *Policing a Free Society,* is considered a seminal work in the field. Most recently, his concepts on problem-oriented policing have been implemented by a series of research projects by the Police Executive Research Forum. Professor Goldstein was the 1989 recipient of the Academy of Criminal Justice Sciences Most Prestigious Award, the Bruce Smith, Sr. Award, for contributions to the field of criminal justice.

ALLEN D. SAPP is an Associate Professor of Criminal Justice at Central Missouri State University. He is the author of numerous articles and papers dealing with child abuse, domestic violence, right-wing extremist groups, and police unionism. His recent research interests and publications have focused on matters of sexual assault and sexual violence. He has served as a trainer and consultant for many law enforcement agencies as well as being the research director for the Police Education Project of the Police Executive Research Forum. He holds a B.S. from the University of Nebraska, M.S. from the University of Southern California, and Ph.D. from Sam Houston State University.

LAWRENCE W. SHERMAN is a Professor at the University of Maryland and President of the Crime Control Institute. His extensive number of books and articles have addressed police use of deadly force, ethics in law enforcement, police education, and many other law enforcement issues. Professor Sherman has also worked with the Police Foundation exploring various issues.

JEROME H. SKOLNICK is a Professor at the University California at Berkeley. He has written extensively on the topic of police examining their behavioral systems, organizational relationships, and operational developments. Professor Skolnick's description of the "working personality" of police officers has become a classic conceptualization on which a significant amount of research has been based. His work on police deception provides important insights into law enforcement officers' behavior as related to self-perception and the working personality.

DARREL W. STEPHENS is the Executive Director of the Police Executive Research Forum. He served as Police Chief in Newport News, Virginia and Largo, Florida and Assistant Police Chief in Lawrence, Kansas. While he was Chief in Newport News, the department gained national recognition for the development and implementation of the problem-oriented policing concept. Having begun his law enforcement career in Kansas City, Missouri, he served as a patrol officer in several assignments as well as supervising and later commanding the department's operations resource unit. He also spent one year as a National Institute of Justice fellow on loan from the KCPD. Mr. Stephens has an extensive background as a consultant in law enforcement and has received numerous national honors and awards. He holds an M.S. in Public Services Administration from Central Missouri State University and a B.S. in the Administration of Justice from the University of Missouri at Kansas City.

PAUL WEST is an Inspector with the Durham Constabulary, Durham England. He received his baccalaureate degree from Oxford University in Physics and an M.S. in Criminal Justice from Michigan State University while on a Harkness Fellowship. Inspector West has held a wide range of assignments and received specialized police training at the Bramshill Police College. He developed the methodology and conducted the research for a Police Executive Research Forum project on police complaint procedures and has developed specialized expertise in examining police misconduct and complaints against the police.

MERVIN F. WHITE received his Ph.D. from the University of Kentucky and currently teaches in the Department of Sociology at Clemson University. His research interests focus on sociological inquiry into citizens' attitudes toward the police, human relations in law enforcement, and juvenile delinquency.